POLITICAL THEORY AND POLITICAL PHILOSOPHY

Seventeen Volumes of Previously Unavailable British Theses

Edited by
MAURICE CRANSTON
London School of Economics and Political Science

A Garland Series

POLITICS AND PHILOSOPHY IN THE THOUGHT OF DESTUTT DE TRACY

Brian W. Head

Garland Publishing, Inc., New York & London
1987

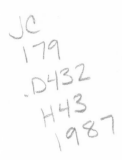

Library of Congress Cataloging-in-Publication Data

Head, Brian.
Politics and philosophy in the thought of Destutt de
Tracy.

(Political theory and political philosophy)
Originally presented as the author's thesis—
Bibliography: p.
1. Destutt de Tracy, Antoine Louis Claude, comte,
1754–1836—contributions in political science.   I. Title.
II. Series.
JC179.D432H43   1987   320'.01   86-26980
ISBN 0-8240-0819-7

All volumes in this series are printed
on acid-free, 250-year-life paper.

Printed in the United States of America

POLITICS AND PHILOSOPHY

IN THE THOUGHT OF

DESTUTT DE TRACY

(1754-1836)

BRIAN W. HEAD

TABLE OF CONTENTS

Page

Preface   1

1. Introduction: the Intellectual and Political
    Background.
    I.   Perspectives on Tracy and the idéologues   4
    II.   Intellectuals and Politics: philosophes
          and idéologues   11
    III. Tracy's life and writings: an outline   36
          Footnotes to chapter one   56

2. Idéologie and the Pursuit of Certainty
    I.   Science and certainty   75
    II.   The concept of idéologie   86
    III. The science of signs and language   100
    IV.   Metaphysics and religion   115
          Footnotes to chapter two   129

3. From Individual Desires to Social Morality
    I.   The will as desire and action   143
    II.   The bases of social existence   159
    III. Social morality   177
          Footnotes to chapter three   198

4. The Science of Social Organization
    I.   From the "social art" to "social science"   208
    II.   Tracy's concept of "la science sociale"   221
          Footnotes to chapter four   243

5. Economics: the Science of "industrie"
    I.   Wealth and "industrie"   251
    II.   Economic classes   266
    III. The problem of inequality   277
          Footnotes to chapter five   296

6. Politics: the Science of "happiness"
    I.   Liberal elitism and the Directory   305
    II.   Critique of Montesquieu   326
    III. Representative government: reason and liberty   345
          Footnotes to chapter 6   359

7. Public Instruction and idéologie
    I.   Public instruction and the Directory   369
    II.   Idéologie in education   385
    III. Defence of the "écoles centrales"   398
          Footnotes to chapter seven   412

Appendices:
          I.   Speech by Destutt de Tracy, 1 December 1791   421
          II. Structure of the Institut National, 1795   422

Bibliography: A. Published Writings of Destutt de Tracy   424
               B. Other Primary Sources   427
               C. Secondary sources and Miscellaneous   447

PREFACE

Destutt de Tracy's long life (1754-1836) spanned several generations of French intellectual life, from the age of Voltaire to the July Monarchy. This study closely follows the text of my doctoral dissertation, entitled 'The Political and Philosophical Thought of Destutt de Tracy', submitted to the London School of Economics and Political Science in December 1979. There has been no attempt to revise the arguments in the light of scholarship which became available since 1978; some acknowledgement of later discussion may be found in articles which have already appeared [1], and in two books which I expect to publish in due course - one on Tracy's notions of ideology and social science, and a second work on the social and political thought of the wider circle of idéologues. In this preface, I make some brief comments on the scope of the present study, and acknowledge the assistance I received during its years of preparation.

The term 'politics' and 'philosophy' are intended to signify the breadth of Tracy's intellectual interests, and to hint at the close connections he saw between understanding human activity and attempting to influence the proper direction of public policy in all spheres of social life. Politics was a central component of Tracy's work. He was a politican during two periods of his life (1788-91 and after 1799); he wrote a treatise on political theory (his Commentaire on Montesquieu); and his writings on law, education, economics and even on language contained important political implications. The term 'philosophy' points to Tracy's preoccupation with issues of epistemology and methodology. At the core of his system of ideas is the notion of idéologie - a philosophical methodology of scientific enquiry which he claimed would provide a guarantee for precise knowledge in the human sciences.

This study is primarily concerned to describe and analyse
the published writings of Destutt de Tracy; it is not an intellectual biograp
based on private papers and archival materials, nor a 'sociology of ideas'
account of the emergence of French liberalism. Historical and biographical
details have been included only to the extent I have judged necessary for a
proper understanding of Tracy's writings, or where I have reported material
which had not previously been used to illuminate his thought.

I have concentrated on the three decades from the calling of the
Etats-généraux to the early years of the Restoration – the period of Tracy's
entire literary production, and the period of his greatest influence and
reputation. The early decades of his life, before about 1788, remain of
little interest for the historian of ideas [2], and the motives for his change
of direction – from a military career towards politics and philosophy – remai
partly obscure. In the same way, the long years of virtual retirement and
ill-health before his death in 1836 are of little philosophical or political
interest except for the historian concerned with Tracy's influence on younger
generations of writers.

I have omitted from consideration some standard topics – such
as Tracy's relations with Henri Beyle (Stendhal) and with Maine de Biran –
topics which fortunately have been treated in depth by numerous historians.
Nor have I here attempted a rounded picture of the idéologues, whose
activities and whose stormy relationship with Bonaparte have been well docume
elsewhere.

I have translated into English all the longer quotations from the
original French texts, occasionally inserting the original terms where
appropriate. Footnotes have been grouped separately at the end of each chapte

I wish to thank Professor Ken Minogue, who supervised the dissertation from its beginnings in 1973. I also benefited from discussions with Professor Maurice Cranston and Dr John Hooper. My research in Paris was aided by a grant from the Central Research Fund of the University of London. I am indebted to the librarians of the Bibliothèque Nationale, the Bodleian Library, the British (Museum) Library, the British Library of Political and Economic Science, and the inter-library loan services of several Australian university libraries. My thanks are also due to Annette Ritchie who typed the drafts in 1978-79.

Brian Head
School of Humanities
Griffith University
Brisbane
                                                            July 1985

Notes

1. B.W. Head, 'The Origin of "Idéologue" and Idéologie"', Studies on Voltaire and the Eighteenth Century, vol. 183 (1980), pp. 257-264; 'The Origins of "la science sociale" in France 1770-1800', Australian Journal of French Studies, vol. 19 (1982) pp. 115-132; 'The Idéologues Revisited', Canadian Journal of Political and Social Theory, vol. 8 (1984) pp. 163-178.

2. For the most detailed account, see R. Emmet Kennedy, A Philosophe in the Age of Revolution: Destutt de Tracy and the Origins of 'Ideology' (Philadelphia 1978)

CHAPTER ONE

INTRODUCTION: THE INTELLECTUAL AND POLITICAL BACKGROUND

I   Perspectives on Tracy and the idéologues

II Intellectuals and Politics: philosophes
    and idéologues

III Tracy's life and writings: an outline

I. PERSPECTIVES ON TRACY AND THE IDEOLOGUES

Tracy and the idéologues have been forgotten and 'rediscovered' several times by historians of ideas. In the period around 1800, securely entrenched in the Institut National, the idéologues enjoyed a reputation, which they took care to encourage, as pioneers in the human sciences. They were then relatively ignored for most of the nineteenth century, until reclaimed by liberal intellectuals of the Third Republic.[1] During the early decades of the twentieth century, the idéologues were again generally ignored, except for the attention of a few specialist historians;[2] more recently there has been a marked revival of interest in their work. There are several reasons for their fluctuating fortunes.

In the first place, the degree of attention and sympathy for their work has been partly related to changing currents of ideas in academic circles. Different generations of scholars have been more or less drawn towards certain themes in the idéologues' writings: for example, their liberal republicanism, their anticlericalism, or their scientific pretensions. This is perhaps clearest during the Third Republic, a period whose debates sometimes echoed those of the 1790s, and again in recent years when the character of the social and political sciences has undergone a close reconsideration. The chequered reputation of the idéologues, then, has partly derived from changing tendencies in intellectua life generally. Secondly, the 'great figures' approach to the study of the history of ideas has worked against the idéologues. The hall of fame of the Enlightenment philosophers accommodated many great names, such as Voltaire, Montesquieu, Rousseau, Diderot and Condillac. There was less room for minor disciples, continuators and acolytes, and the idéologues tended to be pushed into these categories. They were often regarded as having contributed nothing original beyond what had already been said by their illustrious predecessors. Moreover, the 1790s era has been deemed notable mainly for its men of action - political and military leaders, rather than philosophers.

Thirdly, there was a strong reaction in the early years of the nineteenth century against the philosophy of idéologie and its rationalist scientism and optimism. A highly unflattering portrait of idéologie emerged, which has influenced subsequent interpretations. On the one hand, the idéologues were taken to have posited a highly reductionist and materialist philosophy of sensations, in which human thought and action could hardly be distinguished from those of other animals, and where moral and religious experience were dismissed as illusory.[3] There was a movement in philosophical psychology towards a new emphasis on subjective experience (e.g. Maine de Biran), and in literature there was a revival of religious and traditionalist themes (e.g. Chateaubriand). The theory of idéologie was regarded as the last gasp of an intellectually bankrupt sensationalism, a view which still persists.[4] On the other hand, idéologie was discredited by its association with the political rationalism and faith in human perfectibility which had characterised the spirit of the 1790s. Idéologie was variously charged either with responsibility for the persecutions and turmoil of the Revolutionary period, or simply with a shallow and naive optimism which stemmed from its intellectual abstractionism and esprit de système. As if these charges were not enough to destroy the reputation of the idéologues, it has also been suggested that their social and political theory was largely mechanistic, whereas later thinkers increasingly tended to recognize the need to adopt organic models and show more concern for social processes in explaining historical change and continuity. Furthermore, it has been argued by Foucault that the models put forward by Tracy and others for both linguistic and economic analysis, were pre-scientific; in other words, that there was a clear disjunction between the structure of the idéologues' thought in these fields, and the structure of modern philosophy and economic science.[5]

For these reasons, it has become arguable that, at least in some fields, the work of Tracy and the idéologues "left no intellectual traces" and that it was destroyed not so much by Napoleon's persecution as by its own "irrelevance" for the new generations of social and political thinkers.[6] In terms of Kuhn's terminology,[7] idéologie had occupied the position of 'normal' science in the 1790s (though it had always been strongly contested, especially outside its institutional stronghold in the Institut National). However, the ideological paradigm was largely abandoned when it was found unable to satisfy the intellectual demands of philosophical and social analysts in the early nineteenth century. The words of Whitehead might be borrowed to describe aptly this perspective:

> Systems, scientific and philosophic, come and go. Each method of limited understanding is at length exhausted. In its prime each system is a triumphant success: in its decay it is an obstructive nuisance.[8]

The degree of attention and sympathy paid to Tracy's work has reflected the fluctuating judgements passed upon the writings of "ces méconnus, les idéologues".[9] F.-A.-M. Mignet, one of the secrétaires perpétuels of the Académie des Sciences morales et politiques, wrote a study of Tracy in his series of éloges on the idéologues during the 1840s.[10] Mignet had met Tracy and was well acquainted with the family of Tracy's son Victor, and he was able to report a number of family stories about Tracy's beliefs and temperament. Victor's wife, Mme Sarah Newton Destutt de Tracy, wrote a longer essay on the ideas of the old idéologue; this was published privately a few years after Mignet's éloge.[11] These two essays long provided the main source of reference upon

Tracy's life and ideas although showing a distinct lack of warmth for
Tracy's sensationalist doctrines. Their value lay in their 'inside'
knowledge of the subject and their use of some unpublished notes and
papers of the late philosopher. The next landmark was Picavet's large
volume on les Idéologues in 1891, which included a very long and
generous summary of Tracy's writings, and urged a more sympathetic
reconsideration of the idéologues' work in relation to their influence
upon nineteenth-century philosophical and social thought. Picavet's
work remained the major secondary source on Tracy for many decades. A
short and very uncritical study of Tracy's writings as a whole by
Jean Cruet appeared in 1909; Tracy's close links with the liberal and
humanitarian currents of Enlightenment thought were emphasized, but the
analysis remained superficial.[12]

Tracy's life and thought continued to be neglected in most
works on French history and the history of philosophy. When mentioned,
Tracy was introduced as a minor figure in the Assemblée Nationale
Constituante of 1789-91 and in Napoleon's Senate, or simply as the
inventor of the term 'idéologie' and one of a group of sensationalist
philosophers and liberal intellectuals known as the 'idéologues'.
However, studies of particular aspects of Tracy's thought began to
appear: for example, on his psychological and logical writings,[13] his
economic thought,[14] and his political theory.[15] His ideas were also
discussed briefly by those historians mainly concerned with the idéologues
as a group,[16] including their links with the United States,[17] and their
work for the journal la Décade philosophique.[18] Few of the idéologues
have been the subject of a thorough intellectual biography: excellent
studies on the work of Cabanis, Volney, and Sieyès,[19] have not been matched
by works of comparable depth on Daunou, Garat, Ginguené, M.-J. Chénier,
Andrieux, or J.-B. Say.[20] Research in the general field of French

liberalism in the period after 1780 has been growing, partly owing to a new interest in the early development of the social and political sciences and the origins of the theory of industrial society.[21] There have been valuable studies of some influential (and younger) contemporaries of the idéologues such as Benjamin Constant, Mme de Staël, Saint-Simon and Maine de Biran;[22] together with excellent works on important predecessors of the idéologues, including Condillac and Condorcet.[23]

Interest in Tracy's work began to increase in the 1960s and has continued since then. Some of his books were reprinted[24] for the first time since the 1820s, although there was no genuinely critical edition of his writings to complement that devoted to his close friend Cabanis.[25]

The leading commentator on the idéologues, Sergio Moravia, has published several studies which deal with the political and intellectual activities of Tracy's colleagues. His most recent volume, on the thought of the idéologues,[26] includes a substantial discussion of Tracy's 'idéologie' from the viewpoint of the materialistic anthropology of Cabanis and contemporary debates on language and sensationalism. But Moravia has nowhere presented a picture of Tracy's theories as a whole, and has instead taken up selected themes, treated with great erudition. All students of Tracy have explicated the concept of 'idéologie' at greater or lesser length; but few have attempted to discuss Tracy's work in terms of what I regard as the other central themes: namely, social science and liberalism.[27] The approach of my study is to bring together these three concerns, arguing that they are central not only in Tracy's own conception of his writings, but also as the areas of continuing importance in his work and the sources of his influence.

Tracy's writings, in my view, constitute one of the most comprehensive and interesting attempts at the beginning of the nineteenth century to elaborate a liberal theory of man, society, education and politics. Tracy's system of ideas operated on three levels. Foremost in his own hierarchy of priorities was his epistemological concern with the nature and limits of knowledge, the basis for certainties in the various sciences, and the possibilities of conceptual reform as the avenue to intellectual progress. Secondly, Tracy participated in the early French discussions about the possibilities of a social science which, he hoped, would be intimately connected with the realm of public policy in government and public instruction. And thirdly, Tracy sought to elaborate a liberal approach to economic, moral and political questions, and to defend what he saw as the liberal gains made by the Revolution.

These various enterprises were not simply echoes of the philosophes, whose writings had so inspired his admiration. Nor is it true to say that Tracy's work failed to influence later generations of theorists. Tracy was an important link in the chain of French liberalism in politics and economics; he was a methodological precursor of the behaviouralist approaches to the human sciences; and he was a pioneer of social concepts (idéologie, industrie, la science sociale, etc.) which became established in a variety of forms throughout the nineteenth century. While confident that his theory was the only solid foundation for the study of man and society, Tracy recognized that his work was not strikingly original. He claimed to be extending certain traditions of thought, in collaboration with other intellectuals whose specialist knowledge of areas like physiology was necessary for the full development of the human sciences. But he did claim to have provided a solid epistemological base for their further development, and to have introduced a greater degree of coherence among these sciences, arguing that they were all dependent on a proper understanding of the intellectual faculties of man, and thence of his needs and capacities.

Specialist research suggests that the degree of Tracy's influence upon later thinkers has been seriously underestimated by many writers, notwithstanding the claims made in his own lifetime that the philosophy of sensations was already moribund. My own view is that Tracy's influence, whether directly upon figures such as Joseph Rey, Henri Beyle (Stendhal), and Augustin Thierry, or indirectly, as with Auguste Comte and the readers of his translated works in Europe and the Americas, was due to the ambitious yet apparently rigorous character of his quest for certainty in the human sciences, and to the liberal currents in his political and economic theories. Tracy is also of interest to the historian concerned with the origins of social and political concepts. Tracy invented terms such as idéologie[28] (and its derivatives: idéologiste, idéologique). He contributed to the currency of other new terms such as la science sociale. He anticipated aspects of the theory of industrialisme,[29] and the idea of a confederation of Europe.[30] And, according to one learned commentator, Tracy was a precursor of the marginalist conception of economic values.[31]

Tracy's epistemology, social science, and liberalism will be discussed and evaluated throughout this study. The purpose of this introductory chapter is to sketch the biographical and historical context of Tracy's thought, showing the connections between his writings and the political and philosophical debates and problems of his times, and establishing the links between Tracy and the other idéologues. The following section discusses these liberal savants in terms of their group identity, their characteristic political and intellectual concerns, and their reactions to events during the Revolutionary and Napoleonic era. In the final section of this chapter, the main events of Tracy's political and intellectual career are briefly traced, before turning in subsequent chapters to the substantive discussion of his theories.

II. INTELLECTUALS AND POLITICS: PHILOSOPHES AND IDEOLOGUES

Destutt de Tracy has been properly described as one of the most important members - and sometimes as the philosophical leader[32] - of the idéologues. The ideas and activities of these men provide the immediate environment in which Tracy developed his own philosophical ideas and responses to contemporary events and it is therefore appropriate to discuss their ideas and activities. In general terms, the idéologues may be regarded as among the disciples and continuators of le mouvement philosophique in the second half of the eighteenth century, from Condillac's Essai sur l'origine des connoissances humaines (1746) and d'Alembert's 'Preliminary Discourse' to the Encyclopédie (1751), to Sieyès' Qu'est-ce que le tiers-état? (1789) and Condorcet's Esquisse d'un tableau historique du progrès de l'esprit humain (1793).

The philosophes saw themselves as developing a tradition of thought, inspired in many ways by the rationalism of Francis Bacon and René Descartes, which came into conflict with many of the established doctrines of the Church on the nature of man, society and government. The philosophes were gens de lettres and savants, an intellectual élite critical of existing culture and institutions.[33] They tended to support political reforms directed towards civil and legal freedoms, abolition of slavery in the colonies, and a rationalized system of public administration. They argued for religious tolerance and against the entrenched influence of the Church. They sought a more secular outlook in morality, government, and the natural sciences, though many were deists rather than

atheists or agnostics. Some argued that the human species was capable

of infinite progress, and that such progress could be judged in terms

of the greatest happiness of the greatest number of citizens. They

encouraged the popular dissemination of a 'scientific' worldview through

a reformed system of public instruction, believing that education was

the best weapon against oppression and injustice, and that ignorance

was the main enemy of further progress in political, economic and

cultural affairs. Most of the philosophes held that a scientific

understanding of man and society could be successfully pursued, once the

clouds of superstition and prejudice were dispelled, but they were less

concerned to elaborate a systematic theory of man, society and govern-

ment than to attack what they saw as the sources and forms of irrationality

in their own society.[34] As Condorcet wrote:

> Soon there was formed in Europe a class of men who were
> concerned less with the discovery or development of the
> truth than with its propagation, men who whilst devoting
> themselves to tracking down prejudices in the hiding
> places where the priests, the schools, the governments,
> and the ancient corporations had gathered and protected
> them, made it their life-work to destroy popular errors
> rather than to drive back the frontiers of human
> knowledge.[35]

Many of the philosophes were impressed by the English political

and legal system, with its mixed or balanced constitution so admired

by Montesquieu, its civil liberties and legal rights, and its religious

tolerance. They sometimes drew attention to the differences they saw

between England and the more repressive situation in France, which they

attributed to the effects of Catholic orthodoxy and the inefficiencies

of a traditionalist monarchy. This partly accounts for their energetic

criticisms of religious and political orthodoxies, in the name of

"reason, tolerance, humanity".[36] In their polemics against the existing authorities, however, the philosophes did not become champions of popular democracy or of public opinion. Their advocacy of "common sense" did not imply that good sense was already common. They were not moved to discuss in the form of systematic theory the problems of political power and the difficulties of carrying through their desired reforms. Many were content to hope that their policies would be adopted and implemented by an enlightened political élite which would rule in the general interest instead of protecting that of a narrow circle of nobles, courtiers and ecclesiastics. In such a polity, the philosophe and the savant might expect to gain some influence upon the formulation of rational legislation, administration and a more enlightened system of public instruction.

The philosophes have often been accused of favouring a form of "enlightened despotism", as a method of reform from above, and of wishing to take over from the Church its position of defining orthodox opinion.[37] In fact, the most plausible interpretation of le mouvement philosophique suggests that the political theory of the philosophes underwent a sequence of important changes. Montesquieu, in l'Esprit des Lois (1748), had defended the thèse nobiliaire against the monarchy. Most of the Encyclopédistes of the 1750s and 1760s such as Diderot, together with the Physiocrats such as Mercier de la Rivière, defended the thèse royale in various forms as the means of progressive centralized change. The period 1770-1789 saw an increasing degree of support for the thèse nationale, advocating various forms of representative government from republicanism to constitutional monarchy, and a greater currency of Lockean and utilitarian assumptions.[38] The problems of the corn trade, the mounting crisis of French public finances, the reform Ministry of Turgot, and the issues raised by the American War of Independence, provoked an increasing concern with political and constitutional questions, which eventually became transformed into the demand for the recalling of the Etats-généraux at the end of 1788.

The idéologues developed the Lockean and utilitarian currents in social and political thought, generally in the direction of a programme of liberal reforms within the framework of a constitutional monarchy. (Their subsequent republicanism was a pragmatic adjustment to the events of 1791-2 rather than a matter of a priori reasoning, as I will show later.) For the moment, all I wish to claim is that the philosophes were important for the idéologues because of the formers' concern to seek national reform of public finances and administration; civil and legal equality; propagation of scientific ideas and inventions to combat prejudices and to stimulate production and trade; reduction in the influence of the Church; secularization of public authorities; religious tolerance; a national system of education; and their faith in the possibility of a scientific understanding of the individual and society. Some of the main differences between the two generations derive from the idéologues' more sophisticated theories of representative government, political economy, and social science. The philosophes and idéologues represent distinct generations in the development of liberalism, both political and economic, and in the quest for a science of man and society.

The two generations were bridged most clearly in the life and writings of Condorcet and Cabanis. Condorcet (born 1743), was intimately involved with the philosophes in the two decades before the Revolution and his theories on politics, education and social science[39] had a profound influence upon the idéologues and upon the educational institutions created under the Directory in 1795. More impressed by the political doctrines of the American settlers than by the English

Constitution, Condorcet favoured democratic representation and a national system of education including civic instruction. The humanitarian and optimistic strands of the French Enlightenment found their full expression in his _Esquisse,_ completed while in hiding during the Jacobin dictatorship. But for his death in March 1794, Condorcet might well have been deemed an idéologue rather than a philosophe. Cabanis (born 1757) was also an authentic bridge between the generations, because he resided as a young man at the house of the widow of Helvétius after 1778, and became her _fils adoptif._ Mme Helvétius had moved to Auteuil in 1772 after the death of her husband. The _salon_ of Mme Helvétius at Auteuil, a few miles outside the Paris metropolis, became a meeting place for most of the philosophes of the day, and welcomed distinguished visitors such as Franklin and Jefferson.[40] The ties between Condorcet and Cabanis were close: they had moved in the same _salons_ and political clubs; Condorcet's family moved to Auteuil in September 1792 shortly before his proscription; Cabanis had married Condorcet's sister-in-law some years earlier; Cabanis was involved in the preparation for publication of Condorcet's _Oeuvres complètes_ (edition of 1804); and several of Cabanis' writings[41] directly took up themes which Condorcet had made his own. Destutt de Tracy, who had met Condorcet and Cabanis in the political clubs, moved to Auteuil in July 1792 to further his association with the doctrines and intellectual approaches of the _salon_ of Mme Helvétius. After _thermidor,_ the _salon_ of Mme Helvétius was reconstituted under the leadership of Cabanis and Tracy,[42] and the specifically 'idéologue' phase of _le mouvement philosophique_ was born. The composition of this group is somewhat problematic, and deserves some further attention.

The idéologues, as a political and intellectual generation, were born in about the mid-eighteenth century, and reached their intellectual maturity in the 1790s. Historians have taken little care to establish criteria for designating individuals as belonging to the idéologues.[43] Picavet offered a very broad definition of idéologues as "all those who accept the new term [idéologie] and the science it designates, all those who continue the philosophical traditions of the eighteenth century".[44] By defining them in relation to a philosophical viewpoint, Picavet produced a very extensive list of idéologues over three generations, from Saint-Lambert (born 1716), through Condorcet (1743), Tracy (1754) and Cabanis (1757), to the "disciples" and "continuateurs" of all persuasions from Henri Beyle (1783), Thierry (1795), and even to J.S. Mill (1806). Van Duzer also offered a very broad conception of the idéologues, beginning with Condillac (born 1714) and Helvétius (1715), and giving special emphasis to the intellectuals of the 1790s such as Condorcet, Tracy and Cabanis; but he extended the "school" of idéologues to include Bernardin de Saint-Pierre (who, though a fellow member of the Institut National, was their opponent on moral and religious matters).[45] Drucker, more recently, proposed a list of twelve idéologues who were generally accepted as having been members of the group, but he did not provide any principles of inclusion or exclusion. His list consists of Tracy, Cabanis, Volney, Garat, Daunou, Sieyès, Talleyrand, Constant, Andrieux, M.-J. Chénier, Ginguené, and J.-B. Say.[46] The problem is not simply whether each of these men deserves to be called an idéologue (for example, Talleyrand is somewhat odd alongside the others in this list). There is also the difficulty of knowing where to draw the line in admitting others into the group: what of Roederer, La Revellière-Lépaux, Gallois, Pinel, Lakanal, La Roche, Prévost, Neufchâteau, Lévesque, Boisjolin, A. Duval, Praslin, Moreau de la Sarthe, Grégoire, Lambrechts, Laromiguière, Degérando, Lanjuinais?

Were there any female idéologues - for example, Mme de Condorcet and Mme de Staël? Then there are a host of minor figures who might be said to share many of the same beliefs as the leading idéologues.[47] Presumably there were some figures who were identified with the idéologues for a time, before separating themselves from the group: examples might include Maine de Biran, Roederer, and B. Constant.

The problem of the membership and boundaries of the group is to some extent an artifical difficulty imposed upon the historian by the very term 'idéologues'. As I have shown elsewhere,[48] Tracy and his friends did not recognize the term as one of self-identification. It was invented at about the time of Bonaparte's coup of 18 brumaire, and was used to describe disgruntled critics of the new régime and, by extension, all alleged opponents of political stability and social order. Bonaparte himself, who claimed to have coined the term,[49] included various philosophes as well as his contemporary political critics under the rubric of 'idéologues'. For Bonaparte, it described a state of mind, a theoretical approach, characterised by an insistence upon interrogating existing institutions in the light of abstract principles, and upon demanding reforms in the light of these principles. Bonaparte's usage of the term is very modern, suggesting an idéologue 'type' quite distinct from other political roles, such as that of the statesman or the adminis-trator. As such, idéologues included, for Bonaparte, anyone who criticized his régime by appealing to general principles, such as the Rights of Man or the importance of individual liberty. Historians have been too quick to assume that Bonaparte's derogatory label described a well-defined group. To what extent was there a group of idéologues?

Tracy and his colleagues never constituted a cohesive party in either political or philosophical matters, whether at the height of their

influence under the Directory, or during their extended period of
fitful opposition to Bonaparte's increasingly autocratic rule after 1800.
The boundaries of the group remained fluid and informal, in the absence
of a generally recognized leader or a clearly prescribed body of 'official'
doctrine. All that might be said is that they were a circle of friends
who shared many views in philosophy and politics, and co-operated in
spreading their views through journalism, books, political and administrative activities. The idéologues are most readily recognizable in
their salons, especially those of Mme Helvétius at Auteuil and Mme de
Condorcet in Paris; the various legislative assemblies in the decades
after 1789; the Institut National after 1795, especially in the Second
Class (Moral and Political Sciences); their own journals such as la
Décade philosophique and le Conservateur; their work to establish and
defend the educational system of 1795-1802; and their close association
with the philosophical outlook of Condillac, the political views of
Condorcet, and the project of elaborating a systematic science of man
and society. These broad, descriptive criteria would produce a relatively
short list of idéologues, and allow for a changing membership over time,
as some figures became more distanced from and new figures were
attracted to the group.

The diversity of intellectual interests among the idéologues
is quite remarkable. Each individual cultivated his own chosen fields
of interest, ranging from epistemology, education, ethics and economics,
through geography, government and history, to medicine, physiology,
psychiatry, not forgetting literature, linguistics, religion and social
anthropology.[50]

Beneath this diversity, however, there were some common themes
and approaches - an interest in promoting the unity of the sciences; a

belief in the importance of scientifically-based knowledge as a liberating force in society and government; and their conception of an analytical
method, stemming largely from Condillac's sensationalist epistemology,
which they held to be the basis for advances in the human sciences.[51]
Voltaire, greatly admired by Tracy, was the philosophe who did the most
in introducing to a French audience the ideas of the English philosophers
of the new science; he had shown his respect for these men in his
Lettres philosophiques (1734). Bacon was there regarded as "le père de
la philosophie expérimentale" who anticipated many of the important
advances of the following century.[52] Locke was said to have described
the human mind as an anatomist explains the faculties of the human body;
Locke was praised for rebutting the notion of innate ideas, for showing
that "toutes nos idées nous viennent par les sens",[53] and for insisting
that empirical knowledge is quite distinct from such religious revelations
as the immortality of the soul, which can only be supported by faith.
Newton was celebrated for having rewritten mechanics and optics in terms
of a small number of fundamental laws inherent in nature, thus discovering the elementary properties of matter.[54] Similar admiring accounts
were repeated in the writings of other philosophes and savants. The
experimental method, the emphasis on observation, the search for general
laws - such features of English philosophy and science were rapidly
assimilated by many of the French who hoped to find therein the keys to
unlock the secrets of nature and the laws of individual and social
behaviour.[55]

Condillac[56] was understood by Tracy and others to have
distilled the essentials of the scientific method propounded by Bacon,
Newton and Locke, at least in its application to the study of human
action. In his Essai sur l'origine des connoissances humaines (1746),

Condillac claimed to have extended and purified Locke's account of the foundation of ideas in sense perceptions, the derivation of complex ideas from simpler units of sense perception, and the refutation of the hypothesis of innate ideas. In his Traité des systèmes (1749), Condillac developed a methodological critique of l'esprit de système which he detected in the Cartesians, whose metaphysics was not securely anchored in the philosophy of sense perceptions and observation. In his Traité des sensations (1754), Condillac attempted to demonstrate - through the famous metaphor of the statue-man whose five senses were awakened one by one - how the basic concepts of human thought (such as time and space, quantity and quality) could be shown to arise from sense experience and the combination of ideas; they did not require any resort to notions of innate or intuitive ideas. Much of Condillac's approach is summarized in the following passage:

> Judgement, reflection, desires, passions, etc., are nothing
> but sensation itself, transformed in various ways. That is
> why it has not appeared useful for us to suppose that the
> mind [l'âme] draws immediately from nature all the faculties
> with which it is endowed. Nature gives us organs to acquaint
> us through pleasure with what we must seek, and through pain
> with what we must avoid. But nature is limited to that; it
> leaves to experience the task of having us adopt habits and
> of completing the work which it had begun.[57]

The philosophes and idéologues took very seriously the call by Bacon and Descartes for a complete renovation of accepted ideas and beliefs grounded on authority. The instrument for re-evaluating the stock of ideas about man and nature was the scientific method based on observation. For the idéologues, the most significant aspect of the philosophes' thought was not their various doctrines about matter and motion, but their desire to apply the same scientific outlook to social, moral and political questions as had already been applied with success to the physical and biological sciences. The further development of the science of man became the passionate goal of the philosophes and

idéologues. The desire to become the "Newton of the moral sciences"

moved many a writer in the eighteenth century, from Hume and Bentham

in England, to Sieyès, Condorcet and Tracy in France. By the 1790s,

these French theorists were convinced that the human sciences could be

raised to the level of reliability and generality already attained by

the natural sciences. Their intentions were largely practical and

political – they desired to establish a scientific basis for formulating

rational public policy in legislation and education. The human sciences

were seen as the key to destroying the irrational authority and habitual

prejudices of the past, and to reconstructing society and culture on the

foundation of the new scientific knowledge of human faculties and

desires – the only way, in their opinion, of securing the happiness and

liberty of the citizens.[58] If the course of history, on the contrary,

presented a spectacle of misery, unhappiness and oppression, this was

due primarily to ignorance, reinforced by habit and superstition. The

remedy lay in science and education. The philosophes and idéologues

were confident that science was a liberating and humanizing force. They

were impressed by the material benefits which flowed from the applications

of the physical sciences in medicine, manufacturing and the military

arts; they hoped for, and confidently expected, a corresponding series

of social and moral benefits from their mastery of the human sciences.

The sensationalist philosophy and the scientism of the idéologues

attracted a good deal of criticism. But neither Bonaparte nor the Catholic

traditionalists would have accused them of being meddling and doctrinaire

theorists if they had been nothing but epistemologists and dabblers in

the philosophy of science. Extending the philosophe tradition, the

idéologues placed strong emphasis on the need for intellectuals or savants to play a larger part in reshaping political and educational institutions in the light of "reason".[59] Tracy and his friends had called themselves idéologistes to describe their more restricted activities as epistemologists enquiring into the intellectual faculties of man.[60] But the term 'idéologue' was clearly intended by its users to designate men seeking to link abstract ideals and social practices, criticizing traditional sources of moral and political authority, and judging the real world through the intellectual prism of their own ultimate values. L.-S. Mercier, a member of the section on morale in the Institut, and one of the few critics in that company of the Locke-Condillac approach, introduced a note of levity and disdain by describing his opponents as idiologues and idiologistes.[61] More seriously, an anonymous royalist brochure in September 1800 attacked the members of the Institut not only for peddling atheism and a false philosophy, but as "des conspirateurs idéologues" responsible for attempting to undermine the Consulate.[62] Chateaubriand later argued, in his famous defence of the Génie du christianisme (1802), that "our recent idéologues have fallen into a great error, in separating the history of the human mind from the history of things divine, claiming that the latter leads to nothing positive and that it is only the former which is of immediate use".[63]

Given the importance of the politico-practical purposes of the idéologues' work, it is appropriate to discuss briefly their political and educational doctrines[64] in the context of the Revolutionary and Napoleonic era, as a background for understanding Tracy's theories. The idéologues' approach to these questions was broadly within a liberal tradition, but they developed a number of distinctively 'idéologue' positions, some shaped in response to the exigencies of the political

and economic situation in Revolutionary France, and some reflecting
their views on the central importance of language, science and education.

Under the Jacobin regime of 1792-94, several of the idéologues -
who were identified with the political positions of the proscribed
Girondin deputies and Condorcet - suffered imprisonment, or saw their
friends persecuted or guillotined.[65] That experience left an indelible
mark on their political thought: they became even more resolved to
prevent the executive from dominating the legislature, and to ensure
that popular influence upon government remained indirect. They wanted
an end to the turmoil of the Revolution, and the peaceful institutional-
ization of the post-thermidorean republican "settlement". In their own
conception, they tried to steer a middle course between the egalitarian
and demagogic Jacobins, and the counter-revolutionary royalists and
traditionalists.[66] Returning to public life in 1794, they found that
the excesses of the previous two years had brought into disrepute the
symbols and catchwords of the philosophes, and undermined the liberal-
constitutional direction of the reforms of the earlier period (1789-91).
Catholic and royalist publicists argued forcefully that the Terror, the
proscriptions and persecutions were the abominable but logical culmination
of the attempt to reconstitute the social and political order on the
basis of rationalist and utilitarian dogmas of human perfectibility and
the Rights of Man.[67] In defending the philosophical heritage of the
Enlightenment, the idéologues used three main lines of argument.

They claimed, firstly, that the doctrines of Voltaire, Rousseau
and Helvétius were quite opposed to coercion, anarchy or despotism in
any form, and that the philosophes' doctrines in no way condoned the
Terror.[68] On the contrary, the philosophes had sought change through
the peaceful persuasion of education and legislative reform. Secondly,
the idéologues tried to establish a wide gulf between Jacobin practice

and liberal ideals. Robespierre in particular was depicted, often unfairly, as a bloodthirsty despot, an unprincipled monster, a usurper, a shallow demogogue, a sinister manipulator bent upon personal aggrandizement, and a megalomaniac who flouted the elementary Rights of Man while mouthing its language of liberty.[69] For the idéologues, the Jacobins had betrayed the liberal content of the revolutionary ideals of 1789 - the Jacobins were a terrible aberration, not the logical development of the Revolution. Robespierre and his colleagues had voiced their contempt for most of the philosophes (Rousseau excepted), for the intellectual Académies,[70] and for liberal education programmes.[71] Thirdly, the idéologues reclaimed the mantle of true spokesmen for the Enlightenment, and sought to rehabilitate the humane ideals of the Revolution, to purify them of an unsavoury association with Jacobin terrorism, and most importantly, to implement the liberal ideals through rational legislation and a new system of education. To actualize the ideals in society was the best way to demonstrate their practical benefits. Representative government and scientific education could achieve by moderation what despotism and persecution could never accomplish - a prosperous and ordered republic of enlightened and public-spirited citizens.

After the collapse of the Jacobin régime in July 1794, the thermidorean Convention began the task of social and political reconstruction. A number of liberal republicans who were part of the idéologues' circle - such as Daunou, Garat and M.-J. Chénier - were influential both in drafting the new Constitution of 1795 (which established the Directory) and in laying the foundations of a new educational system. The idéologues had always emphasized the rule of law and shown a sceptical distrust of mass political mobilization. The entry of the untutored and politically inexperienced masses into the sphere of government would place enormous strains upon the fledging

institutions, at least until the people had learned to restrain and

moderate their demands and were less amenable to demagogic manipulation.

The common citizens could not be expected to conduct themselves in a

responsible manner so long as they remained under the sway of ignorance,

prejudice and short-term passions. Responsible and patriotic citizens

would not be produced simply by guaranteeing civil and political

liberties to the whole population. The idéologues believed it was

necessary to increase the availability of education, and to revise the

content of all courses taught in the schools. Public instruction was

to become an instrument in the political survival of the republic.[72]

The idéologues' emphasis on creating a new education system

was a continuation of the philosophes' preoccupation with renovating the

stock of ideas in the community and placing central importance on

scientific methods in the study of man. Educational writings attacking

the traditional curricula and teaching methods of the old collèges had

become common after about 1750. Gradually the critics shifted their

focus from giving advice for the instruction of the sons of the nobility,

towards schemes of national public education.[73] The highpoints were

reached with Talleyrand's plan presented to the National Assembly in

September 1791, and Condorcet's plan presented to the Legislative

Assembly in April 1792[74] - neither of which was implemented during the

years of Jacobin control, which coincided with the war against the

first Coalition of European powers. The law of 3 brumaire an IV

(25 October 1795) reorganised the whole system of public instruction in

France,[75] and other legislation established the école normale in Paris

for training teachers.[76] The main provisions of the new system were that

primary schools were revitalized, the numerous collèges of the old régime

were replaced by a system of écoles centrales (at least one in each of
the 89 Departments), the special schools in technical and professional
disciplines were expanded, a number of public festivals (fêtes nationales)
were established, and the moribund Académies were replaced by the Institut
National des Sciences et des Arts, comprising three Classes - Physical
and Mathematical Sciences, Moral and Political Sciences, and Literature
and Fine Arts. Most of the idéologues became members (or associate
members) of the Institut, and were dominant in the Class of Moral and
Political Sciences.[77] The system as a whole was marked in several
respects by the idéologues' outlook - instruction was secular; utilitarian
goals were emphasized; scientific ideas were diffused as widely as
possible; the human sciences were shown to bear upon the formulation of
rational public policy; and curricula, especially in the écoles centrales,
were gradually revised in accordance with Tracy's principles of idéologie,
through the work of the Conseil d'instruction publique (especially in
1799 under Tracy's direct influence).

Under the Directory, the idéologues were very energetic in
furthering the cause of an 'ideological' education and politics.
Historians, indeed, have attributed to them a large degree of influence.
Thus, for Van Duzer, the idéologue viewpoint was the "approved doctrine
of the government".[78] Professor Cranston has claimed that the idéologues'
theories became the "official doctrine of the French republic".[79]
Bréhier noted that the creation of the Institut signified the beginning
of "the golden age of idéologie".[80] These claims require some small
qualifications, as will be shown by a closer examination of the idéologues'
involvement in the education and politics of the Directory. We have seen
above that the educational policies of the Directory were inspired by
idéologue doctrines; several idéologues served on the Conseil d'instruction

publique in the Ministry of the Interior, administering the schooling system; the idéologues also wrote books and pamphlets, established journals, and defended their educational ideas in the legislative assemblies and the Institut. There was a gap, however, between their semi-official status in defining the major doctrines of republican education and in setting the tone of the Institut, and their success in 'reaching' the ordinary population in the provinces. Primary education remained in a relatively depressed condition in the government schools. The écoles centrales had a very mixed reception outside a few large cities, and began to show signs of improvement only just before the Consulat decided to reorganize the system. The école normale in Paris operated only for a few months, early in 1795, before being closed down.[81] Similarly, the fêtes nationales failed to generate any widespread enthusiasm, and the Institut was reorganized by Bonaparte in January 1803 to eliminate the sections devoted to the 'ideological' sciences.

The idéologues of the Institut, wrote Vandal, believed they had a 'calling' to fashion public opinion, and wanted to be a spiritual power complementing the political power of the executive authorities.[82] Given the governmental support for their educational doctrines, it is a little less surprising to find that the idéologues compromised their liberalism by justifying the actions of the Directory in its executive coups against both royalist and Jacobin deputies in the legislature in 1797 and 1798.[83] The idéologues had supported the Directory in order to institutionalize their political and educational doctrines. Their primary concern was to conserve[84] 'moderate' republicanism against the forces of left and right, rather than to protect the institutions of the 1795 Constitution as the ideal form of government. When the Directory seemed too weak to play this 'conservative' role, they looked for a

strong republican General to reintroduce political and social stability.

The 1795 Constitution has often been regarded as the epitome

of idéologue thought on political and constitutional matters. Guillois,

for example, wrote that "the Constitution of year III was ... the

Charter of the idéologues".[85] This is slightly misleading, since they

did not directly frame the Constitution, and since they eventually

supported its overthrow by Bonaparte. Moreover, it is important to

note that the 1795 Constitution was in some respects a more conservative

document than that of September 1791 defining the constitutional monarchy,

and certainly less democratic than the constitution of 1793.[86] For

example, sovereignty was no longer located in the people or the nation,

but in the 'citizens', defined by a property qualification. Voting for

members of the national legislature was restricted to male property-

holders - all male citizens could participate in their local Primary

Assemblies, but only men of property could be elected from among them

to the more powerful Electoral Assemblies, which in turn elected the

deputies to the national legislature. The Constitution was prefaced by

a Declaration of the Rights and Duties of Man and Citizen, which emphasized

the rule of law, asserted the importance of private property as the basis

of prosperity and the social order, and defined the equality of citizens

as a purely civil and legal relationship with no economic implications.[87]

The reaffirmation of these principles was intended as a clear indictment

of the policies and practices of 1793-94, when some of the popular

committees and sans-culottes had pursued a campaign against wealthy

citizens. The Constitution also established a complex series of 'checks

and balances' as a safeguard against executive and/or legislative

despotism: the executive Directory of five members was completely separated from a bicameral legislature, and the power to initiate

legislation lay solely with the lower chamber, the Council of Five

Hundred. The weaknesses and disagreements engendered by this system

help to account for the series of political crises of the Directory

and its ultimate demise in Bonaparte's coup of November 1799.

In formulating the Constitution for the Consulate, Bonaparte

was able to modify the prescriptions of Sieyès and other idéologues to

his own centralist purposes.[88] As soon as the political and cultural

influence of the idéologues was threatened, they reverted to a more

clearly liberal posture of defending individual freedoms, and criticizing

the aggrandizement of the executive, just as they had earlier attacked

the Jacobin threats to liberal-constitutionalism. What kind of liberals

were the idéologues? Were they consistent in their liberalism? It is

necessary to pause a moment to consider some of the main features of

liberal thought, in order to relate Tracy and the idéologues more closely

to their intellectual context.

Liberalism in social and political thought (from Locke to Mill

in England, or from Montesquieu to Constant in France) was generally

characterized by the following aspects: (a) a desire to limit and

specify the powers of public authorities, to prevent the abuse of author-

ity; (b) a belief in progress through the use of reason; (c) a distrust

of traditional sources of moral and political authority; (d) a plea for

tolerance of diversity in religious and political beliefs; (e) protection

of individual freedom of action and expression, providing that others

were not directly harmed.[89] Such doctrines were developed in different

ways by liberal writers. Some were concerned mainly with advocating

certain institutional forms to gain their general objectives (e.g. con-

stitutional devices, forms of judicial procedure, prohibitions against state regulation of economic affairs, etc.). Others were more concerned

with defending certain 'natural rights' of the individual,[90] which were

invoked by social contract theorists as the terms of reference for all

legitimate government. In most cases, liberalism eventually became

associated with a defence of representative government, as the best

instrument for securing the liberties of the citizen. All these issues

were raised at length in the American War of Independence and the later

phases of constitution-making in the American states and in France.

The idéologues were classical liberal optimists in the period

before the Terror, supporting the Constituent Assembly's attacks on

traditional privileges, its rationalistic reorganization of many aspects

of social, religious and political life, and its proclamation of the

Rights of Man and Citizen. After the Terror, they became less optimistic

about the wisdom of universal male suffrage, and all the more anxious to

prevent either a despotic executive or a despotic legislature. Under the

Directory, they supported measures limiting freedom of the press (in

order to curb what they saw as 'extremist' critics of the régime),

provisions which required public officials to have attended a government

school, and other administrative measures designed to encourage patriotism

and civic virtue among the citizens. In this period of their greatest

influence, the idéologues sometimes experienced a tension between their

philosophical commitment to tolerance and pluralism, and their fervent

desire to see their programmes implemented in the face of opposition.

These contradictions in the activities of the idéologues, together with

their support for the Directorial coups of 1797 and 1798, and for Bonaparte

coup establishing the Consulate, appear to have tarnished their reputation

as liberals.

Moreover, it has been claimed that the idéologues, owing to

their desire to establish a "rational and scientific society largely by means of education", paradoxically combined "liberalism with planning".[91]

This claim overstates the extent to which the education system of the

Directory attempted to impose a cultural uniformity. The desire for

uniformity was always balanced by a commitment to a dual private/govern-

ment system of education, by the principle of freedom from outside

supervision in the classroom, and by their ultimate faith in the powers

of persuasion and reason.[92] Moreover, the idéologues were hostile to

state regulation in other spheres of life, especially in economic affairs,

and they were anxious to reduce state expenditures to the bare minimum.

A more sympathetic interpretation might regard the idéologues

as liberal theorists with a schematic style of thought, whose opportunities

to influence state policies occurred at a time when the society and govern-

ment were beset with intractable problems - economic chaos, military

threats, civil and religious conflict, political instability. In the

absence of a favourable climate of opinion, and with very limited

resources, the idéologues supported the Directorial group because they

saw it as attempting to create a pragmatic middle ground between the

political extremes, and as willing to promote a new cultural integration

around principles which the idéologues supported. When it became clear

that the Directory had failed, and that it could only survive through

continued violations of the Constitution, they looked for a republican

General who could become a symbol of integration as the chief executive

in a new representative régime. Their support of Bonaparte showed that

they had recognized that a stable government enjoying public respect

was the essential precondition for advancing their reform programme.

They wanted both order and progress. Indeed, they were correct in antici-

pating that Bonaparte would answer the wishes of a conflict-wearied

population.[93] The Consuls proclaimed that the Revolution was 'completed', and that the struggles were over.[94] It is another matter that the idéologu

misjudged his character and future policies, but in this they were not

alone. Bonaparte had cultivated their favour throughout the Directory

years; they were not to know that he would abandon the doctrines he

professed to admire.

It is ironical that the term _libéral_ was widely used to

describe Bonaparte's political outlook at the time of the transition

from the Directory to the Consulate. In what is perhaps the first

example of the leader of a government proclaiming the 'liberal' nature

of his future policies, Bonaparte's message at the end of the events of

19 brumaire announced that "les idées conservatrices, tutélaires, libérales

sont rentrées dans leurs droits".[95] Bourrienne recalled in his _Mémoires_

that some 'men of good faith' had called Bonaparte "un héros des idées

libérales".[96] Just after the _coup_, the journal _Ami des lois_ - whose views

were generally similar to those of the idéologues - presented a gloss on

Bonaparte's 'liberal ideas', attributing to him a belief in patriotism,

republicanism, the rule of law, charity, political and religious

tolerance, forgiveness of past wrongs, and "all the conceptions of a

strong and generous mind".[97] This _pot pourri_ of vague policies and

sentiments is only marginally related to the mainstream of what historians

have identified as liberal political thought - but herein lies an

important early usage of the term _libéral_ in French politics.[98]

The idéologues' relationship with subsequent régimes may be

briefly sketched. Although the _Tribunat_, _Corps législatif_, and _Sénat_

conservateur, created by the Consulate, contained many of the idéologues,

their power rapidly diminished. The strong executive established by

Bonaparte had no use for a critical, rationalistic and academic

philosophy[99] whose principles were hostile to centralized authority and

to the traditional sources of social and religious integration, upon
which the new régime increasingly relied. When the liberal deputies in
the Tribunate criticized his legislative proposals in 1801, he had them
purged from the legislature.[100] The powers of the assemblies were
steadily reduced, and the Senate was flooded with compliant appointees
who voted constitutional changes giving further powers to the First
Consul.[101] Bonaparte was anxious to "heal the wounds" of the Revolution
by suppressing social and political antagonisms and by drawing upon
traditional loyalties to promote unification and stability. The republican
festivals of the 1790s were gradually abolished, and Catholicism was
re-established in 1802 as the official religion, with priests returning
to their former prominence as educators. The return of the émigrés
changed the intellectual climate,[102] though royalist propaganda was
subjected to the same strict censorship as Jacobin opinions. The écoles
centrales were replaced in 1802 by lycées with more traditional curricula.
Bonaparte abolished the last refuge of the idéologues, the Class of Moral
and Political Sciences, when the Institut National was reorganized in
January 1803, the members being dispersed to other more innocuous Classes.
Bonaparte's work of destroying liberal republicanism was completed by
the reintroduction of slavery in the French colonies in 1802,[103] and
the creation of the Empire with himself as the hereditary emperor
Napoléon Ier in 1804.[104] The republican calendar was thereafter
abolished and la Décade had to become la Revue, until it was forcibly
merged with its conservative rival, le Mercure, in 1807.

The idéologues, having lost all their bases of influence,
increasingly withdrew from political activity of all kinds, in silent
protest against a régime which they could no longer criticize openly.[105]
A few Senators had voted against the creation of the Empire,[106] but

opposition was completely ineffective. A number of Senators (including Tracy and Cabanis) were implicated in General Malet's conspiracy in the summer of 1808, but lack of evidence suggested that the Senators had not been privy to Malet's plans.[107] Malet's attempt to repeat his performance, during Napoleon's absence in Russia in 1812, again showed no evidence that the idéologues were participants in an active conspiracy. However, Napoleon took the opportunity, upon his return, to deliver a famous tirade against the idéologues, whom he blamed for all the problems faced by the nation since he took office:

> We must lay the blame for all the misfortunes suffered by our fair France upon idéologie, that shadowy metaphysics which seeks out with subtlety the first causes on which it bases the legislation of peoples, instead of making use of the laws known to the human heart and the lessons of history. These errors have inevitably led to the rule of bloodthirsty men. Who, indeed, proclaimed the principle of rebellion as a duty? Who flattered the people in attributing to it a sovereignty it was incapable of exercising? Who destroyed respect for and the sanctity of laws in seeing them only as the will of an assembly composed of men ignorant of civil, criminal, administrative, political and military law, rather than as based on the sacred principles of justice, the nature of things and civil justice. When one is called upon to revitalize a state, it is necessary to follow principles that are constantly opposed [to idéologie]. History is the canvas of the human heart; it is in history that must be sought the advantages and disadvantages of various types of legislation. These are the principles which a great empire's Council of State should always keep in view.[108]

After the idéologues had lost their power and influence, it was much easier for them to be characterized as impractical utopians, designers of artificial schemes and blueprints, doctrinaire believers in human perfectibility, and ignorant of the practical requirements for social order and political stability. Under the Consulate and Empire, the term idéologie and its variations became terms of derision. A decade after the fall of Robespierre, the liberal voice was forced into silence and had lost all its institutional sources of influence. There was a resurgence of religious and sentimental literature, a revival of traditionalist theories of political obligation in the writings of Chateaubriand, de Maistre, de Bonald and a number of lesser writers, and a resurrection of the pomp and ceremony befitting an empire founded in part on military prowess. Liberalism resurfaced only in 1814 with the restoration of a constitutional monarchy.

The liberals who remained in the Senate throughout the Empire – including Tracy, Garat, Grégoire, Lambrechts and Lanjuinais – were to play a role in the transition from the Empire to the constitutional monarchy of Louis XVIII. The Allied armies entered Paris, and the Senate pronounced the deposition of Napoleon and his heirs on 2 April.[109] The Russian Emperor Alexander promised that France should have a 'liberal' constitution. A working party of Senators – including Tracy – drafted a constitution which rejected the royalist party's insistence on the concept of divine right, claimed that Louis was "freely called" to the throne by the French people, and which sought a plebiscite to confirm the people's approval.[110] The royalist party eventually prevailed, and the Charte constitutionnelle was proclaimed on 4 June 1814 as having been "granted" by the king to his "subjects".[111] Nevertheless, the terms of the Charter were relatively liberal in proclaiming legal equality, freedom of religion and the press, establishing that Ministers might be members of the legislature, and protecting properties acquired from biens nationaux[112] during the Revolution. Few of the idéologues remained politically active after 1815, and several were omitted from the Chambre des Pairs and the Institut Royal as regicides or for collusion with Napoleon during the Hundred Days. However, the liberal salons and journals of the Restoration carried on the main ideas of the idéologues, some of whom regained a measure of influence in opposition circles.[113] Those few who survived until the eve of the July Monarchy were pleased

to find that Guizot, then Minister for Education, initiated in 1832 the
reconstitution of the former bastion of the idéologues, renamed the
Académie des Sciences morales et politiques.[114]

The relationships between the idéologues and the various régimes
in France after 1789 have now been sketched, suggesting certain continu-
ities in doctrine between the philosophes and the later idéologues. The
main themes highlighted have been their liberalism, their belief in
the importance of science and education, and their desire to elaborate
a science of man and society as a foundation for national government.
With these concerns in mind, we turn to Destutt de Tracy himself. What
follows is a highly compressed outline of Tracy's life and writings,
focussing on those aspects which are most relevent for understanding the
essential structure of his system of ideas.

III. TRACY'S LIFE AND WRITINGS: AN OUTLINE

Antoine-Louis-Claude Destutt de Tracy was born on 20 July 1754,[11]
in Paris.[116] He was descended from the Stutt family in Scotland, whose
sons had always followed a military career. Four Stutt brothers came
to France from Scotland in 1420 to join the cause of the French Dauphin,
the future Charles VII, against England. One of the brothers, Walter Stutt
was ennobled by Letters-Patent in 1474 under Louis XI, and settled on
estates in the Bourbonnais near Moulins. His descendants acquired by
marriage the estate of Tracy in Nivernais in 1586, and that of Paray-le-
Frésil in 1640.[117] The father of the future philosopher, Claude-Charles-
Louis Destutt de Tracy, born 1723, commanded the King's gendarmerie at
the battle of Minden against the Duke of Brunswick in 1759; seriously
wounded, the soldier died several years later, leaving only one child,
Antoine-Louis-Claude, who was prevailed upon to uphold the military

traditions of the family.[118] His education was supervised by his mother,

until at about the age of sixteen he went to complete his studies at the

école militaire in Strasbourg, and also at the University there, which

had a liberal and cosmopolitan character and was a training ground for

the diplomats of Europe.[119] Tracy's fellow students at that time

included Narbonne,[120] Ségur[121] and Talleyrand.[122]

In common with the eldest sons of noble families, Tracy was

rapidly promoted through the commissioned ranks of the army.[123] In

April 1779, he married the great-niece of the Duc de Penthièvre, and

became the colonel of the regiment of Penthièvre Infantry. On the death

of his grandfather Antoine-Joseph (1694-1776), Tracy inherited consider-

able estates in Nivernais and Bourbonnais, and the title of Comte de

Tracy.[124] Tracy divided his time between his regiment, his young family

and his mother and grandparents at the family home of Paray-le-Frésil.

There is little evidence concerning the reasons that Tracy became

dissatisfied with his life as a rich and successful officer of noble

birth.[125] However, it appears that he thoroughly read the works of the

physiocratic economists, including Quesnay, Dupont de Nemours, and the

'revisionist' writings of Turgot. Tracy also read the encyclopédistes

and philosophes, and formed a particular admiration for Voltaire, whom

Tracy had visited at Ferney in 1770.[126] His studies in classical philo-

sophy at Strasbourg confirmed his appreciation of Condillac's sensational-

ist critique of Scholasticism, but there is no evidence that he became

familiar with Kantian philosophy at that time, nor with the particular

form of empiricism developed by David Hume.[127] Together with many young

nobles, Tracy was enthusiastic about the principles contained in the

American Declaration of Independence,[128] supported the administrative

reforms undertaken by Turgot and later by Necker, and was generally attracted to the liberal currents of ideas in politics, economics, religion and education. There is no evidence from these years that he frequented any of the salons in Paris or at Auteuil. Nor did he develop a passion for travel, diplomatic service overseas, or modern languages. He remained content to stay in France, and could read books only in French or the ancient languages.

Tracy's career took a new direction after 1788, at the age of thirty-four years. He became a politician and administrator during the early years of the French Revolution. In August 1788, in the midst of a general movement towards new forms of representation, Louis XVI agreed to the establishment in the Bourbonnais of a provincial Assembly, and four local Assemblies in the larger towns. Tracy was the spokesman for the local Assembly at Moulins when it resolved on 27 November to press for the creation of Etats-provinciaux composed of "véritables représent- ants de la Nation, légitimement et librement élus, au lieu de simples délégués du gouvernement tels que nous sommes".[129] An ordinance on 17 December authorized a meeting of the three états (clergy, nobility and tiers), to consider the question. Two hundred and twenty-five people from the three états met at the Town Hall of Moulins on 22 December and successfully petitioned the King to agree to the creation of Etats- provinciaux on the model of those recently granted in the Dauphiné province. Meetings of the three Orders began on 16 March and each proceeded to nominate commissioners who were to draw up a cahier of principles and demands, and then to meet together in order to formulate a single cahier for the whole province.[130]

Tracy was one of eight commissioners for the Bourbonnais nobility elected on 18 March 1789. In a series of enthusiastic meetings on 21 March, the nobility and the clergy offered to share the burden of taxation and dispense with their monetary privileges; Tracy was among

the deputation sent to the Third Estate informing them of this abnegation.

The proposal to draw up a joint cahier was strongly endorsed by all three

Orders.[131] But after two days of separate meetings to discuss the

articles of their own cahiers, disagreement arose at a joint meeting on

24 March because the nobility refused to accept a proposal for voting by

head at the Etats-généraux rather than voting separately by Orders. The

nobility thereby hoped to negate the doubling of the representation of

the Third Estate agreed by the King at the end of December 1788. So

the plan for a joint cahier was abandoned, and each of the états commenced

electing separate representatives to the Etats-généraux. Tracy was one

of three deputies for the Bourbonnais nobility.[132] The majority of the

Bourbonnais nobility had ultimately been concerned to avoid making major

concessions which would threaten their traditional prerogatives; Tracy

emerged in their debates as the leading spokesman for liberal principles

and leading critic of their privileges. He had urged voting by head at

the Etats-généraux, supported the double representation of the Third

Estate, and was in large measure responsible for some relatively liberal

provisions in the cahier of the Bourbonnais nobility.[133] However, he

had not been successful on some important issues. Article 8 of Section

III of his cahier instructed the representatives of the nobility to

support separate debates and voting by Order at the Etats-généraux, and

article 15 of Section II declared that the rights and prerogatives of

the nobility were never to be renounced.

When the Etats-généraux began meeting on 5 May, Necker, the

King's Minister, initially upheld the separation of the three Orders in

voting. However, on 17 June the tiers renamed itself the National

Assembly, and on 20 June its members and some liberal supporters from other Orders took the so-called Tennis Court oath to continue meeting until a new Constitution had been established. Within a few days the National Assembly had been joined by about 170 clergy and 50 nobles. The King eventually reversed his policy on 27 June, and ordered the unification of deputies from the three Orders.[134] Contrary to the accounts given in some biographies,[135] Tracy had not accompanied liberal nobles like La Rochefoucauld into the National Assembly before the King's change of policy, nor had Tracy signed the Tennis Court oath.[136] Indeed, Tracy and his two colleagues had felt bound to seek the approval of their constituents before complying with the King's command to join the National Assembly. The other two Bourbonnais nobles eventually refused to serve in the new Assembly.[137]

Subsequently, Tracy supported the abolition of noble and other privileges on 4 August, the Declaration of the Rights of Man on 26 August, legislation to establish a Civil Constitution of the Clergy in July 1790, and measures to reform public finances. As an inexperienced politician, probably a little bewildered by the rapid turn of events, Tracy remained independent of factions and parties.[138] He adopted a pragmatic and cautious approach in most of his eighty or more interventions in debates, often concerning himself with administrative detail,[139] rather than high-flown rhetoric. He demonstrated no special gifts for leadership or eloquence in more than a few of his contributions. Only two of his speeches from this period were published. The first was a defence of the work of the Assembly against Burke's attack in the House of Commons on 9 February 1790.[140] The second was a major speech in September 1791 in favour of the rights of blacks in the colony of Saint-Domingue to enjoy equal political rights with white colonists.[141] Tracy was clearly in sympathy with the views of the Société des Amis des Noirs (the antislavery lobby led by Brissot and Lafayette), but he was never a member of that body.[142]

While living in Paris as a deputy in the National Assembly, Tracy had many opportunities to meet and admire the leading political and intellectual figures who gathered in the various salons and clubs. Most important for Tracy's developing intellectual interests, he became a member of the Société de 1789, whose main convenors were Sieyès and Condorcet, and whose members included Cabanis, Garat and Bailly.[143] Moderate constitutionalists such as Lafayette and La Rochefoucauld established the Club des Feuillants in opposition to the Jacobins (or Amis de la Constitution); Tracy was a member toward the end of his political career in Paris.[144] In 1789-90, he also frequented the salon of Adrien Duport, another foyer of anti-Jacobin opinion.[145] However, it may be that Tracy's involvement in these clubs was less a matter of doctrinal purity than of friendships and experiment. For in March 1791, he became a foundation member of the Moulins branch of the Société des Amis de la Constitution (affiliated to the Paris Jacobins), alongside the other deputies from Moulins.[146] The membership of this Club of liberal patriots at this time was no stronghold for sans-culottes and ouvriers of egalitarian views. On the contrary, it was "une société de bourgeois et de lettrés",[147] which regarded as a tragedy for the nation the death of the comte de Mirabeau in April 1791. However, after the unsuccessful flight of the King towards the border in June 1791, the Moulins branch shared in the general radicalization of public opinion: the King's name was struck from their oath of loyalty, and a motion to open their membership was only narrowly defeated. Tracy's regiment had been implicated in protecting the flight of the King, and Tracy felt obliged in the Assembly to declare his devotion to the Constitution and to condemn the complicity of his regiment.[148]

The Assemblée Nationale Constituante completed its work on the new Constitution at the end of September 1791, with great haste and confusion. Tracy was later to argue that a legislative assembly should never take upon itself the dual functions of legislation and constitution-making.[149] The Constituant had declared its members ineligible for the new legislature which met in October 1791, thus depriving the new assembly of all the most experienced politicians, a loss which Tracy regarded as foolhardy.[150] He returned to his home at Paray-le-Frésil, enrolled in the National Guard, and undertook the functions of mayor. Elections for the executive of the Département de l'Allier gave Tracy a place on the administrative Council, and he joined the Commission des Impositions; a few days later (on 19 November) he was elected Président du Département.[151]

The impending war with Austria led to the formation of three French armies in December 1791 by Louis de Narbonne, Minister for War (a friend of Tracy). Tracy returned to active duty as a maréchal-de-camp in the Army of the North under Lafayette, and had some skirmishes with Austrian troops in April-June. Meanwhile, the Jacobins in Paris were attacking the loyalty and integrity of Lafayette and of other constitutional moderates.[152] Tracy, with a heavy heart, considered it prudent to resign from the army in July 1792 and seek a quiet life as an ordinary citizen with his family. Contrary to some accounts,[153] Tracy was not among the group of senior officers with whom Lafayette crossed the border into Austrian-held terrirory on 19 August 1792, after the Jacobin triumph in the Legislative Assembly.[154]

Tracy thus established his residence at Auteuil only in the summer of 1792. There is a strong probability that he had already met, in the Parisian clubs and salons, some of the other inhabitants of Auteuil - Cabanis, Gallois, La Roche, and others who were the centre of the salon of Mme Helvétius. But even if Tracy and Cabanis had already met, it was only after they became neighbours and shared the same intimate circle of political and literary friends that they became intellectual colleagues. Tracy was the debtor in their early exchanges; Cabanis was far more knowledgeable in the physical and biological sciences, and in his understanding of the philosophical heritage of the Enlightenment.

As the Jacobin ascendancy grew in Paris and in provincial towns, it became increasingly difficult for erstwhile nobility like Destutt-Tracy[155] to avoid accusations of sympathy for royalism, or lack of civisme.[156] The loi de suspects in 1793 granted wide powers to local comités de surveillance in seeking out people whose zeal for republicanism was not abundantly manifest.[157] The Moulins comité de surveillance accused Tracy of incivisme and aristocratie, and imposed a large "revolutionary tax", which he claimed was too large for him to pay; they accepted instead the revenues of his properties in the Moulins district.[158] Nevertheless, the commissaire civil in Paris ordered the arrest of Tracy and other residents of Auteuil on 2 November 1793. Cabanis was involved in hospital administration in Paris and escaped the fate of his colleagues. After a few weeks in l'Abbaye prison, Tracy was transferred on 16 December to Les Carmes, where he shared a cell for many months with Jollivet. His attempts to demonstrate his republicanism and patriotism met with no success, and it was more than three months after the fall of Robespierre before he was freed from prison, after eleven months of detention.[159]

After his retirement from the Assembly, local administration, and the army, Tracy had devoted himself to scientific and philosophical studies. In his unpublished manuscripts, Tracy wrote:

> Delivered by circumstances to my penchant for a solitary
> and contemplative life ... I devoted myself to study, less

to extend my knowledge than to become aware of its
sources and bases. That had been the object of my
life-long curiosity. It had always seemed to me that
I was living in a mist which restricted me, and the
most extreme dissipation had never been able to
distract me completely from my desire to know the
characteristics of all our surroundings, how we know
them, and what we are sure about.[160]

Tracy's studies commenced with the study of nature - the
biological and physical sciences; Tracy noted that this emphasis was all
the more welcome under the Jacobin régime, for helping him "forget the
history of men".[161] He began with Buffon's vast work on natural history,[16]
with its broad evolutionary perspectives, imaginative hypotheses, and
detailed classifications. He moved on to the works of Lavoisier and
Fourcroy, who were breaking new ground in establishing the methods and
nomenclature of modern chemistry.[163] Lavoisier was especially important
for Tracy's intellectual development, because Lavoisier claimed to adhere
to Condillac's analytical method in his search for the laws governing the
combination of the elements in physical nature. "M. de Tracy regarded
Lavoisier as a great idéologue, who had perceived most of his discoveries
via the chain of his ideas, before confirming them by experience".[164]
Tracy himself wrote at this time that:

Lavoisier led me to Condillac ... I had previously seen only
his Essai sur l'origine des connoissances humaines ... and
had come away without knowing whether I should be satisfied
or not with it ... In the prison of les Carmes, I read all
his works, which made me go back to Locke. Taken together
they opened my eyes, their conjunction showed me what it was
I was seeking. I saw clearly that it was the science of
thought [la science de la pensée]. The Traité des systèmes
in particular was for me a shaft of light, and, having
found the Traité des sensations neither complete nor free
of errors, I then drew up for myself a short exposition of
the main truths which result from the analysis of thought.[165]

According to Mignet, the summary of truths was written on
5 thermidor [23 July 1794], just a few days before Tracy was expected to
face the revolutionary tribunal and thence the guillotine; Robespierre,
however, was himself overthrown on 9 thermidor and the revolutionary

tribunal never pronounced upon Tracy's case. The table of truths took

a quasi-algebraic form:

> The product of the faculty of thinking or perceiving =
> knowledge = truth. In a second treatise on which I am
> working, I show that three other terms must be added to
> this equation: = virtue = happiness, sentiment of loving.
> And in a third work, I will demonstrate that the following
> must be added: = liberty = equality = philanthropy.
>
> It is for lack of a sufficiently precise analysis that we
> have not yet managed to find the deductions or mediating
> propositions needed to make obvious the identity of these
> ideas. I hope to prove by facts what Locke and Condillac
> have shown by reasoning, that morality [la morale] and
> politics are capable of demonstration.[166]

This strikingly deductivist system of identities provided the

germ for a series of papers and volumes written during the following

fifteen years, Tracy's most creative period of intellectual activity.

Released from prison in October 1794, Tracy returned to his family and

friends at Auteuil. Sixteen months later, he had the good fortune to be

elected as an associate (non-resident) member of the Class of Moral and

Political Sciences in the newly created Institut National. Tracy's

nomination on 18 February 1796, to the section entitled Analyse des

Sensations et des idées,[167] was very curious considering that he had not

yet published anything in that field. Cabanis, a member of that section,

was doubtless reponsible for Tracy's election, having inside knowledge

of Tracy's work at Auteuil. Cabanis' faith proved justified: two months

after his election, Tracy began reading a series of papers in which the

concept of idéologie as a fundamental science of ideas was first

elaborated.[168] Tracy was also very busy serving on commissions of the

Institut responsible for awarding prizes in essay competitions, and

investigating ideas put forward by private citizens.[169] Outside the

Institut, Tracy helped to edit the literary section of the Mercure

français , alongside Lenoir-La Roche, Cabanis, Barbier and others

(1795-98).[170] He also contributed during the Directory period to the

Moniteur, to la Décade philosophique, and possibly (given Cabanis'
involvement) to le Conservateur.

Tracy became increasingly involved in educational problems,
and eventually was directly involved with the administration of the
system of national education established by the law of 3 brumaire an IV
(25 October 1795). The Minister of the Interior established a Conseil
d'instruction publique in October 1798, composed largely of Tracy's
friends at the Institut.[171] Tracy was appointed as a member in February
1799, and drafted a number of circulars designed to improve the quality
of teaching in the écoles centrales and to standardize the curriculum in
accordance with his conceptions of idéologie.[172] He also corresponded
privately with a number of teachers sympathetic to his own conception of
the "science of ideas", and thereby promoted the diffusion of these
doctrines throughout France. By this time, Tracy was confirmed in his
new role of savant and educator. He had refused Bonaparte's offer of
a position as maréchal de camp in the ill-fated military and scientific
expedition to Egypt.[173] Tracy continued to write papers for the Institut
on various themes related to idéologie, including criticisms of Kant and
of Berkeley.

Tracy also wrote several pamphlets of topical and theoretical
interest. The first was an answer to a prize-essay topic "Quels sont les
moyens de fonder la morale chez un peuple?", offered by the Class of
Moral and Political Sciences in 1797 and later withdrawn for lack of
response among the literary public. Tracy's answer appeared in three
issues of the Mercure français in January 1798, and later as a pamphlet.
He argued that law and order was of fundamental importance in society,
and that wise legislation and education were the keys to instituting
public virtue and private happiness.[174] His second pamphlet, an anonymous
digest of Charles Dupuis' l'Origine de Tous les Cultes (1795), appeared

in 1799. Tracy appeared to agree with Dupuis' argument that Christianity

was a permutation of prior religious systems, and that all systems of

worship of supernatural beings have their origins in worship of the sun

and stars.[175] Tracy published a greatly extended second edition of his

Analyse of Dupuis in 1804, in the midst of the Catholic revival in

France.[176] The anonymity of his work was pierced by Napoleon's librarian

in 1806, in his Dictionnaire des ouvrages anonymes:[177] Barbier and Tracy

had worked together ten years earlier on the Mercure français. The final

pamphlet to be noted here, was a defence of the education system established

in 1795, and especially a plea for the retention of the écoles centrales.

The Consulate government after 1800 had begun an enquiry into the operation

of the schools; Tracy's pamphlet, partly based on information obtained

from his work on the Conseil d'instruction publique, argued that minor

changes could greatly improve the idéologues' educational programme and

that drastic reorganization of the system would be irresponsible.[178]

Tracy's plea was ignored – lycées came to replace the écoles centrales,

and all traces of idéologie were removed from the curricula.

Tracy commenced writing in about 1800 a series of philosophical

works intended as texts in the écoles centrales. This decision was partly

a result of his work on the Conseil d'instruction publique, where he

became aware of the acute absence of suitable texts for the new courses

in the schools, and partly a fulfilment of his desire – first formulated

in 1794 – to provide a systematic account of the human understanding in

its various manifestations. The first volume in the series, Projet

d'éléments d'idéologie ..., appeared in 1801.[179] The second volume on

Grammaire (1803), and the third volume on Logique (1805), completed the

first part of the series, devoted to the origin, formation and expression

of ideas in general. The Logique was dedicated to his friend Cabanis, whose conversations and whose <u>Rapports du physique et du moral de l'homme</u>[18]

had guided and inspired Tracy's own studies. Tracy wrote:

> ... the goal that I most desire is that my work might be
> regarded as a consequence of your own, and that you might
> see it as a corollary of the principles which you have
> expounded. Such a result would be extremely advantageous
> for the science itself [idéologie] which henceforth would
> be placed on its true foundation: for, if I deserve such
> praise, the intention of Locke is fulfilled; ... and in
> accordance with his wish, the detailed history of our
> intelligence is at last part of and dependent on <u>la</u>
> <u>physique humaine</u>.[181]

In the meantime, the schools and curricula for which these works were

written had been abandoned in 1802 by the Consulate government; Tracy's

works were not read by students but by the <u>savants</u>.

Tracy had intended his three volumes on epistemology and language

to form the basis for three further volumes on the moral, economic and

political sciences. But works of liberal doctrine could not be published

in Napoleonic France owing to the censorship of views critical of the

Imperial government. Tracy began to establish closer links with

Jefferson in the United States, who had already met or corresponded with

a number of idéologues, and who had been elected in 1802 as a foreign

associate member of the Class of Moral and Political Sciences. Tracy

sent Jefferson several of his publications, and was subsequently elected

a member of the American Philosophical Society in January 1806.[182] Tracy

wrote a critique of Montesquieu in 1806-7 as a basis for his projected

volumes on politics and economics. He sent the manuscript of this

<u>Commentaire sur l'Esprit des Lois</u> to Jefferson in Virginia in June 1809;

Jefferson was sufficiently impressed to undertake an English translation,

published anonymously as <u>A Commentary and Review of Montesquieu's Spirit</u>

<u>of Laws ...</u> (Philadelphia 1811).[183] After writing a manuscript on

political economy in 1810-11, Tracy sent it to Jefferson in November 1811,

but the translation was seriously delayed and appeared only in 1817 as

A Treatise on Political Economy.[184]   In the meantime, the same work had

appeared in France, after the fall of Napoleon, as Elémens d'idéologie,

IVᵉ partie, Traité de la Volonté (Paris 1815).   The anonymous manuscript

of the Commentaire was reprinted in France, apparently without Tracy's

permission, in Liège (1817) and Paris (1819).   He decided to issue an

authorized edition under his own name, which appeared in July 1819.[185]

Tracy's volume on morale was never completed.   He sketched a few ideas,

including a chapter on l'amour which was sent to Jefferson for comment

in 1821 and had been published in an Italian translation in 1819.   Tracy

confessed to a certain timidity which prevented him declaring publicly

his opinions on such sensitive matters in his own country.[186]

Tracy had re-entered politics after Bonaparte's coup of

November 1799, when he was appointed alongside Volney, Cabanis and Garat

among the first thirty members of the Sénat conservateur on 25 December.[187]

It was the Senators who in turn nominated the members of the Tribunate

and the Legislative assembly, and many idéologues were included in these

bodies.   Having been appointed for life, the Senators did not face the

threat of periodic purges which faced their colleagues elsewhere.   On the

other hand, they had no power to initiate legislative debates or to discuss

matters not referred to them by other bodies.   They were the "elders" of

the Revolution, with high status but little power.   Compliance with

Bonaparte's wishes was further induced by handsome salaries, and by the

creation in 1803 of sénatoreries, or revenues from landed estates (none

of the idéologues were thus rewarded).   The Senate was cajoled into passing

a decree on 2 August 1802 proclaiming Bonaparte Consul for Life.   This

became the pretext for issuing what was really a new Constitution two

days later, in which the powers of Bonaparte were greatly extended and

the powers of the other legislative bodies were reduced; the epithet

conservateur was removed from the Senate's title. A further constitutiona.
decree was passed on 18 May 1804 introducing the hereditary principle
and after obtaining approval in a plebiscite, the Empire was proclaimed.
The Tribunate was abolished by a further decree in August 1807.[188]
Tracy and his colleagues had long since become silent partners in the
growing autocracy, taking little part in the Senate's proceedings or in
the pageantry of the Empire. The title of "comte de l'Empire" was
bestowed uniformly upon all Senators - even upon Grégoire (who alone
had voted against the new nobility in March 1808) and posthumously upon
Cabanis (who was granted the title two weeks after his death in May 1808).
There was no effective, organized opposition to Bonaparte after 1802, and
apart from the theatrical interventions of General Malet in 1808 and 1812
(see above, p. 34), there was no open rebellion. In December 1813, when
a committee of the Corps Législatif - including Maine de Biran - dared to
imply that France would be best served by a policy of peace, their mild
protest was met with Imperial rage, and the assembly was dissolved.[190]

The death of Cabanis in May 1808 deprived Tracy of his closest
intellectual colleague. Tracy's sense of loss was immense[191] and in
some respects he never regained his impetus, for he began to lose his
ability to undertake sustained work and he gradually began to lose his
eyesight. Tracy was elected on 15 June to fill Cabanis' place in the
Classe de Langue et de littérature française (later the Académie
française), and his discours de réception on 21 December was an éloge
of his friend Cabanis.[192] After Cabanis' death, Tracy moved from Auteuil
to Paris,[193] where he lived the rest of his life except for visits to his
country estates.

Napoleon suffered reverses in March 1814 and the Allied armies
occupied Paris. The Senate was invited to appoint a provisional government and draft a new Constitution. Talleyrand organized the Senators to

nominate a provisional government of five members (including himself) on
1 April, and Tracy was among the 63 signatories of the Senate's procès-
verbal approving this measure.[194]   On 2 April, a resolution was passed
by the Senate to remove Napoleon and his family from the throne, and it
requested Lambrechts to draft a more detailed resolution for the following day. The Russian Emperor Alexander gave an audience to the Senators,
in which he said: "it is just and wise that France be given strong and
liberal institutions which are in accord with the present lumières. My
allies and I only come to protect the liberty of your decisions".[195]
The next day, the Senate debated and approved the detailed resolution,
drawn up by Lambrechts, specifying the motives for the déchéance of
Napoleon: fourteen considérants were given, listing his infractions
against the liberties and good government of the French people.[196]   There
is some dispute concerning whether Tracy or Lambrechts moved the original
resolution to remove Napoleon from office on 2 April. Tracy apparently
claimed to friends, including Lafayette, that it was he who had moved
the historic decree; if this was the case, it may seem curious that
Lambrechts was selected to draw up a more detailed resolution for the
next meeting. The official reports of proceedings are silent on the
matter, noting only that "a member" proposed the déchéance.

The provisional government organized informal meetings to
consider the general principles for a new constitution; several Senators
were invited to attend these meetings. After a preliminary meeting on
3 April, a committee of five Senators (Tracy, Lambrechts, Lebrun, Barbé-
Marbois, Emery) was asked to draw up the text of a constitution.[197]   The
text was debated at these large and informal meetings on 4 and 5 April.[198]
It was sent to the Senate where the 29 Articles were referred to a

Committee before being passed unanimously.[199] This constitutional
project recalled the Bourbons to the throne as if by popular request,
rather than ancient prerogative. The document was seen, however, as
extremely self-serving, for the Senators had defended their own positions
and revenues as matters of constitutional law (article 6). The royalist
party was able to exploit this unpopular aspect of the document, although
their main disagreement concerned the Senators' attempt to cast the
monarch's authority in terms of social contract theory and national
sovereignty. Eventually, in consultation with the provisional government
instead of the Senate,[200] Louis XVIII was able to proclaim his own
Constitution as a _fait accompli_ on 4 June. Its provisions were generally
acceptable to the constitutional liberals, despite their dislike for
Louis' re-assertion of his traditionalist legitimacy.

Tracy was nominated on 6 June a member of the Chambre des
Pairs (and retained this position after Napoleon's Hundred Days interrupted
the continuity of the restored monarchy). His title of comte was restored
on 31 August 1817.[201] Several of his colleagues, however, were excluded
from royal favour and thus from official positions - Volney, Garat,
Lambrechts, Sieyès, Grégoire. The cynical _Dictionnaire des Girouettes_
took to task the political opportunism and vacillations of public figures
during the previous decades. Each biographical entry was accompanied by
a string of flags indicating how many régimes had been served or accommodated by each subject. Destutt de Tracy received eight "flags". His
entry concluded: "M. de Tracy is a quiet person who, while writing
brochures to stifle his boredom, allows events to pass by - without,
however, forgetting to make use of them to his greatest advantage".[202]
The great survivors and opportunists, however, were men like Fouché,
Fontanes and Talleyrand who each collected twelve "flags" - together with

the Senate ("dit Sénat-Conservateur"), which attracted the particular
scorn of the compilers of the Dictionnaire.[203]

Tracy attended some of the more important debates in the
Chamber, but refused to attend the trial of Marshal Ney.[204] He was more
active outside the Chamber, maintaining a distinguished salon, frequented
by constitutional liberals from the legislature[205] and a variety of
young admirers, who included at various times Henri Beyle, Victor
Jacquemont, Augustin Thierry, Joseph Rey, and a number of young Academicians
including Pierre Flourens. Tracy's only son, Victor (1781-1864), who had
resigned from the army in 1818 after many years of active service, entered
the lower Chamber in 1822, beginning a political career of some thirty
years, mainly among the left-liberal opposition who were attracted to
Tracy's salon.[206] Tracy was involved with B. Constant, Lafayette and
others in establishing a Société des Amis de la Presse in November 1817
to campaign against restrictive censorship.[207] Tracy's four volumes of
Elémens d'idéologie were reprinted in 1817-18, and again in 1824-25 and
1826-27. Several of his works were translated into Italian, Spanish and
German[208] (in addition to the English translations supervised by Jefferson).
Through his secretary, Tracy maintained a wide correspondence with several
young disciples, and a circle of foreigners who sought his advice on
political and other matters.[209] The publication of Tracy's Commentaire
boosted the liberal cause, and occasioned polemical reviews, both flatter-
ing and highly critical.[211] Though increasingly given to bouts of
melancholy,[212] Tracy made a favourable impression on distinguished
visitors, such as David Ricardo[213] in 1822 and Lady Morgan[214] in 1829.

Tracy died in Paris on 9 March 1836, having survived his wife
by twelve years. His old friend Daunou, and the young physiologist
Flourens (secretary of the Académie des Sciences), delivered éloges at

his funeral on 12 March. Tracy's place in the Académie française was taken by François Guizot.[215] His place in the section of Philosophy in the Academy of Moral and Political Sciences was taken by J.-P. Damiron[216] (a disciple of Cousin's spiritualist eclecticism), whose Essai sur l'histoire de la philosophie in 1828 had been severely critical of Tracy and his fellow idéologistes. For Guizot and Damiron, Tracy had been a faithful disciple of eighteenth-century materialism and utilitarianism; but the nineteenth century had, in their opinion, transcended such narrow perspectives, reintegrating the spiritual and the material aspects of human life and thought.[217] For Daunou and Flourens, on the other hand, Tracy's idéologie pointed the way to a precise knowledge of the human understanding and of economic and political organization.   In Daunou's words, Tracy "devoted his whole life to research into and propagation of those truths which can exercise a happy influence on the intellectual, moral and political habits of peoples".[218] Flourens singled out for special attention Tracy's

> method, that instrument of all our progress in every field. It is through it that he [Tracy] has had such a great influence on philosophy, and from there this influence has spread to all the other sciences, which all ultimately draw from philosophy their basic rules; and hence his name, which belongs to two Academies, that of moral and political sciences, and the Académie française, is pronounced with no less respect and acknowledgement in the Academy of physical and mathematical sciences than in the other two.[219]

The partisans and critics of Enlightenment philosophy will always dispute its intellectual value and historical influence. Judgements about Tracy's importance will doubtless be influenced by the observer's position in this debate. Tracy typified a particular strand of late eighteenth-century thought in which reason, truth, liberty and happiness became mutually entwined, as both the means and end of a progressive social and philosophical movement against the forces of ignorance, repression, habit and superstition. In 1798, Tracy wrote: "... la vérité est le seul chemin du bien-être".[220] Tracy's search for fundamental truths about the individual and society, led him back to an enquiry into the operations of the human intellect. In the following chapter, I will examine Tracy's quest for a "scientific" understanding of man, his concept of idéologie as the key to providing certainty in the knowledge of man, his emphasis on the mechanisms of concept-formation and language, and his critique of "metaphysics" and religion.

FOOTNOTES TO CHAPTER ONE

1   Most notably by F. Picavet, whose lengthy study on Les Idéologues
     (Paris, 1891) was the only detailed vue d'ensemble until the recent
     works of S. Moravia. Other important contributions of that period
     included J. Simon, Une Académie sous le Directoire (Paris, 1885),
     and A. Guillois, Le Salon de Mme Helvétius: Cabanis et les
     Idéologues (Paris, 1894).

2   For example, G. Chinard, Jefferson et les Idéologues (Baltimore,
     1925), C.H. Van Duzer, Contribution of the Idéologues to French
     Revolutionary Thought (Baltimore, 1935), and E. Cailliet, La
     Tradition littéraire des Idéologues (Philadelphia, 1943).

3   For example, J.-P. Damiron, Essai sur l'histoire de la philosophie
     en France au XIXe siècle (Paris, 1828); A. Franck (ed.), Dictionnaire
     des sciences philosophiques (Paris, 1844-52), articles on "Destutt
     de Tracy" and "Idéologie".

4   C. Smith, "Destutt de Tracy and the Bankruptcy of Sensationalism",
     in Balzac and the Nineteenth Century, eds. D.G. Charlton, J. Gaudon,
     A.R. Pugh (Leicester, 1972), pp. 195-207. Contemporary criticisms
     of idéologie are reported below in chapter 2.

5   M. Foucault, The Order of Things: An Archaeology of the Human
     Sciences (London, 1970). Foucault argued, however, that in the
     field of medicine and the biological sciences, contemporary figures
     such as Pinel and Cuvier were pioneers of the modern viewpoint;
     Cabanis was not specifically evaluated in this context by Foucault.

6   J.N. Shklar, [review of K.M. Baker's Condorcet], Political Theory,
     vol. 3 no. 4 (November 1975), pp. 469-474. A more general argument
     is found in Shklar, After Utopia: the Decline of Political Faith
     (Princeton, 1957).

7   T.S. Kuhn, The Structure of Scientific Revolutions (Chicago, 2nd ed.
     1970). Cf. S.S. Wolin, "Paradigms and political theories", in
     Politics and Experience: Essays presented to Professor Michael
     Oakeshott ..., eds. P. T. King and B.C. Parekh (Cambridge, 1968),
     pp. 125-152; I. Lakatos and A. Musgrave (eds.), Criticism and the
     Growth of Knowledge (Cambridge, 1970).

8   A.N. Whitehead, Adventures of Ideas (New York, 1933), p. 159.

9   A. Canivez, "Les Idéologues", in Histoire de la Philosophie, tome III
     [Encyclopédie de la Pléiade, tome XXXVIII] (Paris, 1974), p. 99.

10   "Notice historique sur la vie et les Travaux de M. le Comte Destutt
     de Tracy", in F.-A.-M. Mignet, Notices et Memoires historiques
     (Paris, 1843), vol. I, pp. 245-288. This essay originally appeared
     in the Séances et Travaux published by the Académie des Sciences
     morales et politiques, vol. I (1842), pp. 396-434; studies on other
     idéologues also appeared in this series, and were reprinted in
     Mignet, Portraits et Notices historiques et littéraires (Paris,
     2e ed. 1852).

11 Mme Sarah Newton Destutt de Tracy, "Notice sur M. Destutt de Tracy", first published separately in 1847, and reprinted in Essais divers, Lettres et Pensées de Madame de Tracy (Paris, 1852-55), vol. I, pp. 305-404.

12 J. Cruet, La Philosophie morale et sociale de Destutt de Tracy (1754-1836) (Tours, 1909).

13 R. Lenoir, "Psychologie et logique de Destutt de Tracy", Revue philosophique de la France et de l'étranger, vol. 84 (1917), pp. 527-556; O. Kohler, Die Logik des Destutt de Tracy (Borna-Leipzig, 1931); G. Madinier, Conscience et mouvement (Paris, 1938), ch. 3; S. Moravia, "Logica e psicologia nel pensiero di D. de Tracy", Rivista critica di storia della filosofia, vol. 19 (1964), pp. 169-213.

14 E. Allix, "Destutt de Tracy, économiste", Revue d'économie politique vol. 26 (1912), pp. 424-451.

15 V. Stepanowa, Destutt de Tracy: eine historisch-psychologishe untersuchung (Zürich, 1908); P.-M. Imbert, Destutt de Tracy: Critique de Montesquieu (Paris, 1974).

16 R.G. Carey, The Liberals of France and their relation to the development of Bonaparte's dictatorship ... (Ph.D. thesis, University of Chicago, 1947); G. Gusdorf, Introduction aux sciences humaines (Strasbourg, 1960); J.W. Stein, The Mind and the Sword (New York, 1961); S.M. Gruner, Economic Materialism and Social Moralism (The Hague, 1973); S. Moravia, Il tramonto dell'illuminismo (Bari, 1968).

17 G. Chinard, Volney et l'Amérique (Baltimore, 1923); G. Chinard, Jefferson et les Idéologues (Baltimore, 1925); D. Echeverria, Mirage in the West: A History of the French Image of American Society to 1815 (Princeton, 1957).

18 R. Fargher, The "Decade philosophique" and the defence of philosophy... (D.Phil. thesis, Oxford University, 1940); J. Kitchin, Un journal philosophique: La Décade ... (Paris, 1965); M. Régaldo, Un milieu intellectuel (Paris/Lille, 1976).

19 F. Labrousse, Quelques notes sur un médecin-philosophe, P.-J.-G. Cabanis (Paris, 1903); M.S. Staum, Cabanis and the Science of Man (Ph.D. thesis, Cornell University, 1971); J. Gaulmier, L'idéologue Volney 1757-1820: Contribution à l'histoire de l'Orientalisme en France (Beyrouth, 1951); P. Bastid, Sieyès et sa pensée (Paris, 2e ed., 1970).

20 The more important discussions of these thinkers are included in my Bibliography.

21 For example, H. Gouhier, La jeunesse d'Auguste Comte (Paris, 1933-41).

22 For example, P. Bastid, Benjamin Constant et sa doctrine (Paris, 1966); G.E. Gwynne, Madame de Staël et la Révolution française (Paris, 1969); F.E. Manuel, The New World of Henri Saint-Simon (Notre Dame, 1963); L.A. Siedentop, The Limits of Enlightenment ... Maine de Biran and Joseph de Maistre (D.Phil. thesis, Oxford University, 1966); H. Gouhier, Les Conversions de Maine de Biran (Paris, 1947).

23   I.F. Knight, The Geometric Spirit: the abbé de Condillac and the
      French Enlightenment (New Haven, 1968); K.M. Baker, Condorcet: From
      Natural Philosophy to Social Mathematics (Chicago, 1975).

24   A.-L.-C. Destutt de Tracy, A commentary and Review of Montesquieu's
      Spirit of Laws [Philadelphia, 1811] (New York, 1969); Tracy,
      A Treatise on Political Economy [Georgetown, 1817] (New York, 1970);
      Tracy, Eléments d'idéologie, 5 vols. [Paris, 1801-1815] (Stuttgart,
      1974); Tracy, Elémens d'idéologie, vol. I, Idéologie proprement dite
      and vol. II, Grammaire [Paris, 1817] ed. H. Gouhier (Paris, 1970) -
      the later volumes were not reprinted owing to the small demand for
      the early volumes.

25   P.-J.-G. Cabanis, Oeuvres philosophiques, ed. C. Lehec and
      J. Cazeneuve (Paris, 1956).

26   S. Moravia, Il pensiero degli idéologues (Firenze, 1974).

27   In 1973, when I began the present research, there had been no
      intellectual biography of Tracy since Picavet (1891) and Cruet (1909).
      It now appears that several students have been working independently
      on Tracy in the 1970s. The results of their research reached me too
      late for any detailed consideration, but it may be useful to indicate
      how my own work differs from theirs. Dr Barry Garnham's account of
      Tracy's thought [B.G. Garnham, The Social, Moral and Political
      Thought of Destutt de Tracy (Ph.D. thesis, University of Durham,
      1974)] has inevitably dealt with some of the same questions as my
      own study, and I believe that there would be general agreement with
      his view that Tracy's approach was based more on deduction than
      observation. However, Garnham says little about Tracy's liberalism,
      and virtually nothing about Tracy's notions of science and social
      science. Another recent study, by Dr Emmet Kennedy [R.E. Kennedy,
      A Philosophe in the Age of Revolution: Destutt de Tracy and the
      origins of 'Ideology' (Philadelphia, 1978)] has provided a wealth
      of detail about Tracy's life and times. The book is organized in
      a strictly chronological structure, seeking to unite the discussion
      of Tracy's life, writings, and milieu. In its fine detail and use
      of unpublished sources, it is sure to become the standard biography
      of Tracy. As a discussion of Tracy the theorist, it lacks thematic
      unity and overlaps only slightly with my own work. I should add
      that all the documentation in my own present monograph is the
      result of my independent research.

28   B.W. Head, "The origins of 'idéologue' and 'idéologie', Studies on
      Voltaire and the Eighteenth Century, vol. 183 (19), pp. 257-264.

29   The theory of industrialisme was developed by Saint-Simon in 1817-20
      during the Restoration (though his theory of the importance of savant
      and productifs is considerably earlier); Tracy's ideas on political
      economy, were written in 1806-11 though not published in French
      before 1815. Both men were working in the economic tradition of
      Smith (1776), Sieyès (1789) and Say (1803), as will be established
      in chapter five below.

30   Saint-Simon's proposal for a European confederation dates from 1814;
      Tracy's idea was sketched in 1806, but published in French only
      after the Restoration.

31   F.A. von Hayek, The Counter-Revolution of Science (Glencoe, 1955), p. 115.

32   The stronger claim about Tracy's leading position in the group is
     asserted by S.M. Gruner, Economic materialism and social moralism,
     pp. 63, 77; and by R.E. Kennedy, A philosophe in the age of
     Revolution, pp. ix, 333. M. Leroy, however, claims that Cabanis was
     "le chef des idéologues": Histoire des idées sociales (Paris, 1950)
     vol. II, p. 163. The question of leadership is a sterile dispute,
     since the men themselves did not defer to any acknowledged leader.
     This was because of their diversity of interests, and their
     consequent lack of group coherence.

33   The secondary literature discussing the philosophes is vast. The
     most useful overviews include the works of E. Cassirer, P. Gay,
     P. Hazard, K. Martin, D. Mornet, and C. Vereker (see Bibliography,
     part C). L.G. Crocker provides a good definition of the philosophes,
     as "that group of eighteenth-century French writers who, refusing
     to abide by Christian doctrines and dogma and by the authority of
     the Church, searched for the truth in the light of reason and
     experience. They were not (excepting Condillac) systematic philosophers
     in the usual sense, but were primarily combative social and moral
     thinkers, usually with a strong tinge of scientific dilettantism".
     An Age of Crisis (Baltimore 1959), p. xv.

34   All these generalizations about the philosophes assume a unity of
     outlook and temperament which did not exist. On the extent of
     their diversity, and for an argument suggesting an underlying unity,
     see P. Gay, The Party of Humanity (New York, 1971), chapter 4.
     Rousseau is an exception to almost every generalization one might
     venture about the philosophes, so much so that Professor Lough omits
     him from his list of key representatives of the philosophes:
     J. Lough, "Who were the philosophes?", in Studies in Eighteenth
     Century French Literature, ed. J.H. Fox et al. (Exeter, 1975),
     pp. 139-150.

35   Condorcet, Sketch for a Historical Picture of the Progress of the
     Human Mind, trans. J. Barraclough (London, 1955), p. 136. I have
     slightly modified the translation [cf. Esquisse, ed. O.H. Prior
     (Paris, 1933), p. 159].

36   Ibid., p. 137.

37   See, for example, C. Becker, The Heavenly City of the Eighteenth-
     Century Philosophers (New Haven, 1932).

38   See, for example, L. Gottschalk, "Three Generations", in Studies in
     Eighteenth-Century Culture, vol. 2, ed. H.E. Pagliaro (Cleveland,
     1972), pp. 3-12; G.J. Cavanaugh, "Turgot: the rejection of enlightened
     despotism", French Historical Studies, vol. 6 (1969), pp. 31-58;
     A.M. Wilson, "Why did the political theory of the Encyclopedists not
     prevail? A suggestion", French Historical Studies, vol. 1 (1960),
     pp. 283-294.

39   See the works by K.M. Baker on these aspects of Condorcet's thought.

40   A. Guillois, Le Salon de Mme Helvétius, chapter 2; S. Moravia, Il
     tramonto dell'illuminismo, chapter 1; S. Moravia, "La Société d'Auteuil
     et la Révolution", Dix-huitième siècle, no. 6 (1974), pp. 181-191.

41   Most notably, the "Lettre sur un passage de la Décade philosophique et en général sur la perfectibilité de l'esprit humain" [19 April 1799], in P.-J.-G. Cabanis, Oeuvres philosophiques, ed. C. Lehec and J. Cazeneuve (Paris, 1956), vol. 2, pp. 512-519. Tracy regarded Condorcet as "a great philosopher: most others are, I think, merely scribblers". Letter to C. Fauriel, 6 June 1804, cited in J.-B. Galley, Claude Fauriel (Saint-Etienne, 1909), p. 143 n.2.

42   A. Guillois, Le salon de Mme Helvétius, chapter 3 and passim.

43   For an interesting exercise of this kind in relation to the philosophes, see J. Lough "Who were the philosophes?".

44   F. Picavet, Les Idéologues, p. 23.

45   C.H. Van Duzer, Contribution of the Idéologues, p. 72.

46   H.M. Drucker, The Political Uses of Ideology (London, 1974), p. 4.

47   An example is discussed in M. Régaldo, "Profil perdu: l'idéologue Chaussard", in Approches des Lumières: Mélanges offerts à Jean Fabre (Paris, 1974), pp. 381-401.

48   B.W. Head, "The origin of 'idéologue' and 'idéologie'" (1980).

49   There are uses of the term in Parisian journals from early in 1800; Bonaparte's conversations using the term seem to begin a year later, though evidence is very sketchy; Bonaparte was, however, important in popularizing the term. For journalistic uses of the term, in addition to those cited in Head (1980), see the anonymous review of Tracy's Projet d'élémens d'idéologie [1801], in Mercure de France, 6 January 1802, p. 101; and the anonymous review of Cabanis' Rapports du physique et du moral de l'homme [1802], in Mercure de France, 22 January 1803, p. 220, and 29 January 1803, p. 273.

50   S. Moravia has, more than most commentators, drawn attention to the range of their work: see, for example, La scienza dell'uomo nel settecento (Bari, 1970). J.-P. Damiron had remarked, in Tracy's life time, that the thought of the école sensualiste might be usefully understood as being divided between Cabanis the physiologist, Tracy the metaphysician, and Volney the moralist: Essai sur l'histoire de la philosophie en France au XIXe siècle (Bruxelles, 3e ed. 1829), p. 91.

51   Tracy had argued rather unconvincingly in 1802 that the French idéologistes were not strict "disciples" of Condillac, and that each worked independently in developing his own views in the moral, political and "ideological" sciences. If they happened to agree on many things, this was definitely not due to any esprit de système analogous to the Germanic addiction for Kant or Leibnitz. Tracy, "De la métaphysique de Kant", Mémoires de l'Institut National, Classe des Sciences morales et politiques, tome III (Paris, 1802), p. 548.

52   F.-M. A. de Voltaire, Lettres philosophiques, ed. R. Pomeau (Paris, 1964), p. 78.

53 Ibid., p. 84.

54 Ibid., lettres 14, 15, 16.

55 A more detailed discussion of the idéologues' understanding and
    application of such ideas may be found below, especially in chapters
    two and four. It is important to be aware that there were diverse
    ways of interpreting the heritage of Newton and Locke.

56 The abbé de Condillac was a scholar of retiring disposition, not
    at all in the combative mould of most other philosophes. Although
    he wrote some works on political economy and education in his later
    years, his reputation, and his influence on Tracy, was largely
    through his earlier writings on epistemology and scientific method.

57 Condillac, Traité des sensations, in Oeuvres philosophiques, ed.
    G. Le Roy (Paris, 1947), vol. 1, p. 222.

58 The idéologues' practical concerns with politics and education
    suggest that they were closer in orientation to the writings of
    Condorcet and Helvétius than to Condillac, whose more technical
    work they nevertheless singled out for special commendation. For
    a similar view, see C.-A. Saint-Beuve, Portraits littéraires (Paris,
    1880), vol. I, p. 243.

59 Cf. Damiron, Essai sur l'histoire de la philosophie, p. 43: "Napoleon,
    who was hardly fond of their doctrine as science, liked it no more
    as a party". For Bonaparte's remarks about the "theory of signs"
    in March 1798, cf. Guillois, Le Salon de Mme Helvétius, pp. 121-122;
    also P.-L. Roederer, Bonaparte me disait ... conversations notées
    par le comte P.-L. Roederer (Paris, 1942), pp. 11-12.

60 Tracy, Elémens d'idéologie, vol. I (Paris, 3ᵉ ed. 1817), pp. 118, 224, 318, 320,
    360, 362; Tracy, "De la métaphysique de Kant", pp. 560, 596, 604.
    Other usages by contemporaries such as Pinel, Daube, and Laboulinière
    are cited in my article, "The Origin of 'Idéologue' and 'Idéologie'",
    p. 259.

61 L.-S. Mercier, Néologie (Paris, 1801), pp. xlvii-lxi.

62 [Anon.], Etrennes de l'Institut national et des lycées (Paris:
    Moller, an VIII), discussed in a police report of 27 September 1800,
    reprinted in Aulard (ed.) Paris sous le Consulat, vol. I (Paris, 1903),
    pp. 675-677. Earlier usages in January and April 1800 are reported
    in my article (1980).

63 F.-R. de Chateaubriand, Génie du christianisme, ed. P. Reboul (Paris,
    1966), vol. 1, p. 421. The idéologue P.-L. Ginguené savagely
    attacked Chateaubriand's work in a series of review articles published
    in la Décade philosophique, 30 prairial, and 10, 20 messidor an X.
    In his Mémoires d'Outre-Tombe, ed. V. Giraud (Genève, 1946), Vol. I,
    pp. 365-366, Chateaubriand had the last word.

64 Tracy's views on politics and education are discussed in detail in
    chapters six and seven.

65 Tracy, Ginguené and Daunou were imprisoned, but several savants and
    littérateurs lost their lives (Bailly, Lavoisier, Vicq-d'Azyr,
    André Chénier, Condorcet, Chamfort, Roucher, and various Girondin

deputies including Brissot). For various reasons, Sieyès, Garat, M.-J. Chénier and Cabanis survived without having to withdraw from public life.

66 This is the major theme in the political position of the Thermidorean idéologues, and supporters of the Directory from 1794 until the early years of the Consulate.

67 This accusation abounds in the journals and pamphlets of the traditionalist groups in France and elsewhere: see, for example, the writings of Rivarol, La Harpe, de Bonald, de Maistre, Fiévée, Barruel Burke; and the Journal des Débats after 1799.

68 See, for example, F.A. Kafker, "Les encyclopédistes et la Terreur", Revue d'histoire moderne et contemporaine, vol. 14 (1967), pp. 284-295; R. Mortier, "Les héritiers des 'philosophes' devant l'expérience révolutionnaire", Dix-huitième siècle, no. 6 (1974), pp. 45-57; M. Régaldo, "La Décade et les philosophes du XVIIIe siècle", Dix-huitième siècle, no. 2 (1970), pp. 113-130; R. Fargher, The 'Decade philosophique' ... (D.Phil. thesis, Oxford University, 1940), chapter 2; J. Kitchin, Un journal 'philosophique' ... (Paris, 1965), Part III.

69 Cf. Daunou's remarks in his Mémoires, ed. Barrière (Paris, 1848), and in A.-H. Taillandier, Documents biographiques sur P.-C.-F. Daunou (Paris, 1841).

70 The Académie française and the Académie des Sciences were closed by the Convention in August 1793: see R. Hahn, The Anatomy of a Scientific Institution (Berkeley, 1971), chapter 8, and J. Simon, Une Académie sous le Directoire (Paris, 1885), chapter 1. For the Jacobins' attack on the philosophes, see, for example, Robespierre's remarks cited in J. Kitchin, Un journal 'philosophique' ..., p. 101, n.1.

71 Public instruction became a low priority in the face of the war against the First Coalition in 1792-93, though educational projects continued to be debated in the Convention. For one example of a very "illiberal" proposal by the Jacobin deputy L.-M. Lepelletier (championed by Robespierre in July 1793), see H.C. Barnard, Education and the French Revolution (Cambridge, 1969), pp. 119-123.

72 This was a major theme of the educational debates in the Convention in 1794-95.

73 Cf. R. Mortier, "The 'philosophes' and public education", Yale French Studies, no. 40 (1968), pp. 62-76; J.A. Leith, "Modernisation, Mass Education and Social Mobility in French Thought, 1750-1789", in Studies in the Eighteenth Century, ed. R.F. Brissenden (Canberra, 1973), vol. II, pp. 223-238; D. Mornet, Les origines intellectuelles de la Révolution française (Paris, 6e ed. 1967).

74 These reports were reprinted in C. Hippeau (ed.), L'instruction publique en France pendant la Révolution: discours et rapports ... (1881). Daunou paid tribute to Talleyrand and Condorcet when introducing the educational legislation of October 1795: cf. his speech reprinted in Hippeau, op.cit., pp. 476-78.

5   The text is printed in A. Duruy, L'instruction publique et la
     Révolution (Paris, 1882), pp. 375-380; also in Tracy, Elémens
     d'idéologie, 5 vols. (Paris, 1824-26), IV, pp. 383-395, and ibid.
     (Bruxelles, 1826-27), IV, pp. 376-387.

76   Lakanal's report, justifying the creation of the école normale, is
     reprinted in Hippeau, L'instruction publique en France pendant la
     Révolution, pp. 408-422.

77   Simon, Une Académie sous le Directoire, esp. chapter 7. Cabanis
     saw the Institut as "une véritable encyclopédie vivante": Oeuvres
     philosophiques (1956), vol. I, p. 125. The latter remark was
     attributed to Condorcet by M. Lyons, France under the Directory
     (Cambridge, 1975), p. 94. The structure of the Institut is given
     below in Appendix II .

78   C.H. Van Duzer, Contribution of the Idéologues, p. 7.

79   M. Cranston, "Ideology", Encyclopaedia Britannica (Chicago, 1975),
     Macropaedia, vol. IX, p. 194. For an example from a later period,
     cf. D.S. Goldstein, "'Official philosophies' in Modern France: the
     example of Victor Cousin", Journal of Social History, vol. 1 (1968),
     pp. 259-279.

80   E. Bréhier, The History of Philosophy, trans. W. Baskin (Chicago,
     1968), vol. VI, p. 27.

81   The problems of the schools and the reasons for their mixed success
     are examined in more detail in chapter seven.

82   A. Vandal, l'Avènement de Bonaparte (Paris, 1907), vol. I, p. 5.

83   The political history of the Directory is examined in more detail
     in chapter six.

84   Hence the title of the journal edited in 1798 by Daunou, Garat and
     M.-J. Chénier: le Conservateur. Another journal of the same name
     was produced in 1818-1820 by traditionalists including Chateaubriand.

85   Guillois, Le Salon de Mme Helvétius, p. 104. Guillois also claimed,
     in the same sentence, that this Constitution was "the work of Daunou":
     this is to exaggerate greatly his influence in the Commission des
     Onze of the Convention in April-August 1795. Guillois' claims are
     repeated by L. Coser, Men of Ideas (New York, 1965), p. 192.

86   Cf. J. Godechot, Les institutions de la France sous la Révolution et
     l'Empire (Paris, 1951), p. 396. The texts of the various constitutions
     are contained in J. Godechot, Les constitutions de la France depuis
     1789 (Paris, 1970). Tracy noted in 1806 that the people had not
     given strong support to the 1795 Constitution in the plebiscite of
     that year: Commentaire sur l'Esprit des Lois (Paris, 1819), p. 147.
     Tracy and Sieyès were critical of the absence of an independent body
     capable of preserving the Constitution, by adjudicating disputes.

87   The 1793 Constitution, which was never implemented, contained
     provisions which were mildly social-democratic, such as the right to
     education and to subsistence. For a detailed discussion, cf.
     A. Mathiez, "La Constitution de 1793", Annales historiques de la

Révolution française (1928), pp. 497-521. The plebiscite for the 1793 Constitution attracted greater support than that of 1795.

88   Cf. A. Vandal, l'Avènement de Bonaparte, I, chapter 12; P. Bastid, Sieyès et sa pensée, pp. 231-260; R. Guyot, "Du Directoire au Consulat", Revue historique, vol. CXI (1912), pp. 1-31.

89   For general background on these issues, cf. J.P. Plamenatz (ed.), Readings from Liberal Writers, English and French (London, 1965), "Introduction"; W.M. Simon (ed.), French Liberalism, 1789-1848 (New York, 1972); E. Bramsted and K. Melhuish, Western Liberalism: A History in Documents from Locke to Croce (London, 1978); E. Halévy, The growth of philosophical radicalism, trans. M. Morris (London, 1949); K.R. Minogue, The Liberal Mind (London, 1963); K. Martin, French Liberal Thought in the Eighteenth Century (London, 1962).

90   Variously specified in terms of life, liberty, security, property, and even happiness. Each of the French Constitutions of 1791, 1793 and 1795, was prefaced by a different statement of these "rights of man and citizen". These disappeared under the Consulate and the Empire.

91   M. Cranston, "Ideology and Mr Lichtheim", Encounter (October 1968), p. 70. The same author makes a similar point, even more strongly, in his article on "Ideology", Encyclopaedia Britannica (1975), Macropaedia, IX, p. 194: "Their teaching combined a fervent belief in individual liberty with an elaborate program of state planning".

92   This point is developed further in chapter seven.

93   According to C. Fauriel, the French would have supported any government guaranteeing "le repos": Les derniers jours du Consulat [1804] (Paris, 1886), p. 3.

94   On 15 December 1799, the three future Consuls (Bonaparte, Cambacérès and Lebrun) issued the following Proclamation to the French people: "A Constitution is presented to you. It brings to a close the uncertainties which the provisional government brought to external affairs and the domestic and military situation of the Republic. In the institutions which it establishes, it puts at the head magistrates whose devotion seemed necessary to its activity. The Constitution is founded on the true principles of representative government, on the sacred rights of property, equality and liberty. The powers it institutes will be strong and stable, as they must be to guarantee the rights of the citizens and the interests of the State. Citizens, the Revolution is established upon the principles in which it originated: it is over". (Text in J. Godechot, Les constitutions de la France depuis 1789, p. 162). The journals of the day rallied to this theme: see, for example, the Moniteur, 25 nivôse an VIII (15 January 1800), pp. 456-57.

95   Cited in A. Vandal, l'Avènement de Bonaparte, I, p. 400.

96   L.A. Fauvelet de Bourrienne, Mémoires sur Napoléon, le Directoire, le Consulat, l'Empire et la Restauration, 10 vols. (Paris, 1829), III, p. 29.

97   Amis des lois, 7 December 1799, cited in A. Aulard, Paris sous le Consulat, I, p. 42.

98   The first self-conscious usage of the term in a party-political sense is usually credited to the liberales in the Spanish Cortès of 1810-11.

99   Cf. A. Morellet, Mémoires (Paris, 1823), II, p. 120.

100   R. Dutruch, Le Tribunat sous le Consulat et l'Empire (Paris, 1921), chapters 1, 2; A. Gobert, L'Opposition des Assemblées ... (Paris, 1925), pp. 221-233; C. Fauriel, Les derniers jours du Consulat, pp. 20-23; Mme de Staël, Dix années d'exil (Paris, 1966), pp. 4-5, 29, 40. Cf. Lucien Bonaparte, Lucien Bonaparte et ses mémoires (Paris, 1882), II, p. 457: letter to Talleyrand, 12 February 1801: "What you tell me of the miscontents in the Tribunate does not astonish me. Since brumaire, my opinion is clear. There is no peace possible with the execrable faction which hankers for '93".

101   A. Gobert, L'Opposition des Assemblées, chapters 6-9; J. Thiry, Le Sénat de Napoléon (Paris, 1932), passim.

102   Cf. R. Fargher, "The retreat from Voltairianism, 1800-1815", in The French Mind: Studies in Honour of Gustave Rudler, ed. W.G. Moore et al. (Oxford, 1952), pp. 220-237; J.-L.-E. Lerminier, De l'influence de la philosophie du XVIIIe siècle ... (Bruxelles, 1834), pp. 237-239.

103   Fauriel, Les derniers jours du Consulat, pp. 42-47; H. Blet, Histoire de la colonisation française (Paris, 1946), vol. II, chapter 4.

104   G. Lefebvre, Napoleon (London, 1969), I, p. 182ff; J. Thiry, Le Sénat de Napoléon, pp. 130-144.

105   P.-L. Ginguené, Journal de Ginguené 1807-1808, ed. P. Hazard (Paris, 1910); A. Gobert, L'Opposition des Assemblées, p. 359; A. Guillois, Le Salon de Mme Helvétius, pp. 180-182, 197-198; L. Villefosse and J. Bouissounouse, L'Opposition à Napoléon (Paris, 1969), chapters 6, 7; Fauriel, Les derniers jours du Consulat, pp. 97-99; P. Gaffarel, "L'Opposition républicaine sous le Consulat", La Révolution française, vol. 13 (1887), pp. 530-550, and vol. 14 (1888), pp. 609-639.

106   J. Thiry, Le Sénat de Napoléon, pp. 142-143.

107   F. Masson, "Les Conspirations du Général Malet", part 2, Revue des deux mondes, 15 September 1919, pp. 358-389; Aulard (ed.), Paris sous le Premier Empire (Paris, 1923), III, p. 644ff.

108   Address to the Council of State, 20 December 1812, cited in Lafayette, Mémoires (Paris, 1837-38), V, pp. 297-98.

109   The question of whether it was Tracy himself who formally proposed the déchéance is discussed below, p. 51.

110   Articles 2 and 29 of the draft constitution, approved by the Senate on 6 April: see full text in Moniteur, 8 April 1814, p. 385.

111 Préambule to the Charte constitutionnelle, in J. Godechot, Les Constitutions, pp. 218–219.

112 Biens nationaux consisted essentially of the confiscated estates of émigrés, proscribed persons, and the Church. The article upholding the legal rights of the new owners, without further compensation, was an important element in social peace under the Restoration, and a rebuff to the ultras.

113 Cf. G. Weill, Histoire du parti républicain en France de 1814 à 1870 (Paris, 1900), chapter 1.

114 Cf. Séances et Travaux ..., I (1842), pp. 10–11: members included Tracy, Daunou, Garat, Roederer, Sieyès and Degérando.

115 Unfortunately, the date of birth is misreported as 1762 by M. Leroy, Histoire des idées sociales, II, p. 167, and by M. Prélot, Histoire des idées politiques (Paris, 1961), p. 435.

116 Most biographies correctly give Paris as the birthplace. However, the Biographie universelle et portative ..., ed. Rabbe (Paris, 1834), IV, p. 1435, and the Nouvelle Biographie générale, ed. Hoefer (Paris, 1853–66), XLV, col. 562, stated that Tracy was born "in the Bourbonnais", that is, at the family château of Paray-le-Frésil outside Moulins. This information was accepted by G. Rougeron, A.-L.-C. Destutt de Tracy ... (Montluçon, 1966), p. 4, by H. Gouhier, "Introduction historique" to Tracy, Elémens d'idéologie, vol. I (1817; reprint Paris, 1970); p. 5 (with reservations), and by S. Moravia, Il pensiero degli idéologues, p. 319. The correct information was given by F. Potiquet, L'Institut National de France (Paris, 1871), p. 34; F. Picavet, "Destutt de Tracy", La Grande Encyclopédie (Paris 1887–1902), vol. XIV, p. 297; L. de Brotonne, Les Sénateurs du Consulat et de l'Empire (Paris, 1895), p. 4; Biographie Universelle ..., ed. Michaud (Paris, n.d.), XLII, p. 77; Dictionnaire historique et biographique ..., ed. Robinet (Paris, 1899), II, p. 790; Dictionnaire de Biographie française, ed. Balteau (Paris, 1967), XI, col. 116.

117 F.-A.-A. de La Chesnaye des Bois, Dictionnaire de la noblesse (Paris, 1770–86), vol. VI, pp. 201–203, vol. XV, pp. 282f.; F. Michel, Les écossais en France ... (London, 1862), I, 254.

118 Mignet, "Notice historique sur ... Destutt de Tracy", Notices et Mémoires historiques (Paris, 1843), vol. I, p. 247. The death of the marquis de Tracy has been variously estimated at 1761 (when Antoine was less than eight years old) and 1766 (when the boy was at least twelve years).

119 A. Sorel, Europe and the French Revolution (London, 1969), p. 188.

120 Louis de Narbonne, his lifelong friend, Minister for War at the end of 1791, and a companion of Mme de Staël.

121 Louis-Philippe de Ségur, who replied to Tracy's discours de réception in 1808 on his entry to the Classe de langue et de littérature françaises (later renamed the Académie française). Cf. L. Apt, Louis-Philippe de Ségur: an intellectual in a revolutionary age (The Hague, 1969).

122 Charles-Maurice de Talleyrand-Périgord, diplomat and politician, who was influential in almost every régime in France from 1789-1815. Cf. J. Orieux, Talleyrand, ou le sphinx incompris (Paris, 1971).

123 Lafayette, Mémoires, III, p. 276ff; M. Reinhard, "Elite et noblesse dans la seconde moitié du XVIIIe siècle", Revue d'histoire moderne et contemporain, vol. 3 (1956), pp. 5-37; E.-G. Léonard, "La question sociale dans l'armée française au XVIIIe siècle", Annales: économies, sociétés, civilisations, vol. 3 (1948), pp. 135-149; J. McManners, "France", in The European Nobility in the Eighteenth Century, ed. A. Goodwin (London, 1967), pp. 22-42.

124 Mignet, "Notice historique sur ... Destutt de Tracy", p. 250. The estate of Paray-le-Frésil itself amounted to 3,600 hectares in the Restoration period, according to the Dictionnaire de Biographie française, ed. Balteau, vol. XI, col. 118 (on Tracy's son, Victor).

125 However, see the following remarks by Tracy, cited in J.-P.-M. Flourens, Discours prononcé aux funérailles de M. le comte Destutt de Tracy ... (Paris, 1836), p. 11: "I was in that period immediately following the end of one's education, and, having no more very important duties to fill in the career I had undertaken, I could leave myself without scruple to my meditations and to the researches towards which my inclination led me. I devoted myself, then, to considering my fellow men in all times and countries, and to seeking the causes of the most important phenomena such as they offer to the eye of the observer". Tracy's early years have not been well documented, partly because no mémoires appear to have been written, and most of his remaining manuscripts in the possession of his descendants were lost in a fire in 1968. The Cabanis-Tracy correspondence, cited by Guillois, has not come to light. Other collections of correspondence have been disappointingly thin for the understanding of Tracy's theoretical work, with the exception of the letters reprinted in Maine de Biran, Oeuvres philosophiques, ed. P. Tisserand (Paris, 1920-), vols. VI and VII.

126 Some of Tracy's biographers seem to have regarded this visit to Voltaire, when Tracy was only sixteen years, as something akin to an intellectual baptism: Mignet, "Notice historique sur ... Destutt de Tracy", pp. 249-250; Mme de Tracy, "Notice sur M. Destutt de Tracy", p. 307 (and also pp. 397-99 for Tracy's defence of Voltaire in the Restoration years); G. Rougeron, A.-L.-C. Destutt de Tracy, p. 4. The pilgrimage to visit Voltaire was an enterprise common to many young men of the times. Tracy used to call Voltaire "le héros de la raison humaine": Flourens, Discours prononcé aux funérailles de ... Tracy, p. 10, and Mignet, op.cit., p. 284. For one of Tracy's comments in praise of Voltaire, cf. Logique (1805), p. 137n.

127 Picavet, "Destutt de Tracy", claimed that Tracy might have come across Kant's philosophy at Strasbourg. In his book Les Idéologues, Picavet further suggested that Professor Müller discussed Kant and Hume with his students, and that Tracy probably became familiar with Kantian ideas through conversation or through reading the Latin editions of Kant (p. 295). (Cabanis, however, who was able to read German, was definitely familiar with the work of German savants.) J.W. Stein, reinterpreting Picavet, asserted that Tracy became familiar with Kant and Hume at Strasbourg, and developed "a respect

for thinkers whose theories he later contested" (The Mind and the Sword, p. 21). For a broader view of the reception of German literature and philosophy in France, cf. L. Reynaud, L'influence allemande en France au XVIIIe et au XIXe siècle (Paris, 1922). As for Hume, it appears that he was far better known in France as an historian than as a philosopher of mind; and even in the latter role he was seen as analysing the "association of ideas" rather than as urging a suspension of belief in "laws".

128   Cf. L. Apt, Louis-Philippe de Ségur, chapter 2; Lafayette, Mémoires, vol. I. Tracy made frequent reference to American experiences in constitution-making in his Commentaire.

129   J. Cornillon, Le Bourbonnais sous la Révolution française, vol. I (Vichy, 1888), p. 5.

130   Ibid., pp. 8-40.

131   Ibid., pp. 41-48.

132   Ibid., pp. 49-52.

133   For example, Section I of the cahier demanded the concurrence of King and Etats-généraux in all laws (article 3), habeas corpus (article 4), Ministerial responsibility (article 6), liberty of the press (article 11); section II demanded the suppression of certain unpopular taxes (articles 10-13) and reform of public finances; and section III urged the improvement of public education as the best way to "increase the citizens useful to the country" (article 6). Cf. Cahier de l'Ordre de la Noblesse du Bourbonnais ... (1789); also reprinted in Cornillon, op.cit., I, pp. 233-243, and in Archives parlementaires, première série, vol. II, p. 442 ff.

134   For the events of 1789, cf. Cambridge Modern History (1904/1934), VII, chapters 5, 6; A. Cobban, History of Modern France (Harmondsworth 1973), I, p. 136ff; Lafayette, Mémoires, vol. II.

135   For example, Dictionnaire de Biographie française, ed. Balteau, XI, col. 116; Dictionnaire historique et biographique, ed. Robinet, II, p. 790; Biographie universelle, ed. Michaud, XLII, p. 78; J. Cornillon Le Bourbonnais, I, p. 118.

136   Tracy is absent from the list of signatories to the "serment du jeu de paume" of 20 June, in Archives parlementaires, vol. 8, pp. 138-141 and 659-660, and from the list of 47 nobles who were present in the National Assembly on 25 June (ibid., p. 154).

137   F. Picavet, Les Idéologues, p. 298; L. Biernawski, Un département, pp. 137-138; Mignet, "Notice historique sur ... Destutt de Tracy", p. 250.

138   On 30 March 1790, Tracy explained that he belonged to no committee of the Assembly because he valued his independence and because he was already very busy as an independent: Archives parlementaires, vol. XII, p. 443. Subsequently, he served for ten weeks on the Comité des Rapports created in July 1790 (ibid., XXXII, p. 562); and for seven days on the Comité des Colonies in August 1791 (ibid., p. 548) before resigning in disgust, when his argument in favour of the coloured population of the colonies was rejected by the Comité (ibid., XXX, p. 55).

139 One of his early tasks was to serve on a commission of the Assembly
     in January 1790, to establish the boundaries of the new Department
     of l'Allier; Moulins was chosen as the capital. Cf. L. Biernawski,
     Un département, pp. 52-69; P. Flament, "Introduction", Inventaire
     sommaire des Archives Départementales postérieures à 1790, ed.
     F. Claudon and P. Flament, Allier: série L, vol. I (Moulins, 1912),
     pp. i-ii.

140 M. de Tracy à M. Burke (Paris, 1790), a speech of 3 April, rewritten
     on 26 April.

141 Opinion de M. de Tracy sur les affaires de Saint-Domingue, en
     Septembre 1791 (Paris, 1791). See also Tracy's speeches on the same
     subject in Archives parlementaires, XXV, pp. 642-43, 750; XXVI, p. 25;
     XXVII, p. 214; XXIX, p. 627; XXXI, pp. 259-263. The subject of the
     rights of coloured residents of the colonies became Tracy's major
     contribution to the debates in the Assembly. It was the Convention
     Nationale in 1793-94 which finally voted the suppression of slavery.
     Bonaparte's reintroduction of policies of colonial annexation and
     slavery deeply wounded Tracy's sensibilities. In his Commentaire
     sur l'Esprit des Lois, written 1806, Tracy insisted that colonies
     should be freed as rapidly as practicable: (Paris, 1819), p. 136.

142 Tracy strongly denied any link with the Amis des Noirs, in his
     speech on Saint-Domingue, p. 2. Most Enlightenment thinkers were
     hostile towards discrimination on 'racial' grounds. However, an
     interesting exception was Saint-Simon, whose unpublished manuscripts
     show he was persuaded of the inferiority of blacks on the grounds
     that their cranial dimensions were smaller. He deduced an inequality
     of political rights from an alleged physiological difference. (I
     owe this information to Dr John Hooper.)

143 The Société de 1789, a club of savants, officials and businessmen,
     is discussed in more detail in chapter four. The main secondary
     discussions are S. Moravia, Il tramonto, pp. 152-161, and K.M. Baker,
     "Politics and Social Science in Eighteenth-Century France: the
     'Société de 1789'", in French Government and Society, ed. J.F. Bosher
     (London, 1973), pp. 208-230. The membership list is reprinted in
     J.-B. Challamel, Les Clubs Contre-révolutionnaires (Paris, 1895),
     pp. 400-414. (Tracy's name appears on p. 413.) Condorcet and
     Sieyès later joined the Jacobins when the Société de 1789 collapsed.

144 Challamel, Les Clubs contre-révolutionnaires, gives membership lists
     for the Club des Feuillants, p. 286 ff. (Tracy's name appears on
     page 302; circumstantial evidence suggests that he joined between
     July-September 1791.) G. Michon, Essai sur l'histoire du parti
     feuillant, Adrien Duport (Paris, 1924), p. 323, cites Tracy as
     participating in a discussion at the Feuillants.

145 Cf. Lafayette, Mémoires, IV, p. 4.

146 J. Cornillon, Le Bourbonnais, I, p. 120.

147 Ibid., II, p. 109.

148 Archives parlementaires, XXVII, p. 391; cf. p. 547.

149 Commentaire [1806] (Paris, 1819), pp. 167-168.

150 Archives parlementaires, XXIV, p. 622 (7 April 1791); Commentaire, pp. 168-69.

151 G. Rougeron, A.-L.-C. Destutt de Tracy, p. 6; Inventaire sommaire des Archives Départementales, ed. F. Claudon and P. Flament, I, pp. 37-48. Tracy's picturesque address of 1 December 1791, closing the current session of the administrative Council (pp. 47-48), is reprinted as Appendix I below.

152 Lafayette, Mémoires, III, pp. 291-384.

153 For example: [Anonymous], Biographie des Quarante de l'Académie française (Paris, 1826), pp. 102-103 (where Tracy follows Lafayette into Austrian-held territory and both are captured); P. Simon, L'élaboration de la Charte Constitutionnelle de 1814 (Paris, 1906), p. 205 n.1 (where Tracy deserted the army alongside Lafayette).

154 Lafayette, Mémoires, III, pp. 402-405, 490-491.

155 After the abolition of noble titles, the comte de Tracy became the citoyen Destutt-Tracy.

156 Civisme (like its opposite, incivisme) was coined during the early years of the Revolution to denote appropriate sentiments for the citizen who cheerfully performs his duties: cf. F. Brunot, Histoire de la langue française ..., tome IX, Part II, pp. 666-667; [Anon.], Dictionnaire de la Constitution française (Paris, 1791), p. 75; Dictionnaire de l'Académie française (Paris, an VII [1798-99]), II, p. 767; Dictionnaire de l'Académie française (Paris, an X-1802), I, p. 291. Under the Jacobin régime, the need to demonstrate one's civisme was increasingly identified with support for current policies, and became part of an inquisitorial procedure of the popular committees.

157 Cf. R. Cobb, Paris and its Provinces 1792-1802 (Oxford, 1975), who points out that Auteuil was regarded as an area of suspect loyalties under the Jacobin régime (pp. 119, 137-38).

158 F. Picavet, Les Idéologues, p. 302; L. Biernawski, Un département, p. 139; G. Rougeron cites the report of the Moulins comité de surveillance, in A.-L.-C. Destutt de Tracy, p. 7.

159 A. Guillois, Le Salon de Mme Helvétius, p. 90; Mignet, "Notice historique sur ... Destutt de Tracy", pp. 257-58.

160 Cited in Mignet, "Notice historique sur ... Destutt de Tracy", p. 254.

161 Ibid., p. 255.

162 Cf. G.-L. Buffon, Oeuvres philosophiques, ed. J. Piveteau (Paris, 1954).

163 Mignet, op.cit., pp. 255-56.

164 Mme de Tracy, "Notice sur M. Destutt de Tracy", p. 314.

165 Cited in Mignet, "Notice historique sur ... Destutt de Tracy", p. 262.

166 Cited, ibid., p. 266n; repeated in Picavet, Les Idéologues, p. 303.

167 Potiquet, L'Institut national, p. 34. For the structure of the Institut, see Appendix II below.

168 Tracy, "Mémoire sur la faculté de penser", in Mémoires de l'Institut National, Classe des Sciences morales et politiques, vol. I (1798), pp. 283-450.

169 For example, Tracy in 1802 wrote the report awarding the prize on the question of the influence of habit upon thinking to Maine de Biran; earlier, he had assisted in investigating various linguistic systems which claimed to help in perfecting a "universal" language, such as pasigraphie. On the problems caused by the large workload for members, cf. J. Simon, Une Académie sous le Directoire, pp. 108-109.

170 A.-A. Barbier, Dictionnaire des ouvrages anonymes et pseudonymes ... (Paris, 1806-1808), vol. II, p. 69, item 4500; E. Hatin, Bibliographie historique et critique de la presse périodique française (Paris, 1866), p. 26.

171 Cf. A. Duruy, L'instruction publique et la Révolution, pp. 241n, 266-267. This conseil is further discussed in chapter seven.

172 Tracy's letter of appointment, and the text of the circulars, are reprinted in his Elémens d'idéologie, 5 vols. (Paris, 1824-26), IV, pp. 265ff, and ibid. (Bruxelles, 1826-27), IV, pp. 259ff.

173 Cf. Mignet, "Notice historique sur ... Destutt de Tracy", p. 269. On the Egyptian expedition, cf. H. Blet, Histoire de la colonisation française, vol. II, pp. 28-32; C. Herold, Bonaparte in Egypt (London, 1963).

174 Tracy, "Quels sont les moyens de fonder la morale chez un peuple?" (Paris, an VI [1798]), also reprinted as appendix, pp. 435-477, in Commentaire sur l'Esprit des lois (Paris, 1819). See further, chapter three.

175 [Tracy], Analyse de l'origine de tous les cultes ... (Paris, an VII [1799]).

176 [Tracy], Analyse raisonnée de 'l'Origine de tous les Cultes ou Religion universelle' (Paris, an XIII=1804). See further, chapter two.

177 A.-A. Barbier, op.cit., vol. III, p. 10, item 9165.

178 Tracy, Observations sur le système actuel d'instruction publique (Paris, an IX [1801]). See further, chapter seven.

179 It had a second edition in 1804, entitled Elémens d'idéologie, vol. I: Idéologie proprement dite.

180 Large parts of this work were originally read as a series of papers at the Institut in 1796-97 and published in the first two volumes of the Mémoires of the Class of Moral and Political Sciences. The complete work was published in 1802. Tracy contributed a lengthy summary (Table analytique) for the second edition in 1805.

181 Tracy, _Logique_ (1805), p. viii.

182 Cf. G. Chinard, _Jefferson et les idéologues_, pp. 13-15, 20-30; for Tracy's first exchange of letters and subsequent election, see pp. 35-41.

183 _Ibid._, pp. 42-85.

184 _Ibid._, p. 86, and chapter 3 (pp. 97-188).

185 Chinard wrongly reported that the only French edition of the _Commentaire_ was in 1817 (_ibid._, p. 45). Tracy complained in the _Avertissement_ to his edition of July 1819 that an "inexact copy" had been printed in Liège and reprinted in Paris, without his permission (p. v).

186 Tracy, _De l'amour_ (Paris, 1926), translated from the Italian edition of 1819 by G. Chinard. See Chinard's "Introduction", pp. i-vi, and _Jefferson et les idéologues_, chapter 4.

187 L. de Brotonne, _Les Sénateurs du Consulat et de l'Empire_, pp. 2-9.

188 J. Godechot, _Les Constitutions de la France depuis 1789_, chapters 4-6.

189 C. Lehec, "Introduction" to Cabanis, _Oeuvres philosophiques_ (Paris, 1956), vol. I, p. xix.

190 L. de Villefosse and J. Bouissounouse, _L'Opposition à Napoléon_, pp. 320-321.

191 See Tracy's letter of 17 August in Maine de Biran, _Oeuvres philosophiques_, ed. P. Tisserand (Paris, 1930), vol. VII, pp. 346: "Ma pauvre tête m'a abandonné avec mon bonheur et ma santé. Je me sens vraiment comme aliéné". The first Malet affair coincided with this grief.

192 Tracy, _Discours ... pour la réception de M. de Tracy, ... 21 décembre 1808_ (Paris, 1808). Tracy had unsuccessfully contested a vacancy in the same Class in 1803: see J.F. Reichardt, _Un hiver à Paris sous le Consulat 1802-1803_, ed. A. Laquiante (Paris, 1896), p. 402 n.2. Tracy had obviously felt slighted when he had been appointed in January 1803 as a corresponding member of the Classe de l'histoire et de littérature anciennes, after the reorganization of the Institut.

193 Tracy, letter of 15 November 1809, in Maine de Biran, _op.cit._, VII, p. 352.

194 _Le Moniteur Universel_, 2 April 1814, p. 365.

195 _Ibid._, 3 April 1814, p. 367.

196 _Ibid._, 4 April 1814, p. 369.

197 J. de Soto, "La Constitution Sénatoriale du 6 avril 1814", _Revue internationale d'histoire politique et constitutionnelle_, no. 12 (1953), p. 279; P. Duvergier de Hauranne, _Histoire du gouvernement parlementaire en France 1814-1848_ (Paris, 1857-72), vol. II, p. 95;

C. Viel-Castel, Histoire de la Restauration (Paris, 1860-77), vol. I,
p. 241; C.-J.-M. Lambrechts, Principes politiques ... (Paris, 1815),
pp. 3, 88-89; P. Simon, L'élaboration de la Charte Constitutionnelle
(Paris, 1906), p. 28ff.; J. Thiry, Le Sénat de Napoléon, pp. 330-346;
J.-D. Lanjuinais, Oeuvres (Paris, 1832), vol. II, pp. 68-69.

198 Lambrechts, op.cit., p. 89, reported that Tracy missed the discussion
on 5 April because of a confusion about the time of the meeting.

199 The text of the Senators' constitution appeared in the Moniteur
universel, 8 April 1814, p. 385.

200 Tracy in May 1814 was annoyed with the Senate for allowing itself
to be excluded from these negotiations. He also expressed his fear
lest the Bourbons should bring about their own downfall just as the
Stuarts had done - a possibility made more likely by the foreign
occupation and by the fact that "Cromwell" (i.e. Napoléon) was still
alive. (Letter to Maine de Biran, op.cit., VII, p. 365.)

201 Nouvelle Biographie générale, ed. Hoefer, XLV, col. 563.

202 [C. de Proisy d'Eppe], Dictionnaire des Girouettes ... (Paris, 3e
ed. 1815), p. 142.

203 Ibid., pp. 182-193, 446-451, 462-466.

204 Nouvelle biographie générale, ed. Hoefer, XLV, col. 563; also [Anon.],
Biographie des Quarante de l'Académie française, p. 104.

205 Cf. A.-L.-V.-C. Broglie, Souvenirs (Paris, 1886), vol. I, p. 264;
G. Weill, Histoire du parti républicain, chapter 1.

206 Cf. Dictionnaire de Biographie française, ed. Balteau, XI, col. 118.

207 C. Rémusat, Mémoires (Paris, 1958), vol. I, p. 388n; Broglie,
Souvenirs, vol. II, p. 82.

208 I have excluded these translations from the Bibliography of Tracy's
published writings.

209 Mme de Tracy, "Notice sur M. Destutt de Tracy", pp. 330, 393.

210 For example, Thierry's review of the (anonymous) unauthorized 1817
edition, in Le Censeur européen, vol. VII (1818), pp. 191-260.

211 Cf. P.-M. Imbert, Destutt de Tracy, Critique de Montesquieu (Paris,
1974), pp. 175-76, citing the Journal des Débats, 1822. The
Commentaire was reprinted several times in the 1820s.

212 Cf. P. Maes, Un ami de Stendhal, Victor Jacquemont (Paris n.d. [1953]),
p. 306; Mme de Tracy, "Notice sur M. Destutt de Tracy", p. 402.

213 D. Ricardo, Works and Correspondence, ed. P. Sraffa (Cambridge, 1962),
vol. IX, p. 248: letter to Malthus, 16 December 1822.

214 Lady Morgan, France in 1829-30 (London, 1830), vol. I, pp. 133-146:
"The Count de Tracy".

215 Elected 28 April 1836: Potiquet, L'Institut National, p. 170.

216 Elected 17 December 1836: Potiquet, L'Institut National, p. 404.

217 Guizot, Discours ... pour la réception de M. Guizot (Paris, 1836), pp. 9–11, 15; Damiron, Essai (3ᵉ ed. 1829), pp. 77–90 and passim.

218 P.-C.-F. Daunou, Discours prononcé aux funérailles de M. le comte Destutt de Tracy (Paris, 1836), p. 5.

219 Flourens, Discours, p. 13.

220 "Quels sont les moyens de fonder la morale chez un peuple?", reprinted in Tracy's Commentaire (Paris, 1819), p. 456.

CHAPTER TWO

IDEOLOGIE AND THE PURSUIT OF CERTAINTY

I   Science and certainty

II   The concept of idéologie

III   The science of signs and language

IV   Metaphysics and religion

I. SCIENCE AND CERTAINTY

Tracy constantly professed his faith in the importance of facts, observations and rigorous scientific method, and yet his writings often have the appearance of rationalist deduction from basic principles. In exploring this paradox or tension in his work, it is necessary to consider the images of scientific method and scientific laws which were part of Tracy's intellectual borrowings. Why did he believe that methods of observation, analysis, and the search for general causal explanations, were the key to attaining certain or reliable knowledge? What kinds of ideas were to be excluded from the realm of positive knowledge? What was the proper starting-point for reaching a scientific understanding of man and society? Could the models derived from mechanics, optics, astronomy, and the biological sciences be applied directly to the study of man? These and similar questions are the concern of this chapter. In the first place, let us simply note the enormous intellectual excitement generated among savants in the eighteenth century by the scientific advances in the natural sciences. It was commonly believed that a "revolution" in the understanding of nature had commenced after 1600, and that a vast range of useful technological applications of theoretical discoveries were following in the wake of the new outlook. Tracy's remarks on some of the major figures in this confrontation between the moderns and ancients, throws a great deal of light on his conception of science and the appropriate methods for attaining certainty. The writings of Bacon, Descartes, Newton and Lavoisier, contributed in various ways to Tracy's understanding of science and method. (Condillac, another writer of enormous importance for Tracy, will be considered in the following section.)

Bacon was regarded by Tracy as the first _savant_ to insist on experimental and observational methods, as part of his rejection of scholastic philosophy. The _Novum Organum_ (1620) was seen as a call for a new starting point in the search for knowledge of nature and of man. The programme announced by that work had a beneficial effect in encouraging the adoption of experimental approaches, and the rejection of hypotheses founded only on custom and authority. Tracy regarded Bacon's work as so important that he placed a twenty-five page summary of the whole _Instauratio Magna_ as an appendix to his own volume on _Logique_ in 1805.[1] Moreover, in the historical introduction to his _Logique_, Tracy included a very lengthy discussion in praise of Bacon's views.

No progress had been made after Aristotle in the science of human understanding, wrote Tracy, until the works of Bacon – all the scholastic philosophers had merely spun variations of Aristotle's mode of reasoning.[2] "Profound habits of un-reason" had been implanted, and it was Bacon who first had the "admirable and sublime" idea of our need for a _novum organum_, by which to "re-make entirely the human mind, begin all the sciences again, and submit to a new examination the whole of our acquired knowledge, or what we believed we had acquired under the old so-called _organum_". Bacon's call for a new paradigm, based on observation and experience as the foundation of knowledge, was a "decisive" and "unique" step in human history.[3] There followed, in Tracy's exposition a discourse of six pages where Bacon was made to express "some ideological and logical principles with more precision than he actually managed".[4] Among the ideas attributed to Bacon are the following elements of idéologie

But nature does not present us with general principles: it only offers us facts, impressions we receive, and from which we then draw consequences. These so-called first principles, maxims ... are then already products of human art, creations of our intellect. It is first necessary, then, to go back to their elements ...

> ... in this world, you never do anything but see facts
> and draw consequences from them, receive impressions and
> notice their circumstances; in a word, sensing and deducing
> (which is still a form of sensing). These are your only
> means of instruction, the only sources of all the truths
> you can ever acquire ... Observation and experience to
> gather materials, deduction to elaborate them: these are
> the only good intellectual mechanisms (machines). Leave
> all the others to the pedants and charlatans ...[5]

Tracy clearly identified his own idéologie with the Baconian

project of renovating the understanding of man and nature. Bacon's

Novum Organum, he wrote, had the same objective as his own logic of the

sciences, namely, "to show the human intellect· the road to be taken to

increase its knowledge, and to teach it a sure method of reaching the

truth".[6] However, Tracy criticized Bacon's classification of the sciences,

his inability to break completely from the natural science assumptions of

his day, his approach to seeking out the laws of nature, and his failure

to describe accurately the properties and operations of our intellectual

faculties.[7] Bacon had pointed the way towards a new and more adequate

manner of achieving certain knowledge, upon which the practical arts

could safely depend. He was a prophet of a scientific technology. But

he had not been able, in his own work, to give a positive content to the

new sciences, nor to provide what for Tracy was of fundamental importance:

a satisfactory theory of the formation and expression of ideas.[8] Tracy's

criticisms of Bacon are of a quite different order from those directed

against the English Chancellor by opponents of Enlightenment scientism,

such as Joseph de Maistre. Tracy had been excited by Bacon's programmatic

statements (and disappointed with their detailed elaboration). Maistre

was concerned to deflate the extravagant reputation which Bacon had

acquired as a man of science (Maistre judged him as somewhat confused and

incompetent), and especially to attack Bacon's materialistic assumptions

that inductive methods could be successfully applied to all subject matters,

and that general causes could be generated by the study of physical facts.[9]

Hence, Maistre's assertion that "all the enemies of the human race assembled including Cabanis himself are descended from Bacon".[10]

For Tracy and his colleagues, Descartes was also very important as one of the founding fathers of the new scientific outlook. The radical doubt upon which he based his philosophy demanded a new starting point for certain knowledge, locating it in self-knowledge. The quest for certainty, and the clear rejection of tradition and speculation as a basis for knowledge, were important aspects of the Cartesian heritage.[11] On the other hand, Descartes' rationalist image of the physical universe as an ordered and integrated whole, based on matter and motion, was also very influential: the image of the animal-machine, and of the universe as a clockwork mechanism, both found their inspiration in Descartes. He also argued for the unity of the natural sciences, and made mathematics a universal model.[12]

Tracy, however, was mainly concerned with Descartes' contribution to the scientific principles of observational method. Descartes' modest Discours sur la méthode (1637), wrote Tracy, had independently developed all the important insights of Bacon's long and complex work, and with greater clarity and simplicity.[13] Moreover, Descartes had made two important additional contributions. First, he had distilled his method into four principles of general application (briefly: insistence on clear and distinct ideas, decomposition of concepts into constituent parts, production of reliable knowledge by proceeding from simple objects to the most complex, and constant reviews of each stage in the chain of thought).[14] Secondly, Descartes had claimed that the first object of our examination should be the intellectual faculties by which we gain all our knowledge, and that the first thing of which we are certain is our own existence.

The phrase *je pense donc je suis*, wrote Tracy, is the most profound utterance, and is "the only true starting-point for all reasonable philosophy".[15] Yet Descartes should have said, more exactly: *je sens, donc j'existe.*[16] This formula, according to Tracy, would have saved Descartes from many of the errors into which he subsequently lapsed in assuming that thought and extension were two utterly different substances, were mutually exclusive. Descartes' rash assumption in separating thought and extension led directly to the hypotheses of innate ideas, on the one hand, and the impossibility of a void in space, on the other. These false doctrines, said Tracy, since disproved by Locke and Newton respectively, could only have arisen from Descartes' failing to follow carefully his own rules of procedure.[17] A more cautious attention to the facts, to the operation of our intellectual faculties, would have shown Descartes that "thinking and existing are ... one and the same thing" for the thinking subject.[18] Nevertheless, added Tracy, it took a genius to be the first to perceive that all our certitudes derive from the "original fact" that we are sure of our own existence. "By this sublime conception, he [Descartes] replaced all of *la science humaine* on its true and fundamental basis. Therein lies the germ of the true and total renovation desired by Bacon. Bacon said: everything consists of facts deriving from one another, it is necessary to study the facts; and Descartes found the first fact from which all the others are derived".[19]

This alludes to another aspect of Descartes' approach which deserves attention for a full understanding of Tracy's thought: namely, his deductivism. The passage by Descartes which immediately follows the four principles in the Discourse on Method illustrates this point:

> These long chains of reasonings, quite simple and easy, which geometers are accustomed to using to teach their most difficult demonstrations, had given me cause to imagine that everything which can be encompassed by man's knowledge is linked in the

same way, and that, provided only that one abstains from
accepting any for true which is not true, and that one
always keeps the right order for one thing to be deduced
from that which precedes it, there can be nothing so
distant that one does not reach it eventually, or so
hidden that one cannot discover it.[20]

Tracy's adoption of this conception of knowledge as reducible to an

analytico-deductive schema, is a fundamental characteristic of his

thought, as will be shown in more depth when the concept of idéologie

is examined. Tracy's borrowings from Condillac have usually been taken

as his primary intellectual debt; it is arguable, however, that what

Tracy extracted from Condillac, at least in regard to method, had

essentially been said by Descartes.[21]

Newton, more than any other figure, had become a catchword for

the substantive progress of the natural sciences. Where Bacon had merely

announced a programme of research, and Descartes had refined the statemen

of methods (after having made some positive investigations of his own),

Newton had achieved a grand mathematized synthesis of the physical laws

governing the phenomena of astronomy and mechanics, propounding as his

basic principle the attraction of objects in proportion to their mass.

According to Tracy, Newton was the great theoretical systematizer of

previous empirical research, the man who was able to demonstrate that

all the facts, now and in the future, followed the patterns specified by

a few simple laws.[22] Newton symbolized what could be achieved by a

systematic science of nature, but curiously there is no evidence that

Tracy ever tackled Newton's Principia or Opticks in any detailed manner.

Tracy was quite familiar with Newton's place in the development of modern

astronomy, mechanics and optics - for example, he had certainly read the

accounts by Voltaire,[23] Bailly,[24] and Condorcet,[25] and probably several

others. Newton's influence on Tracy remained diffuse and indirect.

The heritage of Newton, however, was by no means clear-cut. Some championed Newton by stressing his differences from Cartesianism (where Newton was seen as an empiricist and inductivist, and Descartes - or at least his disciples - was represented as an a priori metaphysician). Others found Newton too abstractly mathematical and too close to the old deism; they advocated a greater emphasis in scientific research on direct experimentation with the materials provided by nature.[26] Newton was harnessed to competing - or at least complementary - views of science. Part of the explanation for this may be that Newton's Opticks and most of his methodological pronouncements tended to place him as a prudent empiricist, wary of hypotheses and closely guided by experimentation; whereas his Principia provided a vast synthesis of the laws governing matter in motion,[27] a theoretical picture of the world which appeared not inconsistent with aspects of Cartesian rationalism.

What Tracy understood by Newtonian science is best illustrated in some relevant remarks made by J.-S. Bailly, in his historical discussion of the development of astronomy:

> A science is a sum of truths. The object of the elements is to connect (enchaîner) these truths, to present them in their order, from the most simple through to the most complex. But the connected chain of these truths is not the order of their discovery ...[28]

> All the phenomena are connected (enchaînés): the system of our knowledge is ordered just like nature. A single principle serves for us to explain everything, just as a single spring suffices for it to make everything act ... The phenomenon of attraction ... the development of that simple cause will encompass all the present phenomena, and will predict the phenomena to come.[29]

It was the simple structure and the comprehensive scope of the Newtonian system which impressed Tracy - rather than Newton's remarks on the importance of observation, which, after all, had already been said by many thinkers before Newton. Tracy's conception of a "completed" science, such as Newtonian mechanics, dwelt upon its systematic and deductive character, rather than upon the gathering of the observational data which supplied the materials from which the science was fashioned. Knowledge deserved the name of science, wrote Tracy, only when its systematic character

> is advanced enough for us to see the links among the facts, their governance by a few common laws, and their explanation by a small number of general truths. Until this stage is reached, our knowledge of a subject is only a collection of isolated facts without connection ... on the contrary, a science matures with the discovery of a general truth which by itself explains all the phenomena as consequences of the principle.[30]

This critique of the adequacy of undirected empiricism is an important feature of Tracy's thought. For him, a science was not properly developed until "we know the relations which unite these facts and the laws which they invariably follow".[31] The simplicity of an explanatory principle was not a sign of scientific immaturity, but, on the contrary, was a product of the precision found in a mature science. The ontological structure of nature (for Tracy, the only reality which was knowable) was itself ordered, simple, and governed by general laws which direct the behaviour of all phenomena. As the sciences have become more advanced, wrote Tracy, they have had the great merit of being reducible to a smaller number of basic propositions. "That is the proof that all the questions to which they are related have reached that high degree of precision which is very near the solution".[32] Tracy's views on the structure of a scientific theory were by no means peculiar to himself alone; his concerns were widely shared among his contemporaries. One example may suffice here to illustrate the point. Degérando, who had won a prize at the Institut National in 1799 for an essay on the influence of signs upon the thinking process,[33] wrote in his Histoire comparée des systèmes de philosophie (1804) that "the perfection of a system depends above all on three things: the multitude of the phenomena it encompasses, the simplicity of the solutions it presents, and the rigour of the connections between its parts".[34] Tracy would not have disagreed with such a formulation.

Lavoisier was another _savant_ whose work influenced Tracy's conception of science and method. The atomistic and corpuscular theory of the universe - where nature is composed of a myriad combinations of elementary particles - had existed since the ancient world. This theory had been developed in various ways, beyond the form given by Democritus and Epicurus, into the modern physical and biological sciences. One important application was in chemistry, where Lavoisier and his colleagues succeeded in developing a theory of the elements of matter and their possible combinations, giving rise to a new nomenclature for the modern science of chemistry.[35] Lavoisier, in his Traité élémentaire de chimie (1789), attributed his success to following the rigorous analytical method of Condillac, who had put forward the view that a science is a well-made language, i.e., that scientific truth depends upon conceptual coherence and precision.[36]

Tracy, who had studied Lavoisier and Condillac intensively while in prison in 1794, enthusiastically adopted these conceptions in 1796:

> Every science is reducible to a well-made language; and to advance a science is none other than to perfect this language, whether by changing the words or by making their meaning precise.[37]

Similarly, Tracy wrote that "to make a science is to make its language, and to learn the language of a science is to learn the science itself".[38] However, a few years later, when he wrote his Logique, he recognized the ambiguity and paradox implicit in such Condillacian formulae, and found it necessary to clarify the relationship he saw between science and nomenclature. The progress of a science, he said, does not depend simply

on providing it with a more methodical nomenclature. The important thing
is that the meaning of the concepts should "conform to the facts", and
that the meanings should be fixed by men who use the terms in this true
and precise manner. The use of new words could sometimes be useful; but
the words themselves do not "create the science". Thus, for example,
when "our learned French chemists" discovered the theory of combustion,
they recognized that phlogiston - believed to be the cause of combustion -
was not what it had been thought to be: it was not a property of the
combustible objects but something which united with them to produce heat,
light, and so forth. Lavoisier and his colleagues "fixed the meaning" of
these terms in a way which conformed to the facts. Even if they had
retained the term phlogiston, with its new meaning, instead of the new
and more useful word oxygen, they would still have "rectified the science"
by giving the true meaning to its concepts. In this sense, concluded
Tracy, a science is well made to the extent that the ideas represented
in its terminology are correct.[39] Later in the Logique, Tracy went so
far as to criticize Condillac for not having sufficiently distinguished
between "a science, the method it follows, the language it employs, the
ideas it elaborates, and the signs which represent these ideas".
Condillac, said Tracy, had been guilty of hyperbolic exaggeration in
identifying a science with its language or the signs it employed.[40]

Two other aspects of Tracy's views on science and method
should be briefly mentioned. Firstly, in common with his contemporaries,
Tracy borrowed various images, analogies and metaphors, in a fairly
unsystematic way, from the physical, mathematical and biological sciences.
The images are sometimes architectural, arithmetical and geometrical -
elementary particles, building blocks, basic faculties, which combine or
operate to form more complex wholes. Writing in this mode, Tracy sees it

as the task of <u>analyse</u> (in the sense defined by Condillac and Condorcet) to decompose complex reality into its constituent units, the better to re-combine them in a more rigorous and coherent manner. Sometimes the analogies are mechanical and chemical - attractions, aversions, affinities. On other occasions, the metaphor of organic constitution, organization, or system occasionally comes to the fore, especially under the influence of the physiological writings of Cabanis and the natural history and zoology of Buffon's successors. Tracy makes use of each of the above modes or idioms, depending on the subject under examination, sometimes using more than one kind of image, especially in his social theory.

Secondly, Tracy argued for the unity of all the sciences, and for the scientific status of the study of human behaviour. He believed that the same procedural methods and logical structure of scientific explanation were applicable to all the positive sciences. For Tracy, the human and social sciences differ from geology and astronomy only in their subject matter, not in their epistemological status or their susceptibility to comprehension in terms of general causal laws. In making these assumptions, Tracy seems to be firmly placed among the founders of positivist and behaviouralist social science - a judgement which is further discussed in chapter four below, together with the question of how far mathematics might serve as a model for the scientificity of the human sciences. The behaviouralist aspect of Tracy's work, consisted in the assumption that science could only deal with observed effects, and not with first causes. Moreover, in the explanation of social and moral action, Tracy is a considerable distance from those approaches which emphasize the importance of motives, intentions and purposes as causally adequate explanations. Tracy's reductionist account of action in terms of needs and desires all but eliminates intentionality. Tracy's unity of the sciences was achieved on the basis of (i) a determinist view of human behaviour (the complement of the general determinism of the laws of inorganic nature); and (ii) his argument that the certainty of the sciences could be guaranteed and demonstrated only by a correct understanding of man's intellectual operations, which are the substratum of all his forms of knowledge. This is the role played by the theory of idéologie, as the logos of the sciences and the guarantee of their certainty in all fields of investigation.

II. THE CONCEPT OF IDÉOLOGIE

Destutt de Tracy presented his colleagues in the Class of moral and political sciences on 20 June 1796 with a problem of nomenclature: what would be the most appropriate name for the "new" science of ideas?[41] Inspired by Lavoisier and Condillac concerning the importance of nomenclature and conceptual reform, Tracy was keen to find a suitable name for a science which, he claimed, "is so new that it does not yet have a name".[42] The birth of a new science evidently required a baptism; and the best place for this was in the presence of that section of the Class devoted to Analyse des sensations et des idées, whose task was precisely the further development of this science. In seeking a new name, Tracy was not yet proposing a thorough overhaul of all the working concepts of the science of thought: the desire to reform its whole nomenclature would only become widely felt when the science itself had been more systematically studied by savants. The first step was to find a suitable name to mark off the scientific study of ideas from the pre-scientific "metaphysics" of the past, just as it had been necessary for astronomy to separate itself from astrology.[43]

Condillac had been content to use the term métaphysique, albeit
with the qualification that scientific or observational procedures should
be used in the gathering and analysis of facts.[44] Tracy regarded this
term as quite misleading and discredited. The common meaning of
métaphysique, said Tracy, is

> a science which treats the nature of beings, spirits [esprits],
> different orders of intelligence, the origin of things and
> their first cause. Now these are certainly not the objects
> of your research ... Moreover, metaphysics strictly means
> something other than physics: yet the knowledge of the faculties
> of man, as Locke believed, is certainly a part - an important
> part - of physics, whatever [ultimate] cause one wants to
> ascribe to these faculties.[45]

The legislators establishing the Institut had wisely refrained from
using the term "metaphysics" - but the term which they had used was not
very satisfactory. "Analysis of sensations and ideas" was hardly a
suitable name for the new science - it was rather like saying "analysis
of the sources of wealth in a society" instead of "political economy".[46]
Another possibility was the term psycologie, which Condillac had sometimes
used along with Charles Bonnet.[47] However, Tracy argued that psychology
literally meant "science of the soul [âme]"; it would not only be
presumptuous to claim a knowledge of such an entity, but it would give
the false impression that the savants of the Institut were investigating
first causes. On the contrary, insisted Tracy, "the goal of all your
works is the knowledge of effects and their practical consequences".[48]
What, then, was to be the name for this behavioural science to which
Tracy and his colleagues were devoting their attention?

Tracy recommended his own neologism: "idéologie, ou la science
des idées". Idéologie, he said, had a very clear etymological meaning,
based on the Greek eidos and logos, and it made no presuppositions about
causes.[49] Hence, it was a suitable word to express "the science of ideas
which treats ideas or perceptions, and the faculty of thinking or
perceiving".[50] This formulation of the content of idéologie was by no

means neutral, however. Tracy had not only defined the content in behaviouralist terms as knowledge of "effects" and "consequences", but he had also imported a whole epistemological doctrine by his equation of ideas with perceptions and of thinking with perceiving. This perspective was reinforced and extended in the following passage:

> This word has still another advantage – namely, that in giving the name idéologie to the science resulting from the analysis of sensations, you at once indicate the goal and the method; and if your doctrine is found to differ from that of certain other philosophers who pursue the same science, the reason is already given – namely, that you seek knowledge of man only through the analysis of his faculties; you agree to ignore everything which it does not uncover for you.[51]

Here we find not only statements which define the procedures and content of idéologie in terms of "analysis of sensations" and "analysis of [intellectual] faculties", but we also find sharp limits placed upon what is knowable – or what is to be taken as reliable knowledge. Such knowledge according to Tracy, must be derived from analyzing man's faculties, i.e. from investigating the operations of the mind in forming and expressing ideas. Let us examine more closely some of the main themes in Tracy's conception of idéologie.

First, we will take his view that the science of ideas is the fundamental science, necessary for guaranteeing reliable knowledge in all the other sciences. Tracy's reasoning seems to be as follows. All knowledge, regardless of subject-matter, consists of ideas, and their accuracy depends on our capacity for making a series of precise judgements. Knowledge of the processes by which errors arise and by which correct judgements may be formed, is the only basis available for ensuring the reliability of knowledge. The primacy of idéologie over the other sciences arises from the fact that in explaining the general operations of our intellectual faculties, it points out the methods for attaining certainty and avoiding error. Or, as Tracy succintly wrote: "it is necessary to

know our intellectual faculties in order to be sure we are using them

well".[52] In his early mémoires on idéologie, Tracy asserted that it was

"the first of all the sciences in the genealogical order".[53] Indeed, he

went even further, suggesting that

> knowledge of the human understanding is really the only
> science [la science unique]; all the others, without
> exception, are only applications of this knowledge to
> the diverse objects of our curiosity, and it must be
> their guiding light.[54]

Tracy gives two main kinds of reasons for the primacy of

idéologie - one related to scientific method, and the other concerning

the nature of human experience. The first argument is straightforward:

he asserts that all the sciences require a guarantee of their truth-

content; that scientific methods of observation and analysis are the

best procedural guarantees of reliable knowledge; that all the sciences

should adopt such methods; and that idéologie is central because it

clarifies and recommends the logic of scientific method and explanation.

The second argument, however, is more contentious and surprising. Here,

Tracy argues that the science of ideas is fundamental to all our knowledge

because the ideas of an individual are constitutive of his experience of

the world and of his self.

> In fact, since nothing exists for us except through the
> ideas we have, since our ideas are our whole being, our
> very existence, the examination of the manner in which
> we perceive and combine them is alone able to show us in
> what consists our knowledge, what it encompasses, what
> are its limits, and what method we must follow in the
> pursuit of truths in every field.[55]

This doctrine of the primacy of ideas-as-experience is rather anomalous in

what is otherwise a philosophy of monist materialism. The doctrine plays

little role in Tracy's overall conception of idéologie and the human

sciences, but it does suggest the overwhelming residual influence of the

Cartesian cogito in French philosophy.[56]

Tracy's view of idéologie as analytically and logically prior to all the other sciences led him to describe it as la théorie des théories,[57] and to suggest that "the examination of our intellectual operations is the natural introduction to all the branches of studies".[58] Knowledge of our means of knowing is la véritable philosophie première ou science première.[59] But it is quite different from "that first philosophy of which all our ancient authors have spoken so much", for the latter had assumed the truth of their general principles and built their systems on shifting sands.[60] The modern philosophie première, the "first of the sciences in their order of mutual dependence", is simply "the history of our intelligence considered in relation to its means of knowing".[61]

Tracy's assumptions about the genealogical and analytical priority of idéologie led him to reconsider the traditional classification of the branches of learning, propounded by Bacon and by d'Alembert. Bacon's classification, said Tracy, was confused and fallacious,[62] and d'Alembert had erred in following Bacon so closely.[63] Not only was it wrong that theology had been accorded the primary place as a general ontology; but the major categories of memory (history), reason (philosophy, including theology and science), and imagination (poetry) showed a faulty understanding of our intellectual faculties. The proper way to classify the sciences, wrote Tracy, was to distribute them in accordance with "the order in which they are derived from one another and through which they are fortified and inter-related". The science of the formation of our ideas "incontestably" came first, closely followed by the science of their expression and of their deduction.[64] Idéologie was to form "the trunk of the tree".[65] At the end of his Logique in 1805, Tracy drew up a plan which summarized the ambitious and ever-broadening scope of his conception of idéologie, as the new _prima philosophia_ providing the epistemological groundwork for all the sciences. The scheme was divided into nine parts and an appendix as follows:[66]

Elements of Idéologie

First Section: History of our means of knowing. In three parts.

  1st part: On the formation of our ideas, or Ideology strictly defined.

  2nd part: On the expression of our ideas, or Grammar.

  3rd part: On the combination of our ideas, or Logic.

Second Section: Application of our means of knowing to the study of the will and its effects. In three parts.

  1st part: On our actions, or Economics.

  2nd part: On our sentiments, or Morality.

  3rd part: On the rule of some by others, or Government.

Third Section: Application of our means of knowing to the study of beings other than ourselves. In three parts.

  1st part: On bodies and their properties, or Physics.

  2nd part: On the properties of extension, or Geometry.

  3rd part: On the properties of quantity, or Calculus.

Appendix: On the false sciences, which are abolished by knowledge of our means of knowing and their proper use.

Taken together, these sciences would form "the totality of the trunk of the encyclopedic tree of our real knowledge".[67]

Despite the enormous breadth of his ambitions, it should be evident that Tracy's intention was not to summarize all existing knowledge about man and nature, but to recommend and demonstrate the superiority of a particular method of enquiry: _analyse_. According to this method, as elaborated by Condillac[68] (and adopted by Condorcet,[69] and Garat,[70] and Tracy), all phenomena are susceptible to explication in terms of their location in an ordered progression from simple to complex facts; this approach is equally applicable to the study of animate and inanimate nature, and to mathematics. Any idea or concept can be "decomposed" by analysis into its constituent simple ideas which are anchored in sense-experience. Analysis demonstrates how complex ideas are built up from simple elements.[71] The programmatic aspect of this doctrine implies that any ideas which cannot, in this way, be melted down and reconstituted on the basis of simple sense-experience must be expelled from scientific discourse as ambiguous or meaningless, and propositions based on such ideas are false or at least unprovable.[72] Tracy asserts that _analyse_ and idéologie are based upon scrupulous observation of the facts, drawing only those conclusions fully warranted by the evidence, and always preferring "absolute ignorance" to any claim which merely appears to be plausible.[73]

The study of the formation of ideas, based on observation of facts and the analysis of their relationships, was for Tracy _une science expérimentale_.[74] The implication was that there were two kinds of "knowledge" - that modelled on the physical sciences, and that which could hardly be called reliable knowledge at all. Condillac had claimed that there was really only one _science_ - the history of nature - which could be subdivided into two, interdependent, parts: that dealing with facts or experience (_physique_), and that dealing with abstractions or reasoning upon these facts.[75] Tracy, in similar fashion, claimed that there are two kinds of "truths", namely, those of "experience or fact", and those of "reasoning or deduction". The deductive or abstract truths, however, had no validity independently of the facts from which they were abstracted.[76] Idéologie, like all positive sciences, required both types of truths. The scientific genius, wrote Tracy, is one who is able to "discover in the facts those important and very general truths which have not yet been detected - but it can never be a question of creating them out of his own head".[77] When idéologie and the human sciences had become more highly developed, he believed, they would be closer to the positive sciences of nature, especially physiology, than to any purely abstract science such as mathematics whose truths are entirely a deductive system abstracted from the objective world.[78] In idéologie and the human sciences, claimed Tracy, "perfection is not proportional to the number of facts observed, but to the knowledge of the laws which govern these facts".[79]

The problem, in Tracy's conception, was to find a starting point for structuring "the facts" in accordance with the laws governing their inter-relationships. What kind of starting point was appropriate? Would it be a truth of observation or a truth of deduction? Tracy chose the latter, on the analogy of astronomy, which explained all its phenomena "by starting from this single truth, that attraction acts in direct proportion to mass and in inverse proportion to the square of the distance".[80] Once such a secure starting point had been found, the rest of the scientific system would be unfolded in a series of rigorous deductions. If this were accomplished, the system of truths would be complete and entirely "certain". On the foundation of idéologie, the human sciences, according to Tracy, were capable of certainty in the same manner as the sciences of inanimate nature. A whole system of truths about man and society would follow:

> now that we are certain of the formation and filiation of our
> ideas, all that will be subsequently said - on the manner of
> expressing, combining and teaching these ideas, on regulating
> our sentiments and actions, and directing those of others -
> will be only the consequences of these preliminaries, and
> will rest on a constant and invariable base, consistent with
> the very nature of our being. Now these preliminaries constitute
> what is strictly designated as idéologie; and all the consequences
> derived from it are the object of grammar, logic, instruction,
> private morality, public morality (or the art social), education
> and legislation ... We will go astray in all these sciences only
> to the extent that we lose sight of the fundamental observations
> on which they rest.[81]

The secure starting-point for idéologie, the fundamental building-block on which all the "ideological, moral and political sciences" rested, was sense-perception. The methods of empirical observation and analyse (pioneered by Locke and Condillac in particular) had demonstrated to Tracy's satisfaction the truth of the ancient adage "nihil est in intellectu quin prius fuerit in sensu"[82] (literally: there is nothing in the mind which was not previously in the senses). Idéologie was therefore "a system of truths closely tied together, all stemming from this first indubitable fact, that we know nothing except through our sensations, and that all our ideas are the product of the various combinations we make from these sensations".[83] Tracy's insistence on sense-perceptions was, as we saw earlier, a materialized form of the Cartesian cogito. Having assumed that the only fact of which we can initially be certain is our own existence as a sensing being, Tracy's whole system is erected upon this être sensible. The proposition that "man is a sentient being", is the première vérité générale from which he elaborates his entire theory of man and society.[84] Tracy's disingenuous remark that his theories were devoid of presuppositions and that he had elaborated his idéologie purely by observation of man's thinking processes,[85] is clearly misleading. Tracy had accepted the sensationalist paradigm of what constitutes knowledge and what procedures had to be followed to reach the truth, to the exclusion of all other conceptions and procedures.

In Tracy's view, the study of mental phenomena had wrongly been separated in the past from the study of physical phenomena. Descartes, for example, had separated the two spheres, and had concluded that our thinking faculty owed nothing to sense perceptions, and that general principles were the foundation of knowledge. Tracy, following Locke and Condillac, argued that all ideas stem from sense perceptions or simple ideas which are transformed into complex ideas; and that knowledge must

be based on particular facts, not upon a priori or axiomatic principles.

The "artificial" separation of the mental and the physical had been

bridged by empiricist writers like Locke, who, according to Tracy, was

"the first man to try to observe and describe the human intelligence just

as one observes and describes a property of a mineral or a vegetable, or

a noteworthy aspect of the life of an animal: he also made this study a

part of la physique".[86] The study of the human intelligence, as of the

human body, is part of natural history: hence Tracy's well-known claim

that "idéologie is a part of zoology".[87]

Tracy's epistemology assumes, then, that sense-experience is

primary; and indeed, Tracy goes beyond Locke in asserting that sense

perception and thinking are absolutely identical terms.[88] Locke had

allowed the mind a certain independent activity in ordering and recalling

ideas from among the materials provided by sense experience. Condillac

virtually eliminated such independent reflectiveness of the mind by

attempting to demonstrate that memory, comparison and desire consist in

nothing but modifications of sense impressions.[89] However, Condillac

wished to allow that mind was an entity not entirely reducible to physical

operations, and spoke of "l'âme oisive". Tracy, noting the redundance of

such an entity in a thoroughly reductionist sensationalism, obliterated

the distinction between the mind itself and the activities of rearranging

sense perceptions by which it was constituted. His purpose was to deny

any independent reality to a mental or moral realm, and to assert a

naturalistic monism of consciousness and physical environment. Thought

(or perceiving/sensing) consisted of four basic faculties or modes of

operation: simple sensibility, memory, judgement and desire. "This

manner of envisaging it in these [four] elements unveils for us the whole mechanism".[90] All mental phenomena were produced by these modes. Where Condillac had shown that one faculty of the mind gave rise to the next in a generative manner, Tracy collapsed all such operations into aspects of the general sensibility of living creatures, all being "the results of our organization".[91]

Here, Tracy's physiological emphasis becomes important. Tracy takes as a given datum the physical structure and operations of the body, including all the sensibilities involved in consciousness. Whereas the content of ideas was largely determined by experience, education and environment, the structure of the mind itself was stable and predictable owing to its physiological foundation. Even though the innate ideas hypothesis in its Cartesian, Kantian and other versions was incompatible with Tracy's sensationalism, his theory appears to assume that the mind is so structured that its capacities are universally shared throughout the species, owing to a biological or physiological uniformity.[92] Cabanis' notion of the body as having intrinsic organic qualities, made it less dependent on external stimuli for all its operations. Physiology provided, for Tracy, the stable and certain basis which guaranteed that simple sensations were perceived in the same way by men of all ages and epochs.[93] The "certitude of all we know" depended on the physiological necessity that when we perceive X and Y, they are necessarily perceived as such and not as A and B. The same is true for "all beings who are organized like us".[94]

An important question arises concerning the character of the physiological determinism implied by Tracy's doctrine and the extent to which the physiological substructure is modified by the social-environmenta superstructure. This is an area where contradictory elements emerged in Tracy's writings, and he never discussed these problems at sufficient lengt or depth. We will note below, in the discussion of the will (desires) in chapter three, that despite the voluntarist doctrine of motilité, which was later developed by Maine de Biran, Tracy's general reductionism allows no role for genuinely independent volition. On the other hand, his educational doctrines (discussed at the end of chapter three, and in chapter seven) claim that vast changes in patterns of ideas and behaviour are made possible through a rational system of public instruction and legislation. Tracy was deeply influenced by the views of Cabanis on the interaction between the physical and moral aspects of man,[95] but these doctrines were largely taken for granted rather than argued or elaborated.[96]

Tracy's professions of belief in the physiological basis of the intellect, and in the capacity of the physiologists to resolve many of the outstanding problems in the science of ideas, became quite marked in the years after 1796 when he had first argued that idéologie should be divided into two parts. Idéologie physiologique would deal with the physical and biochemical dimensions of human sensibility, and idéologie rationnelle would examine the psychological and logical aspects of the intellectual faculties. Tracy claimed he would confine himself to the latter aspects: "I take our faculties such as they are, and concern myself only with their effects".[97] Nevertheless, a "complete" account of the operations of these faculties would require a unified approach, including the knowledge of a physiologist, mathematician, grammarian, and algébriste philosophe.[98] That the human sciences would require the co-operation of savants of various kinds was partly recognized in the organization of the Institut, where Tracy and Cabanis were both in the section on "Analysis of sensations and ideas". However, the grammarians had, to Tracy's regret,[99] been placed in a different Class; a more strictly "ideological" structure would have united them with the physiologists and idéologistes, for in

Tracy's doctrine, the study of how ideas are expressed (grammar) is merely one aspect of the general study of the origin and communication of ideas.

Tracy plainly believed that intellectual and moral ideas were dependent upon physical faculties, but the claim remained ambiguous. It could have meant only that sense perceptions are necessary materials for the mind and that without the senses there can be no human consciousness. However, Tracy no doubt intended a stronger relation of dependence than the claim that bodies and brains are preconditions of minds and thoughts. Tracy argued, against theories which posit innate or intuitive ideas, that ideas have no autonomy, independence, or innate existence in the mind; further, that all ideas are nothing but transformed and modified sensations, whose content derives entirely from data provided by the senses. Tracy, however, never attempted to demonstrate how the supposed physiological basis of mind shapes and interacts with the processes involved in reflection, judgement or desire. Tracy's reductionist language (idea = sense perception, thinking = perceiving sensations, idéologie = part of zoology and physics) was partly a methodological polemic against what he saw as metaphysical systems of ideas, which had misled men about nature and liberty and which had asserted a dualism between the natural and moral, the physical and the intellectual. Tracy's reductionism was also a confused doctrine, asserting a physiological base of human behaviour, without specifying the relationship between physiology and mind.

Tracy and Cabanis were rapidly identified as promoting the same materialist monism as La Mettrie and d'Holbach.[100] The only new thing about idéologie, wrote a hostile reviewer in 1802, is the title itself. Idéologie "substitutes the movement of the brute for human reason, and sees in man nothing but muscles and nerves". Fortunately, opined the critic, the human heart and the passage of time would leave such demented systems behind, as so much flotsam left on the river bank after the storm.[101] In obliterating reflective reason, "the idéologues saw in man nothing more than Condillac's statue", man being analyzed purely in terms of his physical needs.[102] The ideological analysis of mind, wrote another critic, was just like a "treatise on mechanics" where all one can see are "actions and reactions, moving forces and inertia".[103] The denial of a separate realm for human morality and reason, was to place man in the family of the monkeys. Those who espoused such a view wanted "to lead the moral man to the cemetery".[104]

Tracy's views on the physiological basis of human thought and action remained undeveloped. He did not ask why the mind operated in the ways it did - this was a matter for the physiologists to determine (and in any case, they could do little more than re-describe the processes in physical terms, unless they trespassed into the forbidden area of first causes). Tracy focussed his attention on behavioural effects or operations of the mind, and especially upon the connections between thought and language, ideas and words, the signified and the sign. Here was a field where he expected idéologie to make great progress. Idéologie, as the science des sciences,[105] was particularly suited to the task of clarifying ideas, making concepts more precise, and thereby promoting scientific understanding of phenomena in every field. The priority of idéologie over the positive sciences of man and nature depended on a view of language as the conventionalized set of signs which expresses our ideas, and a view of scientific advance as dependent on clarification of concepts and rejection of those not validated by sense-experience. The scientific language of elements and compounds also had the eminent

advantage, for the philosophe and idéologiste, of lending itself to
what Gillispie has called a "naturalistic pedagogy".[106] Idéologie was
seen to provide a grammar and syntax of nature, and a set of procedural
rules for finding the basic elements (signs, concepts) of any language.
The analysis of language was thus of critical importance for the idéologist
in his role both as scientific observer, and as educator of mankind.
The main features of Tracy's conception of language, and his view of how
language qua knowledge can be perfected, is examined in the following
section.

III.   THE SCIENCE OF SIGNS AND LANGUAGE

A language, for Tracy, is a system of signs whose meanings have
been fixed or formalized by the attribution of conventional meaning to
each symbol.[107] Some languages or sign-systems are more specialized than
others (algebraic notation, for example, or the symbols of chemistry),
but all share certain characteristics. First, language is created and
sustained as a social phenomenon: it is a kind of collective network
through which individuals share experiences and perhaps even contribute
to the enlargement of knowledge. Secondly, a mastery of language involves
a mastery of knowledge, of which the words are the signifers. In Tracy's
view, the ability to manipulate an appropriate language was the avenue
to understanding man and nature. The problem was to ensure that the
words actually designated precise and observable facts, or that general
ideas were squarely based on such facts.

The analytical method of idéologie was invoked to perform this
function - to ensure that the vocabulary and syntax of languages were
consistent with the facts discovered by observation, and with a rigorous
interrelationship of concepts. As Gillispie has aptly remarked, the

Baconian project of a renovation of learning became, in Condillac's work, identified with a "linguistic reform, redesignating words where necessary to make them speak facts, recombining them in a syntax of experience, lending reality to the expression used of the ancient atomists that theirs was an alphabet of nature".[108] Tracy's inspiration was the same, and his model of language was no less atomistic and naturalistic. In the generation of ideas, he claimed, a small number of basic elements, combined in various ways, produce "an almost infinite multitude of ideas, just as a small number of letters variously arranged suffice to represent those ideas. Here as elsewhere, nature shows a remarkable economy of means and profusion of effects".[109]

Tracy's interest in theories of language and the usage of signs was quite different from that of historical philology or pure linguistics. His purpose was far more practical. Ideological analysis was designed primarily to clarify our existing stock of ideas, eliminate vague concepts and false propositions, and provide criteria for rebuilding the human sciences. Tracy rejected all theories which attributed the form or content of language to any divine or supernatural agency. Rousseau had seen language as a divine spark planted in the mind, though its forms were developed by the passions; Maistre and Bonald proposed a theory of innate ideas, and ridiculed the Locke-Condillac account of the development of language through association of simple perceptions. In his desire to establish idéologie as an empirical science, Tracy believed it necessary to overthrow the "innatist" theories and to base the principle of language on its instrumental functions for satisfying human needs. Having established in this way how language evolved and functioned, it would become possible to improve its value as a precise instrument for codifying, communicating and enlarging our knowledge. Tracy's model of language was derived primarily from Condillac, whom Tracy therefore praised as the founder and creator of idéologie.[110]

Condillac had argued that all animate beings have sense impressions or perceptions, and are attracted or repelled by them. But only human beings have the capacity to reflect upon these simple ideas, to compare, combine and judge them.[111] The human faculties of reflection and judgement evolved very slowly over time, but rapidly outstripped the animal world when men began to invent and manipulate artificial signs to designate their ideas. The earliest signs were gestural and verbal, closely connected with immediate desires or passions. Gradually, various graphic forms of communication were developed, of which modern written languages are the highest form. The earliest signs designated sensible objects; gradually more general terms were derived or abstracted from the particular terms.[112] Condillac regarded the use of language as a process which assigned conventional meanings to given signs or words. The use of concrete particular terms was unambiguous because the objects designated were immediately apparent. But the use of more abstract terms was bound to involve confusion and imprecision, because the objects designated were not immediately obvious, and because clear meanings for general ideas depended on a rigorous chain of conceptual relationships founded upon simple ideas.[113] Finally, Condillac noted the importance of repetition and habit, which not only strengthen all our intellectual operations, but also unfortunately confirm us just as much in our badly-formed judgements as in our properly-formed judgements.

Tracy took up these four points concerning the origins of language, the usage of signs, the role of habitual judgements, and the problems of making language more precise. In the first place, Tracy was little concerned to assemble fresh historical evidence on the origin of

language, or to engage in any detailed comparative studies of living
languages. He was generally content to rely on the research of Gébelin
and others in regard to the ancient non-European languages,[114] and on
the large number of grammarians who had considered the development of
the European languages. The earliest form of communication, Tracy
surmised, was a "language of action" by which one's desires were made
known. Gestures and movements would usually be complemented by articulated
sounds of various kinds. Many animals could rightly be seen to have
reached this level of communication.[115]

Wherein lay the distinction between men and other animate
creatures? Was this not a problem for sensationalist philosophy, given
that all animate creatures were defined by their sensibility? Was not
Tracy's definition of man as l'homme sensible a denial of a qualitative
leap between human and other creatures? Certainly Tracy's critics believed
that his emphasis upon sensibility (rather than morality and reason) was
to condemn mankind to a search for purely material satisfactions and a
life without the consolations and inspirations of religion.[116] As
Aimé-Martin wrote:

> To reduce man to his body, is to reduce him to his senses.
> It results from this idea that the brute would have an
> intelligence superior to our own, because the senses of a
> great number of animals are more perfect than those of
> man. This single objection destroys the system of the
> materialists.[117]

Tracy had anticipated this line of criticism in his earliest
mémoires at the Institut. Man is superior even at the level of communication
through gestures or movements: "the organization of man is so superior to
all others that even his language of action can become much more advanced
than that of any animal".[118] It was true that ideas, understood as sense
perceptions, were experienced by all animate species; perceptions or
thinking exist before language, insisted Tracy.[119] But although animals

rapidly attain the degree of intellectual development they require for
their survival, they seldom surpass that level: their instinct is fixed
and limited.[120] No doubt there are many animals whose physical sensibilities are more highly developed in certain fields than human sensibilities.
This, however, does not confer a general superiority among such animals
over the human species, for the animals have only very limited means of
communication with their own species. The fact that our ideas originate
in our sense perception, in no way proves that intelligence is the same
thing as a refined capacity to perceive sensations: "the perfection of the
senses is very far from being the measure of our intellectual capacity".[121]

The superiority of the human species consisted in the ability
to make use of conventional and durable signs, to give permanent form to
ideas, enabling men to combine and multiply their ideas in a variety of
ways in co-operation with their fellows. Tracy no doubt believed that
there was a physiological basis for this human capacity to create and
manipulate signs representing ideas. He assumed, as a given feature of
our physical organization, the capacity of the brain to deal with complex
operations - of comparison, recollection, judgement, desire, etc. More
immediately, however, he pointed out the importance of the human ability
to vocalize a vast range of distinctive sounds - a kind of oral/aural
alphabet - which made available a more flexible and extensive system of
signs than those given by gesture or movement.[122]

Tracy claimed that Condillac was the first philosopher to have
clearly demonstrated our dependence on signs in developing and communicating
our ideas.[123] Hobbes was also praised for having understood the difficulties
and the importance of establishing clear connections between words and
meanings.[124] Signs are necessary to fix in our memory the meanings of, and
the relations between, our ideas; without signs, says Tracy, we could hardly

remember our ideas nor combine them.[125] The use of consciously developed language sets man apart from the beast, and makes it possible for him to emerge from that historical stage where he was dominated by his immediate needs.[126] Language, the symbolic embodiment of rationality, is the instrument of man's perfectibility. Having begun in total ignorance, the human species has profited by shared experience and knowledge, and eventually reached a point where the desire to increase and propagate knowledge developed its own dynamic.[127] Knowledge becomes a cultural possession only by virtue of sign-systems or languages, which are entirely a product of social interaction over many centuries. It is a slow process: our means of knowledge require considerable exercise before they are developed more fully.

> And so we are entirely the product of art [rather than nature], that is, of our work; and we resemble the natural man, or our original mode of existence, as little as an oak resembles an acorn or a chicken resembles an egg.[128]

If signs were the instruments of human progress and reason, it followed that an individual who was denied the opportunity to participate in a linguistic communication system, would be unable to develop his mental capacities to more than an "animal" level.[129] Eighteenth-century materialists and sensationalists, including Diderot, La Mettrie and Condillac, had taken this to be a clear refutation of any innate-ideas hypothesis. Two examples were of particular interest to them, and were widely discussed - the case of deaf-mutes, and the case of so-called "wolf children". The deaf-mute from birth, said Tracy, cannot share in advanced forms of communication, and his intellectual capacities will reach only a limited level, even though he may be considered helped by instruction in gestural language.[130] The enfant abandonné was in a similar position: deprived of social interaction and advanced language skills, his intellect was seriously deficient.[131] The example of

le sauvage de l'Aveyron, captured in 1799 shortly after Tracy's early
mémoires at the Institut, provoked great interest among the idéologistes.
The famous Dr Philippe Pinel, who was pioneering more humanitarian forms
of treatment for the insane, wrote a report on the boy in 1800, on behalf
of a committee of the Société des Observateurs de l'Homme, and concluded
that the boy was an idiot, who had been abandoned because he was incapable
of reaching more than a mediocre degree of intelligence. Dr Jean Itard
subsequently spent several years, with very modest success, training the
boy through techniques developed by Sicard at the Institute for deaf-mutes.

According to Tracy, men in primitive societies learn to make
certain types of judgements with great facility and precision, but only
in a limited area, beyond which they encounter enormous difficulties.
Progress beyond this stage depends on improvements in our language as
an instrument of communication, knowledge, and mastery of the environment.
Without language, said Tracy, "the human species would be condemned to
an eternal infancy".[133] Our communication through the use of signs,
according to Tracy, "is the origin of all our social relations, and has
thus given rise to all our sentiments and all our moral pleasures".[134]

Every language is based on conventional attributions of meaning
to a set of signs. But a convention, according to Tracy, must rest on a
prior mutual understanding between men. The main foundation for this
mutual understanding is the universality of sensible experience - each
man is affected similarly by feelings of joy, grief, surprise, tenderness,
tiredness - and he observes these feelings in other men and understands
the causes. A shared language of action thus arises from our sentiments.[13]
From this "natural and necessary" language of action based on our desires,
there gradually develops a more "artificial and voluntary" language in
which we invent a multitude of signs to represent a wider range of ideas

and relationships.[136] It is necessary, for continued progress, that some

way is found to "render durable these first artificial signs which are

all transient and fleeting".[137] Written languages mark a further stage

in the development of human understanding.

But the practical consequences of adopting a written language

are not uniform, because there are two main kinds of écriture: that based

on pictorial representation of ideas (such as the complex hieroglyphic

languages of China, Japan and the Middle East), and that based on

notation of the tonal qualities of the oral language (such as the

European languages). Tracy argues for the superiority of the second

type, mainly because it is more flexible, simple, and readily learned by

the mass of the people.[138] Even when the vocabulary is very extensive,

all the words of an alphabetical language "are the result of the

frequent repetition of a fairly restricted number of sounds".[139] Tracy

could find no obvious reasons why some civilizations have used hieroglyphic

writing and others alphabetical writing, for such phenomena were not the

result of calculative choice or deliberation. The consequences, however,

were irrevocable. Once a society had adopted one of these forms, it was

virtually impossible to change to the other, since the changes involved

would amount to a complete uprooting of customs, traditions, habits and

institutions.[140] Societies which have adopted the hieroglyphic symbols,

said Tracy, are condemned, as a direct result of their complex and

inaccessible language, and their inevitably rigid social ranks, to achieving

very little further progress.[141] The alphabetical languages, on the other

hand, are more easily taught to everyone. They facilitate the propagation

of knowledge through the development of the printing press, for their

small number of mobile characters are very flexible.[142] The scientific

outlook could be transmitted more readily in alphabetical script, via

textbooks and journals reaching a mass audience. This last factor was
an infinite advantage in the eyes of the idéologues, in the Baconian and
encyclopédiste tradition, for whom the diffusion of ideas and the combattir
of existing prejudices was as crucial as the discovery of new knowledge.

Tracy emphasized that the development of intellectual faculties
depended greatly upon the repetition of ideas in given circumstances,
an exercise which made our judgements more or less rapid and habitual.
It is a "general law" of all our movements, mental and physical, that

> the more they are repeated, the easier and quicker they become;
> and that, the easier and quicker they are, the less they are
> perceptible, that is to say the perceptions they cause in us
> are diminished, even to the point of vanishing, though the
> movement itself still occurs.[143]

Our intellectual development depends on our judgements becoming easier,
more rapid and less perceptible; and these operations are enormously
facilitated by a shared language composed of a multitude of signs, whose
meanings are fixed by conventional usage. However, while familiarity
with the ideas contained in a language is the source of our cultural
progress, there are certain inherent defects in the use of signs which
prevent us from ever achieving perfect communication, the implicit goal
of idéologie.

In the first place, there is a problem of guaranteeing that the
same meaning is always given to a sign by different people. But this is
impossible to guarantee, says Tracy. On the contrary, it is strictly
true that the exact meaning of a sign is known only to the first user –
and even for him, only on the first occasion, because he may be mistaken
in believing that later circumstances correspond exactly with the first
situation.[144] Few people are inventors of signs and of meanings. Language
is generally learned as part of our education in a particular society.
Tracy assumes that there is always a degree of uncertainty and vagueness

in using conventional signs,[145] especially in ordinary language where the sign system is more subject to individual variability in usage. To some extent, we can overcome the difficulty in practice by gaining personal experience of the idea represented by the sign, especially in the case of simple sensations. But this becomes very difficult with complex ideas, for it would be necessary for each man to analyze all the elements composing such ideas, examining their relations step by step, to be sure that the idea had the same content for him as it had for others.[146] Condillac and Tracy believed that brute facts, immediately striking the senses, must be unambiguous and given directly to man by nature, so to speak. Simple sensations would be experienced in the same way by every individual owing to their identical organic faculties, and presumably owing to the passivity of the perception. Complex ideas allowed more possibilities of vagueness, error, or variability in meaning, and the intrusion of faulty memory. Language in use, therefore, is necessarily individualized to some extent, owing to the improbability of each man attaching exactly the same meanings to the same words.[147] This is an inherent problem of complex communications and the use of abstract ideas.[148] Ambiguity can never be eliminated, but idéologie could do much to reduce the problem by showing how to avoid precipitate judgements[149] at least in those specialized languages claiming to be systems of scientific knowledge. Fortunately, not all the defects of language were inherent in complex communication - some defects were caused by ignorance and by habitual errors of judgement: these could be overcome by education and by correcting certain anomalies in the written language.[150]

In searching out the possibilities for improving the accuracy of concepts and of knowledge, Tracy considers the difference between language in general and algebraic analysis in particular. In 1796, he

had confidently urged his colleagues to "imitate the mathematicians",
since they had achieved a rigorous system of certain truths, beginning
from a "palpable" first truth and proceeding slowly "from the known to the
unknown".[151]   Before long he recognized that the analogy was misleading,[152]
and in so doing rejected Condillac's tendency to posit algebraic equations
as the epitome of linguistic exactitude. Tracy's comparison of language
and algebra throws light upon the ideals of his reformist enterprise in
conceptual reform, and also upon the impossibility of attaining a perfect
language for expressing truths about man and society. Tracy began by
asserting that

> ... we can regard as proven that the general effect of signs
> is, in summing up prior judgements, to make easier the
> subsequent analyses; that this effect is exactly that of
> the symbols and formulae of algebra; and that, consequently,
> languages are true instruments of analysis, and algebra is
> simply a language which directs the mind with more certainty
> than others, because it expresses only very precise relations
> of a single type. Grammatical rules have just the same
> effect as the rules of calculus; in both cases, it is only
> the signs which we combine; and, without our being aware of
> it, we are guided by words just as by algebraic symbols.[153]

Tracy immediately qualified his analogy, by insisting on the
distinctive nature of algebra. It is confined to ideas of quantity, which
are invariable and distinct units whose relations are very precise and
certain: providing one follows the rules, one always reaches a correct
conclusion. But most of our ideas are not quantitative, and it would be
mistaken to take algebra as the desired model in our reforms of ordinary
language, whose signs and relationships can never have the simplicity and
precision of quantitative signs.[154]   Algebraic signs are a particularly
clear and limited group of precise symbols; ordinary language is relatively
untidy and imprecise.

> Words are ... formulae which depict in an abridged way the
> results of previous combinations and which relieve our
> memory of the obligation of having these combinations
> presented ceaselessly in all their details ... [B]ut the

> results which these words express are not of a kind as
> simple or precise as those represented by algebraic
> symbols; and the modifications which we make them undergo
> in discourse ... are much more varied and much less
> measurable than those undergone by algebraic symbols ...
> [which] are all perceptible in numerical terms; those
> of words are not so, and that is an immense difference.[155]

In rejecting the model of algebra for a perfected language, Tracy rejected
Condillac's notion that correct judgements are nothing but statements
of identity between the two terms of the judgement.[156] He also unwitting-
ly cast doubt upon the very possibility of a deductivist science of man,
and upon his assumption that the human sciences could be brought to the
same degree of certainty as the mathematical sciences.

Tracy was determined, above all, to show how the study of our
intellectual faculties could throw light on the correct operation of our
judgements. The problem was to understand the mind sufficiently to
enable us to make correct judgements. Given Tracy's view that language
consists of signs and the combinations we make of them, the reform of
language consists in making our signs (concepts) more precise, and in
making the links between them more certain. His ultimate practical
objective was "ideological" education: "to make correct judgements
habitual".[157] This would be a substantial and long-term project of public
instruction, which would never be completely successful, given the inherent
defects of signs. However, some progress could be made.

> ... a complete reform [of words and syntax] is almost
> impossible, for too many habits resist it. To change
> completely a usage which is tied at so many points to
> all our social institutions, would require a unanimous
> consent which cannot even be conjectured, and would be
> a real revolution in society. [But] ... while letting
> this usage subsist, since it cannot be destroyed, it
> would be very useful to point out properly its defects,
> their causes and consequences, and to place alongside
> our existing written language a perfected model of
> what it should be.[158]

Tracy assumes that, for maximum clarity, the written language should represent as exactly as possible the sounds of the spoken language. The latter should be examined carefully by a learned body of experts who would draw up a phonetic alphabet, containing all the sounds and inflections of spoken discourse, and would publish extracts from local and foreign literature in the new phonetic form for the edification of the public. This would fix the pronunciation and prose form of languages as precisely as possible, while leaving their everyday variations "in the grip of routine and [customary] usage". At least the savants of every nation might wish to consult with profit such an écriture universelle.[159] Tracy also hoped that a learned group from within the Institut might desire to take up the matter of perfecting the spelling, pronunciation and syntax of the French language.[160]

Tracy's hopes in these areas were neither unfounded nor ignored. Indeed, many of the problems of language raised by Tracy had been examined by grammarians and idéologistes towards the end of the eighteenth century. Discussions at the Institut on questions concerning the development and reform of language were very common between 1796 and 1803, and some of the idéologistes were involved in revising the Dictionnaire de l'Académie française. One of the most notable initiatives was the series of prize essay topics proposed by the Second Class of the Institut, including three concerned with language. The first, proposed in 1796, was addressed to the question of determining "the influence of signs on the formation of ideas".[162] The second, in 1799, asked contestants to "determine the influence of habit on the faculty of thinking, or in other words, clarify the effects on each of our intellectual faculties produced by the frequent repetition of the same operations".[163] The third such competition announced in 1802, sought essays on the topic: "Determine how one should le-compose the faculty of thinking, and what are the elementary faculties which are to be recognized?"[164] Tracy himself was also active at the Institut pursuing related questions. For example, he was a member of a commission of the Institut appointed to examine the merits of a lexicological system devised by a M. Buttet, who sought to devise rules for giving exact meanings to words by the perfecting of our language. He was also appointed to a commission investigating the systems of pasigraphie, invented by de Maimeux and others, who sought to discover a "universal language" in which ideas were directly represented in symbolic forms other than the verbal forms of conventional languages.[165] Tracy in 1800 presented to the Institut his own critical assessment of pasigraphy.[166] Such a system, he claimed, had all the defects of hieroglyphic languages, and thus could not resolve the problems it set out to overcome.[167]

Tracy had argued earlier, in his "Mémoire sur la faculté de penser", that a perfect language of any type was "a chimera, like perfection in any field".[168] Existing languages had developed in a haphazard manner over many centuries; they were far from methodical or systematic. For a perfect language to be created, it would have to be composed all at once, by a genius with universal knowledge, and devoid of all particular passions but love of truth.[169] A perfected language would in principle be able to represent our ideas precisely in a way which prevented misunderstanding, and might impart to our deductions the same certainty which exists in the languages of quantity.[170] There would be no way, however, that such a language would be widely adopted, by other than a few savants. Moreover, even if it were adopted, it would immediately become disfigured by the conventional usages of spoken language, and by the inherent weaknesses or limitations of our intellectual faculties.[171]

A less ambitious series of reforms would try to improve
spelling and pronunciation;   make syntax follow more closely the "natura.
progression of ideas in deductions"; eliminate vague and euphemistic
expressions;[172] encourage the adoption of new terms wherever needed;
formulate properly methodical nomenclatures in all the sciences; and
correct our ideas by the discovery of new truths, especially in idéologie [17.]
All these things could be done to the French language, making it the
nearest approximation to the needs of savants for precise expression.[174]
But while some such reforms can be made in each conventional language,
Tracy concludes that a universal perfected language (la langue universell
is bound to remain a "dream" - indeed, it is "as impossible as perpetual
motion".[175]

The idéologistes of the 1790s had placed great faith in the
progressive consequences of conceptual reform; it was central to their
conceptions of public instruction and the production of enlightened
and virtuous citizens.[176] This explains why the écoles centrales,
created in the law of October 1795, included a course on grammaire
générale, a subject which, according to Tracy, would demonstrate that
"all languages have common rules which are derived from the nature of our
intellectual faculties", and that this knowledge is necessary "not simply
for the study of languages but is also the only solid basis of the moral
and political sciences, [on which ...] all citizens should have sound
ideas".[177] The science of language was intended to have important and
beneficial consequences for social and moral behaviour.

While Tracy believed that great improvements could be made by
linguistic and conceptual reforms introduced into the education system
by enlightened teachers and administrators, the other side of the problem
was to combat the sources of error and mystification which were institut-

ionalized in positions of influence. The major source of illusions in France, according to Tracy, was the Catholic Church. In the following section, we therefore examine Tracy's views on religion and theological metaphysics, in terms of his desire to reduce the influence of "metaphysics" or of "unscientific" thought.

IV. METAPHYSICS AND RELIGION

Tracy wanted to establish a clear separation between sciences based upon observation and analysis, and bodies of doctrine whose object was

> not to discover the sources of our knowledge, their
> certitude and their limits, but to determine the
> principle and the purpose of all things, to divine
> the origin and destiny of the world. That is the
> object of metaphysics. We place it among the arts
> of imagination, designed to satisfy us and not to
> inform us.[178]

There could be nothing more different in approach, insisted Tracy, than the "old theological metaphysics, or metaphysics strictly defined", and the "modern philosophical metaphysics or idéologie". The latter was the "remedy for all these infirmities" of the mind.[179] "Idéologistes" and "métaphysiciens" were engaged in distinct enterprises.[180] As an "experimental" science dealing with facts and observation, idéologie avoided the "metaphysical" error of believing that general ideas gave meaning to particular ideas, instead of vice versa.[181] Metaphysics tended to separate the mental and material worlds, whereas they should be studied in their essential unity. Metaphysics tended to derogate the reality of man's natural objectivity, and see him as moving in a world of pure thought.[182] Condillac wrote that

> Nature itself points out the order we ought to follow
> in the communication of truth; for if all our knowledge
> comes from the senses, it is evident that the perception
> of abstract notions must be prepared by sensible ideas ...
> If philosophers do not care to acknowledge this truth,
> it is because they are prejudiced in favour either of
> innate ideas, or of a customary usage which seems to
> have been consecrated by time.[183]

The "metaphysics" of Descartes and others, who located the origins of ideas in pre-given categories of the mind, was thus contrasted by Tracy with idéologie, whose basic assumption was that a scientific epistemology would demonstrate the unity of mind and body, of the physical and moral realms, and that all ideas were derived from our sense perceptions. Tracy did not attempt to refute in detail the various theories of innate and intuitive ideas. His procedure was to assert fundamental differences of principle between a priori "metaphysics" (in which Plato and Aristotle rubbed shoulders with Descartes, Malebranche, Leibnitz, Berkeley and Kant) and the philosophy of sensations and experience (whose key figures included Bacon, Hobbes, Locke, Helvétius and Condillac). As a behavioural science, concerned with effects and not ultimate causes,[184] idéologie was utterly opposed to pronouncements by philosophers and theologians claiming to know the purpose of creation or the destiny of man. Such matters could not be resolved by science - they could only be answered in accordance with revealed religion or private faith. The idéologiste's faith in the benevolent powers of reason in social life was held up in contrast to what they saw as the mystifications inherent in acceptance of unverifiable dogmas about man, nature and God.

The idéologues, like the philosophes before them, were involved in a bitter contest with Catholic orthodoxy for political and cultural influence. The Church had been a rich and powerful institution, supported by state authority and the censorship system, until it was disestablished

from its official status, and priests were obliged to swear loyalty to
the civil constitution in 1790. In the following years, the goods of
the Church were confiscated, convents were closed, and refractory priests
were forced to emigrate or face execution. After the Terror and the
forcible de-christianization, there was a slight return towards religious
toleration in 1795-97, before the Directory moved against "royalists"
and anti-republicans in its efforts to bolster its precarious authority.
The separation of Church and State had been formalized in a decree of
February 1795.[185] Tracy and the idéologues strongly supported such moves
to reduce the influence of the Church, not only in politics but especially
in education. As opponents of clerical influence and as sensationalist
philosophers, they were accused by more orthodox believers, as we have
seen above, of destroying the moral stature of the human species by
degrading it to the level of animal sensations and appetites. Idéologie
was accused of being materialist, atheist, and destructive of morality.[186]
These critical claims, however, require certain qualifications.

In the first place, the idéologues, like most utilitarian social
theorists,[187] did not want to destroy morality as such, but to reduce the
authority of the Church in prescribing moral rules, and sought to
found morality upon a rational consideration of human desires and
interests. For Volney and others, moral behaviour was based on natural
laws, or rational principles inherent in social life.[188] The moral
injunctions of the idéologues were not very distant from certain
principles in the Sermon on the Mount.[189]

Secondly, most of the idéologues were deists or agnostics rather
than atheists.[190] They occasionally spoke of a divine providence which
had ordered the universe; and some were active supporters of deist cults
such as théophilanthropie[191] which flourished briefly under the Directory.

Tracy and his colleagues were predisposed, by their scientific
weltanschauung and by their Voltairian ancestry, to be sceptical and
agnostic towards theological revelations about the nature of the universe
and the moral duties of man, and to be distrustful of claims by the
Church to have privileged knowledge of the forms of authority and moral
virtue prescribed by God for mankind.

Thirdly, the idéologues' view of man as anchored in natural
history may be understood not so much as a denial of man's paramount place
in the hierarchy of animal life, but more as a methodological strategy
for a positivist science of human behaviour.[192] The idéologues were
perfectly willing to agree that the human species had a unique capacity
for reason, sentiment and morality. But they wished to demonstrate that
these qualities had a physiological dimension (bordering on determinism,
in one or two cases), and that these qualities were historically developed
through language and social interaction (rather than a divine gift). Ther
would seem to be a clear line of continuity between the idéologues and
Auguste Comte, not only in regard to a thorough-going scientism in their
methodological pronouncements, but also in regard to the three stages
theory of knowledge.

Tracy argued in his Commentaire (1806-7) that there have been
three main stages in the development of reason and civilization. The firs
was typified by despotism, force and ignorance; the second, aristocratic
rule buttressed by religious opinions; and the third, representative
government and the full flowering of reason. Comte's three stages were
the theological, metaphysical and positive stages.[193] The pattern of
evolutionary progress is similar. Both systems obviously owe a great
deal to Condorcet's ten-stage Esquisse of 1793 (and the conception can
be traced back even to Turgot). What is common to Condorcet and his

successors is a view of religion, theology and abstract ontology as
obsolete and pre-scientific explanations of man. Moreover, they are
seen as institutional obstacles to the development of scientific reason.
Condillac had therefore been wrong to retain "natural theology" among
the philosophical principles needed to explain man's place in society
and history.[194] Indeed, Tracy completely excluded theology from the
hierarchy of sciences, where it had traditionally occupied a pivotal
position.[195]

In considering theology and institutionalized religion in their
dual aspect, as systems of knowledge/beliefs and systems of authority,
Tracy made three kinds of criticism. Firstly, he asserted that many of
the doctrines of revealed religion were not merely unverifiable, but
had actually been disproved and exposed by science as mystifications and
illusions about the operations of natural phenomena. Secondly, he
criticized the Church for having resisted and obstructed the search for
scientific knowledge about nature, and for attempting to impose a dogmatic
and illiberal view of morality and the social order. Thirdly, he argued
for a separation of Church and State, and in favour of religious tolerance,[196]
claiming that no religious beliefs should have the status of official
doctrine, supported by public authority. Religious beliefs, in his view,
should be essentially matters of private conscience and faith, not matters
of orthodoxy and authority. Taken together, Tracy's criticisms led him
to support policies designed to reduce the influence of the Catholic Church
in France, and especially in public education, where so many impressionable
young minds could be distorted by unscientific dogmas and superstitions.

The anticlericalism of the 1790s changed after the Consulate was
established by Bonaparte, who decided that the traditional religion was a
necessary basis for the social order.[197] Catholicism was recognized as the

official religion of France by the Concordat of 1802, and Chateaubriand's Génie du Christianisme simultaneously provided a spiritual defence of the Church. The idéologues were outraged by Bonaparte's policies whereby the Church regained a great deal of its erstwhile influence. It was not possible to mount a strong attack upon the Concordat and the revival of Catholicism (owing to censorship), although Chateaubriand's work was ridiculed in the pages of la Décade,[198] and oblique criticisms of the Church and the Concordat were made in articles defending "la philosophie rationnelle" and "la saine morale".

Tracy had observed the changing fortunes of the Church with a watchful eye; he adopted a staunchly and sometimes bitterly anti-clerical position. He had welcomed in 1795 the publication of Charles Dupuis' voluminous l'Origine de tous les cultes, which attempted to reduce religious doctrines to allegories or myths about nature, and especially about astronomical phenomena.[199] Tracy was so impressed by the thrust of Dupuis' erudite volumes, that he wrote some articles for the Mercure français giving a concise summary of the main arguments. The journal ceased publication in January 1798 before all of Tracy's remarks had appeared. Soon afterwards, Dupuis published a 600-page Abrégé of the multi-volume work (1798); but Tracy was not satisfied that Dupuis' summary was sufficiently analytical and didactic to serve the purpose of enlightening the wider reading public. Tracy therefore published, as an anonymous pamphlet, the full text of his Analyse de l'Origine de tous les cultes.[200] A second and expanded edition, also anonymous, appeared in 1804: in the light of the revived influence of Catholicism, it was a veritable political tract.[201]

Dupuis' main argument, wrote Tracy, was that the ancient fables had never been properly understood, because it was not recognized that "all religions are never anything but the worship of nature and its main

agents, the stars, fire and other elements; and because it was not seen

that myths are only the allegorical and symbolic expressions of that

first religion and its celestial aspects".[202]   Christianity could be

understood, in these terms, as essentially the worship of nature and of

the sun, under a variety of different names and symbols.[203]

        The perspective adopted by Tracy and Dupuis was that religious

dogmas were a product of a non-scientific world-view, a product of

ignorance, and had been propagated by priests who preach servility and

fear. The empirical methods of science were foreign to the priests and

theologians, who set themselves up as authorities on the moral and the

natural world.

> Let us conclude, then, that every religious system is, at
> the theoretical level, a supposition without proof, a
> veritable lapse of reason; and, at the practical level,
> it is a powerful force for making men follow certain rules
> of conduct but a sure means of giving them false rules,
> and emanating from an illegitimate authority; hence, that
> all religion may be defined as an obstacle to good logic
> and to sound morality both private and public.[204]

In some lines added to the 1804 edition, Tracy said that even a man

"convinced of the utility and the sanctity of religion, if he wanted to

be just and did not aspire to become domineering and oppressive", would

desire that no religion be taught in the public education system, for

that would impose a uniform doctrine on people of contrary views.[205]

In his Commentaire on Montesquieu two years later, Tracy asserted that

"any government which wants to oppress, is attached to priests and works

to make them powerful enough to serve it".[206]   The critical references

to Bonaparte are unmistakable. Tracy concluded his pamphlet in 1804 by

asserting that

> theology is the philosophy of the infancy of the world,
> [but] it is time that it gave way to the philosophy of
> its age of reason; theology is the work of the imagination,

> like bad physics or poor metaphysics which are born with
> it in times of ignorance and serve as its base; whereas
> the other philosophy is founded on observation and
> experience, and is closely tied to true physics and
> rational logic, which are all the product of the work
> of enlightened centuries; finally, a theologian is
> nothing but a bad philosopher who is rash enough to
> dogmatize on things he does not and cannot know.[207]

Tracy's identification of religion with speculative metaphysics and imagination was joined to an explanation of the historical origins of religious beliefs. Despite the apparent diversity and mutual antagonism of religious cults and sects, they all had a common basis, namely, that they were

> founded on the same idea – fear of invisible forces.
> Saint-Lambert said with good reason: superstition
> is fear of invisible forces. That is how he defined
> it; he could have added: and it is the source of all
> religions.[208]

In seeking the causes of natural phenomena, primitive societies invented various spirits whose task was to ensure that the sun and planets, the rivers and the winds continued to be activated in their customary way. The worship by men of these multitudinous spirits who presided over every-day life, was inevitable for primitive men, with their unsophisticated knowledge of the processes of nature. Later, they imagined a superior being who supervised all the lesser spirits and gave an overarching order to the whole universe.[209] But it was only ignorance of the real causes of phenomena which led men to explain events without a known cause as the product of the will of an unseen being.[210]

Dupuis had especially emphasized the religious significance of primitive astronomy and the mythology of the constellations and signs of the zodiac. "The adventures of all these gods are only allegorical tales about the movements of celestial bodies and their various relations; and thus it is in the heavens that we must find the source and application of all the mythological and theological fables".[211] These myths should not be dismissed without first seeking out their symbolic meanings. Dupuis had claimed that the key to decoding such myths lay in astronomical and physical phenomena.[212] Analysis of these myths showed that the two main sources of human unreason are the personification of abstractions, and the use of metaphorical and metaphysical terminology.[213] In such cases, wrote Tracy, ignorance is preferable to false ideas.[214]

Tracy also elaborated a critique of religion as a social institution in terms of the historical development of a priesthood.[215] In each primitive society there emerged people claiming to recognize more powerful spirits than those currently worshipped, or to know the best means of influencing such spirits, and who thus held sway over credulous people in their locality. Insofar as they did not join with other priests in founding a total religious system and theology, their social effect was relatively harmless.[216] Tracy took a different view of a powerful priesthood which emerged with the growth of societies: religious doctrines became more systematic and the priesthood became an organized and hierarchical body. Priests then became "an integrating and important part of the constitution of the state".[217]

At the height of their power, the priests made their doctrines into a "science" which stifled all other forms of inquiry.[218] They propounded that mauvaise philosophie which is based on imagination rather than observation, conjecture rather than doubt, and which endowed abstractions and essences with reality instead of studying the actual operation of our intellectual faculties.[219] Theologians began to assert the complete spiritualization of the gods and of souls, depriving them of all material attributes. They could then attribute to these "purely imaginary beings" whatever qualities they chose, without fear of contradiction. The only way to disagree would be to deny the very existence

of spiritual powers, and to do so would invite severe punishment.[220]
Theologians established a complete separation of the realm of ideas and
judgement, from the realm of nature and material existence. Hence, they
concluded that all our ideas and sentiments have their source not in our
sensibilities but in another immaterial being, the universal spirit of
God.[221] By giving free rein to their favourite errors - belief in the
real existence of abstract ideas, and belief in the reality of a being
deprived of all its sensible qualities - the theologians generated "a
host of shocking absurdities", in which the Christian religion is
especially prolific.[222]

The early Christian religion, claimed Tracy, consisted largely
of practices and precepts; not dogmas, mysteries and sacraments. But by
the thirteenth century, and throughout the "barbaric" Middle Ages,
Christianity suffered an "excess of theological delirium", full of "far-
fetched dogmas which are truly non-sense" and sustained by a sophistical
language.[223] Such a system of beliefs began to lose ground, however, when
the spirit of observation, experience, and doubt emerged alongside that
of credulity and supposition. The truths based on observation and on the
questioning of received opinion, began to replace the mass of accumulated
errors. Once the facts of man and nature have been properly explained,
Tracy asserted with more hope than conviction, the human mind would not
abandon them again. Theology is like a child's imagination, destined to
give way to a mature reason.[224] Tracy expressed a desire to be rid of

this multitude of different religious systems, which have
done so much harm in the world, caused so often the spill-
ing of men's blood, divided people into what amounts to
hostile groups, prevented commercial and social interaction
among them, especially the communication of knowledge, made
some people into objects of aversion and malediction for
others, and prescribed so many duties so contrary to their
happiness and to reason, particularly that of hating and
detesting those who think differently from themselves.[225]

Dupuis' work had shown, to Tracy's satisfaction, that all the ancient and modern religions of Asia and Europe, which denounced one another so fiercely, were exactly the same apart from some changes in name. There could be no more bitter truth for the priests than this underlying unity of doctrine, for their greatest passion, he wrote, was hatred of their competitors. In that respect, said Tracy, priests are more like charlatans than thieves - for thieves keep a strong loyalty among themselves for their common security, whereas charlatans denigrate their fellows in trying to attract the crowd exclusively to themselves.[226]

Tracy noted that it would be easier for modern Europeans to accept that the ancient religions and myths were based on the worship of nature and the stars, than to see that Christianity was in the same mould.

> Christianity is so close to us, it still rules over
> the least enlightened part of our surroundings, it
> seems to have so little relationship to these brilliant
> fictions: how are we to be persuaded that Christ too
> is only a fantastic being, just one of a thousand
> versions of the sun-god?[227]

Tracy further agrees with Dupuis that Christ was no more a historical figure than were Hercules, Bacchus or Osiris.[228] Nevertheless, it would require a great deal of scientific analysis and demystification to destroy the influence of religious illusions - "for the absurdities have a very strong hold on the human mind when they have an ancient priority over reason".[229] How could this "ancient mass of prejudices and errors" be overturned? The exact analysis of our intellectual operations could demonstrate to educated men that we only truly know whatever falls under our senses, and that all other supposed beings are nothing but "personified abstractions, creations of our imagination". It is necessary to open the eyes of the common man by tracing the origin and evolution of these myths, showing their fundamental similarity and basis in astronomical allegories.[230]

Tracy's ultimate objections to established religions are moral.
Priests who claimed authority over the people, prescribing rules of
belief and conduct, were obliged to demand blind faith in their own
pronouncements. But it was a grave moral error, according to Tracy, to
"make a virtue of stupid servility", and it was an even graver error to
"accustom men to seek their rules of conduct in the will of an unknown
being" instead of finding them in a rational understanding of their own
human needs.[231] Priests hindered men from recognizing the inherent link
between virtue and happiness, and deprived them of the strongest motives
for seeking out the good.[232]

> When I see religious men proclaiming almost unanimously that
> detestable maxim - that without the idea of the life to come,
> man has no motive for being good - I wonder in dread if they
> really want to degrade virtue, if they have sworn to pervert
> all moral ideas, and if their very devil could invent a
> principle better able to cover the world in misery and crime.[233]

In the place of religion - a defective moral system based on false
assumptions and reasoning - Tracy advocated what he termed a morality
"guided by reason", and based on the observation of man's intellectual
faculties. In such a rational morality, we would rouse a man's personal
interest in fulfilling his "true" duties, instead of employing fear to
induce him to fulfil his "imaginary" duties.[234] We will examine the
character of this rational morale of needs and interests in chapter three.

Finally, Tracy argued that religions are "essentially subversive
of true principles of social order or of public morality", for it is the
right of the civil legislature to prescribe the duties of citizens. When
priests claim for themselves this right, they usurp the sovereignty of
the legislature and are often in conflict with it. So they are necessarily
the enemies of all governments of which they are not in command; and where
the clergy does control the state, the liberty of all other citizens is
violated, and equity and social equality are destroyed.[235]

Theologians should not, then, be accorded special privileges; the truth of their doctrines should not be protected from criticism by authority; they should not have special rights to exercise public authority or to form a collective body.[236] Their false doctrines, wrote Tracy, deserved to perish along with the false physics and logic which had so long supported them. Science, believed Tracy, would spell the demise of illusions about man and nature. All the "subtleties of the old theological metaphysics will vanish as soon as we specify the proper meaning of the word, to exist".[237] As soon as the unity of man and nature was fully appreciated, the influence of supernatural explanations of reality would decline,[238] and it would become possible to educate people in the ideological art of forming correct judgements about reality on the basis of observation.

Tracy, despite his fierce condemnation of priests and super-natural doctrines, wanted to avoid being taken for a "materialist" and "atheist". When Cabanis was accused of holding such positions by Mme de Staël, Tracy replied that such terms were not appropriate to describe "men who loudly proclaim not to know what is spirit nor what is matter, and who often repeat that they have never been, and never will be, occupied in determining the [ultimate] character of the principle of thought, for that is irrelevant to everything they have to say about it".[239] The behavioural scientist of mental operations did not wish to be seen as propounding a materialist ontology - that would also have been a false metaphysics, for it dealt with the "first causes" of the universe. On the other hand, he could not resist making anticlerical jibes whenever the occasion arose, as in his remark that "the religion of the Court of Rome ... is a commodity for export and not for consumption".[240]

This chapter has outlined in some detail the main themes in Tracy's epistemology: his views on science and method, his concept of idéologie as a logic of discovery and explanation, his views on the centrality of language in human experience and progress, and his critique of metaphysical idealism. Tracy's thinking subject, certain of his own existence and perceptions, must now be placed in the sphere of action. In the following chapter, we examine l'homme sensible as actor, and Tracy's account of how the individual becomes a social creature.

FOOTNOTES TO CHAPTER TWO

1   Tracy, Elémens d'idéologie. Troisième partie. Logique (Paris, 1805), pp. 563-588. See also ibid., (Paris, 1818), pp. 489-514; Elémens d'idéologie, 5 vols. (Paris, 1824-26), IV, pp. 7-44; Elémens d'idéologie, 5 vols. (Bruxelles, 1826-27), IV, pp. 1-38.

2   Tracy, Logique (1805), pp. 4, 46.

3   Ibid., p. 50. The Baconian programme was also extremely prominent in the conception of the Encyclopédie: see, for example, d'Alembert's Preliminary Discourse to the Encyclopedia of Diderot [1751], trans. R.N. Schwab (New York, 1963). Bacon was also one of the masters of the modern mind identified by D.-J. Garat in his lectures on l'analyse de l'entendement at the école normale in Paris early in 1795: see Séances des écoles normales ... (Paris, 1801), Leçons, vol. I.

4   Logique, p. 57.

5   Ibid., pp. 52-54. Tracy added in a note (p. 54); "Bacon uses the word induction instead of deduction. We will see elsewhere the difference between these two terms and why I prefer the latter". Descartes, of course, used the term deduction.

6   Ibid., p. 62.

7   Ibid., pp. 79-82, 87-88, 105-106. See also [Tracy], "Sur les Lettres de Descartes", La Revue philosophique, 1 June 1806, p. 394.

8   Cf. Condorcet, Sketch for a historical picture of the progress of the human mind [1793], trans. J. Barraclough (London, 1955), 8th epoch, p. 121: "Bacon revealed the true method of studying nature and of using the three instruments that she has given us for penetrating her secrets; observation, experience and calculation. He asked that the philosopher, cast into the middle of the universe, should begin by renouncing all the beliefs that he had received and even all the notions he had formed, so that he might then recreate for himself, as it were, a new understanding admitting only of precise ideas, accurate notions and truths whose degree of certainty or probability had been strictly weighed. But Bacon, who possessed the genius of philosophy in the highest degree, was without the genius of science; and these methods for discovering truth, of which he gave no examples, were admired by philosophers but in no way influenced the course of science".

9   For Maistre's views on science, cf. The Works of Joseph de Maistre, trans. and ed. J. Lively (London, 1965), "Saint Petersburg Dialogues", Fifth Dialogue, pp. 222-237; and especially his Examen de la Philosophie de Bacon, written 1803-1817, published posthumously in 1836, and in Oeuvres complètes (Lyons, 1884), vol. VI. See also L.A. Siedentop, The Limits of Enlightenment (D.Phil. thesis, Oxford University, 1966), vol. II, chapter 8; E.D. Watt, "J. de Maistre and the thoughts of Chancellor Bacon", Australian Journal of Politics and History, vol. 17 (1971), pp. 406-411; R. Lebrun, "J. de Maistre, Cassandra of Science", French Historical Studies, vol. 6 (1969), pp. 214-231.

10   J. de Maistre, Examen de la philosophie de Bacon, in Oeuvres
      complètes, vol. VI, p. 513.

11   Cf. Condorcet, Sketch, p. 132: "Descartes had brought philosophy
      back to reason; for he had understood that it must be derived
      entirely from those primary and evident truths which we can discover
      by observing the operations of the human mind". Cf. ibid., p. 122:
      Descartes "gave a method for finding and recognizing truth ... He
      commanded men to shake off the yoke of authority, to recognize none
      save that which was avowed by reason ...".

12   On Descartes' views on the physical sciences, cf. A. Vartanian,
      Diderot and Descartes (Princeton, 1953); R. McRae, The Problem of
      the Unity of the Sciences: Bacon to Kant (Toronto, 1961).

13   Tracy, Logique, p. 109.

14   See chapter 2 of the Discourse on Method, trans. F.E. Sutcliffe
      (Harmondsworth, 1968), p. 41. Tracy cited these principles in
      Logique, p. 109n-110, concluding that "there is nothing as profound
      nor as just in the whole grande rénovation". The continuity
      between Descartes' four principles and Condillac's methodological
      position is quite striking. Much of Condillac's polemics are
      directed against Cartesians such as Malebranche, who developed the
      'spiritual' side of Cartesian dualism.

15   Logique, p. 111. For Descartes' phrase, see Discourse on Method,
      chapter 4, pp. 53-54.

16   Logique, p. 133.

17   [Tracy], "Sur les Lettres de Descartes", pp. 395-96; Principes
      logiques, in Elémens d'idéologie, 5 vols. (Bruxelles, 1826-27),
      vol. IV, pp. 200-201.

18   Logique, p. 189.

19   Ibid., pp. 189-190.

20   Descartes, Discourse on Method, p. 41.

21   Cf. Tracy, Logique, p. 126. Of course, Condillac substituted
      sensationalism for Descartes' spiritualized dualism, in explaining
      the operations of the intellect. The influence of Descartes upon
      the idéologues has seldom been raised: exceptions include the brief
      remarks by F. Bouillier, Histoire de la philosophie cartesienne
      (Paris, 3e ed. 1868), vol. II, pp. 641-46; F. Picavet, Les Idéologues,
      pp. 1-10.

22   Cf. Tracy, "Mémoire sur la faculté de penser", Mémoires de l'Institut
      National, Classe des Sciences morales et politiques, vol. I (1798),
      p. 320.

23   See the reference earlier (p. 19 supra) to Voltaire's Lettres
      philosophiques (1734); Voltaire also wrote a more detailed Eléments
      de la philosophie de Newton (1737).

24   J.-S. Bailly, Histoire de l'astronomie moderne, 3 vols. (Paris,
      1779-82), especially vol. I, p. xvi, vol. II, pp. 469-471,
      vol. III, p. 331.

25   Cf. Condorcet, Sketch, pp. 148-151. Some of Condillac's remarks on
      Bacon, Descartes and Newton may be briefly seen in his Histoire
      Moderne, in Oeuvres philosophiques, vol. II, pp. 220-221, 230-233.

26   Cf. H. Guerlac, "Newton's changing reputation in the eighteenth-
      century", in Carl Becker's Heavenly City Revisited, ed. R.O. Rockwood
      (New York, 1958), especially pp. 21-24; for a detailed account of
      the early phase of Newton's reception in France (before 1738),
      cf. P. Brunet, l'Introduction des théories de Newton en France au
      XVIIIe siècle (Paris, 1931). The modern account of Newton by
      A. Koyré stresses the abstract theoretico-mathematical character
      of his work upon an idealized nature, rather than his empiricism
      and positivism: cf. Newtonian Studies (London, 1965), and "The
      Origins of Modern Science", Diogenes, vol. 16 (1956), especially
      pp. 20-22.

27   Cf. G. Buchdahl, The image of Newton and Locke in the age of Reason
      (London, 1961), especially pp. 4-5, 11-14; A. Koyré, Newtonian
      Studies, chapter 2.

28   J.-S. Bailly, Histoire de l'astronomie moderne, vol. I, p. xi.

29   Ibid., vol. III, pp. 330-331. That Tracy was familiar with Bailly's
      work is shown in "Mémoire sur la faculté de penser", pp. 319-320.

30   Tracy, "Mémoire sur la faculté de penser", p. 387.

31   Ibid., p. 391.

32   Tracy, Elémens d'idéologie. Seconde Partie. Grammaire (Paris, 2e ed.
      1817), pp. x-xi.

33   Published as Des signes et de l'art de penser (Paris, an VIII [1800]).

34   J.-M. Degérando, Histoire comparée des systèmes de philosophie
      relativement aux principes des connoissances humaines (Paris an XII=
      1804), vol. II, p. 453. A further example may be found in J.-B. Say,
      Traité d'économie politique [1803] (Paris, 2e ed. 1814), "Discours
      préliminaire", pp. xxv-xxvi.

35   A.-L. Lavoisier, Guyton de Morveau, et al., Méthode de nomenclature
      chimique (Paris, 1787).

36   Lavoisier, Traité élémentaire de chimie (Paris, 1789), "Discours
      préliminaire". Like Tracy, Saint-Simon was very enthusiastic about
      this profession of faith in analyse and observation by a successful
      investigator of nature.

37   Tracy, "Mémoire sur la faculté de penser", pp. 325-6. This phrasing
      was repeated in Grammaire [1803] (Paris, 2e ed. 1817), p. 386.

38   Tracy, "Mémoire sur la faculté de penser", p. 416.

39   Tracy, Logique, pp. 32n-33.

40 *Ibid.*, p. 509 and pp. 503-509 passim.   Tracy's critique may have
    been prompted in part by Degérando's attack on Condillac's view
    that science is a well-made language, and that, once appropriate
    signs are found, every science is as simple and certain as
    mathematics: Des signes et de l'art de penser (Paris, 1800), vol. I,
    p. xxxi.

41 The question was posed in the second of a series of mémoires, later
    collected under the name "Mémoire sur la faculté de penser", and
    published in Mémoires de l'Institut National, Classe des Sciences
    morales et politiques, vol. I (1798), pp. 283-450. Evidence for
    the date of the original usage of the term idéologie is given at the
    end of my article (1980), pp.263-4.

42 Tracy, p. 322.

43 *Ibid.*, p. 323.

44 Cf. Condillac, Essai [1746], in Oeuvres philosophiques, vol. I, p. 3;
    Art de raisonner, in *ibid.*, Vol. I, p. 619; and Histoire moderne,
    in *ibid.*, vol. II, p. 229.

45 Tracy, "Mémoire sur la faculté de penser", pp. 322-323.

46 *Ibid.*, p. 322. Cf. Garat's lectures at the école normale in 1795,
    entitled "analyse de l'entendement" - a slightly more Lockean phrase
    than the Condillacian title of Tracy's section at the Institut.

47 Cf. Condillac, Histoire moderne, in Oeuvres philosophiques, vol. II,
    p. 229; Bonnet, Essai analytique sur les facultés de l'âme (1760).
    Bonnet had sought to develop "une psychologie expérimentale":
    see H. Gouhier, Les Conversions de Maine de Biran (Paris, 1947), p. 89

48 Tracy, "Mémoire sur la faculté de penser", p. 324.

49 *Ibid.*, p. 324.

50 *Ibid.*, p. 325.

51 *Ibidem.*

52 Logique, p. 55. Cf. p. 81n: "all that we know, is only an application
    of the science which shows us what we can know and how we can know it"

53 "Mémoire sur la faculté de penser", p. 286.

54 *Ibidem.*

55 *Ibidem.* (emphasis added)

56 One might be tempted to call the above doctrine a form of phenomeno-
    logical Cartesianism, which is distantly related to some aspects
    of modern existentialism via Maine de Biran.

57 Elémens d'idéologie, vol. I [1801] (3e ed. 1817), p. 307.

58 *Ibid.*, p. 207.

59   _Logique_, p. vi.

60   _Ibid._, p. 397.

61   _Ibid._, p. 425.

62   _Ibid._, pp. 79-82, and Tracy, "Sur un système méthodique de
     bibliographie", _Moniteur universel_, 8 and 9 brumaire an VI
     (29 and 30 October 1797), pp. 151-152, 155-156.

63   Cf. d'Alembert, _Preliminary Discourse_, pp. 143-164.

64   _Logique_, p. 80n. These three areas corresponded to the first three
     volumes of his _Elémens d'idéologie_ (1801-1805).

65   _Ibid._, p. 81n.

66   _Ibid._, pp. 520-521. Of these nine parts, Tracy completed four,
     sketched a small part of the fifth, and wrote a preliminary work
     (the _Commentaire_) for the sixth. Some aspects of his conception of
     the final three parts were summarized in chapter 9 of the _Logique_.

67   _Ibid._, p. 519.

68   Cf. Condillac, _Essai_ [1746], in _Oeuvres philosophiques_, vol. I,
     especially pp. 24-27; _l'Art de penser_, in ibid., vol. I, especially
     pp. 747, 769-774; and _Dictionnaire des synonymes_, article "Décomposer",
     in ibid., vol. III, p. 179.

69   Cf. Condorcet's manuscript on the meaning of _analyse_, published by
     K.M. Baker, "Un 'éloge' officieux de Condorcet", _Revue de synthèse_,
     vol. 88 (1967), especially pp. 247-251.

70   Cf. Garat's lectures at the _école normale_.

71   Cf. Tracy, "Mémoire sur la faculté de penser", pp. 307, 327, 339,
     341-342, 355; _Elémens_, vol. I, chapter 6; _Principes logiques_, in
     Elémens, 5 vols. (Bruxelles, 1826-1827), vol. IV, pp. 208-209.

72   Cf. Tracy, "De la métaphysique de Kant", _Mémoires de l'Institut ..._,
     Vol. IV, pp. 569, 580. See also section IV, of the present chapter,
     on "metaphysics and religion".

73   "De la métaphysique de Kant", pp. 550-551; "Mémoire sur la faculté
     de penser", p. 386.

74   "Mémoire sur la faculté de penser", p. 349. Cf. article "expérimentale",
     in _The Encyclopédie_, ed. J. Lough (Cambridge, 1969), pp. 68-81.
     See also note 47 above.

75   Condillac, _Art de raisonner_, in _Oeuvres philosophiques_, vol. I, p. 619.

76   "Mémoire sur la faculté de penser", pp. 377-378, 384. Tracy also
     used the dichotomy "positive" and "conjectural", in his "Supplément
     à la première section des Elémens d'idéologie" [1805], in _Elémens..._
     IVe et Ve parties. Traité de la volonté et de ses effets (Paris,
     1815), pp. 46-47.

77 "Mémoire sur la faculté de penser", p. 378.

78 Ibid., pp. 389-390. Cf. Condorcet, Sketch, pp. 133, 173, 185-186 on the unity of methods among all the sciences.

79 "Mémoire sur la faculté de penser", p. 390.

80 Ibid., p. 388.

81 Elémens, vol. I, pp. 212-213.

82 This was one of the handful of favourable citations by the idéologiste from ancient Greek philosophy: cf. Degérando, Histoire comparée des systèmes de philosophie, vol. II, p. 375, and vol. I, p. 51n; and Cabanis, Rapports, in Oeuvres philosophiques (1956), vol. I, p. 137.

83 "Mémoire sur la faculté de penser", p. 317; also p. 290.

84 Ibid., p. 389. Cf. the anonymous review (signed "P.M.") of Cabanis' Rapports du physique et du moral de l'homme, in Mercure de France, 2 pluviose an XI, p. 219: "The rational-analytical philosophy [claims to] depend solely on facts and experiences. But what is one to make of the principal fact [all ideas deriving from the senses] when one invokes witnesses who disavow it?".

85 Logique, p. 424.

86 Elémens, vol. I, p. xv. The idéologiste Pierre Laboulinière claimed that the science of the understanding should be termed la physique morale, because "idéologie" was too restricted in meaning: Précis de l'idéologie (Paris, 1805), p. 10. A.Comte later made famous the phrase la physique sociale before coining the term sociologie.

87 Elémens, vol. I, p. xiii.

88 Ibid., pp. 24-25; and "Mémoire sur la faculté de penser", p. 326.

89 Condillac, Extrait raisonné du Traité des Sensations, in Oeuvres philosophiques, vol. I, p. 325.

90 "Mémoire sur la faculté de penser", p. 327; cf. p. 336.

91 Elémens, vol. I, p. 53.

92 This seemed to imply that where particular individuals were incapable of performing these common intellectual operations, the immediate cause was physiological - although the physiological 'dysfunction' could have been induced by factors in the individuals' social environment (or indeed, by the very absence of a social environment: see the wolf-children example mentioned in the following section).

93 "Mémoire sur la faculté de penser", p. 414.

94 Ibid., p. 347.

95 Cf. Cabanis, Rapports du physique et du moral de l'homme, in Oeuvres philosophiques, vol. I, p. 126: physiology should be la base commune for the research of the Class of moral and political sciences, to

avoid elaborating "a vain scaffolding which is inconsistent with the eternal laws of nature".

96 Cf. Principes logiques, in Elémens d'idéologie, 5 vols. (Bruxelles, 1826-1827), vol. IV, pp. 251-253; Logique, p. viii. Tracy had provided an analytical summary for the 1805 edition of Cabanis' Rapports, where he attributed to Cabanis the view that the brain is "le digesteur spécial ou l'organe sécréteur de la pensée" (1830 ed., vol. I, p. 29: cf. Cabanis, Oeuvres philosophiques, vol. I, pp. 195-196 for Cabanis' more extended analogy). Tracy repeated that the brain is "l'organe sécréteur de la pensée", in Principes logiques [Elémens, 1826-1827, vol. IV, p. 212]. On one occasion Tracy slips into a monist materialist ontology in speaking of "matière animée" (Logique, p. 190), but this is rare.

97 "Mémoire sur la faculté de penser", pp. 344-345.

98 "De la métaphysique de Kant", p. 604. Moreau de la Sarthe proposed a different division of labour in the general science of man or anthropologie: physical anthropology and moral anthropology, each divided into four sub-sections. Cf. la Décade philosophique, 20 prairial an IX (9 June 1801), pp. 458-459.

99 "Mémoire sur la faculté de penser", p. 326.

100 Cf. J. La Mettrie, l'Homme-Machine (1748) and Paul Thiry d'Holbach, Système de la Nature (1770).

101 Anon. review (signed "G") of Tracy's Projet d'éléments d'idéologie [1801], in Mercure de France, 16 nivose an X (6 January 1802), p. 102.

102 Ibid., p. 101.

103 Anon. review (signed "D.M.") of Chateaubriand's Génie du Christianisme in Mercure de France, 4 thermidor an XI (23 July 1803), p. 214.

104 Mercure de France, 8 prairial an XI (28 May 1803), pp. 461, 463.

105 Grammaire [1803] (Paris, 2e ed. 1817), pp. viii-ix.

106 C.C. Gillispie, The Edge of Objectivity (Princeton, 1959), p. 203.

107 Cf. Tracy, Logique, p. 504; "Mémoire sur la faculté de penser", pp. 401-428; Elémens, vol. I, chapters 15, 16, 17.

108 C.C. Gillispie, The Edge of Objectivity, p. 169.

109 Tracy, "Mémoire sur la faculté de penser", p. 327. A very similar formulation was repeated in Tracy's manuscript of 1806, the so-called "Mémoire de Berlin", published by P. Tisserand in Revue philosophique, vol. 116 (1933), p. 172.

110 Elémens, vol. I, pp. xvi, 214, 322; Logique, pp. 121-129; "Mémoire sur la faculté de penser", p. 290. Tracy was nevertheless critical of several aspects of Condillac's work: cf. Elémens, chapter XI. For Tracy's remarks on Rousseau's recourse to divine agency in explaining language, cf. ibid., pp. 302-303.

111 Condillac, Essai [1746], in Oeuvres philosophiques, vol. I, pp. 10-53.

112 Ibid., pp. 60-103.

113 Ibid., pp. 104-115; Art de penser, in Oeuvres philosophiques, vol. I, pp. 720, 727-730, 738-741.

114 Tracy, "Mémoire sur la faculté de penser", p. 325n. Cf. the erudite studies of Tracy's contemporaries on non-European languages: Volney, Oeuvres (Paris, 1821), vol. VIII, and Lanjuinais, Oeuvres (Paris, 1832), vol. IV.

115 "Mémoire sur la faculté de penser", p. 407.

116 Cf. Bernardin de Saint-Pierre, Harmonies de la nature, in Oeuvres, ed. Aimé-Martin (Paris, 1818), vol. IX, p. 435, and vol. X, pp. 10-24, 30-34, 54-55, 58-59, 78-89.

117 L.-A. Aimé-Martin, "Préambule", to Bernardin de Saint-Pierre, op.cit., vol. VIII, p. vi.

118 "Mémoire sur la faculté de penser", p. 408.

119 Ibid., p. 411; Elémens, vol. I, p. 361.

120 Elémens, vol. I, p. 295.

121 "Mémoire sur la faculté de penser", p. 428. The same point is made, in more detail, in Elémens, vol. I, p. 388, where Tracy concluded that "we are, on the contrary, almost entirely the product of the circumstances surrounding us ... [hence] the importance of education, taking this word in its widest sense".

122 Grammaire, p. 383; Elémens, vol. I, pp. 308, 369-371.

123 Elémens, vol. I, p. 322.

124 Tracy's respect for Hobbes' views on language and logic (as against his social and political doctrines) may be judged from the discussions in Logique, pp. 112-117; and the French translation of Hobbes' Logic, (Part I of De Corpore), appended to ibid., pp. 589-667.

125 Elémens, vol. I, pp. 324-25, 335; "Mémoire sur la faculté de penser", pp. 425-426.

126 Elémens, vol. I, p. 294. Cf. V. Cousin, Fragmens philosophiques (Paris, 1826), pp. 168-169.

127 Elémens, vol. I, pp. 297-298.

128 Ibid., p. 289; cf. p. 388. The teleological metaphor in this quotatio is not typical of Tracy, since his conception of progress does not usually imply foreknowledge of the final destiny of man.

129 Ibid., pp. 292-293.

130 "Mémoire sur la faculté de penser", pp. 408-410.

131 Ibid., pp. 402-403.

132 Cf. Lucien Malson, Wolf Children (London, 1972), which reprints
     J.-M.-G. Itard's reports of 1801 and 1806 on le sauvage de l'Aveyron,
     pp. 91-179. See also Harlan Lane, The Wild Boy of Aveyron (London,
     1977), which contains the reports on the boy by the naturalist
     P.-J. Bonnaterre, pp. 33-48, and by the psychiatrist P. Pinel,
     pp. 57-69, as well as those of Itard. Pinel's report was published
     by Georges Hervé in Revue d'Anthropologie, vol. 21 (1911), pp. 441-
     454. See also the anonymous article in la Décade philosophique,
     10 Vendémiaire an 9 (2 October 1800), pp. 8-18; and Leroy's essay
     in la Revue philosophique [la Décade], 21 March 1807, pp. 513-523.

133 Elémens, vol. I, p. 378.

134 Ibid., pp. 377-378. (Cf. "Mémoire sur la faculté de penser", p. 420.)

135 Ibid., pp. 316-317.

136 Ibid., p. 318.

137 Grammaire, p. 273.

138 Ibid., chapter 5, especially pp. 264-270 and 277-280.

139 Ibid., p. 261.

140 Ibid., pp. 281-284, 288.

141 Ibid., p. 291; and Commentaire [1806] (Paris, 1819), bk. 19, p. 308
     (or Commentary [1811], p. 202).

142 Grammaire, p. 292. Cf. Condorcet, Sketch, pp. 99-102, on the
     importance of printing for the spread of rationality and the
     destruction of prejudice and oppression.

143 Elémens vol. I, p. 266. For a parody of this so-called "law", see
     the hostile review of Tracy's Projet d'Eléments d'idéologie [1801],
     in Mercure de France, 16 nivose an X (6 January 1802), pp. 99-100:
     here, the critic applies this "law" to "explain" how a habitual
     thief acts to satisfy his desires, against all the evidence of
     reason.

144 "Mémoire sur la faculté de penser", p. 412; Elémens, vol. I, p. 384.

145 Elémens, vol. I, p. 383.

146 Ibid., p. 379; "Mémoire sur la faculté de penser", pp. 327, 342.

147 Logique, pp. 57-58, 420-421; Elémens, vol. I, p. 386. Tracy does not
     seem to acknowledge that perception of simple sensations could itself
     be highly selective, not to mention erroneous.

148 "Mémoire sur la faculté de penser", pp. 400, 435.

149 Logique, pp. 166ff.

150 Elémens, vol. I, p. 387; cf. Condillac, Traité des animaux, in
     Oeuvres philosophiques, vol. I, p. 375.

151 "Mémoire sur la faculté de penser", p. 288.

152 Ibid., pp. 384-385, 390.

153 Elémens, vol. I, pp. 339-340; a similar point emerges on p. 323.

154 Ibid., pp. 340n-349.

155 Ibid., p. 342n.

156 Cf. Condillac, Art de penser, in Oeuvres philosophiques, vol. I,
    p. 748. Tracy began his "Mémoire sur la faculté de penser" by
    agreeing with Condillac's view (p. 314), but gradually began to
    criticize it (p. 382) and soon rejected it entirely (p. 392), a
    critique he continued to make in his Logique, pp. 104, 155, 158f.
    Maine de Biran also strongly attacked Condillac on this point, as
    did most of the "revisionists" including Degérando.

157 "Mémoire sur la faculté de penser", pp. 442-443.

158 Grammaire, pp. 359-360.

159 Ibid., pp. 361-363.

160 Ibid., p. 366.

161 Cf. G. Harnois, Les théories du langage en France de 1660 à 1821
    (Paris [1929]); P. Kuehner, Theories on the origin and formation of
    language in the eighteenth century in France (Philadelphia, 1944);
    P. Juliard, Philosophies of language in eighteenth-century France
    (The Hague, 1970); E. Maynial, "Les grammairiens philosophes du
    XVIIIe siècle", Revue bleue (7 March 1903), pp. 317-320; R. Grimsley,
    "Maupertuis, Turgot and Maine de Biran on the origin of language",
    Studies on Voltaire and the Eighteenth Century, vol. 62 (1968),
    pp. 285-307; R. Lefèvre, "Condillac, maître du langage", Revue inter-
    nationale de philosophie, vol. 21 (1967), pp. 393-406; H.N. Bakalar,
    "The Cartesian legacy to the eighteenth-century grammarians", Modern
    Language Notes, vol. 91 (1976), pp. 698-721.

162 Mémoires de l'Institut, tome II, p. 2. The winner was Degérando,
    who expanded his essay into the four volumes of Des Signes et de
    l'art de penser (Paris, 1800). On this work, cf. H.B. Acton, "The
    Philosophy of language in Revolutionary France", in Studies in
    Philosophy, ed. J.N. Findlay (Oxford, 1966), pp. 143-167.

163 Mémoires de l'Institut, tome IV, p. 11. The winner in 1802 was
    Maine de Biran; Tracy drafted the judges' report according him the
    prize, reprinted pp. 207-224, in Maine de Biran, L'influence de
    l'habitude sur la faculté de penser, ed. P. Tisserand (Paris, 1954).

164 Mémoires de l'Institut, tome V, p. 60. The winner in 1805 was
    Maine de Biran: cf. his Mémoire sur la décomposition de la pensée,
    ed. P. Tisserand (Paris, 1952), p. xv.

165 Mémoires de l'Institut, tome III, pp. 1-3.

166 "Réflexions sur les projets de pasigraphie", Mémoires de l'Institut,
    Classe des sciences morales et politiques, tome III (1801), pp. 535-551.

167 Ibid., and Grammaire, pp. 367n.

168 "Mémoire sur la faculté de penser", p. 416.

169 Ibid., p. 415.

170 Grammaire, p. 378.

171 Ibid., pp. 369-380.

172 Tracy evidently is unconcerned about the fate of literature, poetry, and works relying upon subtle imagery. He is concerned essentially with obtaining a standardized language for the expression of scientific truths.

173 Ibid., pp. 382-389; "Mémoire sur la faculté de penser", pp. 417, 414.

174 "Réflexions sur les projets de pasigraphie", pp. 549-550.

175 Grammaire, p. 369. J. Simon, Une Académie sous le Directoire, p. 220, wrongly claimed that Tracy did believe in the possibility of a perfect and universal language. Condorcet, on the other hand, had certainly entertained the idea very seriously: see Sketch, pp. 197-199. On the background to the universal language schemes of the 1790s, see L. Couturat and L. Leau, Histoire de la langue universelle (Paris, 1907), and the excellent work of James Knowlson, Universal language schemes in England and France, 1600-1800 (Toronto, 1975), especially chapters 5-8.

176 Cf. Condorcet, Sketch, p. 191; Talleyrand, "Rapport sur l'instruction publique" [September 1791], in C. Hippeau (ed.), L'instruction publique en France pendant la Révolution: discours et rapports ... (Paris, 1881), pp. 146ff.

177 Elémens, vol. I, p. xxiii-xxiv. In claiming that "all languages have common rules" owing to our common physiology, Tracy seems to be implying a physiological version of innate ideas - at least in the Chomsky sense of "deep structures". Tracy's claim may strike the reader as an example of rationalist faith, rather than as a product of empirical observation.

178 Elémens, vol. I, p. xvi. Cf. "Mémoire sur la faculté de penser", pp. 369, 322-323.

179 Tracy, "Dissertation sur l'existence", Mémoires de l'Institut, Classe des Sciences morales et politiques, tome III (1801), pp. 516-517; see also pp. 529-530. Tracy likened the difference between the old metaphysics and the new science of ideas, to that between astrology and astronomy, or between alchemy and chemistry: Logique, p. 143.

180 "De la métaphysique de Kant", p. 596.

181 Ibid., pp. 569, 580.

182 Ibid., passim; "Dissertation sur l'existence", passim; and "Dissertation sur quelques questions d'idéologie", Mémoires de l'Institut, Classe des Sciences morales et politiques, tome III, pp. 500, 514.

183 Condillac, Essai [1746], in Oeuvres philosophiques, vol. I, p. 117.

184 Cf. Voltaire's work le Philosophe ignorant (1765); and Volney,
     Les Ruines [1791], in Oeuvres complètes (Paris, 1821), vol. I,
     pp. 244-245.

185 A. Dansette, Histoire religieuse de la France contemporaine (Paris,
     1948), vol. I, pp. 65-158; J. McManners, The French Revolution and
     the Church (London, 1969); and F.-V.-A. Aulard, Christianity and
     the French Revolution (London, 1927).

186 In addition to the criticisms cited earlier, pp. 22, 98-99, 103, see
     J.-P. Damiron, Essai sur l'histoire de la philosophie, pp. 25, 88-89;
     de Bonald, Mélanges littéraires, politiques et philosophiques
     (Paris, 1819), vol. I, p. 339.

187 Helvétius and Bentham are clear examples in this context: Cf.
     C. Kiernan, "Helvétius and a science of ethics", Studies on Voltaire
     and the Eighteenth Century, vol. 60 (1968), pp. 229-243.

188 Volney, La loi naturelle [1793], ed. Gaston-Martin (Paris, 1934),
     especially pp. 104-118.

189 Cf. Tracy, Traité de la Volonté (Paris, 1815), pp. 79-80;
     Mme Sarah Newton Destutt de Tracy, "Notice sur M. Destutt de Tracy",
     p. 335.

190 J. Kitchin, Un journal 'philosophique', pp. 158-177. Aimé-Martin
     reported that during a deist peroration by Bernardin de Saint-
     Pierre at the Institut, Cabanis denounced the use of the word 'God':
     Essai sur la vie et les ouvrages de B. de Saint-Pierre (Paris, 1818),
     pp. 244-245. Guillois, in Le Salon de Mme Helvétius, p. 197,
     defended Cabanis' reputation. Cabanis' personal views were clearly
     deist in 1807, in his Lettre à [Fauriel] sur les causes premières,
     in Oeuvres philosophiques, vol. II, pp. 256-298.

191 Cf. A. Mathiez, La théophilanthropie et le culte décadaire, 1796-1801
     (Paris, 1904).

192 Cf. Tracy, Traité de la Volonté (Paris, 2e ed. 1818), p. 499 and
     below, note 239.

193 Tracy, Commentaire, bk. 6, pp. 62-78, and p. 223. Cf. Comte,
     The Crisis of Industrial Civilization: Early Essays, ed. Fletcher
     (London, 1974), p. 134 [written 1822].

194 Cf. Condillac, Traité des Animaux, in Oeuvres philosophiques, vol. I,
     pp. 367, 371, and Art de raisonner, in ibid., p. 619.

195 Tracy, "Sur un systême méthodique de bibliographie"; Logique,
     pp. 520-521.

196 Cf. Commentaire, pp. 232, 387-390.

197 Bonaparte's functionalist view of the integrative power of
     traditional religion, is reported in Voix de Napoléon, ed.
     P.-L. Couchoud (Genève, 1949), pp. 42, 49; Entretiens avec Napoléon,
     ed. L. Pautré (Paris, 1969), pp. 23-26; L. de Villefosse and
     J. Bouissounouse, L'Opposition à Napoléon, pp. 174-175.

198 See above, note 63 to chapter one.

199 Cf. Chateaubriand, Mémoires d'outre-tombe, vol. I, p. 390: Bonaparte exclaimed: "Christianity! Didn't the idéologues want to make of it a system of astronomy?".

200 [Tracy], Analyse de l'Origine de Tous les Cultes, par le citoyen Dupuis, et de l'Abrégé qu'il a donné de cet ouvrage (Paris, an VII [1799]).

201 [Tracy], Analyse raisonnée de l'Origine de Tous les Cultes ou Religion Universelle (Paris an XII = 1804). I have already mentioned above, p. 47, that Tracy's authorship was revealed in 1806 by A.-A. Barbier.

202 Analyse (1799), p. 2.

203 Analyse (1799), p. 3 and pp. 62-77; 1804 ed., pp. 94-116.

204 Analyse (1799), p. 100; 1804 ed., p. 148.

205 Analyse (1804), p. 149.

206 Commentaire, pp. 389-390.

207 Analyse (1804), pp. 158-159.

208 Ibid., pp. xi-xii (Emphasis in original).

209 Ibid., pp. xii-xxiii.

210 "Mémoire sur la faculté de penser", p. 367.

211 Analyse (1804), p. 22.

212 Ibid., pp. 23, 69.

213 Ibid., p. 27; cf. 1799 ed., p. 17 for slightly different phrasing.

214 Analyse (1804), pp. 24-25; "De la métaphysique de Kant", p. 551.

215 Cf. Commentaire, pp. 388-389.

216 Analyse (1804), pp. xxiii-xxiv.

217 Ibid., p. xxv; cf. Commentaire, pp. 35-40, on religion as a form of social control.

218 Cf. Grammaire, p. 6, where Tracy condemns "the despotism of religious opinions".

219 Analyse (1804), pp. xxvi-xxvii; cf. "Sur les Lettres de Descartes", p. 397.

220 Ibid., pp. xxviii-xxx.

221 Ibid., pp. xxxii-xxxiii.

222   Ibid., pp. xxxv-xxxvii.

223   Ibid., p. xxxviii. This depressing view of the Middle Ages is also found in Condorcet, Sketch, pp. 72-89.

224   Ibid., pp. xl-xliv.

225   Ibid., p. xliv.

226   Ibid., pp. xlvi-xlvii.

227   Ibid., p. 95 (emphasis added). The phrase emphasized was inserted in the 1804 edition, to make a stinging comment on the revival of Catholicism. Cf. Analyse (1799), pp. 62-63.

228   Analyse (1804), pp. 113-115.

229   Ibid., p. 29.

230   Ibid., p. 13.

231   Ibid., p. 145. Two years later, Tracy was accused of servility to Condillac's philosophy by a reviewer in la Revue philosophique: cf. J. Kitchin, Un journal 'philosophique', pp. 135-136.

232   Cf. "Quels sont les moyens de fonder la morale chez un peuple?", in Commentaire, pp. 456-460.

233   Analyse (1804), pp. 145-146.

234   Ibid., p. 147; "Quels sont les moyens ...", p. 459; Traité de la Volonté (Paris, 1818), pp. 499-503.

235   Commentaire, pp. 39, 389; Analyse (1804), pp. 146-147.

236   Analyse (1804), p. 158.

237   "Dissertation sur quelques questions d'idéologie", p. 514. Cf. the common contrast between science, on the one hand, and ignorant superstition on the other, e.g. J.-B. Say, A Treatise on Political Economy [1803] (New York, 1880), p. 81n.

238   "Quels sont les moyens ...", p. 460n.

239   Tracy to Mme de Staël, 23 February 1805, reprinted in R. de Luppé, Les idées littéraires de Madame de Staël ... (Paris, 1969), pp. 163-4.

240   Commentaire, p. 98, repeated in Traité de la Volonté (1818), p. 367.

CHAPTER THREE

FROM INDIVIDUAL DESIRES TO SOCIAL MORALITY

I   The will as desire and action

II   The bases of social existence

III Social morality

. THE WILL AS DESIRE AND ACTION

We have seen that, for Tracy, all our ideas come from the perceptions furnished by our senses; simple ideas are those given immediately
by the senses, and other ideas are formed by separating and recombining
simple ideas in complex ways. Our multitude of ideas have been generated
by a small number of mental processes. The faculty of thinking, upon
closer inspection, is seen to be composed of four more specialized
faculties, all of which are modes of sensing or perceiving, and they account
for all the activity of the mind.[1] 1. Sensibility is our faculty of perceiving sensations, which are felt as simple pleasures or pains. 2. Memory
is the faculty of being affected again by a past sensation. 3. Judgement
is the faculty of perceiving relations, comparing and distinguishing
between sensations, memories, simple and complex ideas, or any combination
of these. If we suppose a perception of the relation between a pleasurable and a painful sensation, "there follows at once the desire to experience the one rather than the other."[2] 4. The will, or faculty of
desiring, arises on the basis of our faculty of judgement, which in turn
depends on our capacity to have simultaneous but distinguishable
sensations.

Tracy regarded the individual self (le moi) as the ensemble
of its sensibilities. The self is constituted by its flow of impressions,
judgements and desires. More specifically, the self, said Tracy, is
generally identified with the will, for it is the source of the individual's sense of happiness.[3] The individual is a creature of needs and
has certain means for satisfying those needs. His needs and his means
exist by virtue of his constitution as a desiring being, susceptible to
pleasure and pain, happiness and misery, and as an acting being, capable
of power and influence.[4] There are two main problematical features of
this doctrine of the self as a bundle of desires and consequent actions
to satisfy these desires.

One problem is whether a genuine conception of individuality
and personality can emerge from such a theory, a question which depends
on whether individual desires and actions are seen as determined externally or as significantly controlled by the self. Tracy tackled these
questions through his reconsideration of the old debate concerning free
will and determinism, and through his hesitant attempts to elaborate a
theory of the active subject exploring the external world. These are the
themes discussed in the first section of this chapter. The second problem with Tracy's view of the self as an ensemble of sensibilities, is
his implicitly atomistic conception of individuality. How can Tracy
account for social affections, social co-operation and social conventions
and institutions on the basis of his view of the self as pursuing the
satisfaction of desires springing from its senses? Tracy's conception
of the sources of social integration are considered in the second section
of this chapter, and the final section examines some of his views on the
role of law, education and social morality in producing a secure and
enlightened society.

In his early "Mémoire sur la faculté de penser" in 1796, Tracy
ascribed a crucial role to what he called the faculty of motilité,
or faculty of perceiving our own movement and resistance to this movement by external objects. Motilité allowed us to distinguish between
ourself and externality, and between various objects. Without the comparative judgements made possible by motilité, we could not attain knowledge
of the existence of external bodies, nor develop our faculties of
judgement and will.[5] Motilité, said Tracy, involved experience of the
sensation of effort.[6] Here, Tracy came close to locating the generation
of knowledge in the active subject, rather than simply in human sensibilit

Tracy's emphasis on the motilité of the willing and acting
subject was continued in another paper read to the Institut in 1799.[7]
Here Tracy showed that there was an important difference between Condillac

doctrine in the original edition of the Traité des sensations (1754), where knowledge of external objects was attributed to our sense of touch, and Condillac's revisions of that work, published posthumously in the Oeuvres of 1798, where he recognised the importance of bodily movement and the sensation of resistance to this movement by external objects.   Tracy's doctrine of motilité, with its potential for further development towards a philosophy of effort or active willing, raised the possibility that Tracy's formula je sens donc j'existe might have been modified to accommodate the active subject: e.g., je veux donc j'existe, or perhaps j'agis donc j'existe.   It was left to Maine de Biran[8] to develop this potentiality in Tracy's doctrine of motilité, because the first volume of Tracy's Elémens in 1801 specifically withdrew the activist or voluntarist implications of the doctrine and insisted that every act of the will had to be understood in terms of a sequence of "prior facts".[9]   It is necessary to examine these two doctrines in Tracy's writings on the will, showing the difficulties Tracy faced in outlining a consistent sensationalism, and leading us to a critical consideration of his conception of liberty as the power of the individual to satisfy his desires.

One of the interesting questions posed by Tracy in 1796 concerned the extent to which the will might be regarded as "free" and "active". Tracy suggested that all our faculties "are in part determined and in part voluntary, that is, they sometimes act without our will and sometimes in accordance with our will".[10]   He dismissed the notions of complete free will and complete determinism as equally false extremes. He illustrated the notion of a balance between voluntary and involuntary aspects of action in reference to the various faculties described above. We cannot shut off our reception of simple sensations; we receive them whether we are seeking or avoiding them. However, we are able to concentrate our attention upon certain sensations to such an extent that others go unnoticed. In the same way, we cannot prevent memories from

entering our consciousness, but we are able to recall ideas at will and

can train our mind to become highly proficient at doing so. Our judge-

ment may also be seen as partly independent, in the sense that we are

obliged "by our organization" or constitution to perceive a relation

which clearly exists between two ideas - without this inner "necessity",

we could never achieve certain knowledge. On the other hand, we can

control our judgements insofar as we examine certain relationships rather

than others and focus our attention on certain perceptions and memories

rather than others.[11]

Motilité is also partly independent, at least in the beginning.

In new-born infants, for example, any sharp disagreeable sensations will

cause involuntary movements and sounds. Agreeable sensations, Tracy

speculated, were more likely to cause a contented passivity, rather

than action, at least until the infant learned to communicate expressions

of pleasure. The movements of new-born infants, before they acquire

any "knowledge", may be regarded as independent of the will, however

intentional these movements appear, as in suckling. These involuntary

movements are commonly called instinctive. Instinct is more highly

developed in other animal species but plays some part in human behaviour.

However, until the notion of instinct is further clarified by the

physiologists, said Tracy, only movements which are the product of

prior knowledge and judgement of relations should be taken as voluntary.

There are many cases of such voluntary action, where a certain effect

is intended. On the other hand, there are certain movements which

remain independent of our will no matter what our age and experience,

such as those involved in our organic growth and conservation.[12]

Finally, Tracy showed the simultaneous existence of both

willed and unwilled aspects of the will or desire. The determined or

passive aspect is that we cannot prevent ourselves from desiring agreeable perceptions or the absence of disagreeable perceptions.

> But it is only our first desires which are the necessary
> [determined] effects of our organization; the more
> complex desires formed on their foundation depend more or
> less on the influence our will has established over the
> action of our judgement and other faculties; we have the
> capacity to examine these complex desires, to formulate
> them only after a reflective act of our judgement, and
> to correct or change them if our earlier judgement was
> hasty or false. Our will is, then, involved in the
> formation not only of our knowledge but of our passions.[13]

Having outlined the operation of the faculties, Tracy returned
to the question of whether our sensibility is an active or passive
faculty. The answer, he said, depends greatly on the meaning of the
term "active". Perceiving a sensation is certainly an action of our
faculty of perception; in that sense it is true that we are active when
perceiving. But if "active" means performing an action freely and
voluntarily, while "passive" means doing it by necessity or forcibly,
then we are passive when we perceive a sensation without having desired
it, and active when we experience it only after an express act of will.

The notion of being "free", according to Tracy, consists in
being able to act in consequence of one's will: freedom, then, means
the capacity to satisfy one's desires.[14]   Can it be said that our will
is free in this sense?   In the absence of prior experience and judgements,
our first desires must be "forced and necessary, deriving inevitably
from the nature of things and their relation to our organization. In
this case, our will is only a rigorous consequence of our sensibility:
it is not free".[15] But such cases are not typical of most human experience.
Tracy therefore reasserts at length the difference between simple and
complex desires:

> But if by the question 'Is our will free?' we mean to ask
> if our most complex desires are forced and necessary con-
> sequences of our organization and of our simplest desires,
> without the intermediary of our will, we can reply ...
> that we can very often summon at will the perception of a
> sensation or a memory, and of specific relations among
> them; that we thereby draw new habits, ... new signs,

> ... and new knowledge, the basis of desires which did
> not exist in all these elements. So, these desires,
> based on elements produced by continual acts of our
> will, cannot be regarded as necessary and forced con-
> sequences of our first desires. Thus it cannot be said
> that our most complex desires are mechanical results of
> our organization, as are the simplest desires; moreover
> the former are as different among individuals as the
> latter are similar. Our will has influenced their
> formation; the will is thus free in that sense. [16]

Tracy seems to have established a continuum between relative
degrees of voluntary intervention. A simple perception implies automatic
attraction or aversion to the receiver; the desire which follows it is
thus necessary and forced. But whenever our will helps to select and
arrange our perceptions (which is virtually always), the desire which
follows these perceptions is not completely forced. [17]

Tracy appeared to be alarmed that this doctrine might imply
a dualism between the organic and the intellectual aspects of human
behaviour, and sought to re-impose a theoretical unification through
the doctrine that every action, strictly speaking, has a cause in a
previous perception. Tracy's notion of scientific explanation assumed
that every "effect" must have, at least in principle, a causal chain
of prior effects. Thus he claimed, in a highly determinist and
reductionist manner, that even the most "complex" desire is also a
"necessary" result of the simple and intermediate desires which preceded it. Tracy agreed with Condillac's belief:"if we knew the chain
of all the causes and all the effects, we would find that everything
in existence is so necessarily: otherwise, why would it exist?"[18]
Tracy believed that without such an insistence on causality, one would
relapse into idealist metaphysics. In the physical realm, he said,
we commonly attribute to chance whatever escapes our limited understanding of causes; likewise in the mental realm, we wrongly attribute
to a free and independent will all our acts of desiring, even though

all these acts are the effects of a prior chain of causes and effects.
However, said Tracy, the question of whether our desires are really the
necessary results of prior perceptions is of little consequence. The
important facts for the idéologiste are that our faculties depend in
most cases on our will; that we are free and happy when we are able
to act in accordance with our will, but unhappy and forced when our
will is frustrated; that we have the capacity to regulate our will,
and indeed it is in our interest to do so.[20]

In the "Mémoire" of 1796, the doctrine of motilité held that
our faculties of judgement and the will cannot develop before we have
obtained a knowledge of external bodies, through their resistance to
our movements. Our bodily movements and the perception of resistance
were an involuntary result of our sensibility for we were not at birth
capable of perceiving relationships and having desires. This doctrine,
however, was fundamentally modified in the first volume of the Elémens
in 1801, and further in the second edition in 1804.   Tracy now argued
that knowledge of external objects is gained only because we perceive
their inertia or resistance to our willed actions. This revised doctrine is made possible by collapsing the conception of will into the
general faculty of sensibility. We now find that the will operates
before, or simultaneously with, our first sensible perceptions.[21]

> ... everyone knows that many sensations have the
> inherent property of being agreeable or disagreeable
> to us. Now, what is finding a sensation agreeable
> or disagreeable, if it is not to make a judgement
> about it, to perceive a relation between it and our
> faculty of feeling? And ... is not this to feel at
> the same time the desire to experience this sensation
> or to avoid it?   All these operations, then, can be
> and actually are united in a single fact, in the per-
> ception of any single sensation. I was wrong to deny
> it, and to have asserted that our faculties of judging
> and willing cannot begin to act until we have experienced
> the sensation of movement and that of resistance....
> Indeed there is no sensation of resistance, properly
> speaking, unless there is a previous sentiment of will.[22]

Tracy provided an example: we are all aware, he said, that a sharp pain makes us feel the "need" (besoin) to move away, quite independently of whether we know we are being harmed. This need is itself a "desire", albeit an unreflective desire. It is therefore possible, he concluded, that "the first of all the movements made by each of us was accompanied by our will".[23] The outcome of such a doctrine, in my view, is to obliterate the distinction he had earlier drawn between instinctive or determined behaviour, and more or less voluntary behaviour. "Instinctive" actions, he noted in the new doctrine, "include judgement and desire".[24] Congratulating himself that his "new theory is founded on positive facts",[25] Tracy doubtless believed that the physiological theories of Cabanis would be consistent with his revised doctrine. In fact, Cabanis was never so bold as to claim that instinct includes judgement and desire. Tracy, in expanding the sphere of the will into areas such as instinctive behaviour and actions of new-born children, virtually obliterated the distinction between voluntary and involuntary actions.

A related difference between Tracy's two positions is that the distinction drawn in his early writings between "needs" (besoins) and "desires" (désirs) is eliminated. Tracy in 1796 had agreed with Condillac that "all our faculties arise from a single origin, sensation; they are developed by a single principle, need [besoin]; and they are exercised by a single means, the connection of ideas".[27] Tracy also agreed with Condillac that needs are based on pleasures and pains, and that needs give rise to desires. However, he criticized Condillac for subsequently extending the term "need" to include certain ideas involving judgements or comparisons between various pleasures and pains.[28] Need is the simple sensation of pleasure or pain, and desire is the more complex idea based on comparison or judgement.[29] In this view, our first needs, resulting directly from our organization, are simple perceptions, immediate products of our sensibility, and precede all knowledge of relations. Comparative judgements about the relation of these sensations lead to the desire to experience one or avoid others. Every pleasure and pain is in itself a need; but need becomes desire only when our judgement introduces ideas of relation and comparison.[30] These distinctions were quite compatible with the involuntary vs. voluntary distinction.

In the revised theory, however, "needs" and "desires" are indistinguishable; indeed they are portrayed as synonyms[31] just as "sensations" and "ideas" had earlier been identified with one another. "Desires" now extend from the most "instinctive" to the most "reflective" actions.[32] Tracy's main reason for this all-embracing or monist conception of the will is that many sensations are immediately experienced as either pleasurable or painful. Tracy tried to justify this position in the essay he wrote in 1806 for the Academy of Berlin's competition on the topic "Are there immediate internal perceptions?" He began by repeating his fundamental view that all ideas are the product of our sensations transformed in various ways and that our intellectual operations consist entirely of perceiving, remembering, judging and desiring.[33] One might object, he noted, that by this simple classification one is forcing into the same category phenomena which are often distinguished. For example, it is common to distinguish between instinctive and reflective wants, those which are more obscure or more precise, stronger or weaker, and all kinds of wishes, dispositions and inclinations which are not volitions in any settled and positive way. Moreover, there are cases where we change our mind, and give way to a stronger will. However, these diverse mental phenomena are only variations on a common theme, all arising from the fact that

> we are so constituted that certain affections,
> certain modifications of our being please us and
> others displease us, some appear more agreeable
> to us than the others, and so we are capable
> of the sentiment of preference. This sentiment
> is the common basis of all these intellectual
> acts [of will]. Without it, none of them would
> exist .... Thus I was justified in collecting under
> the general faculty of the will all those acts whose
> basis lies in some kind of preference.[34]

All acts of the will, according to Tracy, are based on the

inherent tendency of animate beings to feel pleasure or pain in certain

sensations; the acts of will consist in furthering one's pleasurable

perceptions and minimizing the unpleasant ones.[35] The ultimate reason

why we experience some as desirable and others as undesirable is un-

known.[36] (This was an area where Tracy expected the physiological

idéologistes might eventually throw some light.) What is known by ex-

perience is that the faculty of desiring determines our well-being.

"Desire ... is inherently an enjoyment if it is fulfilled and a suffering

if it is not. Hence our happiness or misfortune depend on it. And if

by error we venture to desire things which are essentially harmful ...

we are inevitably unhappy".[37]

Tracy ultimately reaches a contradictory and confused position.

On the one hand, he wants to claim that the will is the faculty which

transforms into actions all the results of our other faculties, that it

"directs the movements of our limbs" as well as "the operations of our

intelligence": the will controls the ways we use our "mechanical" and our

"intellectual" forces.[38] The causal links, however, are too complex

and hidden to demonstrate: it would never be possible by scientific

observation to prove that a given desire is the "cause"of action taken

to satisfy the desire.[39] All we can say with confidence is that there s a "correspondence" or a "parallel" between our intellectual phenomena

f desiring and our "mechanical, chemical and physiological acts".[40]

rdinary language holds that the will is the cause of voluntary actions

hich follow it. Tracy concedes there is little harm in admitting such

sage, so long as the causal desires are understood as merely a shorthand

xpression for the complex chain of causality, including all those organic

"internal movements" which are the immediate causes of our actions.[41]

But on the other hand, Tracy asserts that the will is not "free"

because we are unable to control whether or not we experience a desire.[42]

There is an ultimate "necessity" underlying all our actions, in the sense

that there is no action without a sequence of prior causal facts.[43]

Properly posed, he claims, the question of free will may be reduced to

whether our will is "dependent solely on itself". The answer is that it

cannot be independent of prior judgements and sensations, and therefore

the will is not really "free".[44]   The very question of "free will",

wrote Tracy in the Commentaire, is misleading. The question tends to

arise only because in some situations we appear to have alternative choices

available, whereas in other situations our conduct is virtually forced upon

us. In the first case, our "free" choice is really an "illusion", claimed

Tracy, because every act of will is caused by whatever determinations

(however weak) led to its taking one direction rather than another.[45]

Tracy's strict insistence that every phenomenon is determined

(because every phenomenon has a cause) is a good illustration of his

scientism, and of his refusal to concede ground to any spiritualist

interpretation of man's faculties or of man's place in the universe. Tracy

assumes that "facts" are causally inter-related in a complex web, and the

task of science is to find the causal sequences underlying each given
"effect". If a causal chain remains hidden, it is only a matter of time
before the sequence is revealed - a matter of making further observations
asking the correct questions. In principle, the unknown is "not yet
known" rather than "unknowable", always providing that the inquiry is
directed at understanding processes (effects) rather than ultimate causes
of reality.

Tracy's scientistic view of causality also has significant
consequences for his approach to the moral and political sciences. Firstl
it implies the possibility of a social technology. If every idea/percept
and every need/desire has a determinate cause, it is possible in principl
to alter the causal sequence by re-education or re-direction to produce
different ideas and desires. (This implication will be examined more clos
in the last section of this chapter.) Secondly, his behaviouralist
approach leads to a particular view of the content of the moral and
political sciences. _Morale_ is no longer to be seen as a code of moral
precepts (derived from tradition or revelation), but a study of the
character and consequences of our actions in terms of their effects on
our happiness. An expression of intention is no longer a sufficient
explanation for an action, nor is it an adequate measure of the moral
qualities of that action. Virtue, wrote Tracy, is to be judged by
the _effects_ of our actions upon the happiness and well-being of humanity.
Economie is to be understood, again in behavioural terms, as the study
of the actions we take to satisfy our needs/desires, and their consequences for our happiness. And finally, _législation_ is the science
which examines the policies available to public authorities to "direct"
the actions of the citizens so as to increase their happiness.[47] It is

clear that the scientific study of the will leads directly, in Tracy's approach, to a search for institutional methods for securing the welfare and liberty of the citizens, just as we saw earlier that the study of the formation of ideas leads directly to a search for ways of perfecting our faculty of judgement. How is Tracy's doctrine of the will related to his conception of liberty and happiness?

We saw earlier (p.45) that in 1794 Tracy had seen an identity between liberty and happiness. This conception was elaborated in his early mémoires at the Institut, where he asserted a fundamental inter-dependence of the concepts of liberty, power and happiness.

> The more I have considered it, the more I am persuaded that being free consists in being able to act in consequence of one's will, and that the word _liberty_, however it is used, signifies nothing but the power to satisfy one's desires. Now, since it is clear that the well-being, the happiness of a sentient being, of a being susceptible of desires, consists in the accomplishment of these desires, it follows that liberty and happiness are two ideas essentially inseparable for it, or rather that it is absolutely the same idea considered under two different aspects, that of its means and that of its goal. Thus, to mention in passing, the truths of morals, ... politics, ... and physics and mathematics, ... are at the same time means of our happiness and liberty, well-being and power.[48]

Several years later, Tracy repeated that

> the idea of _liberty_ arises from the faculty of willing; for, with Locke, I understand by liberty the power to execute one's will, to act according to one's desires .... Thus there would be no liberty if there were no will; and liberty cannot exist before the birth of the will.[49]

The will has the capacity to regulate most of our movements, to direct the use of almost all our faculties, and thereby to create all our means of enjoyment and power. For Tracy, our liberty or the power to execute our will

> ... is thus the remedy of all our ills, the accomplishment
> of all our desires, the satisfaction of all our needs, and
> consequently the foremost of all our goods, that which produces
> them all and includes them all. It is the same thing as our
> happiness; it has the same limits, or rather, our happiness
> cannot be of greater or lesser extent than our liberty, i.e.
> than our power to satisfy our desires.[50]

Tracy's conception of liberty is defined not only in terms of
an absence of restraints upon action, but also in terms of the actual
accomplishment of our desires (= happiness). It is not a strictly
"negative" conception of freedom as absence of impediments (as in Hobbes)
although this remains the most important strand of his liberalism.[51] The
additional element is Tracy's concern that one criterion of freedom is
the degree to which one has the capacity or power to satisfy one's desires
and thereby attain happiness.

Tracy's concern with positive outcomes, as well as with absence
of restraint, was perhaps related to his experience of politics in the
early years of the Revolution, when "liberty" was invoked to justify all
kinds of illiberal measures jeopardizing the welfare and happiness of
many citizens. But his concern with happiness, as something more than
an absence of restraint, may also be seen as a characteristic of a social
philosophy which assumed that certain kinds of actions should be
encouraged and others discouraged. Tracy was not indifferent to the
ways in which men used their freedom to act. He wanted to promote the
sentiments of benevolence, modesty, frugality and civic-mindedness and
to discourage behaviour which was anti-social, malevolent, prodigal or
mean. He also wanted to promote scientific perspectives and to combat
various sources of obscurantism and prejudice. He wanted to encourage

talents and industry of all kinds, and to abolish traditional constraints upon such activities. It is not surprising, then, that Tracy sometimes wanted to suggest or prescribe what men should do with their freedom. Yet he remained unattracted to doctrines which sought to define and enforce a systematic view of how all men should behave.

Tracy gave some attention to the concept of "constraint" as the opposite of liberty. Constraints prevent us from satisfying our desires and thus cause suffering rather than happiness. Constraints may take many different forms, and there are several ways of trying to overcome them. Some constraints, the effect of physical forces, are direct and immediate: other constraints, the effect of moral and intellectual considerations, are more indirect though no less "real" in their effect.[52] In some cases, the constraints might be insurmountable, imposed upon us by our natural capacities. It is wise to abandon desires which are confronted by insuperable obstacles of this kind. Freedom commences only on the basis of our recognition of necessity, and a knowledge of our capacities.[53] In other cases, certain of our desires can be accomplished only at the cost of abandoning other desires, or by creating additional unwanted effects. Tracy here sees the need for a prudential calculation of relative advantages and disadvantages, in order to choose between alternative courses of action. Tracy claims that it is in our interest to study the nature of the obstacles or constraints upon the satisfaction of our desires, and to adopt the means which are most likely to achieve our goals.[54] Our interest, in other words, is to increase our liberty or power, and to use it well, "that is, to use it so as not ultimately to impede or restrain it".[55] Such calculations of long term interests would require a highly developed faculty of judgement, to the improvement of which Tracy had devoted much of his writing on idéologie.

The above conceptions of liberty and constraint were drawn
at the level of individual desires and their realization or frustration.
Tracy encountered certain difficulties in making the transition from
this level of individuals as collections of desires, to the level of
society and history. The individual self was defined as the composite
of one's sensibilities, or as a collection of desires,[56] and not, as
with Marx, in terms of the ensemble of one's social relations.[57] How
could the desiring individual obtain his satisfactions when competing for
scarce resources with other individuals?   How is society possible in such
a situation of endemic conflict? How do rules, duties and rights arise?
How are they enforced? Is such enforcement a constraint upon the liberty
of the individual, and if so, should it be resisted? The gap between
analysis at the level of individual will and that of social practices or
institutions is very wide in Tracy's theory, as in most forms of utilitarian social theory. Tracy adopted two main strategies for bridging the
gap. One, an extension of his analysis of individual will, attempted to
show by an analytico-deductive method how diadic and wider social
relations may be seen to evolve from interaction between desiring wills.
Tracy "deduces" the origin of rights and duties, and the institutions of
law and property, in such a manner. His second approach is more genuinely
social in character. Here, he takes men's sociality as more or less
inherent in their existence and as a precondition for a truly "human"
existence. Language and sympathy, for example, are seen as intrinsic
to the evolution of the species; and various forms of co-operation, as
in the division of labour and commerce, add a further dimension to the
strength and integration of society. These explanations of social
existence are examined briefly in the following section.

II. THE BASES OF SOCIAL EXISTENCE

Tracy sought to deduce the bases of social practices and conventions from his naturalistic concept of the individual qua will. He claimed that the desiring self, or what he sometimes called the moral personality, attained an awareness of its separate identity through its faculty of motilité. One's personality or self-consciousness arose through a recognition of one's separation from other personalities and from external objects.[58] This self-awareness entailed an understanding that the self was the "exclusive proprietor" of its body and its actions.[59] The concept of property, he claimed, appertains only to a desiring and acting being, who has needs and means, and thereby possesses something.[60] The notion of property as private and exclusive arose from the fact that the desiring and acting self had been endowed by nature with a "necessary and inalienable property, that of his individuality". This "natural and necessary" property was the analogue of all subsequent forms of property which have been established by conventional understandings among men in society. The very ideas of "mine" and "yours" were claimed to follow naturally from the elementary distinction between myself and any other self.[61] For Tracy, private property was an ontological fact of human existence. It was merely vain speculation, in his view, to enquire whether the institution of property was advantageous or not to men, as if it depended on our whim to change our mode of existence.[62] Private property, then, originated in our "inalienable possession" of our individuality and its faculties. Tracy claimed to have demonstrated "how the sentiment of personality or the idea of self, and that of property which necessarily stems from it, are derived from our faculty of willing"[63]

Tracy's "deduction" of private property from the concept of the desiring self is a clear example - albeit a faulty application - of the method of _analyse_. Taking the isolated individual as his secure and certain starting-point, Tracy discovers a host of other concepts implied in the first, like a nest of boxes. Locke had also argued that private property was an inalienable or natural right of the individual, but his reasoning was based mainly on a right arising from labour upon and usage of land and resources, subsequently guaranteed by social conventions.[64] Tracy, who also adopted a labour theory of value,[65] did not apply it in this case to explain the origin of private property (though he later used the labour theory to suggest how to make best use of one's property). Tracy's approach is all the more surprising because even a physiocrat like Dupont de Nemours followed Locke's account of the origins of private property in terms of mixing one's labour with nature.[66] The main error in Tracy's deduction of private property from the concept of the desiring individual, stemmed from his failure to see a distinction between possession-as-use and possession-as-exclusive-entitlement or control. Tracy acknowledged that the individual, with exclusive control of his own faculties through his will, "needed" to appropriate from nature the materials to satisfy his wants. But Tracy was wrong to believe there was a logical derivation of private and legally-guaranteed private property from the fact that we must make use of external objects to satisfy our wants.

Just as personality and property were linked to Tracy's view of the desiring individual, so were the concepts of rights and duties. Rights, according to Tracy, come into existence only because a desiring and acting being is weak, vulnerable and subject to deprivations of various kinds; a being which did not experience pleasures, pains or deprivations would not require rights.[67] In acting upon one's general right to satisfy one's desires, one is only acting in accordance with the "laws of one's own nature" and obeying the "conditions of one's existence" as a sentient being.[68] Similarly, duties are attributable only to desiring and acting beings who are obliged to interact. A being incapable of action (a being with no "means") would have no duties towards others. Duties are modes of regulating the ways in which we use our powers or means.

According to Tracy, everyone has a general "duty" to satisfy his wants and "to employ his means as well as possible" for the satisfaction of his desires.[69] This general duty, upon further analysis, is found to contain the specific duties of "properly assessing" the desires which are to be satisfied, studying the means available, "restraining" one's wants and "extending" one's means as much as possible. For one's unhappiness, said Tracy, is a consequence of one's wants outstripping one's means to satisfy them.[70] It is clear that a number of prudential maxims, purporting to be derived from natural necessity, have been inserted into Tracy's scientific analysis of desires, means, rights and duties, as if the maxims could be deduced from the nature of l'homme sensible. It is also clear that the concept of "duty" (especially in the form of a "duty to oneself") is identical with individual self-interest. This identification of duty and interest appeared in Tracy's early mémoires at the Institut, where he noted that we not only have the ability to regulate our will, but also "we have the duty, that is to say the interest, to do so."[71]

Rights and duties in society are held by Tracy to have an analogu in nature, or in the natural condition of man. Wishing to exclude all "metaphysical" conceptions of rights and duties, Tracy believed that a scientific analysis would locate them in man's "natural" constitution, i.e. his needs and capacities. The task of analysis was to show the natural (or scientifically-based) analogue of social conventions. By following the "natural" rules arising from such an analysis, Tracy believed (in the manner of the physiocrats) that man would be following the only morality which was compatible with his human nature and thus his happiness.

One of the most striking examples of Tracy's deduction of interes rights, duties and moral rules from an abstract consideration of the isolated individual, is presented in his "Mémoire sur la faculté de penser". Starting with the proposition that man is a sentient being with desires, Tracy rapidly deduces that man has the "interest to satisfy his desires", that man has the interest to possess the "power" to satisfy his desires, and thus that "man has the interest to be free".[72] Man's interes is seen to extend, upon further analysis, to the development of his faculties, his education, his respect for the similar interests of others (so that they will respect his interest), and his recognition that social operation increases his physical and intellectual abilities. It is finally seen that the "duties and utility" of social existence consist in these objectives. "All this is implicitly contained in this first truth, that man is sentient".[73] Tracy found no difficulty in moving from the level of brute facts of individual existence to the levels of social organization and moral prescriptions. All were seen as outcomes of the

concepts of need and interest, which Tracy saw as the basic mobiles of
all human action.[74]

The natural right of the individual to seek to satisfy his
desires is a right common to all animate creatures, in Tracy's view. It
is also the interest (or duty) of the individual to do so for his survival.
Tracy illustrates this by suggesting that nature itself is a system of
absolute laws which man can ignore only at his own peril, for to infringe
such laws is to break the laws of one's own nature.[75]

> ... every duty presupposes a <u>penalty</u> which follows its
> infraction, a <u>law</u> which pronounces this penalty, and
> a <u>tribunal</u> which applies that law. In the present
> example, the penalty for making poor use of his means
> is for the individual to see results less favourable
> to, or even destructive of, his satisfaction. The
> laws which pronounce this penalty are those of his
> organization as a desiring and acting being; they
> are the conditions of his existence. The tribunal
> which applies these laws is that of necessity itself,
> against which he cannot protect himself.[76]

This metaphor of natural necessity as a legal system gives us several
clues concerning Tracy's attitude to morals and legislation. It is
apparent that "nature" penalizes men owing to their lack of knowledge,
or carelessness, towards the operation of necessity. It penalizes
ignorance, error or negligence, rather than immoral intentions. Moral
behaviour is the accomplishment of one's duty, but we have already seen
that duty is identified with interests. Tracy's "moral" prescriptions
for human conduct, in the face of the necessities of men's organization
and their environment, are reducible to prudential and utilitarian maxims
urging moderation, self-restraint and mutual respect for one another's
interests.

Tracy finally examines the conception of rights and duties as applied to men in society. First, he takes up Hobbes' discussion of the state of nature (a term not used by Tracy), where individuals could not properly communicate with their fellows nor make conventions with them. Such a situation would be similar to that of man's relations with animals, but would not be a state of war where each man sought the destruction of the other as the only means of ensuring his own preservation. Rather than a state of complete mutual hostility, men would generally live in a state of mutual indifference or separation (étrangeté), each seeking his own satisfactions, and unable to attain mutual understanding or conventional modes of resolving differences.[78] Interaction would be humanized to some extent by the natural sympathy of men for their own kind, which would become quite strong in cases of sexual relations and sentiments of parenthood. But in the absence of mutual understandings and conventions, quarrels would be frequent for there would be no conception of justice or injustice and no limitations placed on one's rights and duty to satisfy one's wants.

The ancient Greeks, continued Tracy, had located the origin of laws and justice in the period when men's relations became stabilized in agricultural pursuits, and hence they called Ceres the legislator.[79] But they should have gone even further back to the origin of the first conventions, and thus acknowledged the central importance of language.[80]

> Hobbes, then, was quite right in establishing the basis of all justice on conventions; but he was wrong in saying that the earlier condition is rigorously and absolutely a state of war, and that this is our true instinct and the desire of our nature. If this were so, we would never have escaped it .... It has always struck me as highly remarkable that this philosopher, who ... is perhaps the most to be commended for the rigorous concatenation and close connection of his ideas, should have reached this fine conception of the necessity of conventions, the source of all justice, despite having started from a false or at least imprecise principle (the condition of war as the natural state) ... [81]

Language, the basis of convention, is also for Tracy one of the necessary conditions of social existence.

Tracy also examines the claim made by some versions of the social contract theory that men sacrificed a portion of their liberty in entering society in order to secure the remainder. Tracy tends to agree with Rousseau rather than Locke in arguing that the individual's liberty can be increased by his social relationships. For Tracy, the individual who constantly strengthens his social interaction with his fellows and is linked to them through social conventions, does not expect to suffer a net loss of liberty, or to diminish his capacity to execute his will. If the individual renounces certain types of action, it is so he may be assisted - or at least not opposed - in other areas which he regards as more important to him.[82] "He consents that his will should be restrained a little, in certain cases, by that of his fellows; but that is so it may be much more powerful over all other beings, and even over his fellows on other occasions; so that the total mass of power or liberty which he possesses should be increased".[83] The object of "true society", based on justice, "is always to increase the power of each one, by making that of others concur with it, and by preventing them from mutually harming one another."[84]

Tracy generally avoided contractual explanations of social order, despite the utilitarian calculus alluded to above. He was aware that the desires of individuals were bound to conflict, and that society would be improbable if such conflict could not be regulated. But he resisted a contractual theory even though he sometimes used its language concerning natural rights and the purposes of political association. He was aware, with Hume and Adam Smith, that there was no historical basis

for a rationalistic contract between ruler and the ruled or among the
associated members of a society. Tracy believed that men were incapable,
by their very organization and needs, of living either an isolated and
atomistic existence or in a condition of total hostility. Tracy acknowledged that a social order "does not commence ... on a particular
day or by premeditated design. It is established imperceptibly and by
degrees."[85] The human species had always lived in communities of
various types. And yet, the achievement of a high degree of social co-
operation and harmony among individuals with diverse wants and capacities
had to be seen as the triumph of "art" over "nature".[86] Herein lay man's
historical progress and further evidence of his superiority over the
animals.

Tracy's historical appreciation of man's sociality is not entirel
consistent with his psycho-physiological conception of man as a desiring
creature seeking to maximise his satisfactions. The dualism became explici
in Tracy's later writings, where he distinguished between two major aspects
of human existence. La vie organique ou intérieure denoted all those
aspects of life concerned simply with the "conservation" of the individual'
body, and included a preponderance of involuntary organic actions.[87] La
vie animale ou extérieure, on the other hand, denoted those aspects of
life in which the individual is placed in "relations" with others. The
relational aspects of life, according to Tracy, consisted of

> the use of our various senses and the operation of our
> faculty of movement, of speech and of reproduction,
> functions which effectively place us in relations not
> only with our fellows and all the beings which surround
> us, but even with the diverse parts of ourselves which
> we learn to know separately and distinctly.   [88]

This distinction between two modes or sides of our human existence corresponds with a distinction between two orders of sentiments, needs and interests. The one is essentially self-centred and the second is essentially other-centred. The sentiments of individual personality and private possessions are part of our vie organique: they are tied to our fundamental structure of existence and are the unalterable precondition of everything we do, whether as new-born infants or as fully socialized adults. All morality must come to terms with this aspect of our human existence. Each person necessarily has "a host of interests" peculiar to him; and since everyone else is in the same position, it is inevitable that their interests will be in opposition. On the one hand, then, our vie organique or biological substructure ensures that men are often in conflict and are bound to suffer since their desires will be frustrated.[89]

On the other hand, our vie animale or relational activities lead us into forms of co-operation and association which are the source of our moral and material progress. The study of économie demonstrates that associated individuals are more intelligent, wealthy and powerful than isolated individuals and that the help of our fellows is necessary even to meet our needs of conservation. Nature gives us "a great attraction to each other", which "strongly counter-balances the mutual opposition of our individual interests". We are naturally drawn together, but not only for mutual satisfaction of our material needs for survival. "Nature has given us real needs for [social] relationships and has even made them obligatory [très-impérieux]. This is doubtless why men everywhere live in associations called societies".[90] For Tracy, then, the desiring individual undergoes a metamorphosis at the level of social relationships. This is because "the basis" of his social

interaction is his natural "need to sympathize" (besoin de sympathiser),

a sentiment which Tracy identifies in a Rousseauean fashion with an

"original goodness".[91]   Sympathy, and not any malevolent sentiment,

is the basis of la vie de relation.

> I call the need to sympathize, or sympathy, that
> disposition which leads us to associate ourselves
> with the sentiments of our fellows and even with
> those of all animate nature; which makes the sight
> of grief a sorrow to us and that of joy a pleasure
> to us; which makes us in need of being pleased when
> we are unhappy and makes our happiness incomplete
> unless it is shared; and finally, which makes the
> sentiment of loving agreeable for us to experience
> and to inspire, and makes the sentiment of hating or
> being hated painful and sad for us.[92]

The importance of this principle for Tracy's science of human

behaviour is that it is an observable and inherent part of human

existence, and also that it tends to heal the breaches opened by

individuals' conflicts of interests.

> ... the sentiment of sympathy derives as necessarily
> from our life of relation, as the sentiment of personality
> derives from our life of conservation. It is this
> powerful attraction which brings us close again to
> our fellows at times when our individuality draws us
> apart. It is what softens the hard and repelling
> aspects of individuality.[93]

Tracy acknowledges that the reconciliation of these twin

principles is highly desirable but cannot be taken for granted. Owing

to the clash of wants, personal interest is the "first cause of all

our hateful passions", whereas sympathy is the "source of all our

benevolent passions". Personal interest is not always a bad or harm-

ful thing. It gives us the ability to increase our powers and over-

come the problem of privation and scarcity; and, "properly understood", it can lead us to forms of co-operation. But we must beware lest it lead us to consequences which are ultimately harmful to our own interests.[94]   Mutual benevolence remains the "great law of our happiness".[95]

The concept of sympathy had been widely discussed among the social and moral writers to whom Tracy's philosophy was indebted in various degrees. Rousseau, in his Second Discourse on the Origin of Inequality, had discussed men's natural sentiments in terms of two complementary and sometimes conflicting principles: amour de soi, which roughly corresponded to Tracy's egoistic drives, and pitié, which corresponded to Tracy's conception of sympathy and compassion.[96]

Hume and Smith had placed great importance on sympathy in explaining social conduct.[97]   Their writings (especially those of Smith) had attracted widespread attention in France. Smith's Theory of Moral Sentiments (1759) had been translated into French in 1774, and a new translation of the seventh edition was published in 1798 by the widow of Condorcet. She appended a series of eight Letters on Sympathy (addressed to Cabanis), in which sympathy was defined as "the disposition we have to feel in the same manner as someone else".[98]   Cabanis had included a discussion on sympathy in his Rapports du physique et du moral de l'homme in 1802.[99]

Tracy's first discussion of sympathy dates from 1796, in his "Mémoire sur la faculté de penser". He began by proposing the doctrine that in our relations with animate beings the part of them we want to possess is their will. This is because their will affects our own pleasures and pains, depending on whether it is in conflict or conformity

with our own will.[100]   Once we recognize another being as a creature of
will, he becomes precious or otherwise to us only by virtue of his will.
The pleasure we gain from finding the will of another conforming with
our own and our desire that it should be so "are necessary results of our
sensibility".[101]   This desire to influence and possess the will of
others "enters into all our moral sentiments, or those which relate to
our fellows; and on close analysis, it is seen to be the principal
cause of our desire for power, wealth, glory, honour and even the
frivolous pleasures of vanity; accordingly, by more or less false
judgements, we believe all these things suitable for reconciling other
wills to ours".[102]

The same desire for a correspondence of wills underlies the
charm of true friendship and true love. It gives us a need for the
esteem of others, and even for self-esteem.

> There arises from this the pleasure of our moral
> sensibility, of philanthropy, of all that we
> properly call the good sentiments, i.e. those
> favourable to our fellows. In fact, we are quite
> sure of being in basic accord with them when we
> wish their good, though we might often wish them
> a good that they are not aware of, or even which
> they disregard.[103]

This same desire to possess the will of others is also the reason we
value their frankness and confidence and want them to count on our own
truthfulness, so that there is a reliable understanding of each other.
It also accounts for our shyness in the company of strangers, whose
will towards us is unknown. Finally, it is the source of our hatred,
envy, jealousy and distrust, insofar as the wills of others are seen
to be in conflict with our own.[104]   In short, for Tracy, "the need
to possess the will of our fellows is the source of all our social and
even our anti-social affections".[105]

At a later point in his "Mémoire", Tracy introduces the importance of sexual relationships and the reproduction of the species for
the development of social bonds. Imagine, he writes, a meeting in the
forest between two of the celebrated enfants abandonnés, a girl and a
boy who had no experience of human society. Their natural need for
sexual relations would draw them together and they would soon learn to
communicate and give pleasure to each other.

> ... and there is the birth of the great social need, the
> need to possess the will of one's fellow. We have already
> seen that it is the source of all morality. From it also
> stems their mutual need to express their affections and to
> know those of their companion, in a word, to communicate. [106]

To the pleasures of sexuality and communication through language, are added
the affections of parenthood whereby the mother, at least, is obliged
to live in permanent society with another human being, her child. In
this way, says Tracy, it can be seen how all aspects of our social and
moral life may be derived from the simple physical needs of our organization:

> ... from the need for reproduction there arise all our
> moral sentiments and all our means of developing our
> ideas, for, in giving us the need to possess the will
> of our fellows, it[reproduction] gives us the need to
> communicate with them. [107]

Tracy had intended to write a treatise on morale, or the
social effects of moral sentiments, as the fifth part of his Elémens
d'idéologie. It was never completed. The introductory chapter had
established the general principles of two types of sentiments, discussed
above, arising from our vie de conservation and our vie de relation.
The natural desire of sympathy was as firmly rooted in human life as
the more narrow desire of egoistic satisfactions. In the subsequent
chapter, Tracy had intended to analyze the various moral sentiments and
their social consequences, beginning with a series on benevolent sentiments

to be followed by a series on malevolent sentiments. But only the
very first of such discussions was ever written, the chapter on l'amour.
The French edition of his Traité de la Volonté included only a few pages
of Tracy's discussion of love - in a final note, he wrote that he no
longer hoped to complete his volume on morale, and that "this fragment
will be my last work".[108]   In fact, however, Tracy had completed by 1813
an extended analysis of love and its social forms. He withheld this extend
discussion from the French editions from 1815 onwards, claiming he did
not want to publish his personal views on such sensitive matters.[109]   But,
as we saw above (p.49), he allowed the full text to appear in an Italian
translation of the treatise on the will in 1819, [110] and he also sent the
complete manuscript to Jefferson in 1821.[111]

The fragment on love in the French edition presents only a
general perspective, claiming that love is the most important of those
benevolent sentiments which are conducive to sociality and happiness.
Love, writes Tracy, has two main aspects, physical and sentimental.
On the one hand, Tracy acknowledges the great influence of le besoin de
la reproduction on our vitality and our temperament, and suggests it can
be the most violent of all our passions when felt in all its force. But
physical passion and the attraction of beauty is only a part of love.
Love is also a sentiment of attachment between individuals, in which
sexual enjoyment may be less important than the pleasure of loving and
being loved.[112]   Forced enjoyment is unsatisfying and even distressing,
and enjoyment which is too easily obtained lacks the sentiment which
provides its full savour.   The consent of participants is "one of its
charms", and sympathie is "one of its greatest pleasures".   The full
development of love in the human species consists of "friendship enhanced

y pleasure", or "the perfection of friendship". Such a sentiment is
the pinnacle of our existence as beings of desire and action.[113]

In the more extended discussion, published in the Italian
edition, Tracy was critical of various formal restrictions upon the relations between men and women, which were especially inhibiting for women,
and urged a liberalization in such relationships. He gave a generally
favourable account of marriage as the main institutional basis of love,
though he urged that divorce should be made easier where a particular
marriage had broken down.   The details of these remarks on institutionalized relations between the sexes are of some interest, but are only of
marginal relevance to the present study. It may suffice to cite his
remarks at the conclusion of the chapter on love:

> In resumé, I say that the need of reproduction attracts
> and brings together the two sexes; to this need is
> joined that of sympathy, which enlivens it even more.
> This is the most important of all our inclinations ;
> through it, the human race is perpetuated and society
> is established, for society is not composed of isolated
> individuals, and a man or woman taken separately do not
> constitute a complete and perfect whole: they are only
> simple fractions. The family is the true social unit,
> rather as we have seen in my Grammar that propositions
> are the true elements of discourse and that words taken
> in isolation have no value by themselves.[114]

We have seen that Tracy posits a view of man as a desiring
individual who seeks to maximize his satisfactions. At the same time,
he posits the view that man is an essentially social being who is
drawn to his fellows initially by his sexual and communicative needs.
This is associated with the doctrine that men are inherently sympathetic
towards the feelings and needs of their fellows, seeking their approval
and esteem, and extending their sphere of shared meanings through gestural
and verbal communication.   All of these pictures of "natural man" are

true, according to Tracy, for they are all aspects of man's natural capacities and inclinations. The clash between individual and social sentiments (arising from the natural opposition of personal interests) is recognized by Tracy as inherent in man's social life, as a dualism rooted in human nature itself. The resolution he proposes depends largely on the use of reason to formulate rules ensuring that the interests and liberty of each are protected as much as possible from others' unregulated selfish pursuit of wealth and power.[115] (This is the realm of legislation and public morality which will be examined in the following section.) At the same time, Tracy expects that men's natural sympathy, love and communication will draw them together in relations of mutual trust and co-operation. But there is another dimension of sociality mentioned by Tracy, the concept of society as "a series of exchanges".

In the first chapter of his study of économie, society is examined purely in relation to "our most direct needs and our means of satisfying them", rather than in relation to moral sentiments and moral duties. From the economic aspect, "society is purely and solely a continual series of exchanges".[116] This is true of the most primitive and the most advanced societies. Exchange, claims Tracy, is "an admirable transaction in which the two contracting parties always both gain; consequently, society is an uninterrupted succession of advantages springing up ceaselessly for all its members".[117] Reverting to the contractual metaphor, Tracy claims that exchange is evident in the very first convention or agreement among men, wherein they promise mutual security, without which society cannot exist. This convention

is a real exchange - "each renounces a certain way of using his powers,

and receives in return the same sacrifice on the part of all the

others". On the basis of this security, men enter into a multitude

of economic relationships which consist in (a) rendering a service

to receive a salary, (b) bartering some merchandise for other goods, or

(c) taking part in some work in common. In each case, there is an

exchange, in which one mode of activity is pursued as being more

advantageous than another.[118]

Tracy insists that exchanges undertaken "freely and without

constraint" are always to the benefit of both parties, because each

prefers what he obtains over what he gives. The fact that some indivi-

duals miscalculate their relative advantages and suffer a loss, does not

impinge on the essence of free exchange, which is to be advantageous to

both parties; and so Tracy concludes that from the economic aspect,

"the true utility of society is to make possible among us a multitude

of such arrangements".[119] Over a period of time, this host of small

particular benefits produces the wonders of perfected society, far

distant from the conditions of primitive societies. The accumulated

material riches and intellectual skills of a civilized society constitute

"the general good" in which everyone shares.[120] Only the human species

is able to make exchanges based on such conventions; hence, only man

has a true society, "for commerce is the whole of society, just as labour

is the whole of wealth".[121]

The great effects of civilized society are entirely a product

of "the reciprocity of services and multiplicity of exchanges".[122]

Relations of exchange, says Tracy, have three remarkable effects. In the

first place, social or collective labour is far more productive than
that of men acting independently; co-operation allows many tasks to be
accomplished which could not have been undertaken successfully by individuals acting alone. Secondly, the same is true of the generation,
preservation and diffusion of knowledge and skills, through communication
and language. Intelligence increases rapidly when many contribute to
resolving problems, and the results of invention become the general property of all. Thirdly, where several men labour reciprocally for one
another, each may devote himself in a division of labour to the
occupation in which he is most skilled and thus be more efficient and
successful. These "three great benefits of society" - namely,
"concurrence of force, increase and preservation of knowledge, and the
division of labour" - are the result of reciprocity and exchange, and
are responsible for all the advances of civilized society.[123]

Tracy's emphasis on individuality as the irreducible basis of
human existence is complemented, then, by his theory that sympathy, co-
operation and exchange are the basis of man's social existence. These
factors, mediated through the development of language[124], broaden the
limits of men's experience and "socialize" them in the values and expectations of their fellows. The process of socialization has a "natural"
basis in the sense that reproductive and communicative desires are
inherent in man's constitution, but the institutional forms and convention
of society are the historical work of many generations. They represent
what Tracy called the triumph of "art" over "nature" though he also
insists, in the style of the physiocrats, that social institutions have an
analogue in natural relationships[125] so that the disjunction between
nature and "true" society is not complete. Tracy's insistence on the

importance of a kind of social instinct in man plays a large part in his

account of how society and social progress are possible. But there

remains the critical problem of how to reconcile individual and social

interests, how to identify and counteract those desires and actions which

are anti-social, or destructive of the liberty and happiness of one's

fellow citizens. To what extent can education, in the broadest sense,

encourage certain kinds of desires and weaken or repress others? These

are the questions to be examined in the final section of this chapter.

III. SOCIAL MORALITY

The reconciliation of private and general interests, according

to Tracy and the idéologues, must be the work of reason and experience.

The most powerful influence upon the social conduct of the citizen is

his education, taken in the broadest sense. A distinction was drawn

between the terms instruction and education. [126] Instruction denoted

formal schooling and the teaching of specified curricula. Education, on

the other hand, was a term of much wider scope, commonly taken to include

the moral education of the citizen, imparted often by the family or the

Church; the values and restraints embodied in the criminal and civil

law; and the ideas engendered by social institutions as a whole.

Liberal theorists were concerned that all citizens should be sufficiently

instructed in their rights and duties as citizens (as well as in their

occupationally-related skills) in order that a free society could be

maintained. But they were opposed to the suggestion that governments

should become involved in prescribing moral rules or defining an

exclusive doctrine for inculcation in schools. [127]

Utilitarian and liberal social theorists, such as Helvétius and Beccaria,[128] had claimed that men's ideas and values were products of their environment, their education and their habitual modes of acting and thinking. To change those ideas and values, it was necessary to change their environment, education and habits. Tracy and the idéologues became deeply involved in attempts to reform the curricula taught in the system of public instruction under the Directory, discussed in Chapter Seven. Our focus here, however, is more limited, taking up Tracy's views on educating citizens in matters affecting the public interest. He believed that the two great instruments of enlightened reform and social harmony were legislation and public instruction. Tracy supported a programme of "civic education" in the broad sense, as did all the French writers on social and moral questions in the 1790s.[129] He had several reservations, however, concerning the effectiveness of direct moral and civic instruction, and called attention to the importance of the more indirect influences such as the probity of government, the rigorous enforcement of legal codes, and the effects of legislation in creating various kinds of incentives for citizens to act in ways which contributed to public order and social co-operation.

Tracy's writings on _la morale_ attempted to avoid moral preaching and exhortation. He claimed only to demonstrate the social effects of various sentiments and actions, leaving to legislators the task of defining the laws appropriate to a "sound" and "rational" morality. _Morale_, he said, is a "science" based upon "experience and reflection". It is "the knowledge of how our various inclinations and sentiments affect our happiness".[130] The scientific study of moral sentiments, he wrote, does not consist in deriving precepts of virtue, but the

> examination of those of our perceptions which include a
> desire, the way they are produced in us, their conformity
> or opposition to the real conditions of our existence,
> the solidity or futility of their motives, and the
> advantages or disadvantages of their effects. [131]

> I do not claim to give any rules for conduct. I do not
> aspire to state principles or establish maxims [of moral
> action].... I simply wish to write the history of our
> affections, sentiments or passions and show their conse-
> quences. May each person then make his own laws for
> himself or even for other people if he thinks he is able. [132]

Tracy's wish to maintain a distinction between an objective

science of moral sentiments (studying origins and consequences rather

than motives and injunctions) and a more practical guide for the creation

of virtue, sometimes became blurred. Part of his scientific enterprise

was to examine how certain kinds of sentiments and actions affected

human happiness, and he clearly believed that those which led to misery

and hostility were contrary to individual and public interest. Tracy's

thoughts were never far removed from the practical problems of "regulating

our desires and actions in the manner best fitted to make us happy". [133]

A complete knowledge of our intellectual faculties, he wrote, was the

precondition for such strategies: the alternative was "a blind routine

devoid of principles". The "art" of finding individual happiness, he

continued, "consists almost entirely in the avoidance of holding

contradictory desires ..., in guarding ourselves as much as possible

from physical harm..., and in obtaining the goodwill of our fellows and

our own self-esteem..."[134]

The question of public _morale_ - or what I have chosen to call

social morality - was discussed directly in Tracy's pamphlet of 1798:

Quels sont les moyens de fonder la morale chez un peuple?   The

question had originally been proposed in that form as a subject for a prize essay competition by the Institut in 1797, but had later been withdrawn because no entry was deemed worthy of the prize. Tracy then decided to write a reply to the original question and his essay appeared in the _Mercure français_ in February-March 1798 and as a pamphlet later that year. Tracy again republished the text as an appendix to his _Commentaire_ on Montesquieu in 1819. The essay question was of great interest to the idéologues; Roederer[135] and J.-B. Say as well as Tracy discussed this topic. J.-B. Say wrote an essay sketching the moral and social organization of a utopian republic (Olbie) where legislators and educators made civic virtue profitable for the citizens.[136]

Writing in 1798, amid the relative turbulence and social unrest of the Directory period, Tracy's main concern for a social morality lay in creating stability and security, rather than the more "ideological" values of liberty and individual rights. Tracy was emphatic that the most effective way to prevent major crimes from being committed was to ensure that all offenders were arrested and punished. The important thing, he wrote, is not that the penalties be severe, but that they are known to be inevitable. "The most useful principle of _la morale_ ... is that every crime is a certain cause of suffering for he who commits it." The enforcement of the law is the essential base of _la morale publique_, and the public officials engaged in this task are "the true supports of society".[137] Tracy adopts a deterrent theory of punishment, rather than notions of vengeance or rehabilitation. (This emphasis on the repression of crime led some commentators to specul ate on the influence of his military background.)[138]

Tracy made some specific recommendations concerning the organization of the various branches of law enforcement. The police or constabulary (la gendarmerie nationale) undertake the dangerous task of arresting criminals, a task where their gentler sensibilities are likely to be undermined and they are thus more exposed to moral corruption than other citizens. Their self-esteem and devotion must be encouraged by their superior officers and their promotion should be in accordance with fixed regulations. Tracy recommends that payment be proportional to the number of arrests, in order that the gendarme finds it in his interest to perform his duties well. The efficiency and stability of the gendarmerie would be improved by being controlled by a single permanent head, rather than by a succession of short-term appointees who are bound to create uncertainties and confusions.[139] Jailers or prison officers have one major responsibility - to prevent the escape of prisoners. The jailers should be punished in some way if they neglect this supreme duty. The prisons and the gendarmerie should be brought under the same system of authority, for they share the same principle: namely, that it is in the greatest interest of society that no criminal should escape punishment.[140]

The jury system, wrote Tracy, is a fine institution insofar as the jurors are independent of authority and not prejudiced for or against the accused; the liberty of the subject is thereby protected. But the minds of the jurymen are often influenced by the period in which they live: in times of turbulence and factional dispute, they may behave like 'party" men, whereas in times of peaceful calm they may become too sympathetic and lenient towards the accused. In either case, they would have lost the proper degree of objectivity and concern for the public interest. Judges ought to be as independent as possible both of governments and of those who come before the courts. For this reason, Tracy said, they should be well-paid, appointed for long terms of office, and itinerant. Public prosecutors, on the other hand, should be dependent on the government and more easily dismissed for simple negligence.[141]

The laws should recognize that the severity of punishment shou be proportional to the crime and to the temptation of committing it. Criminal procedure should enable the accused to conduct a proper defence; but it should also be sufficiently rigorous to ensure that guilty people are punished. Our understandable concern lest a single innocent person be convicted in error may sometimes lead us to let guilty people escape their just punishment. But cases of mistaken conviction were fairly rare in Tracy's view. It is better to err on the side of strictness, because mistaken convictions do not lead to a general decline in moral behaviour[1] whereas the continued freedom of criminals is a threat to social morality and security.

In summary, Tracy's first principle for the establishment of la saine morale is to make the punishment of crimes virtually inevitable. But the legislator or political leader will also be concerned with suppressing all other kinds of roguish and dishonest behaviour. While he cannot punish all such actions directly, he can influence matters so that the culprits suffer financially by their conduct and/or suffer the loss of their reputation if public opinion has been suitably influenced by sound institutions. Dishonest behaviour is further discouraged by well-organized civil tribunals; costs granted against those who bring a civil suit in bad faith; strong measures against fraudulent bankruptcy; exclusion from government offices of all men whose "reputation" is unsavoury; and by the practice of employing men in the province of their birth, where they are judged by those who are familiar with their past conduct. (Officials who are dépaysés can be dangerous, said Tracy, and he added in the 1819 text that there were quite a number of distressing examples in contemporary France.[143])

The friends of liberty should not be too quick to condemn the activities of the police even though its powers could potentially be used in an oppressive way. Providing that the accused are brought speedily before the courts, little harm can be done, especially if the governmental authority as a whole is soundly based. A system operating with small imperfections is preferable to a system paralyzed by restrictions, all the more "because the second basic principle of la morale is certainly to make the success of dishonesty as difficult as possible."[144]

If all crimes and dishonesty were punished, men would be led towards the good and happy life, but the law cannot be so efficient or all-encompassing. Laws are subject to human weaknesses in their formulation and execution; there is a world of difference between the certainty and power of the laws of nature and the laws established by men to regulate their societies, which are only conventions.[145] Some ancient philosophers, seeking to eliminate the possibility of men harming each other and to destroy the very root of immoral behaviour, located it in private property. This erroneous view, wrote Tracy, is rebutted by the fact that individuality could not be suppressed even where the product of one's labour became communal property: there would still be conflict over the division of such communal goods. Each man always has property in his ideas, his labour and the products of his labour. Rousseau was wrong in declaring that private property was the cause of all crime; but at least he was more consistent than the ancients in concluding that society was the source of all vices and that a condition of isolation would be required for individual integrity.[1]

For Tracy, individuals necessarily have distinct and sometimes opposing interests. Since these cannot be eliminated, the task is to "reconcile and contain" them.[147]

> The nature of men is such that they cannot be associated without having distinct and opposed interests and yet they are obliged to draw closer in order to help one another and even to exist. What, then, can they do?.... They set up common rules to prevent themselves from using their frequent opportunities to harm one another. These rules are the laws which we have mentioned, those which punish crimes and restrain misdemeanours. They are the true supports of la morale; they cannot prevent opportunities for evil, but they can forestall the harmful effects; they are good laws.[148]

But in our present societies, "established before an understanding of the true interests of men",[149] not all laws have these beneficial effects. There are some "obscure", "useless" and "impractical" laws which may even create new sources of evil and harm and bring public authority into disrespect. Tracy lists a number of examples: laws which create opposing interests in different classes; laws which prohibit actions which are innocent in themselves; negligent administration or disorder in public finances; institutions which promote errors, prejudices or superstitions; and laws which seek to upset the "eternal nature of things", such as that which substitutes paper money for gold.[150] On the other hand, the opportunities for harm are reduced by legislative and administrative actions which

> tend to base all interests upon the general interest, to draw all opinions towards reason, their common centre, ... to restore to all citizens the full exercise

> of individual liberty which is not harmful;
> and ... simplicity, clarity, regularity and
> constancy in the actions of government ... [151]

All legislative and administrative activities, wrote Tracy, have an important influence on _la morale_, insofar as they increase or diminish the occasions for bad conduct. Our efforts should be directed towards reducing the opportunities for new offences, and in this task "the most powerful of all our moral means ... are repressive laws and their full and complete execution".[152]

Tracy believed it was merely illusory (_chimérique_) to hope that all occasions for mutual harm could be removed; the essential thing was to reduce men's desire to commit harmful actions. Legislation and the execution of the law were not sufficient in this regard. It was also necessary to use "all the indirect manners of influencing the inclinations" of the citizens. Of course, everything in the world has _some_ degree of influence on our dispositions and feelings. However, claimed Tracy, the essential thing to grasp is that since our acts of will are consequences of our acts of judgement (a proposition he takes as "proven"),

> it follows that to guide the one, it is necessary only
> to direct the other; and that the only way to make
> something wanted, is to have it judged as preferable.
> Thus, all these diverse means of acting for good or
> bad upon the inclinations of men are ultimately reduced
> to indoctrinating them well or badly. [153]

This doctrine, implying the possibility of educative control of men's beliefs and values, was inconsistent both with Tracy's later theory of the will and with his liberal approach to educational issues. A brief explanation is necessary.

Tracy's early theory of the will held that our "desires" are a product of "judgements" we make, using the raw material supplied by our immediately perceived "needs". Desires, on this rationalistic view, were directly related to "our true or false knowledge". Hence, concluded Tracy, "in order to direct and regulate our desires, it is only a question of correcting our judgements, and here we find the only solid foundation for all morality".[154] Proceeding on this assumption, Tracy concluded that the problems of education and of morality would be resolved if men's capacity for making "good judgements" was improved to the extent that it became "habitual".[155] However, Tracy does not seem to have noticed that his later doctrine of the will, in which "desires" may be immediately given without the mediation of judgement and comparison,[156] undermines the likelihood that a rationalist educative process - aimed at improving logical inferences - could control undesirable passions.

Secondly, Tracy's use of the term "indoctrinating" the people appears to be an instance of illiberal enthusiasm for the correctness of his own "rational" morality. However, we cannot take his term "indoctrinating" too literally, since he immediately goes on to say that direct instruction in matters of la morale is ineffective. Moral education, on the contrary, is acquired mainly by experience and example. If our environment was so perversely arranged that virtue was punished and vice rewarded, direct moral instruction could do nothing to change that unfortunate system. But if, by wise laws and their enforcement, men could see that vice was punished and rational co-operation rewarded, there would be a close link established between virtue, reason and happiness.

Moral notions and responses are learned, insists Tracy: they are not innate in our minds from birth, nor are they identical in all individuals or in all cultures. Tracy expresses astonishment that his hero Voltaire, who had attacked "so many metaphysical prejudices" and shown that religion was a "human creation" of many cultural and historical varieties, should have believed that la morale is divinely implanted in us and that this explains why its essential principles are similar everywhere.[157] That murder and theft are regarded as crimes in all societies did not convince Tracy of the uniformity or the divinity of moral notions. Men living in association understand rapidly that killing or harming one another undermines the advantages of their social existence, and that if they break their conventions their security and happiness is jeopardized. Such truths are so obvious that everyone can understand them. But beyond these simple truths, there is great scope for disagreement, misunderstanding and ignorance about moral notions.[158] Knowledge of la morale, the science of our sentiments and their effects on our happiness, is dependent on our understanding of idéologie and la physique. That is why "la morale is always the last of the sciences to be perfected, always the least advanced, always that on which opinions must be the most divided".[159] It was almost as if there were as many ways of seeing and feeling as there were individuals - a far cry from any uniformity of moral notions.

Tracy believed that it was laudable to wish to improve the social morality of the adult citizens, but it was inappropriate to make such an attempt through the direct teaching of moral doctrines. Very few adults had the time or the desire to follow a long course of instruction , and even fewer had the ability to grasp a closely reasoned

188

system of ideas. In an elitist fashion, Tracy claimed that only the

legislators were really obliged to have a comprehensive and rigorous

understanding of la morale; other citizens need only to know some of

the most important principles, rather as craftsmen practising their art

make do with a few proven rules and ignore the learned theories on which

they are based.[160] Tracy made the same point a few years later in his

Analyse of Dupuis: it is unnecessary to make the common man understand

the finer points of philosophy, providing that he is clearly presented

with the distilled results.[161] A similar dichotomy was to pervade Tracy's

detailed discussions of public instruction (see chapter seven below).

The general thrust of Tracy's notion of moral socialization is

that we are much more strongly influenced by "the truths we have ourselves

deduced from observation of our surroundings" and which are constantly

drawn to our attention by experience, than by those truths we have been

taught directly.[162] Thus the public festivals established by the education

law of October 1795, and the moral catechisms of Volney, Lachabeaussière

and Saint-Lambert, would be of little consequence. Moral instruction of

citizens could only "impart in a few minds the abstract truths of sound

morality", and help to advance the scientific theory, but could do

nothing to spread the practice of a rational morality. The teaching of

adult citizens can result in "a few more enlightened speculative

moralists", but can never make the bulk of the citizens suddenly more

virtuous.[163]

The individual has three kinds of needs relative to morale

which have to be satisfied, said Tracy: physical needs, the need to

gain the goodwill of his fellows, and the need for his own self-respect.

To satisfy these needs, he has correspondingly to avoid punishment, blame and remorse. He has to act through one of these motivations in seeking

to act in a morally sound or "virtuous" manner, that is, to be "useful

to his fellows and to himself".[164]   Direct moral instruction influences

mainly the third motivation (which is the least influential in most

men). The other two motivations are developed and shaped by the various

institutions of society. Hence the irrelevance of direct instruction,

and the central importance of social experience and practices, for the

moral education of the citizens.

> Legislators and rulers - these are the true teachers of
> the mass of humanity, the only ones whose lessons have any
> efficacy. Moral instruction ... is completely in the acts
> of legislation and administration.[165]

Public authorities thus do not have to rely solely upon repression and

punishment: they are also able to discourage dishonest and anti-social

impulses through their legislative and administrative activities. These

men can accomplish a great deal in encouraging and maintaining a social

morality, guided by a reasoned understanding of

> political truths, which teach us so to arrange our relations
> with our fellows that their desires are the least harmful and
> the most helpful in the accomplishment of our own.[166]

Tracy gives a number of examples contrasting the influence

of the teacher and the legislator. A moral theorist may demonstrate

that allowing pecuniary interests to reach into family affairs is des-

tructive of inner happiness. On the other hand, the legislator who

establishes equal inheritance can virtually eliminate at a stroke all

sentiment of rivalry and all suspicion of dissembling affection. In

the same way, the legislator who establishes a divorce law abolishes

most marriages of interest and maintains all other marriages by the

possibility of their being dissolved.[167]   A teacher may urge that we

should take reason as our guide and claim that reason alone suffices to demonstrate that we have a real interest in being just; but he will urge in vain. The legislator, however, can terminate the payment of priests and stop their involvement in civil affairs and in teaching, with the result that after ten years, everyone implicitly will agree with the teacher without his having said a word.[168]   A teacher may strive to show that virtues and talents are the only precious qualities; but public opinion on such a matter will be determined by "whether the law recognizes or forbids equality of conditions".   It would be a waste of effort to demonstrate that success in the sciences was the most meritorious way of serving one's country, if it were seen that a clever scoundrel could acquire more consideration and credit in one year than a great man by a life's work. A theorist might demonstrate that a man who earns a comfortable living by honest and useful industry gains more inner satisfaction than one who lives by shameful deceit or who languishes in idleness.   But, Tracy noted,

> if a thousand roads are open to get rich by plunder and fraud,
> or to receive great benefits from the state without deserving
> them, everyone will rush in; whilst, if all the means of
> gaining a too hasty fortune are prevented by an economical
> administration of state finances, by a great security and
> great facility for loans ..., by a great liberty to under-
> take all forms of industry ...; if, finally, the prompt
> dispersal of acquired wealth is promoted by equality of
> inheritance ..., you will soon see everyone devoting
> themselves to useful work and adopting the values of an
> active life and a modest existence.[169]

In the same way, it would be in vain to preach loyalty to friends and respect for the innocent, if the law facilitates denunciations and allows confiscations, leading to a multiplication of betrayals and unjust condemnations. A large number of sequestrations will do more to make administrators into scoundrels, and vice versa, than all the instruction in the world could ever do to prevent this happening. And if public officials are suddenly involved in buying and selling property on a large scale, three quarters of them will become speculators, receiving bribes and violating their duties, despite all the philosophical and religious sermons and even despite the surveillance of the law itself. Public opinion cannot in itself be an effective check on such activities if so many people are involved.[170]

Tracy sums up his position on how to provide a moral education for adult citizens: first, and most important, "the complete, rapid and inevitable execution of the repressive laws". Second, "an exact balance between the income and the expenditure of the state". When the state is heavily indebted, warns Tracy, the way is open for fortune-hunting and discontent, the weakening of justice and the impoverishment of the people as a whole. The state should never raise the interest rate and increase the number of idle rentiers by its loan-raising activities. Tracy also recommended several other measures which he believed would promote a sound social morality: civil equality and the abolition of privilege and hereditary power; the non-payment of priests and their exclusion from educational and other public offices; the uniformity of laws and administration; divorce; equal inheritance; freedom of industry, commerce and credit-finance.[171]

If these measures were implemented,

> crime would be punished, reason strengthened, domestic
> happiness assured, equality maintained to the extent it is
> possible and useful, economy made necessary, and work made
> honourable. I can scarcely imagine what else would be
> desirable to lead men to virtue and I have not yet said
> anything about public instruction in the strict sense. [172]

Tracy regarded these institutional devices for forming public and private morality as a necessary background to any direct moral instruction

provided by the schools and public festivals. In cases where there is a
breakdown in public finance and government functions, costly remedies such
as public instruction are seen as irrelevant. Moreover, the mere multiplication of teachers and of moral catechisms does not give citizens the
necessary incentive and time to study. Recalling, no doubt, the turmoil
of the recent past, Tracy pointed to the dependence of public instruction
on rational and stable social institutions.

> Suppose a nation excited by lively passions, upturned by violent
> movements, where greedy men are unrestrained, where almost
> everyone is impoverished, where all fortunes are made or
> destroyed overnight, where no existence is assured, no
> reputation intact and no-one lives in his usual dwelling;
> and imagine if you can the profound indifference for your
> schools and festivals and their complete uselessness.

> Suppose, on the contrary, a people in the circumstances des-
> cribed earlier, who have been made hard-working, modest, sensible,
> happy and prosperous; do you doubt that the desire for ins-
> truction and common enjoyments would be quick to develop?
> Public festivals would be established, schools would be [173]
> desired.

Tracy concluded his essay with a few remarks on the moral education of children. The child's moral education is readily formed in the
family circle if the parents have acquired good habits and have been
"formed, so to speak, by wise institutions". But if society is given over
to prejudices, vice and disorder, the satisfactory moral education of
children is not possible.[174] Tracy insisted again on the superiority
of experience and example over direct instruction in moral education.
Our early sentiments and inclinations are formed not so much by "classes,
sermons and public exhortations", but by our surroundings, by what we
experience in those moments we are not being "indoctrinated".[175] The
corrupting influence of parents and institutions imbued with bad
principles would completely negate the benefits of sound moral
principles imparted in formal instruction. The essential point was that
direct attempts to inculcate certain modes of conduct are unsuccessful.

But "arrange the circumstances in a favourable way and what you desire
will happen without you appearing to have been involved". This was true,
concluded Tracy, in regard to "the project of making men rational and
virtuous". [176]

In the pamphlet edition of <u>Quels sont les moyens ...</u> (1798)
Tracy added a brief Supplement (wisely omitted from the 1819 edition)
where he attempted to "apply" these principles to contemporary events
in France. How could one explain the increased crime rate, the exaspera-
ted passions and the general level of disorder, in which "the best citizens
are those who suffer most"?[177] The common answer, he noted, was that
the Revolution has undermined the moral order.[178] But what could be the
meaning of this alleged "de-moralization"? If it simply drew attention
to the increase in crime and dishonesty, it would not constitute a causal
explanation but only a restatement of the facts. If it meant that
the republican government had corrupted our morals, this was surely to
exaggerate how fast our moral sentiments actually change.

> ... the present is always, so to speak, the disciple of the
> past, and we are motivated today by the habits, passions
> and ideas contracted or acquired under the old social
> order. If these were the causes of our present evils, it
> would be necessary to attribute them all to the <u>ancien
> régime</u>, so foolishly lamented. But let us yet be just -
> that would overstate the reproaches it deserves, since in
> that society these same habits, passions and ideas did not
> lead to the same consequences.[179]

Could it be, then, that the so-called de-moralization arose because the
principles of the new social order were destructive of <u>la morale</u>? This
was to call into question Tracy's fundamental belief in the rational
superiority of the new system over the old . The new system "professes more
respect for men's natural and original rights" than for later usurpations,
it places reason above prejudice and habit, it consults the interests

of the majority rather than the minority.[180]   Such a system was

directed towards justice, not corruption. Moreover, he claimed, the

critics of the new order had mainly attacked its alleged impracticality

rather than its sublime principles of reason and justice.

Why then, was there more corruption under the new system,

devoted to reason, than under the old system, founded on errors?

> It is because the domestic and external troubles which have
> accompanied this great and sudden reformation, have further
> increased the needs of the state and consequently the disorders
> of the administration, and have reduced the effectiveness of
> repressive laws at the very time they were most necessary.
> Owing to these two circumstances, the practice of la morale [181]
> has deteriorated, though its theory has been advanced.

Refusing to admit that his principles were in any way threatened by the

defects of social practice, Tracy consoled his readers that the decline

was only "temporary".   It was caused by the difficulty of establishing

the new order, rather than inherent in its essential character.   The

new political institutions, wrote Tracy optimistically, have deep roots

and are likely to overcome the problems of la morale in the near

future.[182]   Less than two years after these words were written, the

Directory collapsed; Bonaparte pledged himself to restore law and

order, and to this end encouraged the revival of traditional moral bonds

in the place of the morality of reason advocated by the idéologues.

Tracy's successor at the Academy of Moral and Political

Sciences, J.-P. Damiron, claimed that the corruption and materialism of

the Directory period had been directly attributable to the official

adoption of sensationalist philosophy by the intellectual and political

élite.   Utility was not an adequate criterion for a moral philosophy.

It led to an emphasis on the satisfaction of material needs above all lse and offered little resistance to a despotism which promised

o provide for such needs. Its ethic was that of l'industrialisme, which

aw government only in terms of physical and material objectives.[183]

he utilitarian ethic was widely criticized by opponents of the idéologues.

entham's pleasure/pain principle and Helvétius' sensual concept of

appiness were attacked in the pages of the Mercure [184] and other journals.

Tracy certainly believed that material satisfactions were impor-

ant to well-being and happiness, but he was far from believing that

hey were the essential element of public and private morality. Nor did

e hold that criminal actions by the poor should be excused owing to

heir imperative material needs: he did not lapse into an environmental

eterminism that eliminates the concept of moral responsibility.[185]

e might well have agreed with Burke and Durkheim that it is essential

or men to put moral chains upon their own appetites.

A more serious objection against Tracy's "project of making

en rational and virtuous",[186] is the elitism of his claim to know how

individual and social interests may be reconciled and how social virtue

may be recognized and promoted. One commentator has described Tracy's

conception of morality as "the hygiene of desires", [187]   and another

has likened the idéologues' programme to an "educational totalitarianism

attempting to shape minds and hearts".[188]   The thrust of these

criticisms is that Tracy's doctrine was ultimately manipulative: an

educated élite, proficient in ideological analysis of ideas and desires,

would determine what kinds of ideas and actions were compatible with

reason and virtue. The ordinary people, unable to understand the grand

design at a philosophical level, would be given practical precepts

telling them how to conform with the higher truths.[189]   These criticisms are exaggerated, as will be seen in later chapters. It is true, however, that Tracy left himself open to such charges by failing to provide, alongside his concern with techniques of social integration and progress, a defence of a private sphere of individuality or an intellectual and moral pluralism. His criticism of direct moral inculcation in 1798 had been cast in terms of its ineffectiveness, not its illiberalism.

Tracy's epistemological position implied that there was ultimately only one correct judgement on any given issue; the problem was to find that solution and to convince others of its rectitude. Upon examination, however, the content of the "virtuous" social conduct he advocated amounted to little more than honesty, benevolence, prudence and moderation. Such qualities of conduct had little connection with the Jacobin "reign of virtue", nor with any political programme in which loyalty to the current régime took precedence over other principles of conduct. Moreover, Tracy always refrained from any "solutions" based on coercion or indoctrination: he believed that the future lay with those whose case was most in accordance with science and reason. Persuasion and demonstration would suffice in the long run to inaugurate a peaceful and prosperous society of individuals, each pursuing his own satisfactions as he saw fit, mindful of the consequences of his actions upon the interests of his fellows. In the short term, the educated élite were in a position to use their influence to steer social institutions in the general directions pointed out by analysis of human nature and human needs. Tracy and the idéologues grasped their opportunities under the Directory - and failed to have any lasting impact upon the lives of the ordinary people. By the time he wrote his Commentaire in 1806, Tracy was much more explicitly committed to a gradualist or evolutionary perspective regarding moral and political reform, though his faith in the ultimate triumph of reason continued unabated.

We have seen in this chapter that Tracy's conception of the individual as a creature governed by pleasures and pains posed several problems for developing a theory of society or of the social basis of individuality. Tracy's derivation of social institutions from analysis of the faculties of the individual is implausible and leads him into contractual explanations which he elsewhere rejects as unhistorical. His second strategy, positing man's "natural" need for social interaction and the esteem of others, provides some basis for a theory of sympathy and language as the foundations of social existence, and leads to an economic analysis of society as a system of utilitarian exchanges for mutual benefit. The contradiction arising between man's egoistic impulses and his civilized benevolence is not resolved, but the institutions of government and public instruction are seen as instruments of an on-going reconciliation between these two sides of human behaviour. It is now necessary to discuss Tracy's science of social organization and examine his conception of the relation between social science and public policy.

FOOTNOTES TO CHAPTER THREE

1   "Mémoire sur la faculté de penser", pp. 336, 343, 327ff.

2   Ibid., p.332.

3   Elémens, Vol. I, p.248; Traité de la Volonté (1815), pp. 65-71; "Mémoire sur la faculté de penser", p. 311n.

4   Logique, p. 433; Traité de la Volonté (1815), pp. 83-92.

5   "Mémoire sur la faculté de penser", pp. 302, 313, 335, 338, 343.

6   Ibid., p.333; also p.338. These are the only occasions in his published writings where Tracy described action in terms of "effort": it was a word which appealed greatly to Maine de Biran in his attempt to elaborate a more activist conception of the self.

7   "Dissertation sur quelques questions d'idéologie", in Mémoires de l'Institut, Vol. III (1801), pp.491-514.

8   Regrettably there is no space to discuss Maine de Biran's revisions of Tracy's viewpoint. Their widening disagreements are documented in their detailed correspondence from the years 1804-1814 published by Pierre Tisserend in Vol. VII of Maine de Biran, Oeuvres philoso-phiques (Paris, 1930), pp. 227-366; see also Cabanis' letters to Biran in ibid, pp. 209-225. Biran's gradual rejection of the philosophy of sensations, as propounded by Tracy and Cabanis, has been ably discussed in H. Gouhier, Les Conversions de Maine de Biran (Paris 1947), esp. Ch.3; and P. Tisserand, "Introduction", pp. vii-lxiv, to Maine de Biran, L'influence de l'habitude sur la faculté de penser (Paris 1954); and by S. Moravia, Il pensiero degli idéologues (Firenze 1974), pp. 457-529.

9   Elémens, Vol. I, p.247.

10   "Mémoire sur la faculté de penser",p.346.

11   Ibid., pp. 347-8.

12   Ibid., pp. 349-350.

13   Ibid., pp. 350-1

14   Ibid., pp. 362-3. Cf. Elémens, Vol. I, p.252.

15   Ibid., p.364.

16   Ibid., pp. 364-5.

17   Ibid., p. 365.

18   Ibid., p.366.

19   Ibidem.

20   Ibid., p.368.

21   Elémens, Vol. I [3e ed. 1817] ed. Gouhier (Paris, 1970), pp. 115, 141-2, 153, 239-251 (cf. also p.433).

22   Ibid., pp. 149-150.

23   Ibid., pp. 150-1.

24   Ibid., p.151n.

25   Ibid., p.152.

26   For Cabanis' remarks on instinct, see Rapports, in Oeuvres philoso-phiques, Vol. I, pp. 558-562. There is no space to develop the differences of emphasis between Cabanis and Tracy. In his summary of Cabanis' physiological doctrines in the 1805 edition of the Rapports, Tracy showed a tendency to adopt an even more uncompromising materialism than his mentor: cf. Tracy, "Table Analytique", in Cabanis, Rapports (1830 ed.), Vol. I, pp.23-65. On instinct, see pp. 56-7 of the "Table analytique".

27   Condillac, Traité des animaux, in Oeuvres philosophiques, Vol. I, p.379.

28   Condillac, Traité des sensations, in ibid., Vol. I, p.228.

29   Tracy, "Mémoire sur la faculté de penser", p.354.

30   Ibid., pp. 356-7.

31   Traité de la Volonté (1815 ed.), "Introduction", pp. 84, 86, 88, 96.

32   Ibid., p.83.

33   Tracy, "Mémoire de Berlin", published by P. Tisserand in Revue philosophique de la France et de l'étranger, Vol. 116 (1933), at pp. 170-2.

34   Ibid., p.173.

35   Traité de la Volonté (1818), pp. 476-7; Elémens, Vol. I, p.245.

36   Elémens, Vol. I, p.130 (cf. also p.429); Traité de la Volonté (1818), pp. 502, 504.

37   Elémens, Vol. I, p.68.

38   Ibid., p.69; Traité de la Volonté (1815), p.110.

39   Traité de la Volonté (1818), pp. 478, 494-6; cf. Elémens, Vol.I, p.234.

40   Ibid., p.480.

41   Ibid., p.505.

42   Elémens, Vol. I, p.70.

43   Traité de la Volonté (1815), pp. 109-110; Traité (1818), pp.501-2.

44   Elémens, Vol. I, pp. 246-7.

45   Commentaire, pp. 142-3.

46   Traité de la Volonté (1818), p.503; Elémens, Vol. I, p.249; Logique, p.436. An anonymous critic of Tracy's first volume on idéologie drew attention to Tracy's recommendation that intentionality be abandoned as unscientific and his view that every desire is the result of a prior sequence of causes. This doctrine "would soon dispense with [our need for] a civil and criminal code." (Mercure de France, 16 nivôse an X [6 January 1802] , p.100.)

47   Logique, pp. 437-9 (see also pp. 391-5).

48   "Mémoire sur la faculté de penser", p.363.

49   Traité de la Volonté (1815), pp. 108-9. The same point is made in Elémens, vol. I, p.252; Commentaire, pp. 141-2, 227-8.

50   Traité de la Volonté (1815), pp. 110-111; cf. Commentaire, p.144.

51   Cf. Tracy's defence of the liberty of the King's aunts to emigrate in Feb. 1791, on the grounds that what the law does not forbid is the area of free action: Archives parlementaries, XXIII, p.497.

52   Traité de la Volonté (1815), p.111.

53   Ibid., p.113; also Traité (1818), p.262.

54   Traité (1815), p.112.

55   Ibid., p.113.

56   Cf. "Mémoire sur la faculté de penser", p.311n - 312: here, Tracy uses the metaphor of a ball (as in dancing) to describe the self as an ensemble of elements, subject to change, yet unified.

57   Cf. Marx, "Theses on Feuerbach", No. 6.

58   Traité de la Volonté (1815), pp. 65-71.

59   Ibid., p.73.

60   Ibid., pp. 56-7.

61   Ibid., pp. 74-6.

62   "Quels sont les moyens...", in Commentaire, pp. 448-450; Traité de la Volonté (1818), pp. 263-4. Cf. Proudhon's criticism of Tracy's doctrine in Qu'est-ce que la propriété? [1840], ed. E. James (Paris 1966), pp. 100-3. Marx made similar criticisms.

63   Traité de la Volonté (1815), p.82.

64   J. Locke, Second Treatise, section 25 ff: cf. Two Treatises of Government, ed. Laslett (New York 1965), pp. 327 ff.

65   Traité de la Volonté (1815), pp. 92-102.

66   Cf. Dupont de Nemours, De l'origine et des progrès d'une science nouvelle [1768] , ed. A. Dubois (Paris 1910), p.11.

67   Logique, p.433.

68   Traité de la Volonté (1815), pp. 117, 119, 135.

69   Ibid., pp. 128, 135. The physiocrats also claimed that one's natural duty is to care for one's own needs (and to respect the liberty, person and property of others).

70   Ibid., pp. 120-1, and 112-3.

71   "Mémoire sur la faculté de penser", p.368.

72   Ibid., pp. 380-381.

73   Ibid., pp. 381, 383.

74   Commentaire, pp. 16-17. Tracy adds, however, that while need and interest are correctly seen as general explanations of human action, they tell us too little about any particular action to be truly explanatory. However, this qualification remained undeveloped elsewhere.

75   Commentaire, pp. 2-5 ; Traité de la Volonté (1815), pp. 118-121.

76   Traité de la Volonté (1815), p. 120.

77   He also includes a curious discussion of the proper relationship between men and animals, in the light of their conflicting rights and lack of mutual communication (ibid., pp. 123-6). His "conclusion" is that we should avoid both extremes of violent destruction or exaggerated sentimentality in our dealings with animals, and regulate our behaviour in accordance with the extent to which reciprocal relations of benevolence and habit can be established between man and beast.

78   Ibid., pp. 128-9.

79   This was also the view of the physiocrats. Cf. also the "four-stages" theory of social evolution, mentioned in chapter five.

80   *Traité de la Volonté* (1815), pp. 130-1.

81   *Ibid.*, pp. 131-3.

82   *Ibid.*, p.115; *Commentaire*, pp. 161, 219.

83   *Ibid.*, p.116.

84   *Ibid.*, p.137.

85   *Ibid.*, p.115.

86   *Ibid.*, p.132 n.

87   *Traité de la Volonté* (1818), pp. 507-8.

88   *Ibid.*, p.508.

89   *Ibid.*, pp. 512-513.

90   *Ibid.*, p.514.

91   *Ibid.*, p.515.

92   *Ibidem.*

93   *Ibid.*, p.516.

94   *Ibid.*, p.517.

95   *Traité de la Volonté* (1815), p.79.

96   Cf. J.-J. Rousseau, "Discourse on the Origin of Inequality" [1754], in *The Social Contract and Discourses*, trans. G.D.H. Cole (London 1973), esp. pp. 64 ff.

97   For discussion of these writers' views on sympathy, cf. G. Bryson, *Man and Society: The Scottish Inquiry in the Eighteenth Century* (Princeton 1945), esp. chapter 6; G. Morrow, "The significance of the doctrine of sympathy in Hume and A. Smith", *The Philosophical Review*, vol. 32 (1923), pp. 60-78; R. Lamb, "A. Smith's System: Sympathy not self-interest", *Journal of the History of Ideas*, vol. 35 (1974), pp. 671-682.

98   Cf. A. Smith, *Théorie des Sentimens Moraux ...,* traduit de l'Angla: ... par S. Grouchy, Veuve Condorcet [Suivie de huit lettres sur la sympathie] (Paris 1798), vol. II, p.357.

99   Cf. Cabanis, *Oeuvres philosophiques*, vol. I, pp. 158-9, 563-578.

100   "Mémoire sur la faculté de penser", p.359; cf. *Principes logiques,* in *Elémens d'idéologie*, 5 vols. (Bruxelles 1826-27), IV, p.220.

101   "Mémoire sur la faculté de penser", p.360.

102   Ibidem.

103   Ibid., p.361.

104   Ibidem.

105   Ibid., p.385.

106   Ibid., p.404.   The implications of sexual desire for the growth
       of population was discussed by Tracy in Traité de la Volonté, Ch.9.

107   "Mémoire sur la faculté de penser", p.405.

108   Traité de la Volonté (1818), p.523 (= 1815 ed. p.576).   The fragment
       on l'amour occupies pp. 518-521 (1818 ed.) and pp. 568-573 (1815 ed.)

109   Cf. G. Chinard, Jefferson et les Idéologues, p.209 (letter of
       Tracy to Jefferson, 22 February 1821).

110   Destutt de Tracy, De l'amour, ed. Chinard (Paris 1926): for the
       date of composition, see p.33n.

111   Chinard, Jefferson et les Idéologues, pp. 208ff.

112   Traité de la Volonté (1818) pp. 519-520.

113   Ibid.,   p.521

114   De l'amour, pp. 59-60. One might be forgiven some surprise that
       Tracy suddenly finds in his last writing that "the family" is
       the "true social unit". Had he started from such a "basis", his
       social theory must surely have taken a different direction.

115   Cf. Traité de la Volonté   (1818) pp. 517-518; cf. Traité (1815)
       p.137.

116   Traité   (1818) p.131.

117   Ibid.,   pp. 131-2.

118   Ibid.,   pp. 132-3.

119   Ibid.,   134, 135.

120   Ibid.,   p.136.

121   Ibid.,   p.143.

122   Ibidem.

123   Ibid., pp. 144-6. The physiocrats had also noted the importance
       of "exchange" as a principle of social progress: cf. R. Meek,
       Precursors of Adam Smith (London 1975), p.111 (Quesnay and Mirabeau).

124   Cf. Elémens, vol. I, pp. 377-8;   "Mémoire sur la faculté de penser", p.420.

125   Cf. Traité de la Volonté (1815), pp. 74-5.

126   Tracy, "Mémoire sur la faculté de penser", p.287; Louis de Bonald, Mélanges (Paris 1819), vol. II, pp. 311-319; B. Constant, Mélanges (Paris 1829),pp. 240-254: Condorcet, Selected Writings, ed. K.M. Baker (New York 1976), pp. xxvii-xxviii of "Introduction"; C.H. Van Duzer, Contributions of the Idéologues, pp. 95.

127   B. Constant, loc. cit.; Condorcet, "The Nature and Purpose of Public Instruction" [1791], in Selected Writings, esp. pp. 122-134.

128   Cf. Helvétius, De l'esprit, [1758], ed. F. Châtelet (Paris 1973), pp. 492-501; I. Cumming, Hélvetius (London 1955); A. Keim, Hélvetius (Paris 1907). On Beccaria, cf. D-J. Garat, Mémoires historiques sur la vie de M. Suard ... (Paris 1820), vol. II, pp. 203-8. Tracy cited Beccaria's view that "the most certain means of rendering a people free and happy is to establish a perfect method of education" - title page of Commentary (Philadelphia 1811).

129   Cf. Dictionnaire de la Constitution française (Paris 1791), article "Instruction publique", pp. 257-9; A Sicard, L'éducation morale et civique avant et pendant la Révolution (Paris 1884).

130   "Quels sont les moyens" [1798], in Commentaire, pp. 458-9.

131   Logique, pp. 436-7; cf. ibid., pp. 392-3.

132   Traité de la Volonté (1818), pp. 475-6.

133   Elémens, vol. I, p.72.

134   Ibid., p.73. Cf. "Quels sont les moyens", in Commentaire, p.462, and "Mémoire sur la faculté de penser", p.363.

135   P.-L. Roederer, Oeuvres (Paris 1853-9), vol. V, pp. 151-2, 156-8; and 107-129 on moral catechisms. For a completely different view see L.-C. Saint-Martin, Réflexions d'un observateur (Paris, 1798).

136   J.-B. Say, Olbie, ou essai sur les moyens de réformer les moeurs d'une nation (Paris an VIII [1800]). A slightly abridged version was reprinted in Say's Oeuvres diverses (Paris 1848), pp. 581-615. Olbie was favourably reviewed in la Décade, 20 ventose an VIII (11 March 1800), pp. 476-485.

137   "Quels sont les moyens", in Commentaire, p.438. Cf. Logique, p.395, on the meaning of the term "police".

138   Cf. R. Lote, "Histoire de la philosophie", in G. Hanotaux (ed.), Histoire de la Nation française (Paris 1920-24), XV, p.531 and 531 n.1: Destutt de Tracy was "a former colonel who had retained in his theories a little military rigidity", and who "recommended the recourse to the gendarme in matters of morality". La Grand Encyclopédie before 1850, claimed that "Destutt de Tracy is one of those materialists who replace God with a gendarme": [cont.]

38 [cont.]   cited in J. Cruet, La philosophie morale et sociale
de Destutt de Tracy (Tours 1909), p.156. Finally, E. Joyau
claimed that Tracy "simply wanted recourse to gendarmes and
squadrons of cavalry to fortify the teaching of morality":
La philosophie en France pendant la Révolution (Paris 1893),
pp. 174-5.

39   "Quels sont les moyens", pp. 439-440.

40   Ibid., pp. 440-1.

41   Ibid., pp. 441-2.

42   Ibid., pp. 443-4. Of course, Tracy adds, if a man is deliberately
victimized by means of the legal system, this is an "atrocious"
crime and likely to lead to others.

43   Ibid., p.446.

44   Ibid., p.447.

45   Cf. Commentaire, pp. 2-5.

46   "Quels sont les moyens", pp. 448-9.

47   Ibid., p.450.

48   Ibid., p.451.

49   Ibidem.

50   Ibid., p.452. The vehement opposition to paper money was in part
a response to the amazing depreciation in value of government
assignats during the 1790s.

51   Ibid., p.453.

52   Ibid., p.454.

53   Ibid., p.455.

54   "Mémoire sur la faculté de penser", p.356; cf. Elémens, vol. I,
pp. 67, 73.

55   Ibid., pp. 442-3; Elémens, vol. I, pp. 273-4.

56   Traité de la Volonté (1815), pp. 83 ff; and also above, p. 148f.

57   "Quels sont les moyens,"p. 457.

58   Ibid., pp. 457-9.

59   Ibid., p.460.

60   Ibid., p.461.

161   Analyse (1804), p.148.

162   "Quels sont les moyens", p.462.

163   Ibid., p.463.

164   Ibid., p.462.

165   Ibid., p.463; cf. Elémens, vol. I, p.213.

166   "Mémoire sur la faculté de penser", p.363.

167   "Quels sont les moyens", p.464.

168   Ibid., p.465.

169   Ibid., p.466.

170   Ibid., p.467.

171   Ibid., pp. 468-70. Cf. his summary of "Quels sont...." in
       De l'amour, pp. 28-29.

172   Ibid., p.470. In his later writings, Tracy also drew attention
       to the detrimental consequences for morality of luxury: cf.
       Traité de la Volonté (1818), pp. 350, 368-9; and Commentaire,
       pp. 79 ff.

173   "Quels sont les moyens", pp. 471-2.

174   Ibid.,   pp. 474-5.

175   Ibid., p.475

176   Ibid.,   p.477.

177   Quels sont les moyens ... (Paris an VI), p.33.

178   Cf. Lafayette, Mémoires, vol. III, p.384, where Tracy's close
       friend attributed la démoralisation of the Revolution to the
       breakdown of law and order after the Jacobin victory in the
       Legislative Assembly in August 1792.

179   Quels sont les moyens ... (an VI), p.34.

180   Ibidem.

181   Ibid., p.35.

182   Ibidem.

183   J.-P. Damiron, Essai sur l'histoire de la philosophie ...,pp.11,2⁵

84 Cf. review of Bentham's Traités de législation (1802), and of an anonymous work on Seneca and Helvétius, in Mercure de France, 3 vendémiaire an XI (25 September 1802), esp. pp. 21-23 and ibid., 9 thermidor an XII (28 July 1804), esp. p. 263.

85 Traité de la Volonté (1818), pp. 296-297.

86 "Quels sont les moyens", in Commentaire, p. 477.

87 A. Canivez, "Les Idéologues", p. 109. The concept of "hygiene" comes from the writings of Cabanis: cf. Oeuvres philosophiques, vol. I, p. 109 and vol. II, pp. 221-225.

88 M. Régaldo,"Lumières, élite, démocratie: la difficile position des idéologues", Dix-huitième siècle, no. 6 (1974), p. 207.

89 For a different kind of élitism among the philosophes, in which only the masses were held to require the moral discipline of religion, cf. R.I. Boss, "The development of social religion", Journal of the History of Ideas, vol. 34 (1973), pp. 577-589.

CHAPTER FOUR

THE SCIENCE OF SOCIAL ORGANIZATION

I   From the "social art" to "social science"

II Tracy's concept of "la science sociale"

I. FROM THE "SOCIAL ART" TO "SOCIAL SCIENCE"

The argument of this chapter is that Tracy's conception of a science of society is deeply indebted to the physiocratic conception of the "social art", by which legislation and education would lead men to a prosperous society which conformed to the "laws of nature". In order to demonstrate this orientation in Tracy's writings, it is necessary to examine the original usages of the term "social art" in the work of the Marquis de Mirabeau and the abbé de Baudeau, and to show how the concept of a "social science" and a "science of social organization" evolved from these early discussions. The earliest usages of the term "social science" are examined, before turning in the second section to Tracy's own conception of social science as the scientific basis for social policies aiming to increase the happiness of the citizens.

The attempt to elaborate a science of society[1] in France and Great Britain after 1750 took several different directions. A distinction might be drawn between the approach found in the Scottish Enlightenment (Ferguson, Millar, Hume, Smith, and others) and that of the physiocrats or économistes (Quesnay, Mirabeau, Baudeau, Dupont de Nemours, and others) The Scots were more historical and empirical in their approach, and developed a conception of a "social" level of reality whose qualities were distinguishable from the multitude of individual actions. The social could not be explained purely as the sum of its simple components. The French économistes also developed a conception of society distinguishable from individual action, but analytically based upon the satisfaction of individual needs. Their writings were less historical and empirical, and more concerned to posit a desirable order of society conceived as an abstract system of rights, duties, interests and exchanges. The intention of their science œconomique, wrote Mirabeau, was to make men recognize their interest in

> the order which must prevail among them for their own
> happiness, to rectify the natural ideas of those who
> have some, and to give them to those who have none.
> What I mean by 'natural ideas' is very simple; it is
> reflection on the means of assuring one's subsistence.
> It is the first and most necessary idea for every man
> driven by needs and desires he wants to satisfy ...[3]

> I do not claim to make them into scholars or statesmen
> but it is at least necessary that they know this inter-
> dependence of the interests of all, so that they see
> the advantages of the order which assures the property
> of all ... The whole society is formed by individuals
> who must all know the order to which their happiness
> is attached ...[4]

For the physiocrats, the miseries and disorders of human history were caused not by "human nature", but by ignorance of our true interests and a consequent subjection to unbridled passions.[5] Men's reason and intelligence had to be lifted above a blind conformity to established routines if they were to understand their rights and duties, and recognize "the order which must be established among them for their greatest possible benefit, guaranteed to all by the laws of nature". The foundation of such a society is

> public knowledge of those rules and conditions conceived
> in all their purity prior to all human falsification. If
> this distinct, developed and considered knowledge is the first
> bond of society, the first duty of society is thus the
> instruction by which this knowledge must be spread and
> inculcated among everyone in an intelligible and continuous
> way.[6]

Knowledge of the "natural" order to which society should conform, and a general education in the rights and duties of such an order - these were the main elements of the physiocratic approach to a "science of order".[7] The establishment of such an order was the task of the "social art". Mirabeau appears to be the first writer to have used this phrase: it is important to clarify what he meant by it, and how it was elaborated by the abbé de Baudeau.[8]

Mirabeau claimed in 1770 that it was God's will that men live in society, for man can do nothing by himself and his successes are derived from co-operation with his fellows. Continual labour is necessary to avoid privation and death. "Thus, God wills that the social art [l'art social] conforms to the wisdom of the natural laws on which he makes us depend, and that it be taught to children ...".[9] This guidance is not like blind obedience to a command whose rationale remains obscure, but is given so that men will know their true condition , play their parts in society and in the great "universal harmony of nature". The central thread of all forms of instruction equipping men for their tasks in society must be "economic instruction, or knowledge of the rights and duties of man in accordance with nature, the only constant and unchanging measure of his social rights and duties".[10] Casting aside the doubts of some writers concerning whether man's reason "can attain the knowledge necessary for reforming the errors in the administration of States", Mirabeau attacked those who asserted that "it is only by experience acquired through practice that one can learn how to govern properly a kingdom".[11] These stick-in-the-muds, he wrote, have not understood that "experience" always develops hand-in-hand with ignorance. It is rare for experience to perceive its own deficiencies. Experience proceeds via cases, it admits no general rules, it is not readily transmissible, and is unaware that popular opinion is what makes the law. "The latter assertion is a truth of physics, impregnable, and easily demonstrated by details".[12]

In short, the "social art" consisted in so arranging government and education that the "natural" laws of human subsistence and sociability were the guiding light of all public policy and individual conduct. The physiocrats saw man's "perfectibility" as one of his most important

characteristics.[13] His satisfactions and enjoyments of all kinds could
be best guaranteed by conformity with a reasoned appraisal of the laws
derived from nature, or in this case, from the needs and capacities of
his own nature. Divested of their providential rhetoric, and their
exaggerated conception of the role of agriculture, these physiocratic
doctrines played an important part in shaping the assumptions of the
idéologues in regard to a science of society.

A more extensive discussion of the "social art" appeared in a
work by the abbé de Baudeau in 1771.[14] He distinguished between three
types of human activity (or "art") through which the objects of nature
are produced in forms which satisfy our needs. The "fertile" or "productive art" consisted in raising animals, growing crops, and extracting
minerals - in a word, producing raw materials. The "sterile" or "unproductive art", by contrast, consisted of fashioning raw materials for the
satisfaction of diverse and often specialized human wants.[15] The "social
art" consisted of aiding the economic arts by attending to the social
arrangements facilitating their free development.[16] These arrangements
were the necessary conditions for the growth of wealth and satisfactions.
The "social art" consisted of three main activities: instruction, protection
and administration.

> The art of exercising authority, of perfecting it
> continually, is what I call the social art, the first of
> them all, the principle and cause of all the others ...
> The exercise of authority (that is, instruction, protection,
> administration, which are the causes of the prosperity of
> empires) thus forms the object of the social art.[17]

Instruction gives men the capacity to expand their knowledge, their benevolence and their satisfactions. The legal code and public force protect
every individual's personal liberty and property. The tasks of "administration" consist of preparation of the soil and provision of equipment for
primary industries by private owners, together with maintenance of public

properties and transport systems by public authorities. The perfection
of this "social art" leads to improvements in material and cultural
enjoyments.[18]

The conception of a social art devoted to the perfectibility
of man through education, government and economic production, was
ressurrected by E.-J. Sieyès during the agitation and pamphleteering
leading up to the calling of the Etats-généraux. According to Sainte-
Beuve, Sieyès believed he had made the term his own and given it its
definitive content.[19] The term was used frequently in his brochures
Vues sur les moyens d'exécution ... (1788), Essai sur les privilèges
(1788), and Qu'est-ce que le Tiers-état? (January 1789). The essential
point in Sieyès' usage was that the social art consisted in a set of
principles for the realization of a rational social order in which men
were free and happy in the enjoyment of their rights. The social art
was not an empirical science of how societies have actually functioned in
the past, nor a description of contemporary society, but was concerned
with what should be.[20] For Condorcet, the social art designated the
means by which the "rights of man" were to be extended and guaranteed
throughout society. The result would be not only the sovereignty of
popular will, but the reconciliation of private interests with the general
interest.[21]

Early in 1790, Sieyès and Condorcet, together with Lafayette,
Bailly and other liberal notables, founded an academic discussion group
devoted to the development of the moral and political sciences. The
group, known as the Société de 1789, consisted of politicians, scientists,
littérateurs, businessmen and administrators, who wanted to promote a
peaceful and rational solution to the constitutional problems facing the
monarchy.[22] The main objective of the organization was defined by its

eaders as "research into the principles and means of perfecting the
ocial art" and applying its principles to the constitution and the
appiness of the whole nation.[23] According to the "Regulations" of the
ociety, the social art was a "general science of civilization", which
ad only been studied in a fragmentary way in the past. It was necessary
o attempt to create a "common method" for studying the diverse aspects
f this science, and to rally to this cause all the enlightened minds of
ll countries. A "commerce of thought" should be established, and
embers of the Society would thus become "not a sect nor a party, but a
ompany of the friends of mankind and ... dealers in social truths".[24]

The journal of the Society was to be "a collection of mémoires
n the various parts and on the overall character of l'économie sociale,
r even observations on events bearing upon the principles and progress
f this science, as new as it is extensive".[25] The journal was to include
nder the rubric "social art" the following types of questions:

> dissertations, memoirs, notes on the principles of
> constitutions, of legislative bodies, of governments,
> and of administrations, on agriculture, commerce,
> finance and public instruction, on the laws and
> tribunals; in short, on all the elements of the
> social system, and their relation to the will of
> nature and the happiness of men.[26]

In his defence of the Society against radical critics, Condorcet
reaffirmed that it was established to "develop and spread the principles
of a free constitution, and, more generally, to seek means of perfecting
the social art in all its extent". It avoided short-term political
expediency, instead seeking out the "general" and "universal" principles
underlying the "nature of man and things".

> We have regarded the social art as a true science founded,
> like all the other sciences, on facts, experiment, reasoning,
> and calculation; susceptible, like all the others, of an
> indefinite progress and development, and becoming more useful
> the more widely its true principles are spread.[27]

Condorcet and his colleagues were trying to bring together into one enterprise several elements - theoretical and practical, moral and technical, economic and political, "art" and "science". The only test for whether a subject came within the scope of the "social art" was whether it affected the prosperity and happiness of free citizens - an impossibly vague criterion on which to build a unified science of social organization.

Tracy and Cabanis, together with several other idéologues, were members of the Société de 1789.[28] It is even possible that they met there. In any case, they were deeply imbued with a desire to contribute to what Cabanis called la science de l'homme, comprising physiology, analysis of ideas, and morality;[29] and to what Tracy after 1801 increasingly began to call la science sociale (discussed in the following section). Cabanis used the term "social art" with exactly the same meaning as that of Sieyès and Condorcet, in his discussions of constitutional principles at the end of 1799.[30] Tracy also used the term "social art" at various times.[31] On other occasions, he expressed the idea without using the term, for example in his first paper at the Institut in April 1796: ideological analysis of the formation of ideas is the proper basis for the arts of grammar, logic, instruction, education, morality, "and finally the basis of the greatest of the arts, for whose success all the others must co-operate, that of regulating society in such a way that man finds the most help and the least hindrance possible on the part of his fellows".[32] The same point was made five years later in similar terms: the applications of idéologie would include "grammar, logic, instruction, private morality, public morality (or the social art), education, and legislation ...".[33] Tracy was much clearer in 1801 that these were "sciences" rather than "arts", but the distinction between these terms tended often to be blurred in the thought of the idéologues.

hile fully aware of the analytical distinction between sciences and

rts, theories and applications, they were so concerned with the

ractical consequences of their meliorist theories that they tended to

se a variety of terms fairly indiscriminately.

The original usage of the term social science (la science

ociale) dates from the early years of the French Revolution, and is very

losely related to the rationalist concern for an ordered and prosperous

ociety of free and happy citizens. Scholars have gradually discovered

arlier usages of the term than were commonly recognized. It was well

nown that Fourier (1808) and the Saint-Simonians had used it. More

mportantly, the educational law of October 1795 establishing the

nstitut had created a section entitled Sciences sociales et législation

n the Class of moral and political sciences.[34] Thus, the term had a

emi-official status in the classifications of the sciences and arts during

he period 1795 to 1803, after which the Institut was thoroughly

eorganized to eliminate the "ideological" sciences.

Professor Baker has recently traced the term "social science"

o a pamphlet written in December 1791 by D.-J. Garat, a member of the

ociété de 1789 and a leading idéologue at the école normale and the

nstitut.[35] Writing a year after the collapse of the Society, Garat

ought to revive its principles and objectives. The co-operation of

cholars was necessary to complete the work of the encyclopédistes and

hilosophes. The isolated truths discovered by a Rousseau or a

lontesquieu were not a sufficient basis to establish a just social order.

hese, and similar discoveries, were important as "the first data of

ocial science [la science sociale] but they do not constitute that

cience".[36] Condorcet also began to use the new term in his draft plans

resented to the Committee on Public Instruction of the Legislative Assembly,

nd in the materials written for his Esquisse (1793).[37]

Baker wisely refrained from claiming Garat's usage as the earliest instance of the term social science. My own research has shown that the term was used nearly three years earlier by another leading member of the Société de 1789 and of the idéologue group. Sieyès wrote his famous pamphlet Qu'est-ce que le Tiers-état? in November-December 178 The anonymous first edition was published in January 1789, and several revised editions rapidly followed. At the end of chapter 3 of the first edition, there occurred the following sentence:

> If we now turn to considering the same subject according to the principles appropriate to illuminate it, that is, according to those which form the social science [la science sociale], independently of all particular interest, we will see this question in a new light.[38]

In all subsequent editions, however, the phrase "social science" was replaced by the phrase "science of social order" [science de l'ordre social]. Sieyès had evidently decided that the earlier term was not sufficiently familiar or precise to convey his meaning.

The section of the Institut on "Social science[s] and legislati included Daunou and Cambacérès. Daunou's approval of the new term may be inferred from his role in drafting the legislation establishing the Institut. Cambacérès, who became Second Consul after the 18 brumaire, read a paper at the Institut on 25 February 1798 entitled "Discourse on Social Science".[39] The question Cambacérès took as his starting-point was the problem of guaranteeing a social order:

> The art of making a society happy consists in forming a single spirit among all the diverse minds of a people, and in placing laws upon their passions without putting chains on their liberty. To unite and reconcile men, is the goal which must be attained by those who seek a rapid progress towards public happiness.[40]

Men's need for the co-operation of their fellows and for a secure existence, he wrote, gave rise to useful arts and sciences, authoritative laws for ordering their passions, and moral restraints and hopes to lend support to social authority. "Arts, laws and morality, these are thus the principal means of civilization and the true elements of social science".[41] Cambacérès proceeded to deduce the functions and utility of agriculture, industry and commerce, the role of property as the basis of social stability, and the special role of government in guaranteeing the property of all.[42] The moral notions of goodness, honesty and justice were implanted by nature in the human heart. Morality was a necessary adjunct to the power of the legislator, and served as an internalized regulator of individual thought and action.[43] All the sciences contribute to civilization. They have social origins, and they help in their various ways to perfect society. The sciences grow through cumulative efforts, and in turn they extend the social relations of men in ideas, tastes and labour. "But not all the sciences have civilization as their object: they have only an indirect influence on it. This is what distinguishes political economy, legislation, and morality from the other sciences. The direct object of these three sciences is civilization".[44]

Social science, in the view of Cambacérès, is concerned not merely to describe the operations of economic, legal and moral forces in society, but to show how they affect the happiness of the citizens. "Social happiness [le bonheur social] consists of the enjoyment of rights and of property". Now, the maintenance of prosperity, and the securing of these enjoyments by legal and moral means, constitute both "the happiness and the goal of society and of social science". The three aspects of social science are all concerned with the goal of "perfecting our social relations", though by different means: political economy deals with relations of "interest", and considers man's physical faculties; legislation deals with relations of authority and considers men's rights; morality deals with relations of sentiment and examines men's passions and duties.[45]

One can infer from this, concluded Cambacérès, that "the social science is truly none other than the science of man". The great problem addressed by social science was "to determine the best uses of the individual's faculties, of his rights and his passions".[46] There had never before been a time when nations were more obliged to concern themselves with "social science and the perfecting of society".[47] And yet progress in this field of science was slow. A few discoveries had been made, but a spirit of intolerance had hindered the emergence of truth. "There is no science more than social science which needs to be thus perfected. This science is almost yet to be created. Most of its principles are still uncertain, and indeterminate".[48] It was for the free peoples to develop the science, founded not on belief and authority, but on experience and truth.

The abbé Grégoire, a member of the section on Morale at the Institut, read a paper in March 1796 claiming that while some progress had been made towards liberty and happiness, there was still a great deficiency in knowledge among most nations concerning their means of obtaining these goals.[49] "The social science, one of the most necessary, is precisely the most backward".[50] Political economy had few established principles; and there was only a sparse knowledge of statistics (la statistique), so important for a detailed understanding of the facts required by economic theory. The science of government had been repressed by despotic régimes, which persecuted those who dared reveal the rights of the people. Only a few nations had by now understood "the two great principles of the separation of powers, and representation".[51] The political rights of man were expressed and practised in very few countries. Yet such "political truths are not beyond the understanding of the common man". It was the task of philosophers to establish principles. The more widely these were known, the more possible it would be to reduce the number of laws: this would be a measure of "the progress of the social art".[52]

The duty of a "free régime" was to bring the sciences and arts to the people (vulgariser, pour ainsi dire, la science ...), and to " disseminate notions which are immediately applicable to the happiness of men".[53] One could not be free without enlightenment, and one could not properly exercise that freedom without social virtue. It was therefore very important for education to spread the "precious sap" of moral notions "through all the branches of the political tree".[54] In short, the effect of the sciences and arts was to raise the capacities of men, and "increase the sum of their happiness".[55] The savants had a special task of increasing the circulation and propagation of knowledge. The Institut National, in organizing an extensive network of co-operation among scholars, would undertake, as it were, "a general crusade against prejudices".[56]

Such professions of faith in the progressive role of social science and its concern to promote the happiness, liberty and security of the people, formed the climate of opinion in which Tracy developed his own ideas about the nature of a general science of man in society. The leaders of the Société de 1789, and later the savants of the Class of moral and political sciences, assumed that the science they wished to establish was "new". This was because the conception of the "rights of man", embodied in a "free constitution", was a recent development both in philosophy and in political practice: the ancients thus had not been able to conceive of a social art or social science in this modern sense. The idéologues recognised that social science was underdeveloped, and subject to strong resistance by the accumulated habits and prejudices of the past. They were also convinced that social science was a direct guide to public policy: it would establish principles which could direct legislators, educators, and producers concerning the best ways to attain the happiness of a free people.

It was much less clear in what ways social science would be "based" on observation and facts of experience. The success of the natural sciences was an obvious source of programmatic statements, emphasizing empirical data and rigorous respect for the facts. But the idéologues persisted in basing their social theories on variants of a philosophy of natural rights, and a philosophical psychology of human needs; these rights and needs were seen as the foundation not only of social science but of a legitimate social order. Their work was often as much concerned with prescription as with description. They tended to blur the distinction between a science of what _is_, and a science of what _ought to be_. At the same time, however, several of the idéologues moved more clearly in the direction of the positive or empirical sciences - physiology and medicine, anthropology, statistical and economic studies.[57]

Tracy, like most of his contemporaries who were impressed by the scientific revolution, was more inclined to announce the importance of the new outlook than to explain how scientific research actually develops or to demonstrate the relation between empiricist methods and rationalist explanations. The scientific genealogy claimed by the idéologues was undoubtedly weighted in favour of the empiricist tradition. However, as I have pointed out previously, their work in the human sciences was often greatly indebted to a rationalist framework in which certain principles were deduced from a basic proposition, and empirical phenomena were explained in terms of these principles. They assumed that a rational and ordered structure underlay all human behaviour, and that all phenomena could be located within a complex causal chain patterned like the laws of nature. Tracy and the idéologues were determined to raise the moral and political sciences to the level of certainty found in mechanics following Newton's laws of matter and motion, or in chemistry following Lavoisier's theory of elements and compounds. The creation of an Academy of Moral and Political Sciences was sure to accelerate the progress of these sciences. Such a body had been prefigured in the educational reports of Talleyrand and Condorcet in 1791-92. Tracy expressed his support for this idea in notes written a year after his arrival at Auteuil.[58] The creation at the Institut of a Class of Moral and Physical Sciences, in the education law of October 1795, was the fulfilment of their hopes, and the major reason for their institutionalized influence over science and culture under the Directory.

II. TRACY'S CONCEPT OF "LA SCIENCE SOCIALE"

In his first paper to the Institut in April 1796, Tracy urged upon his colleagues the need to "create the theory of the moral and political sciences, which have languished until now in a disastrous uncertainty". The sciences were ultimately justified, he claimed, by their "utility". But before such practical applications could be successfully made, it was necessary to have a correct theory on which to base them. The enlightened minds of Europe therefore looked to the Institut in the hope and expectation that it would "establish the moral sciences on a stable and certain foundation".[59] Tracy, however, defined in practical terms the underlying problem to be tackled by the human sciences: namely, "having understood the faculties of a species of animate creatures, to discover all the means of happiness of which these beings are capable".[60] Tracy thus affirmed the view that the objective of the social art or social science was le bonheur social.

Tracy drew several parallels between the history of the natural sciences and the agenda for the new sciences of man. The Académie des Sciences had been established in 1666 to develop the physical and mathematical sciences; 130 years later, the moral and political sciences were now granted similar recognition, which would greatly assist their progress and dissemination. In astronomy, Copernicus had changed men's conception of the physical universe, and his work had been extended by Galileo and Kepler. According to Tracy, Locke may be seen as the Copernicus of the human sciences, Dumarsais as the Galileo, and Condillac as the Kepler who did most to advance the new paradigm of knowledge.[61] Tracy looked forward to the appearance of a Newton of the human sciences, a man whose work would systematically incorporate existing knowledge in a few fundamental laws, and whose work would allow important applications for increasing human happiness.[62]

Tracy refrained from claiming for himself the title of a Newton of the moral sciences, though the image must have had a powerful attraction for system-builders such as Tracy and Sieyès. One of Adam Smith's students, John Millar, attributed this laurel to the author of the Wealth of Nations.[63] Mme de Staël in 1791 described Sieyès as the Newton of politics,[64] and at the turn of the century she still believed in the possibility and desirability of a science of politics, founded jointly upon notions of calculation and morality.[65] The desire for certainty in the moral and political sciences was a driving force behind Tracy's reduction of their methodology to a consideration of concept-formation, taking his cue from Condillac's view that the sciences could not be perfected "unless we endeavour to render their language more precise".[66]

The truths composing the human sciences, he wrote, could reach

the same degree of certainty as those of the mathematical sciences. Too often, it is true, the reality of their relations is difficult to perceive, owing to ignorance of the way these ideas are formed, the multitude of elements which compose each idea, and the imperfections of the signs by which we calculate them. But this is all the more reason for us to give their connections all the clarity

[évidence] which can stem from the good order of a
methodical deduction. Let us then return carefully
to the very origin of the whole system. Let us
imitate the mathematicians, who do not fear to
begin with a truth so obvious that it seems point-
less to express. Let us follow them further in their
procedures; let us advance, like them, from the known
to the unknown, without being discouraged by the slow
and lengthy journey. For it is above all the moral
sciences which have suffered from the sway of prejudices ...[67]

Tracy's faith in the possibility of certain knowledge about man and

society was unshakeable. The obstacles could be identified - ignorance

and illusions were the main problem; and these could be overcome by

scientific education and wise legislation. The complexity of ideas and

defects in the usage of signs, could be tackled by a methodical ideo-

logical analysis. "This science [of ideas] is positive, useful, and

capable of a rigorous exactness".[68] In these opinions, Tracy was only

voicing the typical idéologue viewpoint.

Lakanal, in introducing the law establishing the école normale

at the end of 1794, had claimed that the superiority of the principles

of the new social order could be demonstrated in the same rigorous way

as in the "most exact" sciences. "The more progress made by human reason,

the more this demonstration will become clear".[69] By using analytical

methods, which alone could renovate the human understanding, the moral

sciences would be "submitted to demonstrations as rigorous as the physical

and exact sciences". The principles of our moral "duties" would be widely

diffused among the people, and inequality of knowledge would be remedied.

"Analysis" was thus the "indispensable instrument of a great democracy".[70]

Cabanis also expressed confidence in the rigorous character of the human

sciences: it would be possible to obtain "results which increasingly

approached the highest level of probability, the only type of certainty

which the practical sciences allow, especially those whose object is the

moral aspects of man".[71]

Tracy's conception of science assumed that there were general truths, principles and causes underlying the complex facts of experience. The observer must rely upon empirical enquiry, but the genius is the man who discovers those general truths which bind together the multitude of discrete facts. Some sciences, according to this criterion, were more developed than others. Botany, zoology and mineralogy, for example, had not yet reached their maturity, because they were still preoccupied with the collection, classification and cataloguing of facts. They had not yet discovered those general laws from which the properties of particular phenomena could be deduced. Astronomy, physics and chemistry were highly advanced, because general principles (such as the law of attraction) had been discovered, which could explain all the past, present and even future phenomena.[72] How did the science of man measure up to these standards?

The human sciences tended to lag behind the others, wrote Tracy, because of ignorance, habits of thought, vested interests, and our need to obtain first an adequate understanding of nature.[73] The consequence of the illusions which obstruct the understanding of human behaviour, was that the theoretical side of the human sciences was poorly developed, despite the abundance of facts about man and society accumulated throughout history.

> Social science [la science sociale], for example, is certainly very rich in data: ... for history has preserved an infinite number of details on the numerous changes which have occurred in different human societies ... However, despite this over-abundance of observations, it can be said that social science hardly merits the name of a science so long as it has no recognized and systematic principles with whose aid we can explain and even predict the happiness and misery of diverse societies and see them only as necessary and constant results of proven laws. It seems to me, in truth, that it is now possible to trace this code, in setting out from this first general truth: man is a sentient being. But this has not yet been done; and that is enough reason that unfortunately I take social science as an example of an emergent science.[74]

Tracy's notion of a developed social science, as a set of systematic principles explaining the happiness of a people, is very close to the concept of the social art championed by Sieyès and Condorcet in 1790. And in locating the starting-point of social science in man as a sentient being, Tracy was in accord with Condorcet's formulation in his Esquisse.[75] For Tracy, the possibility of increasing the level of social happiness depended on our ability to formulate general scientific laws explaining individual and social behaviour. A science, he wrote, "is useful only for the light it sheds on all the arts which depend on it; and so long as that theory is incomplete, the rules it provides for these arts can only be groping approximations".[76] The governmental and educational "arts" of ordering the social environment so as to maximize welfare and happiness were dependent on a "social science" which explained the principles involved.

All the aspects of the human sciences had an underlying unity, in Tracy's view. And if the various branches of human knowledge seemed at present to be separate and distinct, that was only because their relationships had not yet been sufficiently elucidated. If all these sciences were fully developed, it would be clear that

> the totality of the science of man [la science humaine] would be contained in a small number of propositions and that, to unite all the branches to their common trunk, a fundamental proposition would have to be found, from which all the basic propositions of every particular science are derived. Then we would really have a complete knowledge of all that exists, and we would clearly see that all the subsidiary truths are only consequences of a primary truth, in which they are all implicitly contained, and of which they represent only partial developments.[77]

This optimistic faith in the unity and perfectibility of the sciences recalls not only the "tree of knowledge" conceptions of Bacon and d'Alembert, and a belief in uniform methods of observation and analysis in scientific research, but also a reductionist search for a fundamental and general truth from which all our knowledge can be shown to be deducible.

Tracy returned to the subject matter of social science in his educational writings of 1799 and 1801. After joining the Council of Public Instruction in February 1799 as an advisor to the Minister of the Interior, Francois de Neufchâteau, Tracy drafted a number of circulars to teachers in the secondary schools (écoles centrales) in the months of August and September.[78] The courses on legislation and history were of direct concern to the development of Tracy's notion of a social science (though the term social science was not used in secondary curricula). His circulars on these courses will be examined here, while those on other subjects will be discussed in chapter seven along with his general ideas on public instruction.

In his circular to teachers of legislation in the écoles centrales, Tracy pointed out that there was some confusion about the content of the course and its relation to other studies; some teachers had asked for guidance.[79] The course on legislation, he advised, should not deal with areas which might later be taught in an école spéciale for professional training in jurisprudence, political economy, government or diplomacy. It should provide only the knowledge required by "all citizens who have the time and means to undertake a careful education" beyond the level of primary instruction. The course should give young people "sound principles of private and public morality, with the necessary developments to make them into virtuous citizens who understand both their own interests and those of their country".[80] The course on legislation was most closely linked to that on general grammar (one of the key areas of idéologie); the generation of our ideas and sentiments should be studied before commencing the course on legislation. This was because "the general principles of morality must necessarily be established at the beginning and they can be derived only from a knowledge of our intellectual faculties".[81]

The course on legislation should preferably be studied before that on history, since "it is necessary to have some well established principles in order to read history without danger". If one reads history without a prior grounding in rational morality, one might imbibe more false ideas than "useful" knowledge.[82] The content of the course should include:

1. the elements of _morale_, drawn from an examination of the nature of man and his intellectual faculties, and based on his interest, properly understood, and on his invincible desire to be happy; that is what is called natural right;

2. the application of these principles to the organization of the body politic, to the code of criminal, civil and commercial laws, and to its relation with foreign nations - i.e. public law, criminal and civil law, political economy and the rights of nations - always showing what _should_ be alongside that which _is_, in order to accustom [students] to judge the one in terms of the other.[83]

The circular concluded by stating that most of these points should be regarded as useful advice rather than firm regulations, and suggested that teachers might like to add some additional, more specialized material owing to the present absence of any _écoles spéciales_ for those professions depending on the moral and political sciences.[84] Despite the friendly tone of the circular, it wished to prescribe a particular kind of approach to moral and political questions.[85] The analysis should begin from an understanding of human nature: man's needs, interests, intellectual faculties, rights. Institutions and practices should then be judged in the light of these ideal principles. This is a clear example of Tracy's ideological conception of social science.

The circular to professors of history in the _écoles centrales_ was more detailed. It reported that the teachers' lesson plans reflected "a great variety in their manner of envisaging and treating their subject".[86]

The circular noted that the government had initially been unwilling to provide detailed instructions to the teaching profession, preferring to draw on the "fruits of experience" rather than precise and centralized direction. (Daunou, indeed, had championed the freedom of teachers from state regulation in October 1795, a principle established earlier by Condorcet.[87]) But the time had now arrived when more detailed guidance seemed to be necessary.

Three major objectives of the history course were stated in extremely general and vague terms. (i) To provide a general knowledge of events in world history. (ii) To understand the causes of the progress and temporary regressions in the sciences, arts and social organization and the "constant relation between men's happiness and the extent and accuracy of their ideas". This was the genuinely "ideological" objective. (iii) To enable students to further their researches should they so desire. History lessons, then, "should present a summary picture of universal history", together with a guide to sources for deeper study in each area, and advice on how to use and interpret historical authors.[88] There was, however, the problem that the writing of history really demanded a good knowledge of all the sciences. This problem became especially acute when the historian dealt with

> metaphysics, morality, the social art, and political economy.
> These sciences, the most important of all for those who want
> to observe and judge the actions of men in society, still
> have no well established fundamentals: the metaphysics which
> serves as their basis is only just emerging from chaos, and
> it has hardly been generally recognized that it should consist
> simply in the examination of our intellectual faculties.
> History, in this respect, might then serve just as much to
> preserve ancient prejudices as to bring about the discovery of
> true principles. The latter are found more by meditation
> than by [empirical] example.[89]

This sums up in many respects the idéologues' view of the human sciences. The search for true principles in history (presumably those which confirmed the moral and political perspectives evidenced in Condorcet's Esquisse and Volney's Les Ruines), was seen to be more important than the examination of facts. The accidental imbibing of "prejudices" engendered by the old metaphysics is prevented by reliance upon the sensationalist philosophy of idéologie. The history course in the schools should, then, be preceded by the courses on general grammar (idéologie) and legislation, to provide a suitable preparation for understanding the broad canvas of human history.[90]

The conception of history emerging from this document has been criticized as narrow and biased: the real objective was not to understand history, claimed Duruy, but to glorify the established moral and political order of the French republic. In support of this interpretation, Duruy cites a letter by Lagrange, president of the Council of Public Instruction, to the Minister of the Interior (6 May 1799): a circular to the professors of history was needed, said Lagrange, to show them "the real viewpoint from which the course should be considered, and the new benefits for republican morality and for philosophy which should be derived from this properly directed instruction".[91] There is no doubt that Tracy and the idéologues wished to impart their distinctive conception of the human sciences to the courses taught in the écoles centrales. However, they were never in a position to impose their views upon teachers - the organizational mechanisms did not exist even if they had wanted a strict régime. Any attempt at authoritarian control over public education would also have been inconsistent with Tracy's philosophical faith in the primacy of reason and persuasion, his willingness to accept a dual system of state and private schools, the absence of compulsory education, and Tracy's belief that direct moral instruction was ineffective.

For Tracy and the idéologues, historical writing should be leavened by sound moral principles. The authority of facts had to be countered by the authority of reasoned principles, the basis of social science. While Volney[92] and Daunou[93] in some of their work may be exempted from such criticism, it is generally true to say that Tracy and the idéologues treated history with grave suspicion. The past was the arena of prejudice and oppression, as Condorcet had demonstrated. The past should therefore have as little hold as possible over the present and future. Politics or social science was essentially concerned with what should be, not with what exists.[94] (This will be further confirmed below in considering Tracy's commentary on Montesquieu.)

Tracy's Observations (1801) on the educational system established under the Directory also raised the question of a social science. History and the moral sciences, wrote Tracy, are alike insofar as everyone knows some history and everyone has a little system of moral notions, even without being aware of it.[95] These habitual ideas and sentiments determine most of their behaviour: should these ideas be left to chance? On the contrary, it is necessary that students are taught history and the moral sciences, but the first step is to learn "the sound principles of morality and the social art. The principles are the model against which it is always necessary to judge events".[96] Those parts of the course on legislation and moral sciences dealing with "public morality or social science", need to be taught by giving many practical examples; just as in the history course, it is necessary constantly to "relate the facts to the theory".[97] Tracy made similar remarks in regard to the study of the positive laws of a society. Such study, wrote Tracy, should be seen as "an application of the principles of morality and of social science".[98] The study of law, like that of history, tends to lead to the false identification of what is with what should be, unless the student has first received a proper training in principles.[99]

Tracy increasingly came to use the term social science, rather than social art, after 1801. He used the phrase "moral and social sciences" in his Analyse raisonné of Dupuis in 1804,[100] and substituted the term "social science" for Cabanis' term "science of man" in his Table analytique (1805) for the second edition of Cabanis' famous work on the physical and moral aspects of man.[101] The question of a science of social organization was raised at the end of Tracy's Logique (1805). The sciences of morality and economy gave rise to a third science, that of "directing" our sentiments and actions in order to "produce the happiness of the desiring being, for happiness is the goal of the will just as truth is the goal of the judgement".[102] Tracy regarded this as a new type of scientific enterprise, in the same way that idéologie, as the science of the formation and expression of ideas, was new.

> Could this science [of social happiness] be so new, then, that there is no appropriate name for it, and we do not yet even know how to designate it? I fear so. For that which we usually call the science of government rarely concerns itself with the objective we have just indicated, and that known under the name of social science only covers part of the subject, since it does not include education, nor even perhaps all the branches of legislation. Now, the system of principles needed to guide men to their highest degree of well-being must include the principles of behaviour and control of men of all ages, and in all circumstances. Thus here we have another science still to be named. However, with suitable precautions, we can use the common expressions ...[103]

These three sciences, dealing with the actions, desires and guidance of the will, formed a "natural" sequence. The first, economy, provided a knowledge not only of the ways in which we satisfied our physical needs and gained material wealth, but also of the intellectual and moral consequences of our actions, and their influence on the happiness of the individual and society. Such a work would not provide us with "the theory of social science",[104] but it could indicate the elements which would have to be included. The second science, morality, "follows quite naturally, for it is very easy to evaluate our various sentiments

and their different degrees of merit and demerit, when we well understand

all the consequences of the actions to which we are led [by these senti-

ments]".[105] The new social science also follows readily from the

previous knowledge:

> for as soon as one understands the generation of our
> sentiments, one knows the means of cultivating some
> and uprooting others. Thus the principles of education
> and legislation are discovered, and the science of
> man as a desiring and acting being is complete.[106]

Such a complete treatise on the operations and guidance of the will would

be the "most important" work one could undertake, given the present state of

knowledge: for it would be "the basis of a methodical and certain theory

of all the moral sciences".[107]

Elsewhere in his Logique, Tracy gave a similar sketch of the

content of that social science which rested on the foundations of the

moral and economic sciences: on this occasion, he used the term "science

of legislation" rather than "social science".

> Taken in its broadest meaning [legislation] denotes the
> knowledge of the laws which must govern man in all
> circumstances and in all the stages of his life. Thus
> it includes not only the science of the laws which govern
> the interests of individuals, the laws which determine
> the social organization, and those which establish the
> relations of the society with foreign nations: but also
> the science of the laws which must guide children. The
> science of legislation comprises that of government and
> that of education. For government is only the education
> of men, and education is the government of children.
> Except that, in the first case, the main attention is
> given to actions, because they have an immediate effect;
> while in the other case, the main concern is to guide
> sentiments ... [The] goal of the science of legislation
> is to guide [diriger] the sentiments and actions of man ...[108]

The study of positive laws should be related to the science of legislation

in the broad sense. Otherwise, legal studies are only "knowledge of what

is ordered", without consideration of "what should be". It would have

"no theory and no principles", a "simple history of what is".[109]

Tracy never wrote the treatise on political and educational matters, or social science, which would have constituted volume six of the projected nine volumes of the Elémens d'idéologie (see above, p. 91). In abandoning the total project in 1813, after writing the beginnings of his volume on moral sentiments, Tracy wrote:

> I would have left it to the philosophers and legislators to draw consequences from these [foregoing volumes] and to propose the political, civil, moral and penal laws best suited for developing our talents and virtues, for stifling or repressing our bad inclinations , and for assuring our happiness. I would, however, have perhaps ventured to make known my opinions on three important points, in separate pamphlets: namely, religious ideas, the organization of society, and the instruction of youth.[110] This is what would have gone into the third part of the Treatise on the Will, the sixth volume of my Elements of Ideology.[111]

The significant omission from this list of materials relevant to the sixth volume in social science was Tracy's Commentaire sur l'Esprit des Lois. As mentioned earlier (pp. 48-49), Tracy's Commentaire was written in 1806-1807,[112] but could not be published in Napoleonic France because it contained a critique of all forms of illiberal and unrepresentative government. Tracy sent the manuscript to Thomas Jefferson in Virginia, who was sufficiently impressed to undertake an English translation, published anonymously under the title A Commentary and Review of Montesquieu's Spirit of Laws.[113] Tracy's authorship was heavily disguised - Jefferson respected Tracy's wish to be taken for a Frenchman who had fled to America to escape "the tyrannies of the monster Robespierre".[114] Similarly, a French edition of the Commentaire in 1817 remained anonymous. Tracy claimed not to have authorized that edition (printed in Liège and reprinted in Paris two years later). But despite his official disclaimers in his authorized edition in July 1819, the text of the 1817 edition was so close to the original that it was obviously based on a manuscript copy, rather than a retranslation from the American edition.[115] Tracy's edition in July 1819 publicly acknowledged his own name as author. He included

a few notes updating his opinions on some points, but failed to remove

from the text those passages which gave the impression that the author

had been living in America since the Jacobin régime.[116] Tracy noted in

his preface of 1807 that he had begun to make critical remarks on the

important subjects discussed by Montesquieu, and soon realized "that the

collection of these opinions would form a complete treatise on politics,

or social science" if it were correctly and systematically executed.[117]

But Tracy had decided to retain the order of presentation of material in

Montesquieu's classic treatise, in order to do justice to that great

author and facilitate comparisons between Montesquieu's opinions and his

own. So Tracy did not write a systematic work on politics or social

science, though he hoped that the Commentaire would have "contributed

effectively to the advancement of social science, the most important of

all the sciences for the happiness of men,and that which is necessarily

the last to be perfected for it is the result and product of all the

others".[118]

The argument in the Commentaire gives us further evidence about

Tracy's conception of a social science, even though the work is not the

systematic treatise he had once contemplated. Tracy's commentary is

inadequate as an account of Montesquieu's thought; Montesquieu's division

of material simply provides Tracy with a framework for presenting his

own views, with little attention to the finer details of the work he

criticizes. Tracy wants to extract the rational kernel of the Esprit des

Lois, and to ignore the mass of historical detail irrelevant to this

central concern. Very often, Tracy finds nothing of substance in

Montesquieu's discussion of a subject; on other occasions, he asserts

that Montesquieu's categories and explanations are defective and replaces

them with his own conceptions. A major example, discussed below in chapter six, is Tracy's replacement of Montesquieu's tripartite typology of government (monarchy, republic, despotism) by his own two-fold division into governments which uphold the rights of man and those which are based on particularistic forms of privilege.

The Commentaire is in some ways the most historically informed of Tracy's writings, and yet it evidences a view of historical facts which seems to contradict Tracy's professed concern for empirical analysis as against speculative philosophy. A number of later commentators have made this point rather forcefully.

> Destutt de Tracy, in commenting on Montesquieu, discovered that the great historian remained too slavishly grounded in history, and he went about remaking Montesquieu's work by constructing the society that ought to be rather than observing the society that is.[119]

These criticisms suggest that the conception of la science sociale envisaged by Tracy and his colleagues was closer to political philosophy than to a behavioural social science based on observation and the collection of data. The idéologues indulged in a good deal of speculative and deductive reasoning, and, with a few notable exceptions, not much empirical analysis. Moreover, a certain view of history emerges: history is seen to some extent as a moral tale of man's misery, caused by ignorance, superstition, and oppression; followed by man's progressive liberation and redemption through the flowering of reason, which allows man to control nature and to establish social institutions which secure his happiness, prosperity and freedom.[120] Historical data, in this view, is tainted by its association with the dark ages of domination and prejudice; history could thus all the more readily be ignored as a source concerning the patterns of social behaviour.

The idéologues wanted to create a new set of social facts, a new pattern of social organization, to be shaped by an enlightened élite of politicans, administrators, entrepreneurs and educators, in accordance with the rationalist tenets of idéologie. "Social science" was invoked as a set of principles concerned with the perfection of social and political institutions, judged by the criteria of reason, freedom, happiness and justice - which for Tracy were interdependent. Politics, wrote Tracy, is the "science of human happiness".[121] The economic, political and educational content of such principles will be discussed in the last three chapters of this study.

Tracy's discussion of how to establish a rational moral order, and his emphasis on the importance of the general interest, show clear links with the utilitarian stream of political and moral writings. Is it possible that he derived his terminology from Bentham, who clearly also wanted to be a Newton of the science of man? There was a clear overlap of approach and language on many levels, as Tracy's disciple Joseph Rey implied in his writings.[122] It is very unlikely that Tracy was influenced by Bentham, since Tracy did not read English and Bentham's works did not begin to appear in French translation until Etienne Dumont edited and translated some of Bentham's legal writings in 1802. Tracy may have heard about Bentham from Gallois, or indirectly from his reading of other authors. But it seems unnecessary to suggest this, since he shared many ideas with the physiocrats, Helvétius, Beccaria (whose most influential work on crimes and punishments was translated into French in 1766 and was republished many times), and Condorcet (who had experimented with mathematical solutions to the problems of rational calculation of political choices). Tracy's version of utilitarianism is all the more interesting for its critical attitude to quantitative methods in the calculation of individual and public interests or in other aspects of the human sciences.

We have already seen (above, pp. 110-111) that Tracy developed
an early suspicion of arithmetical or algebraic calculations applied to
explain human behaviour. In the first volume of his Elémens d'idéologie
in 1801, Tracy pointed out that quantitative measures were the only forms
of absolute truth, but they could not readily be applied to all types
of phenomena.[123] Aspects of time, space and motion could be measured
with great precision and certainty, even in relation to human beings -
their age, location, volume, weight, etc. could be calculated and compared.
But their other aspects - beauty and goodness, for example - could not be
measured precisely in quantitative terms.[124] The intensity of our desires
could not be measured, Tracy noted in his first mémoire.[125] In the moral
and political sciences

> We have no precise measures to evaluate directly the degrees
> of energy of men's sentiments and inclinations, their goodness
> or their depravity, the degree of utility or danger of their
> actions, the consistency or inconsistency of their opinions.
> That is what makes research in these sciences more difficult
> and their results less rigorous.[126]

However, Tracy continued, it might be possible to make some use of
calculation by measuring opinions, actions and sentiments indirectly,
in terms of their effects. An accurate measurement of these effects
might serve to evaluate the causes. Even in cases where considerable
uncertainty remained, there were boundaries within which one might be
sure of the truth.

> Thus, for example, it may be impossible to determine how
> much more preferable is a particular sentiment or social
> institution over another; but it is impossible not to
> recognize that one leads to absolutely bad results and
> another to absolutely good results; and that is enough
> to stop us saying that these [moral and political] sciences
> are completely uncertain ...   [The degree of certainty of
> all the various sciences] depends on the extent to which
> the objects of each science are reducible to quantities
> measurable by exact units ...[127]

The use of calculus in the various sciences thus depended on whether the
objects could readily be measured in terms of fixed quantitative units.

The use of numbers and calculus in subjects where they were not appropriate was merely a case of charlatanism and bogus scientism.[128]

Tracy returned to some related questions in writing a
"Supplement to the first section of the Elements of Ideology" (1805),
published as an introduction to his Traité de la Volonté (1815). He
included a twenty-page discussion on the "theory of probability"
(developed by Condorcet and Laplace), and on its limited uses in the
human sciences.[129] This theory should not be seen as a separate science
in itself nor a substitute for a sound logical basis of inquiry. The
theory of probability consisted of two parts: (i) the collection and
evaluation of relevant data, and (ii) the calculation or combination of
the data. In the case of historical events, the collection and evaluatio
of data depended on knowledge of the circumstances in question, and of
the authors who had described them - it thus depended on, and was part
of, the science of history.[130]

In the case of examining the probable results of a social
institution or of the deliberations of a political assembly, the relevant
facts are the details of the social organization, and the dispositions and
intellectual operations of these men. Thus, it depended on knowledge of
"social science", morality, or idéologie.[131] The collection and
evaluation of data, then, should be recognized as highly variable,
depending on the subject matter to which the theory of probability is
applied. The calculation itself is simply an application of the science
of quantities, rather than a separate science. The mathematicians who
developed the calculus of probability applied it with great success to
simple fields like games of chance, lotteries, or interest on money -
fields where the choice and evaluation of data presented no difficulties.[1]
But when they tried to apply their theorems to more subtle and complex
areas, their results became distorted by neglecting those considerations

which are not amenable to quantification.

> This is why we have seen great calculators, after the most
> learned combinations, give us forms of voting which are
> quite defective, for they have not taken account of a
> thousand circumstances inherent in the nature of men and
> things, attending only to their numerical circumstances.
> That is why Condorcet himself, when he tried to apply the
> theory of probabilities to the decisions of assemblies
> and especially to the judgements of tribunals, either
> dared not to make any claims about actual institutions,
> limiting himself to reasoning on imaginary hypotheses,
> or was often led to expedients which were absolutely
> impractical or which had inconveniences worse than those
> he sought to avoid.[133]

Condorcet had placed great hopes upon mathematical methods for

the future development of the human sciences, but recognized that much

work remained to be done in perfecting such methods. Tracy argued that

Condorcet's hopes for the utility of a social mathematics could be

realized only by severely restricting the scope of calculus. The theory

of probability is concerned to determine the likely effects of a given

set of causes, or to determine the likely causes of a given set of

effects. Now since only those objects which can be assigned a numerical

or quantitative value can be successfully subjected to calculus, it

follows that there are many objects which cannot be analysed in that

way, even when the data collected is very detailed. Tracy noted the

particular problem of the human sciences.

> Assuredly the degrees of capacity and probity of men, the
> energy and strength of their passions, their prejudices and
> habits, are impossible to evaluate in numbers. The same is
> true of the degree of influence of certain institutions or
> certain functions, the degree of importance of certain est-
> ablishments, the degree of difficulty of certain discoveries,
> and the degree of utility of certain inventions or processes.[134]

If we attempted to determine numerically the "frequency and extent of

their effects", we would not only be obliged to aggregate as similar a

multitude of quite different data, but we would also find it impossible

to "clarify the changes and variations in concurrent causes, influential

circumstances, and a thousand essential considerations".[135]

In order to avoid the pitfalls of a false calculation, it was first necessary to understand which subjects could not properly be subjected to quantitative analysis of this kind.

> It is for the science of the formation of our ideas, the science of the operations of our intelligence, in a word for sound idéologie, to identify these cases, make known their nature, and show us the reasons why they are so refractory. And it will render a great service to the human mind in preventing it in future from making erroneous usage of one of its finest instruments.[136]

Tracy asserted that, despite these limitations, the utility of probability theory in the moral sciences was not entirely destroyed:

> ... for if the various shades of our moral ideas cannot be expressed in numbers, and if there are many other things relative to social science which are equally incapable of being estimated and calculated directly, these phenomena are related to others which often make them reducible to calculable quantities ...[137]

While, for example, the degrees of value we attach to desirable things cannot be directly measured in figures, some objects have other qualities which are calculable or comparable, in terms of their weight, size, etc. And while the energy and durability of our bodily faculties cannot be directly estimated, we can judge them indirectly by their effects.

In the moral sciences, wrote Tracy, many phenomena are susceptible to quantitative calculation, but many are not; the important thing is to discriminate carefully between the two. There are also situations where the facts are an inextricable mixture of types, some refractory and some amenable to calculation, in which case the use of such calculation is likely to produce great distortions.[138] We must be aware, he noted, of "how delicate and subtle is the calculation of all moral and economic quantities, how much precaution it requires, and how imprudent it is to want to apply indiscreetly the rigorous scale of numbers".[139] Where quantitative calculation is inappropriate, we must have recourse to ordinary language for our analysis.[140]

Tracy, despite his sensationalism, had reached an awareness that human actions and feelings were qualitatively different from purely physical phenomena. His philosophy of sensibility, despite materialist nuances, avoided the implication that human behaviour could be ordered and judged by quantitative criteria alone. A felicific calculus alone would remain incomplete, and present a distorted picture of social reality. Nevertheless, Tracy clearly felt that this limitation on the utility of mathematical reasoning was unfortunate for the "scientificity" of the moral and political sciences. While insisting that a great deal of human action and feeling could not be measured, he appeared to regret having to abandon his positivist enthusiasm of 1796: "let us imitate the mathematicians".[141]

Having rejected the mathematized model for social science, what alternatives did Tracy have? He also rejected an historical approach, modelled on perhaps Ferguson or Montesquieu. He also rejected a conservative social theory of the type put forward by Burke, wherein men's reason was embedded in their slowly evolving institutions and habits of thought (rather than exemplified by a capacity for rational critique of that system). For Tracy, the variety exhibited by human societies did not disturb his conception of a single unfolding human nature, the unity amid the diversity. For the philosophes, societies could be "arranged in an 'ideal' series, representing the 'natural order' of the development of mankind. This 'natural order' was accepted as applicable [both] to the progressive stages exhibited in the historical series and to the differences of culture discoverable in the present".[142]

Tracy's starting-point for his science of man and society was his view of human nature: man is a creature of biological and social needs. Finding the correct starting-point, he wrote, is the "most difficult" part of the task.[143] "In order for a single fact to become

the indisputable basis of a vast system, it must be seen to be sufficient
to produce all the observed phenomena".[144]   Tracy's first and general
fact was that man is located in a natural-social world where he begins
with nothing but his needs and capacities, both of which are shaped by
his environment.   Just as an individual's capacities grow, as he acquires
more abilities and understanding, so do those of the human species.
Man begins with nothing but his perfectibility.   History is the unfolding
of his perfectibility.   The science of man attempts to demonstrate how
to maximize his successes or happiness in the economic, cultural and
political realms.   These form the subject of the remaining chapters.

FOOTNOTES TO CHAPTER FOUR

Cf. R. Hubert, Les Sciences sociales dans l'Encyclopédie (Lille, 1923); P. Gay, The Enlightenment, vol. II: "The Science of Freedom", chapter 7; H. Gouhier, La jeunesse d'Auguste Comte, vol. II.

Cf. G. Bryson, Man and Society (Princeton, 1945); D. Kettler, The Social and Political Thought of Adam Ferguson (Columbus, Ohio, 1965); D. Riesman, Adam Smith's Sociological Economics (London, 1976); R. Meek, Social Science and the Ignoble Savage (Cambridge, 1976), chapters 4-6; A. Swingewood, "Origins of Sociology: the case of the Scottish Enlightenment", British Journal of Sociology, vol. 21 (1970), pp. 164-180. On the physiocrats, see G. Weulersse, Le mouvement physiocratique en France de 1756 à 1770, 2 vols. (Paris, 1910); H. Higgs, The Physiocrats (London, 1897); R. Meek, The Economics of Physiocracy (London, 1962); E. Fox-Genovese, The Origins of Physiocracy (New York, 1976).

Marquis de Mirabeau, Leçons économiques (Amsterdam, 1770), pp. xxxi-xxxii.

Ibid., pp. xxxiv-xxxv.

Ibid., pp. ix-xi.

Ibid., pp. xxx-xxxi.

Ibid., p. xlii.

The use of this phrase by Mirabeau and Baudeau was mentioned, without further explanation, by K.M. Baker, "The Early History of the term 'Social Science'", Annals of Science, vol. 20 (1964), p. 215n.16.

Mirabeau, Leçons économiques, p. v.

0 Ibid., pp. vi-vii.

1 Ibid., pp. xii-xiii.

2 Ibid., p. xiii.

3 Ibid., p. iv. See also C.R. Lefure de Beauvray, Dictionnaire social et patriotique, ou précis raisonné de connoissances relatives à l'économie morale, civile et politique (Amsterdam, 1770), pp. 402-407 on perfectibility, and pp. 499-507 on sociability.

4 Baudeau, Première introduction à la philosophie économique, ou analyse des états policés [1771], in Eugène Daire (ed.), Physiocrates, pp. 655-821.

5 Ibid., pp. 658-660.

6 Ibid., p. 663.

7 Ibid., p. 664.

18 Ibid., pp. 664-666, 669, 707, 820.

19 C.-A. Saint-Beuve, "Sieyès", Causeries du lundi (Paris, 1874), vol. V, p. 195.

20 Cf. Roberto Moro, "L'arte sociale e l'idea di società nel pensiero politico di Sieyès", Rivista internazionale di filosofia del diritto, vol. 45 (1968), pp. 226-266; Paul Bastid, Sieyès et sa pensée (Paris, 2e ed. 1970), especially pp. 386-389.

21 Condorcet, Sketch [1793], especially pp. 128, 184, 192.

22 For discussions of the Société de 1789, see J.-B. Challamel, Les Clubs contre-révolutionnaires (Paris, 1895), pp. 391-443; C. Perroud, "Quelques notes sur le Club de 1789", la Révolution française, vol. 39 (1900), pp. 255-262; S. Moravia, Il tramonto dell'illuminismo (Bari, 1968), pp. 152-161; K.M. Baker, "Politics and Social Science in eighteenth-century France: the 'Société de 1789'", in French Government and Society, ed. J.F. Bosher (London, 1973), pp. 208-230.

23 "Règlemens de la Société de 1789", reprinted in Challamel, Les Clubs contre-révolutionnaires, p. 393.

24 Ibid., pp. 392, 393.

25 Ibid., p. 393.

26 Ibid., pp. 393-394.

27 Condorcet, "On the Society of 1789" [1790], in Selected Writings, pp. 92, 93.

28 Tracy and Cabanis appear on the membership list reprinted in Challamel, op.cit., pp. 413, 402.

29 Cabanis, Rapports, in Oeuvres philosophiques, vol. I, p. 126.

30 Cabanis, "Quelques considérations sur l'organisation sociale en général et particulièrement sur la nouvelle constitution", 16 December 1799, in Oeuvres philosophiques, vol. II, especially pp. 464-465, 470, 482. The term also appeared in his Rapports, in ibid., vol. I, p. 160.

31 Elémens, Preface to 1801 edition (3e ed. 1817), p. xxvi; Grammaire [1803] (2e ed. 1817), p. 5; Observations sur l'état actuel de l'instruction publique [1801], in Elémens, 5 vols. (Bruxelles, 1826-1827), vol. IV, p. 347; Commentaire [1806-1807] (Paris, 1819), pp. 233, 387.

32 "Mémoire sur la faculté de penser", p. 287.

33 Elémens, vol. I, p. 213. Tocqueville wrote, many years later, that in the French revolution, "the aim was to establish a social science, a philosophy, I might almost say a religion, fit to be learned and followed by all mankind": Recollections (New York, 1959), p. 75.

34 See Appendix II below. Many of the official documents of this
    period also referred to this section as "science sociale et
    législation".

35 K.M. Baker, "The early history of the term 'social science'", Annals
    of Science, vol. 20 (1964), especially pp. 218-219; Baker, Condorcet
    (Chicago, 1975), p. 391.

36 D.-J. Garat, December 1791, cited in Baker, as above.

37 Baker, "Early History", pp. 219-220.

38 Emananuel-Joseph Sieyès, Qu'est-ce que le Tiers-état? [1789],
    édition critique by Roberto Zapperi (Genève, 1970), p. 151. [Cf.
    the English translation, What is the Third Estate? (London, 1963),
    p. 87.] Sieyès also uses the phrases "science de l'état de société"
    (p. 175: English trans. p. 117) and "l'architecture sociale" (p. 176:
    English trans. p. 118).

39 J.-J. Régis de Cambacérès, "Discours sur la science sociale",
    Mémoires de l'Institut National, Classe des Sciences morales et
    politiques, vol. III (1801), pp. 1-14.

40 Ibid., p. 1.

41 Ibid., p. 3.

42 Ibid., pp. 3-7.

43 Ibid., pp. 8-9.

44 Ibid., p. 10.

45 Ibidem.

46 Ibid., p. 11.

47 Ibid., p. 13.

48 Ibid., p. 12.

49 H.-B. Grégoire, "Réflexions extraites d'un ouvrage ... sur les moyens
    de perfectionner les sciences politiques", Mémoires de l'Institut
    National, Classe des Sciences morales et politiques, vol. I (1798),
    pp. 553-555.

50 Ibid., p. 554.

51 Ibid., p. 555. These two principles were also identified by Cabanis
    in December 1799 as two of the great triumphs of the social art:
    Oeuvres philosophiques, vol. II, p. 470.

52 Grégoire, "Réflexions", pp. 555, 556.

53 Ibid., p. 557.

54 Ibid., p. 558.

55   Ibid., p. 560.

56   Ibid., p. 563-565.

57   Cf. S. Moravia, "Philosophie et Médecine ...", Studies on Voltaire and the Eighteenth Century, vol. 89 (1972), pp. 1089-1151; Moravia, La scienza dell'uomo nel settecento (Bari, 1970); Moravia, Il pensiero degli idéologues (Firenze, 1974), parts 3 and 4: G. Gusdorf, Introduction aux sciences humaines (Paris, 1960), Part 4.

58   Cited in Mignet, "Notice historique sur ... M. Destutt de Tracy", p. 258.

59   "Mémoire sur la faculté de penser", pp. 285-286.

60   Ibid., p. 288.

61   Ibid., pp. 318-319; "Dissertation sur quelques questions d'idéologie" p. 493.

62   "Mémoire sur la faculté de penser", p. 320.

63   D. Reisman, Adam Smith's Sociological Economics, p. 38.

64   Saint-Beuve, "Sieyès", p. 196. E. Dumont, the collaborator of Mirabeau and of Bentham, reported Sieyès' claim to have perfected the science of politics: Recollections of Mirabeau ... (London, 1832), p. 53n.

65   Cited in W.M. Simon (ed.), French Liberalism 1789-1848 (London, 1972), pp. 61-63.

66   Condillac, Oeuvres philosophiques, vol. I, p. 117.

67   "Mémoire sur la faculté de penser", p. 288.

68   Ibid., p. 318.

69   J. Lakanal, 23 October 1794, in Hippeau (ed.), L'instruction publique ... (1881), p. 416.

70   Ibid., pp. 416-417. Paul Dupuy suggests that this speech was largely the work of Garat, though delivered by Lakanal: Le Centenaire de l'Ecole Normale (Paris, 1895), pp. 54-71.

71   Cabanis, "Quelques considérations", in Oeuvres philosophiques, vol. II, p. 466. Condorcet's Esquisse was also a powerful source of faith in the certainty and progress of the human sciences: cf. Sketch, pp. 133, 173, 185-186.

72   "Mémoire sur la faculté de penser", pp. 387-388.

73   "Quels sont les moyens", in Commentaire, pp. 459-460, 473.

74   "Mémoire sur la faculté de penser", p. 389.

75   Cf. Condorcet, Sketch, 9th stage, p. 128.

76   "Mémoire sur la faculté de penser", p. 390; cf. p. 286. That the sciences were to be seen as "useful" was also assumed by Condillac: Oeuvres philosophiques, vol. II, pp. 234-235.

77   "Mémoire sur la faculté de penser", pp. 391-392.

78   Reprinted in A. Duruy, L'instruction publique et la Révolution (Paris, 1882), pp. 433-448; and in Tracy, Elémens d'idéologie, 5 vols. (Paris, 1824-1825), vol. IV, pp. 268-289; and ibid., 5 vols. (Bruxelles, 1826-1827), vol. IV, pp. 262-283.

79   Duruy, op.cit., pp. 439-440.

80   Ibid., p. 441.

81   Ibidem.

82   Ibid., p. 442.

83   Ibid., p. 441.

84   Ibid., p. 443.

85   Cf. the memorandum cited by Duruy, p. 232, where an unfortunate teacher was criticized for failing to use a utilitarian and sensationalist theory of morality.

86   Ibid., p. 433.

87   Daunou, 19 October 1795, in Hippeau (ed.), L'instruction publique ... (1881), p. 479: "freedom of domestic education, freedom of private establishments of instruction ... freedom of teaching methods".

88   Duruy, op.cit., p. 434. Recommended authors included Dupuis, Chastellux, Ferguson, Voltaire, Condillac and Goguet (ibid., p. 438).

89   Ibid., p. 435.

90   Ibidem.

91   Ibid., p. 293.

92   Volney's Ruines (1791) and Loi naturelle (1793) were highly rational-ist; but his Leçons d'histoire (1795) has been called the first attempt to apply objective methods to the study of the human sciences: J. Gaulmier, "Volney et ses 'leçons d'histoire'", History and Theory, vol. 2 (1962), p. 65.

93   Daunou attained a considerable reputation as an historian after 1819 when he took a chair in history at the Collège de France. See his Discours d'ouverture ... (Paris, 1819), and the remarks by A.G. Lehmann, "Sainte-Beuve and the Historical Movement", in The French Mind, ed. Moore et al. (Oxford, 1952), pp. 259-260. For a more detailed and hostile view, see B. Plongeron, "Nature, Méta-physique et Histoire chez les Idéologues", Dix-huitième siècle, no. 5 (1973), pp. 375-412.

94 Cf. the remarks by Sieyès in Saint-Beuve, "Sieyès", pp. 193-194, and Bastid, Sieyès et sa pensée, pp. 386, 388.

95 Observations sur l'état actuel de l'instruction publique [1801], in Elémens d'idéologie, 5 vols. (Bruxelles, 1826-1827), vol. IV, p. 346

96 Ibid., p. 347.

97 Ibidem.

98 Ibid., p. 362.

99 Ibidem.

100 Analyse (1804), pp. i, x.

101 Cabanis, Rapports (1830 ed.), vol. I, p. 23 ("Table Analytique" by Tracy).

102 Logique (1805), p. 438.

103 Ibid., pp. 438-439.

104 Ibid., pp. 441-442.

105 Ibid., p. 442.

106 Ibid., p. 443 (emphasis added).

107 Ibid., p. 444.

108 Ibid., pp. 393-394.

109 Ibid., p. 395.

110 This is an obvious reference to Tracy's Analyse of Dupuis, his Quels sont les moyens ..., and his Observations.

111 Traité de la Volonté (1818 ed.), pp. 522-523. Tracy used the term social science in the Traité, p. 279 (1818 ed.), and pp. 33, 44 (1815 ed.).

112 Evidence for the date of composition appears in the text itself, pp. v, 65n, 91. See also Cabanis' letter to Maine de Biran, 8 April 1807, in Maine de Biran, Oeuvres philosophiques, vol. VII (Paris, 1930), p. 225. Cf. Lafayette, Mémoires, V, p. 288.

113 Philadelphia, 1811. On the events surrounding the American publication, from Tracy's sending the manuscript in June 1809, see G. Chinard, Jefferson et les idéologues, chapter 2, esp. pp. 43ff.

114 Commentary (1811), p. 1. That Jefferson himself wrote this prefatory letter by "the author to his fellow citizens" of the U.S.A., is shown in Chinard, op.cit., pp. 62-63.

115 This is further shown by Tracy's letter to Jefferson, 11 April 1818, in Chinard, op.cit., p. 180.

116 Cf. Commentaire (1819), p. 168n.

117 Ibid., p. vii. In a letter to Jefferson of 4 February 1816, Tracy
acknowledged that the Commentaire, together with his Observations
on education, contained "the germ of all my ideas on legislation":
Chinard, op.cit., pp. 165-166.

118 Commentaire, p. viii. The term science sociale was also used on
pp. 166, 187, 223, 224, 226, 237, 280.

119 H. Taine, Les origines de la France contemporaine, vol. I ("1'Ancien
Régime"), p. 264. For similar remarks, cf. Georges Sorel, The
Illusions of Progress [1908], (Berkeley, 1972), p. 96; Mignet,
"Notice historique sur ... M. Destutt de Tracy", p. 277; Guillois,
Le salon de Mme Helvétius, p. 104; G. Elton, The Revolutionary Idea
in France (London, 1923), pp. 28-30.

120 See especially Condorcet's Esquisse; Cabanis' "Lettre sur ... la
perfectibilité", in Oeuvres philosophiques, vol. II, pp. 512-519;
Cabanis in le Conservateur, 30 September 1797, pp. 236-238:
"Sciences, philosophie". Tracy noted in his Discours of December
1808 that Cabanis at the time of his death had been planning a
major synthetic study demonstrating the means available for the
improvement of man (pp. 19-20).

121 Commentaire, p. 308.

122 J. Rey, Traité des principes généraux du droit et de la législation
(Paris, 1828); Théorie et pratique de la science sociale (Paris,
1842).

123 Elémens, vol. I, p. 194. (Cf. Condorcet, Sketch, pp. 181, 190-191,
and Condillac, Art de penser, in Oeuvres philosophiques, vol. I,
p. 768.)

124 Ibid., p. 195.

125 "Mémoire sur la faculté de penser", p. 380.

126 Elémens, vol. I, pp. 198-199. Tracy noted the inherent variability
of our moral ideas in Principes logiques (Elémens, 5 vols., 1826-27,
p. 246).

127 Elémens, vol. I, pp. 199-200. Tracy later followed Cabanis in
describing moral certainties in terms of probabilities, a lesser
degree of certainty than in the mathematical sciences (Discours,
December 1808, p. 14).

128 Elémens, vol. I, p. 200n-203.

129 Cf. Traité de la Volonté (1815), pp. 30-50.

130 Ibid., p. 33.

131 Ibid., pp. 33-34.

132 Ibid., p. 36.

133 Ibid., pp. 37-38. The works of Condorcet to which Tracy refers are the Essai sur l'application de l'analyse à la probabilité des décisions rendues à la pluralité des voix (1785), and the posthumous work Eléments du calcul des probabilités et son application aux jeux de hasard, à la loterie et aux jugements des hommes (1805). For discussion of Condorcet's views on "social arithmetic", cf. K.M. Baker, Condorcet, pp. 167ff, 330ff; G.-G. Granger, La mathématique sociale du marquis de Condorcet (Paris, 1956); C.C. Gillispi "Probability and Politics", Proceedings of the American Philosophica Society, vol. 116 (1972), pp. 1-20.

134 Traité de la Volonté, p. 41.

135 Ibid., p. 42.

136 Ibid., pp. 43-44.

137 Ibid., p. 44.

138 Ibid., pp. 45-46, 48-49.

139 Ibid., pp. 106-107.

140 Ibid., p. 47.

141 "Mémoire sur la faculté de penser", p. 288.

142 F.J. Teggart, Theory and Processes of History (Berkeley, 1960), p. 9

143 "Dissertation sur quelques questions d'idéologie", p. 512.

144 Ibid., p. 493.

CHAPTER FIVE

ECONOMICS: THE SCIENCE OF "INDUSTRIE"

I   Wealth and "industrie"

II   Economic classes

III The problem of inequality

I.   WEALTH AND "INDUSTRIE"

Economics, in Tracy's theory, is the science which studies "the effects and consequences of our actions considered as means to provide for our needs of all types, from the most material to the most intellectual".[1]   Economic science then, should be distinguished from its etymological meaning of household management, and from its common meaning of carefully managing the goods in one's possession.   The term "political economy" generally meant "the science of the formation and administration of the wealth of a political society".[2]   It is true, wrote Tracy, that the science named - somewhat improperly - political economy has discovered "some important truths on the effects of property, industry and the causes which favour or hinder the formation and growth of wealth".   But economics really should go back to the origin of our needs and of our power to act, for it is really the study of "the history of the use of our powers for the satisfaction of our needs".[3]   (As if to express his dissatisfaction with the term "political economy", Tracy sometimes used the term "social economy"; however, his work was republished in 1823 under the title Traité d'économie politique.)

Tracy's approach to economic theory is based on his view of man as a desiring and sentient being, whose actions consist in attempting to satisfy his needs or wants - material, social, intellectual. The concept of wealth is accordingly related by Tracy to this conception of man: "to be rich is to possess means for satisfying one's needs, and to be poor is to lack such means".[4]   Something is useful or desirable, and thus an object of wealth, only by virtue of contributing in some way to the satisfaction of a need or desire.   Without such desiring, the notion of possessing sufficient or insufficient means

would not arise. The things which we regard as our riches, our means
of satisfying our desires, do not consist only of physical objects
such as precious stones, metals, landed property, a utensil, a
dwelling, or a stock of food, as the physiocrats had implied.

> The knowledge of a law of nature; the habitual use of a
> technical process; the use of a language to communicate
> with our fellows and increase our powers by theirs, or
> at least not to be disturbed by theirs in the exercise
> of our own; the enjoyment of conventions made and
> institutions created in this spirit; these too, are riches
> for the individual and the species, for they are things
> useful towards increasing our means, ... and with the
> least possible obstacles, whether on the part of men or
> of nature, which is to increase their power, their energy
> and their effect.[5]

All such things which contribute to our well-being we call
our "goods". These goods arise from the proper employment of our
faculties, in accordance with the laws of nature. It is only by
intelligent and careful application of our labour and energy to the
materials at hand that we can find precious stones, make use of
metals, produce crops, or fabricate a dwelling or a utensil.[6] Our
original wealth and possessions consist simply in our physical and
intellectual faculties. All our subsequent goods stem from the
active application of these faculties to the satisfaction of our needs,
and the value they have for us is created through our labours.[7] At
this point, Tracy attempted to "deduce" the labour theory of value
from his premise of man as a desiring and acting being. Given that
our physical and moral faculties are our only original wealth, and
that the use of these faculties (work or labour) is necessary to
obtain all our goods, it followed, wrote Tracy, that the value of
these goods arises from the labour involved.[8]

But labour itself has two kinds of value: "natural" and
"conventional". The first, "natural and necessary" value, is
measured by the amount of labour necessary to provide for the

individual's basic needs of survival (whether he satisfies his own needs directly, or whether he labours for another in return for goods sufficient to satisfy these needs). This is the minimum necessary cost of labour, that which furnishes the subsistence of the individual labourer.[9] The second form of value is "contingent", generally "conventional", and much more "variable" than the first; it stems from the value of what is produced, rather than from the costs of sustaining the producer(s). The price of labour is agreed upon between contracting parties at the time. Moreover, it also depends on the wants and means of the employer who profits by it, rather than simply on the basic needs of the labourer himself.[10] Tracy allows, however, that not even the "natural" value of labour is entirely fixed and invariable. On the one hand, there is some variation in determining which needs are regarded as basic and indispensable in a given time and place, "and the flexibility of our nature is such that these needs are restrained or extended considerably by the influence of the will and the effect of habit".[11] On the other hand, favourable circumstances of climate and soil will allow basic needs to be satisfied more rapidly or by a smaller amount of labour; whereas in unfavourable circumstances, the amount of necessary labour will increase.

Tracy's emphasis on the role of individual and social labour in the production of wealth or enjoyments, was developed in opposition to the physiocratic theory of production. Tracy's concept of the desiring and acting self appeared to be incompatible with the physio-cratic view that man's wealth was anchored in his dependence on rural production. In the same way, Tracy's emphasis on the importance of individual rights and education became incompatible at the political level with the physiocratic defence of a strong centralized monarchy to implement their economic doctrines. It is necessary to sketch

the main lines of the debate between the defenders of physiocratic
orthodoxy and its critics. The main point at issue concerned what
should be called "productive" activities. The older doctrines were
overthrown by a new version of the labour theory of value.

The idea that labour, applied to the raw materials supplied
by nature, is the source or cause of wealth and enjoyments has had a
long history, beginning with isolated remarks by the ancient
philosophers and proceeding to a fuller development during the
Renaissance. By the seventeenth century, many writers were under-
lining the connections between labour and wealth.[12] With Locke, the
labour theory had been associated with a moral justification for
property rights - one has a natural right to hold property by virtue
of one's labour embodied in such property.[13] But the labour theory
of value which emerged towards the end of the eighteenth century was
quite distinctive, insofar as it assumed social conditions in which
labour was freely available for purchase on the open market, and in
which wages were seen as part of the cost of production of goods. In
the writings of Adam Smith, the labour theory had become generalized
into the notion that a society has an aggregate fund of labour which
may be used in various ways to produce a range of useful goods and
services, whose quantity depends on the availability of skills and
on the proportion of people engaged in useful labour.[14] A full understanding of Tracy's views requires an outline of the physiocratic
outlook and the new doctrines formulated by Smith and J.-B. Say.

The physiocratic viewpoint developed largely as a critique
of mercantilist doctrines, which had stressed that a nation without
its own gold or silver mines should attempt to increase its national
wealth by accumulating precious metals by means of a favourable trade
balance, promoting exports and restricting imports as necessary.[15]

preoccupation with a bullionist conception of wealth and its

lary of a permanently favourable balance of trade, were rejected

e physiocrats, who argued that the wealth of a society consists

tially in useful goods, not in money itself, which is merely

ium of exchange. But the physiocratic conception of wealth was

f restrictive, arguing that the only "productive" activities were

which resulted in a material surplus (produit net), and that

ulture was the fundamental producer of such goods. Manufacture

ommerce were "useful" and "necessary", but were not genuinely

uctive". Investment in agriculture, and the use of efficient

-scale techniques, were the best ways to increase national wealth;

urplus output could be traded externally for goods which were too

cult or costly to produce domestically. Physiocracy thus had a

y of economic growth, and definite policy implications for govern-

- whatever assisted agricultural investment and output should be

raged; whatever diminished such investment should be discouraged.[16]

Society was divided by the physiocrats into three broad classes.

t, the productive are those who are engaged in agriculture, fishing

ining - though the primary emphasis is on the agricultural

epreneur rather than the labourers in the fields. Second, the

ile or unproductive, including manufacturers, artisans, merchants,

essional men, and their servants: those who fail to produce a net

lus above their expenses (wages and profits are held to be included

uch expenses). Third, the proprietary class which consists of

owners, and others supported directly from the taxation levied on

rietary revenue (including the monarch and those who perform public

tions in Church and State).[17] The growth of the public sector had

e limited for two main reasons: firstly, the physiocratic philosophy

ree trade was inimical to a high level of government regulation of economic life. Secondly, since public expenditure had to be funded from taxation paid by the landed proprietors, a growing public expenditure would have to be met by rising taxes which would divert funds from agricultural investment.

The physiocratic outlook also assumed that society should reflect a natural order. "Political economy" was a quest for the natural laws of economic life. Government should follow these natural laws as far as possible - to flout them was to court economic and social disaster.[18] The natural order conception of economy and government was supplemented, however, by a psychological theory of wants and their satisfaction, a theory which was developed more fully by other writers (including Condillac in 1776), and underlay the utilitarian and post-Smithian political economy.

Smith and J.-B. Say began with the proposition that agricultural manufacturing and commercial activities are equally productive of wealth; hence, the special status accorded to agriculture in the physiocratic doctrine was unjustifiable.[19] But although Smith agreed that all goods and services having an exchange value or market price contributed to aggregate national wealth, he qualified this view by drawing a distinction between "productive" and "unproductive" labour, as between the labour of an artisan (who fabricates an object which can be sold) and that of a domestic servant (whose services, though deserving payment, "seldom leave any trace or value behind them").[20] For J.-B. Say, however, the notion of productive labour may be extended to include even the philosopher.[21]

Smith was largely responsible for the classical labour theory of value, distinguishing between use-value and exchange-value in a commodity, and regarding market price as determined primarily by the quantity of social labour embodied in the commodity.[22] Say was somewhat critical of this labour theory of value, regarding it as a one-sided response to the physiocratic doctrine that value is conferred only by the raw materials won in the agricultural and extractive industries, i.e. that values are conferred essentially by nature rather than by labour. For Say, value is conferred by some combination of labour, capital, and natural resources and powers.[23] Value, for Say, can only be determined by market exchanges. Underlying market prices, however, is the fact that goods can "satisfy the various wants of mankind" and this constitutes their utility. For Say, the production of wealth is the creation of utilities. But Say left aside the issue of whether market price reflects the actual utility of goods, save for his remark that the two measures will tend to coincide in proportion to the liberty of production and commerce.[24]

Tracy followed closely in the "classical" tradition which followed the overthrow of physiocracy. Writing in about 1810, Tracy noted that some fine works of political economy had been produced by Turgot and Smith, but "no-one has shed more light on the subject than Mr. Say, the author of the best work I know on these matters."[25] According to Tracy, not even Smith and Say had been sufficiently rigorous in excluding all traces of physiocratic thought from their own superior systems.[26] However, Tracy willingly follows them in their conception of production in terms of utilities.

> What, then, do we do in our work, in our action on the things
> around us? Nothing but effect changes in their form or place,
> making them useful for the satisfaction of our needs. That is
> what we should understand by to produce; it is to give things
> a utility they did not have. Whatever our work, if it does
> not result in utility it is fruitless; if it does so, it is
> productive.[27]

Tracy therefore mounted a sustained attack on the physiocratic conception of the sole productivity of primary industry. It is "an illusion", he wrote, to believe that producing primary goods is more productive than their subsequent fabrication or transportation. The

sowing of seed to produce crops is no more creative than producing

flour and bread from wheat, or producing cloth from hemp. "In both

cases, there is a production of utility, for all these tasks are equally

necessary to fulfil the desired end, the satisfaction of some of our

needs". In the same way, the man who nets fish is no more creative

than he who dries or salts the catch, or takes the produce to market;

and the man who digs in mines is similarly placed to he who smelts the

metals, makes tools, or takes them to those who require them. "Each

one adds a new utility to that already produced; consequently, each is

equally a producer".[28]

The primary producer, the manufacturer and the merchant all must

study the laws and the forces governing the objects of their activities,

to turn them to the desired effect. "It is wrong, then, to have regarded

agricultural industry as essentially different from all other branches

of human industry, where the action of nature intervened in a unique

manner."[29] Moreover, the very attempt to specify which activities

should be included in that category of agricultural industry

has always remained obscure. If one includes fishing and hunting,

why not herding animals? If one includes the collection of salt from

lakes dried by the sun, why not the production of salt by chemical and

mechanical methods? If one includes the mining of ore, why not the

extraction of the metal from the ore in refining? At what stage in the

process of transformation does one draw a line between producing and

fashioning? How shall we classify those who collect wood in forests,

or peat from the fields: are they agriculturalists, fabricators or

carriers?[30] To take cultivation in the strict sense, who is the true

producer: he who sows or he who harvests? he who ploughs or he who

fences? he who fertilizes the field, or he who shepherds the flocks?

According to Tracy, they are all workmen who concur in the same productive process.

These confusions and mysteries arose from the falsity of the theoretical principle of the économistes. They were poor metaphysicians, who had not understood the nature of man, especially his intellectual faculties; and not seen that labour is our sole original wealth. They were led into many errors by their "false idea of a sort of magical virtue attributed to the land."[31]

> The truth is simply that all our useful labours are productive, and those relating to agriculture are the same [in all respects] ... A farm is a real manufactory; everything there operates in the same way, by the same principles and for the same end. A field is a veritable tool, or a store of first materials if you will ... In every case it is an instrument necessary to produce a desired effect, just like a furnace, or a hammer, or a vessel.[32]

Tracy conceded that primary industry in the most general sense was the most necessary activity and came first in time, since a thing must be procured before it can be used. But that did not mean it was uniquely productive, for most of its products still had to be worked up to become useful things. On the other hand, taking agricultural industry in a narrow sense, it did not come first in time (since men were hunters, fishermen and shepherds before farmers), nor was it the sole source of primary materials; it remained very important for our subsistence, but could not be regarded as uniquely productive. In short, agriculture "is a branch of manufacturing industry", and has no distinctive character which separates it from other industries.[33] "Let us conclude that all useful work is truly productive, and that all the labouring class [la classe laborieuse] of society equally deserve the name productive."[34]

In a neat reversal of the physiocratic doctrine, in which the unproductive or sterile class were mainly occupied in manufacturing and commerce, Tracy condemned as passive and sterile the landed proprietors

and other wealthy investors who were not actively seeking to increase

production. It is a criticism found in the opening pages of Sieyès'

celebration of the Third Estate as the truly productive class,[35] and a

doctrine taken up vigorously by Saint-Simon and the advocates of

industrialisme.[36]

> The truly sterile class is that of the idle, who do
> nothing but live nobly, as it is termed, on the product
> of labours undertaken before them, whether this product
> is realized in landed estates which they lease or rent
> to a labourer, or whether it consists of money or effects
> which they lend for a premium, which is still leasing.
> They are the real frelons de la ruche ...[37]

According to Tracy, the labouring class, which directly

produces all wealth, may be divided naturally into two groups: the

manufacturers (including agriculturalists) who fabricate and fashion

things; and the merchants, who transport them (for the utility of

merchants consists in making goods available where they are wanted,

otherwise they would only be parasitic speculators).[38] It is not clear

from this division where Tracy wished to classify the professions, who

neither fabricate objects, nor transport them, but provide services

which he regarded as of immense importance for social progress.

Production is extremely varied, for there are many different

kinds of "utility", some more solid and real than others. A thing may

be termed "useful" if it is capable of procuring any advantage, even a

frivolous pleasure - for what we desire is to multiply our enjoyments

and diminish our sufferings. These utilities can be graded in terms of

how strongly we desire the object, and this degree of desire may be

measured in terms of the sacrifices we are prepared to make to obtain

the object. If I am willing to give three measures of wheat for one

object and twelve measures of wheat for a different object, it follows

that I desire the second four times as much as the first.[39] Or even if

I personally do not estimate their relative value in this way, I could not obtain them more cheaply, and that is the value generally attached

to them. Market price is the real measure of value.

> In the state of society, which is nothing but a continual
> series of exchanges, the values of all the products of our
> industry are determined in this way. This fixation, no
> doubt, is not always founded on very good reasons; we are
> often poor judges of the real merit of things; but, in
> relation to wealth, their value is none the less that
> assigned by general opinion. It may be thus seen,
> incidentally, that the greatest producer is he who per-
> forms the most expensive type of labour, no matter if it
> be a branch of agricultural, manufacturing or commercial
> industry...[40]

Tracy, as we saw earlier (p.252), subscribed to the labour

theory of value, on the grounds that labour - our physical and intellectual

capacity - is our only method of creating utilities or satisfying our

wants. Echoing the Lockean viewpoint, Tracy claimed that goods become

the property of a person only "because he has previously applied some

kind of labour, whose fruit is assured to him by social conventions".[41]

In obtaining such goods by exchange, we are in effect paying for the owner's

past labour, without which the goods would have no value. This

"natural and necessary" value of labour "is the sum of indispensable

needs whose satisfaction is necessary to the existence of he who executes

the labour during the time he is working".[42] However, the "natural"

values have little influence in modern market societies, in Tracy's

view; hence the distinction between natural and conventional value is

of little practical importance. There is no guarantee that the

"natural" price of labour, in terms of the subsistence needs of the

labourer, will be met. Tracy places the weight of his theory of value

upon market prices:

> But here, where we speak of the value resulting from the
> free transactions of society, it is clearly a matter of
> the conventional and market value, that which general
> opinion attaches to things, rightly or wrongly. If it
> [the price of labour] is less than the wants of the
> labourer, he must devote himself to another industry or
> perish; if it is exactly equal to his wants, he subsists

with difficulty; if it is greater, he becomes rich,
provided however he is economical. In all cases, this
conventional and market value is the real one in relation
to wealth; it is the true measure of the utility of production, since it fixes its price.[43]

The actual determination of market price is not simply the
abstract reflection of individual opinions about the value of an object.
In other words, it is not a simple average of individual estimates. It
depends on market conditions of supply and demand, or the relative needs
and means of producer and consumer, buyer and seller. Market price
depends on variable circumstances, and "the equilibrium of resistance
between sellers and buyers."[44] This depends in turn on a host of
factors, including the relative scarcity of goods in demand and the
ability of purchasers to pay a given level of prices.[45]

Tracy concludes his discussion of the value of labour by
pointing to the historical importance of advances in productivity per
unit of labour as a result of improved technology. For example, the
invention of a machine which can manufacture in one day three times as
many commodities as could a single craftsman, will boost the available
social stock of goods and decrease the average cost per unit of output.
However, the individual's income as a machine-operator is unlikely to
be higher than his former income as a craftsman. This new technology
is not "more productive" for that individual than previously, since
his income remains constant, but it will be more productive for
society taken as a whole, since the commodities are produced more
cheaply. The consumers, who are the mass of the population, are the
main beneficiaries of technical progress and the division of labour.

That is the great advantage of civilized and enlightened
society - everyone finds himself better provided in every
way, with fewer sacrifices, because the labourers produce
a greater mass of utility in the same time.[46]

That is the reason, wrote Tracy, why the standard of living

of the poor classes in various historical periods should not be measured solely by the relation between a day's wages and the price of grain. Though bread may be the most important expense of the poor labourer, he also has other needs which may be better satisfied even when his ability to buy bread remains constant.

> If the arts have made progress, he may be better lodged,
> better clothed, and have better drink for the same price.
> If society is better regulated, he may find a more constant
> employment for his labour, and be more certain of not
> being troubled in the possession of what he has gained.
> ... [But] the elements of this calculus are so numerous
> that it is very difficult, and perhaps impossible, to make
> it directly.[47]

Tracy concluded that labour or industry is the fundamental "source of all our joys and riches",[48] and the means by which historical progress has been achieved.

> Our manner of living is completely artificial. We owe
> to nature, that is, to our organization, nothing but our
> sensibility and our perfectibility: we owe all the rest
> to our industry.[49]

But this emphasis on "industry" should not be confused with the later development of "industrial capitalism" or "industrial society", typified by machine production.[50] France at the beginning of the nineteenth century was still a largely agricultural society, with very few centres of machine manufacture. The concept of an industrial revolution did not emerge until the 1820's. Moreover, many of the families who profited from manufacture and commerce used their wealth to acquire noble offices and the attendant prestige of the landed proprietors.[51] The debate between the defenders of physiocratic orthodoxy - urging the political and economic dominance of landed wealth - and the champions of the labour theory of value was by no means resolved in a political way by the events of the Revolution. The Dictionnaire de la Constitution Française (1791),[52] the writings of Germain Garnier,[53] and even some members of the Class of moral and political sciences under the Directory,[54] continued to uphold the primary position of landed property in opposition to the mobile capital of the entrepreneur and merchant.

One policy upon which both theories could agree was the doctrine of freedom from government regulation[55] - free trade, internally and externally; the abolition of corporative privileges and monopolies; allowing market forces to determine the costs and opportunities for each sector of the economy. This was the "liberal" element in Tracy's economic theory: industry should be free from "artificial" or institutional restraints. Freedom of industry and commerce was the best way to ensure economic growth and progress. This was the main contribution of economics to the social science of happiness.

> Economic science is a major part of social science; it is
> even its goal insofar as we desire that society is well
> organized only because enjoyments [moral and material] are
> thereby more numerous, more complete and more peaceful ...[56]

In assuming an inter-relationship between wealth, happiness, and freedom of industry and commerce, Tracy was in accord with the notion of "commercial society" which had been developed by numerous writers in the second half of the eighteenth century. In the Philosophie Rurale (1763) of Mirabeau and Quesnay, four kinds of societies were identified, in accordance with their different "modes of life" or socio-economic organization: hunting, pastoral, agricultural and commercial.[57] For the physiocrats, the wealthy commercial societies were seen to develop alongside the agricultural, in an international division of labour. For Smith and his successors, however, commercial societies were a more advanced type in the evolutionary pattern, destined to supersede the agricultural societies, and promising a level of abundance far beyond that of previous social forms.[58] At the Institut, the evolutionary pattern was firmly endorsed, as in the paper read by Lévesque in February 1796 contrasting the opportunities for progress and civilization in urban life (la vie policée) with the prior stages of savage and pastoral societies.[59] For Tracy, the "perfection of society", from an economic viewpoint, would be "to increase greatly our wealth while avoiding the extremes of inequality."[60] The physiocrats had also believed in the policy imperative of increasing abundance; the difference was that Tracy believed that further social wealth could not be expected from agriculture alone.

The new economic order which he saw gradually emerging in the last quarter of the eighteenth century involved a new class structure and division of labour. Production was not a process to which everyone contributed in the same way, nor from which all benefited to the same degree. The remaining sections of this chapter take up the question of economic classes and Tracy's analysis of the problems of inequality.

II. ECONOMIC CLASSES

Tracy's critique of the physiocratic doctrine was developed on two levels. The first was a disagreement about the proper definition of "productive" activity. The second and related theme, which has not been sufficiently recognized by previous commentators, concerned the degree of economic and political importance which should be attributed to the "proprietary" class. Tracy did not disagree with the physiocrats' view that the tenant-farmers who were directly responsible for agricultural production were genuinely "productive": he merely wanted to extend this concept to other branches of activity, to those occupations in manufacture, commerce and services which had been called "sterile" industries by the physiocrats. As we have seen, Tracy's criterion of production was that of utility, as determined by market prices, instead of the physiocratic concept of an agricultural surplus.

Secondly, Tracy sharply criticized what he saw as the physiocrats' exaggeration of the economic and political importance of the "proprietary" class. In the physiocratic theory, this class contained a somewhat heterogeneous group of economic functions: (i) the owners of rural estates, who leased their lands to tenant-farmers in return for some form of rent; (ii) the sovereign authority of the nation, responsible for law and order; (iii) servants of the sovereign, engaged in public instruction, defence or administration of the realm. The latter two groups were supported from revenues derived from taxes paid by the landowners. According to Baudeau, whose explanation of the proprietary class was quite detailed, it could also be called "the class of nobles".[61] The identification of the proprietor with the nobility (and additionally with the monarchy and the ecclesiastics) raised grave doubts concerning the legitimacy of the proprietary class in the eyes of the liberals after 1789.

As Tracy wrote, the proprietary class were the idle (<u>les oisifs</u>) "who do nothing but live nobly, as it is termed, on the product of labours undertaken before them".[62] Here was the germ of a theory of exploitation: the idle landowners were seen as an unproductive and parasitical class, who themselves performed no important productive functions but retained an economic surplus in the form of rents. As will be seen later, however, Tracy does not develop the radical possibilities of such a theory; he rather urges that landowners use their capital in a more enterprising way, taking up active entre-preneurial functions instead of passive <u>rentier</u> functions. The present section discusses the implications of the differences which Tracy recognized between the economic roles and incomes accruing to land-owners, entrepreneurs, and labourers. It is first necessary to note some of the revisions in the physiocratic theory of economic classes made by economic thinkers after 1776, when Condillac's work on commerce and government[63] appeared at the same time as Smith's <u>Wealth of Nations</u>.

Unlike the three-class model of the physiocrats, Condillac had recognized only two major economic classes: the landed proprietors living on rents; and the <u>salariés</u>, among whom he grouped the entre-preneurial farmers who leased the lands of the proprietors, as well as the labourers who were employed by these farmers.[64] Condillac denied that the <u>salariés</u> were unproductive workers, for they added to the value of goods or provided valuable services.[65] Similarly, in the works of Adam Smith, classical political economy rejected the unique qualities attributed by the physiocrats to ownership of agri-cultural land, and attempted to show how land, labour and capital are inextricably united in the production of wealth. For Smith,

> The whole annual produce of the land and labour of every country ... naturally divides itself ... into three parts;

the rent of land, the wages of labour, and the profits of stock; and constitutes a revenue to three different orders of people; to those who live by rent, to those who live by wages, and to those who live by profit. These are the three great, original, and constituent orders of every civilized society, from whose revenue that of every other order is ultimately derived.[66]

In the same way, J.-B. Say noted crucial differences in the functional roles and sources of income of landed proprietors (rent), labourers (wages), and capitalist entrepreneurs (profits). It was sometimes possible, according to Say, for a single individual to combine the roles of proprietor, labourer, and capitalist in certain circumstances; but usually the roles were divided among three functionally distinct classes of society.[67] In the writings of Say and Tracy, a particular emphasis was given to the active role of the entrepreneur in initiating profitable productive activities, by contrast to the passive role of the landowner or investor whose income (rent or interest) is essentially a return on idle capital.

For Say, all productive activity may be seen to involve three operations or aspects: knowledge of the properties of phenomena and the laws governing them; application of this knowledge to a useful purpose; and the manual labour required to execute the task.

> These three operations are seldom performed by one and the same person. It commonly happens that one man studies the laws and conduct of nature, that is to say, the philosopher or man of science; of whose knowledge another avails himself to create useful products, being either agriculturalist, manufacturer or trader; while the third supplies the executive labour under the direction of the first two, this third person being the operative workman or labourer.[68]

This division into "theory, application, and execution" is found in all branches of industry, and the wealth of a society depends upon the development of a high level of skill in all three types of activity.[69]

Tracy adopts Say's view that all branches of modern industry - agricultural, manufacturing and commercial - involve a functional division of labour between those specializing in scientific knowledge,

rganizational skills, and manual labour. "Theory is the work of the
avant, application is that of the entrepreneur, and execution that of
he ouvrier".[70] (Significantly, the role of the "mere" owner of land
s omitted, being regarded as either redundant, or positively obstruct-
ve.) Each of these three types of worker derives an income from the
rofits resulting from their co-operative production. But each must
ring to the production process a certain amount of investment (avances).

The savant is obliged to undergo a long and expensive
ducation; the entrepreneur requires not only a certain education but
ust have enough money to obtain facilities and materials for production
nd to pay workers; even the poor workman must have learned certain
kills or acquired some tools of his trade, and must have been sustained
or some years either by his parents or by a public institution. All
hese forms of capital investment are made possible by a surplus of
roduction over consumption, a surplus which gradually builds up in a
ociety as it becomes richer and more civilized.[71] The various
"capitals" of these three classes of productive worker give rise to "a
reat diversity in incomes [salaires]". The savant, whose knowledge
an lower the costs of production and boost productivity, "will
ecessarily be sought after and well paid", so long as his knowledge is
f practical utility and does not become commonplace.[72] The poor
orkman, who has only his physical labour to offer, will always be
educed to a very low wage, which can even fall below subsistence level
nless manual labour is temporarily in short supply. The savant and
he workman are both dependent financially on the entrepreneur. "This
s in the nature of things", according to Tracy. For theoretical
nowledge and manual labour are not enough for production:

> above all there has to be an enterprise, and he who undertakes
> it is necessarily the one who chooses, employs, and pays those
> who co-operate in it. Now, who is the one who can do this?
> It is the man who already has the funds by which he can meet

the first expenses of establishment and supplies, and pay the wages until the moment of the first returns.[73]

The entrepreneur holds a special status in the political economy of Say and Tracy. Among French writers, the distinction between the passive owner of capital (receiving interest on his invest-ment) and the entrepreneur (receiving profit on his enterprise)[74] was more fully developed than among the British writers, who tended to use a single category of profit on capital or stock.[75] Richard Cantillon, in his Essai sur la nature du commerce (1755), stressed the role of the entrepreneur as a risk-bearer; Baudeau saw the agricultural entrepreneur as bringing together intelligent innovation and capital wealth; whereas Turgot emphasised the need for an industrial or merchant entrepreneur to commit large capital funds to initiate productive activity.[76] Say's concept of entrepreneurial activity highlights the planning, super-visory and co-ordinating functions, above the functions of supplying capital, innovations, or bearing risks. The entrepreneur is the key element in production because he puts all the factors to work to achieve a given task. Moreover, he is a universal mediator between all the economic classes, and between producers and consumers; he is at the intersection of several economic relationships.[77] In this sense, Say's entrepreneur performs a universal social function, found in most historical stages of economic life and not specific to capitalist society. (On the other hand, Say adds a number of observations on how the entrepreneur mobilizes capital and other resources in a competitive market society, where the typical economic unit is a one-owner enter-prise, subject to market uncertainties or the levels of supply and demand for certain goods and services.)[78]

Tracy largely adopts Say's explanation of the profit of the entrepreneur in terms of the market price of his specialist labour.

Say had argued that the price of entrepreneurial labour is potentially
very high because two main factors limit the supply of such labour:
access to large funds, either his own or borrowed; and business acumen
and managerial skills. Those who do not have "the requisite capacity
and talent" are bound to fail, owing to the degree of risk in such
enterprises.[79] In a similar way, Tracy argues that the essential
determinant of profit is the quantity of utilities produced by the
entrepreneur for which consumers are willing to pay a price which
exceeds the costs of production:

> It is commonly said that the rewards of the entrepreneur,
> wrongly called salaries since no-one promises him anything,
> should represent the price of his labour, the interest on
> his capital and the recompense for risks undertaken ...
> [But] these are by no means the factors which cause his
> good or bad success; this depends solely on the quantity
> of utilities he has been able to produce, on the needs of
> people to obtain them, and on their ability to pay for
> them ... [80]

The entrepreneur's position is less predictable than that of the wage-
earner who is bound by contract to receive an agreed income. The
entrepreneur is "subject to uncertainty", for he may lose all his
investments or may make a handsome profit.[81]

For Tracy the role of the entrepreneur is starkly contrasted
with that of the idle rich. The idle capitalist (capitaliste oisif) who
receives nothing but a fixed income in the form of rent or interest on
his capital, does not personally direct any productive labour. Rather,
his capital (whether land, money or equipment) is hired to others whose
industrie effects an increase in productive wealth. Indeed, says Tracy
in mild indignation, the rent or interest received by idle capitalists
is a levy or deduction from the products of the activity of les citoyens
industrieux.[82] If these idle rich are employers, it is found that their
employees are engaged in domestic service, or in catering for the
luxurious tastes and enjoyments of their employers. The expenditure

of this whole class of the idle rich is devoted to their personal
satisfactions, and although they provide subsistence for many
personal servants, the latters' labour is "completely sterile".[83]

This appears to be an inconsistency in the economic thought
of Tracy and his colleagues. Production had earlier been defined in
general terms as production of utilities for which there was a market.
Domestic labour and production of "luxuries" seem to fall within the
broad definition of production as creation of utilities, but Tracy
rejects their proper inclusion. His reasons appear to be moral and
political as much as purely economic. There had been a continual
debate throughout the eighteenth century (not to mention earlier
periods) concerning what constituted "luxury", and whether it was
socially, morally and economically desirable. The consequences had
been seen either as corrupting (Rousseau), a positive incentive to
economic growth, employment, and useful arts (Montesquieu, Esprit des
Lois, bk. VII), or as a product of human nature – the inevitable desire
for wealth and enjoyment (Saint-Lambert[84]). Most authors described
luxury either as extravagant personal consumption, or more or less as
that level of consumption typical of wealthy societies where basic
needs had been met. The physiocrats described luxury in terms of
expenditure by the proprietary and productive classes directed towards
the "sterile" class, instead of being directed into rural investment
and maintenance of their properties. Luxury, said Baudeau, is an
"excess of sterile expenditure".[85]

Tracy's first discussion of luxury, in his Commentaire on
Montesquieu, followed in the spirit of the physiocrats (allowance made
for their different concepts of "sterile" expenditure). "Luxury
consists essentially in non-productive expenditure."[86] However, since
most forms of consumption would fall under this heading, Tracy introduced

the notion of "unproductive" expenditure which is "not necessary".[87]

This raised further problems, since the concept of "necessary"

was so variable, according to circumstances;[88] yet Tracy persevered

with the concept. His essential argument was that luxury consumption

was not a source of national wealth, even if it was taken as a _sign_ of

individual wealth and prestige. A business could only increase its

profits by savings and reinvestment, not by wasteful display. The

same, wrote Tracy, was true of national wealth: a high proportion of

luxury expenditure would channel capital into areas of lesser utility

from the viewpoint of economic growth.[89] The production of an economic

surplus in society could only be achieved by careful management of

resources – économie in the sense of savings – rather than by consuming

everything immediately.

A better use of resources was that which produced things

of "lasting utility".[90] In the case of a proprietor leasing his

property, or lending his money at interest, the relevant questions

concerned how the borrower made use of the capital, and what use the

proprietor made of the interest or rent.[91] Generally speaking,

proprietors had made poor use of their rental incomes; and therefore

the _rentiers_[92] were engaged almost entirely in unproductive or luxury

consumption. Under the _ancien régime_, wrote Tracy, most of the useful

labour in France was directed towards providing the "immense revenues of

the court and all the opulent class of society", revenues which were

mainly used in luxury expenditure: e.g.,employment of numerous servants

to care for the gratifications of a small number of men. As soon as

these resources were freed for productive uses, a great burst of

national energy took place, with almost everyone engaged in some form

of useful work.[93] Luxury, according to Tracy, was thus a cause of

economic weakness and misery for the majority. "Its real effect is to destroy continually, by the excessive consumption of some men, the product of the labour and industry of others".[94] Luxury on a large scale was made possible only by vast inequalities of wealth: great fortunes, rather than mere idleness, were the main cause of excessive luxury. For this reason, industries which allowed sudden large accumulations of wealth in a few hands were less desirable than those where progress was steady, requiring skills, knowledge or other worthy qualities.[95]

In short, luxury, or "superfluous and exaggerated consumption", is destructive of accumulated utilities and cannot be a source of further wealth. Luxury is also undesirable from the moral viewpoint, since it encourages vanity, frivolity, greed and various forms of depravity.[97] Tracy conceded that some degree of luxury was inevitable, since the taste for superfluous expenditure partly arises from man's natural desire for new kinds of enjoyments, which are made possible by industry and reinforced by habit.[98] However, the main point he wished to emphasize was that the activities of proprietors or rentiers are generally "unproductive" insofar as their expenditures are devoted to personal gratifications and ostentatious display. Tracy's conception of liberty and happiness was tied to a view that productivity should be maximized. The economic functions of the old class of noble proprietors had become redundant, in his opinion, as soon as the social and political order sustaining their elevated and privileged position had been undermined. The "consumption of this species of capitalists is absolutely pure loss from the standpoint of reproduction",[99] and a diminution of acquired national wealth. Their revenues being fixed, there was no way they could increase the wealth of the community or employ an expanding workforce.[100]

The capitalistes industrieux or active capitalists are quite ifferent in their economic functions.

> The second class of capitalists who employ and pay the wage-
> earners, consists of those we have called active. It includes
> all the entrepreneurs of every kind of industry, that is, all
> the men who, having more or less substantial amounts of
> capital, use their talents and industry in improving their
> capital rather than lending it to others, and who thus live
> neither on wages nor revenues but on profits. These men not
> only increase their own capital, but all those of the idle
> capitalists as well. They take on rental their lands, houses
> and money, and make use of them so as to derive profits
> greater than this rent. Thus they have in their hands almost
> all the wealth of society.[101]

By withdrawing from circulation only a modest amount of profit
or their personal and family needs, the entrepreneurs return to the
eproductive process the large and increasing amounts of capital they
ontrol. For their enterprises to grow, their profits must be higher
han their costs, including both their private consumption and the rent
or interest payable to the idle capitalists; if they are successful,
hey expand their business and engage a larger number of employees.[102]
n this way, it is the production of active capitalists which is
esponsible for initiating and maintaining the growth of wealth and
ts circulation among the various classes of society.

> The entrepreneurs of industry are really the heart of the
> body politic, and their capital is its blood. With their
> capital, they pay the wages to most of the salariés; pay
> rents to all the idle capitalists, owners of land or
> money; and through them pay the wages of all the other
> salariés ...[103]

The idle rich, on the contrary, are to be understood as des-
troyers of wealth, not creators. The source of wealth lies in production,[104]
and not in the consumption of luxuries or in the employment of domestic
servants to satisfy one's private whims. Consumption which does not
generate further production is useless from the viewpoint of national
wealth. The very revenues which pay for the employees of the idle rich
are generated by les hommes industrieux who borrowed the land or money
from the capitalistes oisifs.[105]

> ... those who live on wages, those who live on rents and
> those who live on profits, form three essentially different
> classes of men; and it is the latter who maintain all the
> others, and who alone increase the public wealth and
> create all our means of enjoyment. That must be so, since
> labour is the source of all wealth and since it is they
> alone [the entrepreneurs] who give a useful direction to
> current work, in making a productive use of accumulated
> labour.[106]

Capital which returns merely a fixed rent or interest can only be

consumed, and is thus lost forever; capital which is put to use by

productive entrepreneurs is the source of all increases in national

wealth. Montesquieu had believed that the personal expenditure of the

rich, derived from their rents, was the source of subsistence for the

poor masses. But Montesquieu did not understand the nature of these

revenues, for they were really only rents levied on industrie,and were

dependent on the productivity of industry.[107] "Economically speaking,

then, luxury - exaggerated and superfluous consumption - is never good

for anything". The only good consequence might be that such spending

would bring about the ruin of the oisifs and release their capital into

the hands of la classe industrieuse.[108]

Tracy noted that powerful men of property were hardly able to

understand that their unproductive consumption was useless from the

viewpoint of national wealth, or that their dissipation of great wealth

rendered no great service to the state. Their exaggerated sense of

their own importance had been largely accepted by their employees, who

depended on such spending and could not envisage any alternative source

of employment. Some landed nobility, obliged to abandon their landed

estates during the Revolution, had wrongly believed that the villagers

would have no source of income, when in fact it was the tenant-farmers

who hired most of the labourers; and the same nobility wrongly believed

that the peasants who took over their property would be condemned to

poverty. Tracy, while condemning any threats to "private property and justice", asserted that "the absence of a useless man" would make virtually no difference to the economic order, and that the suppression of feudal rights had greatly benefited the country by opening up more opportunities for the productive classes.[109]

We have examined in some detail the differences seen by Tracy between the economic roles of the <u>rentiers</u> and <u>entrepreneurs</u>; we turn now to examine the <u>salariés</u>, especially in relation to Tracy's view of the causes of and remedies for economic inequality.

III. THE PROBLEM OF INEQUALITY

Tracy saw economic inequality as a problem to be understood and tackled, not simply as an eternal fact of life. He recognized that there were different levels of inequality, some more readily overcome than others. What types of inequality were least acceptable to him? Those which prevented a man from exercising his natural rights to life, liberty and property. Slavery or bondage was the worst form of inequality; it was incompatible with "civilized" society, in Tracy's view. The second type of inequality which he attacked was inequality of instruction, skills or knowledge. While it was obvious that everyone had different talents and instructional needs, it was necessary for all men to receive a basic instruction to equip them for citizenship and their occupation. Ignorance was the servant of repressive élites. Thirdly, there was economic inequality, examined in the present section.

This form of inequality arose mainly from the different prices commanded in the market by different types of labour. Tracy was concerned that extremes of wealth and poverty led to moral corruption and to material misery or stagnation. He opposed all doctrines of economic egalitarianism, owing to his belief in the

sanctity of private property, and to his desire to encourage talents
and industry. But he wished to see a levelling of the extremes: the
prodigal extravagances of some types of luxury expenditure, and
the deprivations of the poorest classes who lacked skills or
opportunities for work.[110] He wished to see a system in which higher
wages were accepted as desirable both for the wage-earners and for
the expansion of the market system. His strategies for attaining a
more equitable distribution of wealth were not, however, thoroughly
developed. Other than his proposal that inheritances be equally
distributed among the children of a marriage, and his great emphasis
on increasing the availability of general and specialist education,
Tracy's recommendations amounted to little more than appeals to
reason and philanthropy, on the one hand, and faith in the benefits
of economic growth, on the other.

In accordance with the labour theory of value, Tracy
recognized the economic importance of manual workers and endowed
their labour with a certain moral dignity denied by physiocratic
notions of the sterility of industry. The manual labourer could even
be said to have a small amount of capital - his tools, and skills -
but he was always bound to depend for wages on an employer. Generally
speaking, the market price of his labour was likely to be very low,
because his skills were not very scarce or highly developed. Having
nothing to offer but his manual labour, his wages were likely to remain
near a subsistence level, and were in danger of falling even lower
in some circumstances.[111] It is a general law of the market, wrote
Tracy, that while the "most necessary" labour is the most constantly
required and employed, "it is in the nature of things that it is
always the lowest paid: it cannot be otherwise".[112] Production of
commodities in common usage required only a relatively low level of

skills, whether in fabricating or agricultural industry. It was important that the price of such commodities should be kept low, for it was the poor who were most dependent on such items: the poor could not afford higher prices. But there was a vicious circle implicit in the situation of the poor, because

> it is on the lowest price to which these [commodities] can be reduced, that the lowest price of wages is regulated; and the workers, who labour in their manufacture, are necessarily included in this latter class of the lowest wages.[113]

Tracy argued that there was a "natural" and inevitable inequality in the distribution of wealth. Every individual held some property by virtue of possessing his own individuality and his faculties; but a natural inequality prevailed because individuals had different talents and abilities. Modern societies facilitate the development of such abilities, and consequent inequalities. "This natural inequality is extended and manifested in proportion as our means are developed and diversified".[114] It is impossible to eliminate inequality, he believed, since it is grounded in human nature for individuals to possess property and to have unequal talents. Could anything be done to reduce inequality? Tracy held that it was not the task of government to enforce economic equality. Such measures could not succeed, for they were too much against 'nature' to be durable. Conflicts over the distribution of communal goods, or over the sharing of communal toil, would replace disputes over the defence of private property, and the general consequence "would be to establish an equality of misery and deprivation, by extinguishing the activity of personal industry".[115]

Tracy was aware, then, that there were inherent tendencies towards economic inequality stemming from the division of labour in modern society. What is more, he conceded that a conflict of interests was inherent in the operation of market forces.

> The frequent opposition of interests among us, and the
> inequality of means, are thus conditions of our nature,
> as are suffering and death.... I believe that this evil
> [inequality] is a necessary one, and that we must submit
> to it ...[116]

In a society based upon "the free disposition of the faculties of the

individual, and the guarantee of whatever he may acquire by their

means", everyone exerts himself in various directions and all are

involved in exchange relationships. "The most able gain, and the most

economical amass wealth".[117] The system of private property usually

entailed a freedom of disposal. Tracy was concerned that inherited

wealth was a means of acquisition without labour; it was a mechanism of

perpetuating and aggravating inequalities. Tracy believed that there

were simple legislative remedies which could ensure that these

unearned riches were more evenly divided.[118]

In a new and industrious nation such as the United States,

where the land had not all been taken up, the ordinary citizens could

obtain vacant land and live in relative comfort. But where such land

was entirely occupied, scarcity dictated that those who had few

resources were obliged to work for those with larger resources.[119]

Competition for jobs diminished the price of labour, and their problems

were compounded by producing more children. The poorest families

could scarcely manage to eke out a precarious subsistence.[120]

In such conditions, could it be said there was a major social

division between proprietors and non-proprietors? Tracy rejected this

proposition, together with the physiocratic view that the landless

poor should be termed non-proprietors. The poor, he claimed, are

proprietors at least of their individuality, their labour and the wages

of this labour. They have a need to conserve such property, and thus

they have an interest that such property be respected. No-one, even

those who commit crimes against property, can afford to deny the right of each individual to security of property.[121] Moreover, the physiocrats

wanted to restrict the term proprietors to those owning landed estates:

whereas land is actually just one form of capital among others, including

money and industrial equipment. "It would be more reasonable",

continued Tracy, "to divide society into the poor and the rich, if one

knew where to draw the line of demarcation".[122] But this would be mis-

leading in relation to property, since "the poor man has as much

interest in the preservation of what he has, as the most opulent man".[123]

The conflict of interests in society is a many-sided

phenomenon. One can detect in the division of labour and unequal

rewards

> the germ of opposing interests, which are established between
> the entrepreneur and wage-earners, on the one hand, and
> between entrepreneur and consumers, on the other hand; among
> the wage earners themselves, among entrepreneurs ..., and
> finally among consumers themselves ...[124]

An examination of these diverse interests and the passions they arouse,

shows that all groups "seek the support of force" to buttress their

interests and conceptions, or at least they seek "prohibitive regulations

to constrain those who obstruct them in this universal conflict".[125]

The consumers, being the whole of the population, cannot form a special

interest group: their interest is the "universal interest", and they

can be protected only by the general laws or by universal liberty. But

those who have a particular over-riding group interest form a separate

body and appoint agents to further their cause.[126] Tracy particularly

had in mind the lobbyists of wealthy interests. Wage-earners had been

forbidden the right to organize trades unions by the legislation of

1791, on the grounds that all "corporate" interests should be suppressed.

The poor could nevertheless be "formidable", in time of trouble, "that

is, when the secret of their strength is revealed to them and they are

excited to abuse it".[127]

If the major social division was not that of proprietors vs non-proprietors, what could it be? Tracy claimed that the key division of interests in society was "that between the salariés on the one hand and those who employ them, on the other".[128] The "two great classes" were thus the employers and those receiving salaries and wages.[129] The defect of this classification, he said, was that somewhat different types of people were included in each category: a minister of state would rub shoulders with a day-labourer among the salariés, and the smallest master-workman would be bracketed with the richest idle capitalist. But there was one essential difference of interest between the two classes: the wage-earners wanted to maximize their wage levels, and the employers wanted to pay low wages. Tracy claimed that the entrepreneur's apparently clear interest in paying low wages was not really as obvious as might be assumed, for he required the consumers to be able to afford to buy the commodities he put on the market. If they did not have enough money, the level of demand would fall, and the entrepreneur might not be able to sell his products at above his costs of production.[130] Tracy was far from championing the interests of entrepreneurs against the consumers. He remarked that since the interest of consumers if that of everyone, it is to be regretted that

> modern governments are always ready first to sacrifice the salariés to the entrepreneurs by constricting the former with apprenticeships, corporation privileges and other regulations; and secondly, to sacrifice the consumers to these same entrepreneurs by granting the latter certain privileges and sometimes even monopolies.[131]

Tracy thus defended the general interest (consumers) and the majority interest (salariés) against certain restrictive practices which interfered with the operations of the free market. He had noted the inherent tendency of the market to depress the price of labour, and believed it was incumbent upon public authorities to adopt policies of economic liberalization in order to promote an expanding economy and to relieve the worst aspects of poverty.

In common with the physiocrats, and most liberal writers of his day, Tracy strongly denied that there were any permanent and legitimate bases for class antagonism in society, on which a serious conflict of interests might emerge. The physiocrats had asserted a unity of interests among the three classes, based upon economic prosperity: the interest of the "cultivator" or producer must prevail.[132] Condorcet had regarded conciliation of interests as one of the highest tasks of the "social art", and he argued that "all the classes have only one interest": to protect the right of everyone to enjoy and increase his property.[133] Tracy also denied there were permanently hostile class interests.

> ... although each of us has particular interests, we change so frequently our roles in society, that often we have in one respect an interest contrary to that which we have in another, so that we find ourselves linked with those to whom we were opposed the moment before. This means, fortunately, that we cannot form groups which are constantly enemies.[134]

This notion of changing and cross-cutting loyalties, taken up via Tocqueville into modern political sociology, is one of Tracy's arguments against a class analysis of modern society. People are bearers of several economic roles, which draw them in different directions, both at a given moment and over a longer period of time. Tracy proposed a second argument against the conception of a fundamental clash of class interests: the shared or common interests which underlie all our social and economic life.

> ... in the midst of all these momentary conflicts, we are all constantly united by our common and immutable interests as proprietors and as consumers; that is, we all have a permanent interest, first, that [private] property be respected, and secondly, that industry should be perfected,

or in other words that manufacturing and transport [commerce] should be in the best possible state.[135]

In short, everyone has a general interest in seeing that the economy is expanding, through the free development of the faculties of each individual.[136]

However, the problem of economic inequality could not be entirely resolved through the natural operation of market mechanisms. What other options were available? Tracy did not condone the political or industrial mobilization of the masses to influence market forces or public policy in a direct manner.[137] Instead, he argued that the community as a whole should be made to understand that everyone benefits in the long term by a system of relatively high wage levels. He enunciated the general principle that "the laws should always tend to protect the weak, whereas too often they are inclined to favour the powerful."[138] Tracy never showed in detail how this principle should be applied in particular cases. But in the present context of income distribution, the implication is fairly clear: there should be a wage structure high enough to alleviate poverty and to generate consumer demand, yet not so high as to undermine the profitability of business.

Tracy's primary concern appears to be a limited defence of the interests of les pauvres or les simples salariés: "humanity, justice and policy equally require that, of all the interests, that of the poor be the most consulted and the most respected."[139] In other words, Tracy felt that the interests of the poor majority were of a different order from the particular advantages and desires of other groups and individuals, whose needs were not matters of physical survival. While it was true that the poor also had many wants of a petty kind, more importantly they shared a fundamentally precarious economic existence.

"Humanity", wrote Tracy, "does not allow interests of that kind to be placed in the same balance with simple conveniences".[140] Justice, he continued in a utilitarian vein, obliges us to take account of the relative numbers of the interested groups (le nombre des intéressés).

> Since the lowest class of society is always by far the
> largest, it follows that whenever it is in opposition
> with the others, what is useful to it should always be
> preferred.[141]

Policy (la politique) also demands that the interests of mere wage-earners be protected, because whenever the lowest class of society is too miserable, "there is neither activity, industry, knowledge, nor real national strength; ... nor interior peace well established."[142]

Assuming a distinction between desires and interests,[143] Tracy claimed that the "true interests" of the poor were consistent with reason and the general interest. This perspective dissolved those "prejudices" according to which the struggle between the poor and the rich was seen as an eternal part of the social order.[144] The first interest of the poor man, insisted Tracy, was the maintenance of the right to hold property, an interest he shared with the rich man even though their relative wealth was very different. Property, he repeated, included personal as well as fixed and moveable property. Security of property was valuable to the poor man not only to guarantee his own actual possessions, but to protect the capital of his employer. "Thus he has a direct interest not only in the conservation of what he him- self possesses, but also in the conservation of what others possess".[145] Since property in one's own person is the "source" of all other forms, Tracy derives the moral maxim that one should respect the other's person in the same way one wishes other forms of property to be res- pected. "Leave him the free disposition of his faculties and their employment, as you wish him to leave you that of your lands and capitals".[146]

The second interest of the poor man is that he should receive a high price for his labour. Tracy understands how unpopular such a doctrine would be with employers.

> All the superior classes of society - here including even the smallest owner of a workshop - desire that the price of wages be very low so they can obtain more labour for the same amount of money. They desire it with such passion that, whenever they can and the laws permit them, they even use violence to attain this end. And they prefer the labour of slaves or of serfs because it is even cheaper. These men do not fail to say, and persuade, that what they believe to be their interest is the general interest, and that the low price of wages is absolutely necessary for the development of industry, for the extension of manufacture and commerce, in a word for the prosperity of the state.[147]

Tracy conceded that if the price of labour was so high that goods could be imported for a much cheaper price, domestic manufacture and employment would collapse. Such a wage level would not be in the interest of the poor because it would lead to vast unemployment. However, this situation would only be temporary, for market forces would rapidly lower the price of labour, and the labourers would be willing to work for smaller wages. If wages are too high even where labour is in good supply, the cause lies in bad workmanship and inefficiency. It would then be necessary to combat "the lack of skill, the ignorance and the laziness" of the workers, which are the "true causes of languor in industry wherever it is encountered".[148]

Such defects among workmen were typically the product of economic and moral misery. The greed of employers blinded them to this fact. The northern parts of the United States, for example, were characterized by high wages and a general vigour and prosperity; whereas the southern states employing slave labour were relatively stagnant even though they produced valuable commodities. Such examples illustrated a general truth in all societies:

> Wherever the lowest class of society is too wretched, its
> extreme misery and resulting abjectness is the death of
> industry and the principle of infinite evils, even for its
> oppressors.[149]

The slavery of the ancient world, the slavery in contemporary European

colonies, and the serfdom of feudal Europe, had led to enormous "errors

in economy, morality and politics". The popular disturbances in many

nations of Europe, and even the problems caused by the enormous poor

tax in England and by the large numbers of wretched men who had to

be restrained by force, were all evidence of the general proposition:

> that when a considerable proportion of society is suffering
> too greatly, and is consequently too brutalized, there will
> be neither repose, nor safety, nor liberty possible even
> for the rich and powerful. On the contrary, these first
> citizens of a state are much more truly great and happy
> when they are at the head of a people enjoying an honest
> comfort, which develops in them all their moral and
> intellectual faculties.[150]

Tracy was vague concerning how such a system of moderately

high wages might be introduced or maintained. He rejected the tactic

that the poor should employ violence to obtain the desired level of

payment, for their first interest was to respect the property of

everyone. But equally he did not want the rich to determine wage

levels in a one-sided way. He simply hoped that the free disposition

of labour, and the free market, would ultimately become a more

humane mechanism for determining the price of labour; yet he had

earlier shown that market forces generally tended to depress wage

levels.

The third interest of the poor man was that his wage or

income should be constant. This was more useful to him than any

temporary or extraordinary increase in his income, which might

encourage improvidence and wasteful consumption and soon turn into

misery. The constancy of wage-levels was part of a wider interest, namely, that the price of basic commodities should vary as little as possible. "For it is not the price of wages in itself that is important, it is their price compared with that of the things necessary for life".[151] The lowest wage levels were closely related in the long run to the price of goods necessary for subsistence. If the cost of necessities fell, the labourer benefited temporarily but without lasting utility. If their price increased, the poor suffered great distress; consequently, they would become more anxious to offer their labour, which unfortunately would drive down the price of labour even further, so that they were paid less at the very time they needed to be paid more. In times of distress, noted Tracy, it was always found that wage levels declined, because there was a surplus of labour on the market; "and this lasts until the return of prosperity or until they perish".[152] In short, it was desirable that the price of commodities, especially those important for subsistence, should be "invariable". The best method of achieving this goal was not government price regulation – as had occurred both during the ancien régime and under the Jacobin régime of 1793–4 (the law of the maximum).[153] It was better

> to leave the most complete liberty to commerce, because
> the activity of speculators and their competition make them
> eager to take advantage of the smallest fall to buy, and
> the smallest rise to sell again; and in this way they
> prevent either one or the other from enduring or from
> becoming excessive. This method is also that which is the
> most consistent with the respect due to property, for the
> just and the useful are always united.[154]

The sudden expansion or contraction of particular industries could have a similar effect upon the employment and fortunes of the poor as did variations in the prices of basic commodities. Tracy alluded to a contemporary debate about the relative prosperity and stability of agricultural and commercial nations, and he cast doubt upon the qualities attributed to agricultural nations.[155] The latter were more exposed, in his opinion, to large fluctuations in the price

of grain because, in the event of a domestic crop failure, the cost

of transporting imported grain to inland regions was extremely high.

Imported supplies were little more than a psychological consolation,

for they did not resolve the problems of hardship and misery.[156] By

contrast with agricultural nations (which have large landlocked hinter-

lands), commercial nations had sufficient seaports to ensure that all

areas could be readily supplied by imports in a time of trouble. On

balance, commercial nations provided a better standard of living: they

were less prone to the possibilities of starvation caused by crop

failures; and, providing their industry and commerce developed

"naturally" rather than by a forced and "exaggerated extension", severe

fluctuations in prosperity could be avoided.[157]

Such a conclusion tied in with Tracy's general assumption

that society - understood as "continual commerce" - was the source of

our power, resources, and happiness.[158] Wherever a commercial nation

was found to be stagnant, the cause was not commerce itself, but such

factors as a very unequal distribution of wealth, which is "the greatest

and most general of evils".[159] Such cases only illustrated the truth

that "the human race is happy from the development and increase of its

means, but ever ready to become unhappy from the bad use it makes of

them".[160] Tracy summarized the interests of the poor as follows:

> the poor man is a proprietor as well as the rich; in his
> role as proprietor of his person, his faculties and their
> product, he has an interest that he be allowed the free
> disposition of his person and his labour, that this labour
> should procure sufficient wages for him, and that these
> wages should vary as little as possible. That is, he has
> an interest that his capital should be respected, that this
> capital should produce the revenue necessary for his
> existence, and that this revenue if possible should be
> always the same. And on all these points, his interest
> is consistent with the general interest.
> But the poor man is not only a proprietor, he is also a
> consumer, for all men are both. In the latter role, he

> has the same interest as all consumers, that of being
> provisioned in the best and cheapest way possible. It
> is necessary for him, then, that manufacture should be
> very skilled, communications easy, and relations multiplied;
> for no-one has a greater need for being supplied cheaply
> than a man with few means. [161]

Some writers had argued that the development of machine
technology, simplifying the labour process and increasing the productivit
of industry, should be seen as opposed to the interests of the poor.
Say[162] and Tracy disagreed. By reducing the labour time embodied in a
commodity, production costs were reduced, and the market price for the
poor consumer was lower. Tracy argued against those who complained that
machines would replace labourers and create vast unemployment. Wage-
earners were paid, he claimed, out of the total capital funds available
to the employers. If there was a saving of funds in one area, those
funds would be diverted into new channels of investment, and the same
number of workers could thereby retain employment (if the new investment was profitable). The best way to increase the total funds available for new investment (and thus further employment) was to make
manufacture more efficient and productive; this was the only way our
wealth could increase. If this was not true, we could advocate the
proliferation of useless labour to keep everyone employed. But this
would actually divert funds away from productive labour, and no useful
goods would be produced to satisfy our needs and to increase our
social wealth.[163]

The argument in favour of machines and other advances was
extremely simple, said Tracy: useful labour is more useful that useless
labour.[164] Tracy used the same arguments to refute criticisms of the
construction of roads and canals, or improvements in communications and
commercial relations. The poor could only benefit from the development
of commerce and transportation, in the same way they benefited from

the development of industry. Moreover, a highly developed commerce was more likely to make prices more constant, protecting the interest of the poor and of society at large. Even if there are short-term fluctuations as a result of industrial and commercial innovations, this is not enough to outweigh the long-term substantial benefits of such progress.[165]

We have seen that Tracy acknowledged a "necessary opposition between our particular interests", but he emphasized that "we are all united by our common interests as proprietors and consumers". It would, therefore, be "wrong to regard the poor and the rich, or the wage-earners and those who employ them, as two essentially hostile classes".[166] The true interests of the poor coincided with those of society at large. But while men's interests may be objectively united, it was necessary to take account of another "condition of our nature", namely, our inequality of means. It has sometimes been asserted, wrote Tracy, that inequality is a useful benefit for which we should thank Providence. On the contrary, he said, inequality is an evil "because it is a powerful support to injustice". Justice — our "greatest good" and sole means of conciliation — is on the side of the weak.[167]

In the case of brutal and savage society, inequality of power is manifested directly in the physical subjection of the weak by the strong, and severely limits the extent of social relations. In civilized society, such personal subjection or inequality tends to be greatly reduced, for "the object of social organization is to combat the inequality of power"[168] typified in the Hobbesian state of nature. Those cases where slavery has been introduced are worse than primitive societies. But in general, society manages to reduce inequality of power among men, and thereby establishes security. This allows a

development of men's faculties and of their wealth, or means of
existence and enjoyment: such are the advantages of society. These
benefits are particularly facilitated by modern societies ruled by
representative government.[169] But economic growth brings inequalities
of new kinds: the more our faculties are developed, the greater are
their inequalities and soon there exists "inequality of wealth,
leading to inequalities in education, capacity and influence".[170]

Having diminished the effects of personal and physical
inequalities, and provided security for individuals to develop their
abilities, society should attempt to overcome the worst effects of
the tendency towards inequality of wealth: always by gentle means,
eschewing force, and remembering that "respect for property is the
fundamental base of society and its guarantee against violence".[171]
Inequality of wealth is an evil because it brings about inequalities
of education, capacity and influence, and tends to re-establish an
inequality of power, thus undermining the advantages of civil society.

Tracy here underlined his distinction between active and idle
capitalists, arguing that the "great fortunes" are held by the idle
rich, who employ no labour except for their pleasure, instead of by
the entrepreneurs of industry who are the only ones able to increase
the national wealth.

> wherever you see exaggerated fortunes, there you will see
> the greatest misery and the greatest stagnation of industry.
> The perfection of society, then, would be to increase
> greatly our riches while avoiding their extreme inequality.[172]

But even if the general principle is clear, the means and difficulties
will differ markedly in each society according to circumstances. A
poor agricultural society with limited commercial relations might well
avoid gross inequalities for a long period. But in the case of conquest,
or if very scarce commodities are produced, a part of the population

will benefit disproportionately. Various other factors influence

the degree and the distribution of national wealth:

> the different characters of peoples, the nature of their
> governments, the greater or smaller extent of their
> knowledge, and above all of their understanding of the
> social art at those moments which decide their fortune ...[173]

While nations may differ in circumstances, the terms of the

problem remain the same. Society, having provided security for persons

and their property, brings about the development of their faculties

and their wealth; this growth leads towards a very unequal distribution

of wealth and thus towards that inequality of power which society was

originally established to constrain.[174] In short,

> all may be reduced to the following truth, which has not
> always been sufficiently understood: the multiplication
> of our means of enjoyment is a very good thing, their too
> unequal distribution is a very bad one and the source of all
> our evils. On this point also, the interest of the poor
> is the same as that of society.[175]

We have seen that for Tracy, the tendencies towards economic

inequality should be resisted, in the interests not only of the poor

but of the community as a whole. The material standard of living of

the wage-labourers should be protected, by adequate wages, stable

employment, and constant prices of commodities. Public instruction and

vocational training could improve the price of their labour in the

market. Employers should be made to understand that everyone benefits

from a well-trained workforce and from moderately high wages, for the

circulation of wealth is raised and demand for goods is maintained.

Moreover, if the poor are assured of their subsistence, they are less

likely to seek violent solutions to their economic problems, and social

harmony is thus ensured.

Philanthropy[176] was necessary to deal with the poverty caused by

temporary fluctuations in various sectors of agriculture and manufacture

or by problems in trade and commerce. Beggary and vagabondage were another matter: they were a social evil, to be eliminated by rational education, laws and institutions.[177] But the overall solution to the problem of poverty lay in continuous growth in productivity and national wealth. The entrepreneurs were the key to such economic growth, and the idle rich _rentiers_ who obstructed the optimal use of productive capital were the main brake upon economic progress. Tracy believed that economic growth was paradoxically both the cause of inequality of wealth, and equally the only peaceful solution to the problem of inequality. Tracy did not examine the paradox in a systematic way, nor suggest reasons why the labourers would be led to understand that their sectional interests as the suffering poor were outweighed by their universal interests as proprietors and consumers. Unlike Say,[178] Tracy did not envisage a society where wage-labourers could achieve anything more than frugal comfort; and even this would be possible only in a society which had an abundance of resources and industry. He looked forward to a society in which the various forces of production could develop rapidly, unrestrained by the landowning class of the _ancien régime_, or by government inter-ference with the natural operation of market forces. He identified the sufferings and vulnerability of the labourers under the market system and proposed some general humanitarian principles to protect them from material deprivation and moral degradation.

Tracy believed that the complete liberalization of commerce and industry, and the application of science to productive processes, would be the best guarantee of general prosperity. The division between the men of skill and education, as well as capital, on the one hand, and the ordinary labourers on the other, was seen as the major feature of the modern division of labour. This division between the educated and uneducated, even more than that between the rich and the poor, was prominent also in Tracy's political and educational philosophy.

These themes will be examined in the remaining chapters.

FOOTNOTES TO CHAPTER FIVE

1   Logique, pp. 437-438.

2   Ibid., p. 437. On the origin of the term political economy, cf.
    W. Letwin, The Origins of Scientific Economics (Westport, 1975),
    p. 217; and J.-B. Say, Traité d'économie politique (Paris, 2e ed.
    1814), "Discours préliminaire", pp. xiii-xv.

3   Logique, pp. 391-392. For the term "social economy", cf. Traité
    de la Volonté (1818), p. 289, and also the quotation on p. 213 above,
    from the Regulations of the Société de 1789.

4   Traité de la Volonté (1815), p. 96.

5   Ibid., p. 97.

6   Ibid., p. 98.

7   Ibid., p. 92-95.

8   Ibid., p. 99. (Tracy's theory of value is praised by Victor Cousin,
    "Adam Smith", Séances et Travaux de l'Académie des Sciences morales
    et politiques, vol. 10 (1846), p. 449.)

9   Ibid., pp. 100-101, 105.

10 Ibid., pp. 101-102.

11 Ibid., pp. 102-103.

12 R.L. Meek, Studies in the Labour Theory of Value (London, 1958),
    chapter 1.

13 J. Locke, Second Treatise, chapter 5.

14 A. Smith, The Wealth of Nations [1776], ed. Skinner (Harmondsworth,
    1974), pp. 104-106.

15 J. Viner, "Mercantilist Thought", International Encyclopedia of the
    Social Sciences (New York, 1968), vol. 4, pp. 435-442.

16 A. Bloomfield and W.R. Allen, "The Foreign-Trade Doctrines of the
    Physiocrats", and J.J. Spengler, "The Physiocrats and Say's Law of
    Markets", in Essays in Economic Thought, ed. Spengler and Allen
    (Chicago, 1960); and the references cited in footnote 2 to chapter 4.

17 Mirabeau, Leçons économiques (Amsterdam, 1770), Leçon XXVI: "Classes
    sociales", pp. 112-119; Dupont de Nemours, Abrégé des principes de
    l'économie politique [1772], in E. Daire (ed.), Physiocrates (Paris,
    1846), p. 376; Baudeau, Première introduction à la philosophie
    économique [1771], in Daire (ed.), Physiocrates, especially pp. 669,
    692, 711; Baudeau, Explication du tableau économique [1767], in
    ibid., p. 852.

18 Dupont de Nemours, De l'origine et des progrès d'une science nouvelle
    [1768], ed. Dubois (Paris, 1910), pp. 7, 11, 35; Le Mercier de la

Rivière, L'Ordre naturel et essentiel des sociétés politiques [1767],
ed. Depitre (Paris, 1910), chapter XLIV: Dupont de Nemours, Abrégé,
p. 378; Quesnay, Le Droit Naturel, in Daire (ed.), Physiocrates,
pp. 46, 52-55.

19   Cf. Say, Traité d'économie politique, book 1, chapter 2; M. Dobb,
Theories of Value and Distribution (Cambridge, 1973), chapter 2;
R.L. Meek, Studies in the Labour Theory of Value, chapter 2.

20   Smith, Wealth of Nations, book 2, chapter 3, pp. 430-431. Smith
includes churchmen, lawyers and public servants among the "unproductive".

21   Say, Traité d'économie politique, book 1, chapters 7 and 13.

22   Smith, Wealth of Nations, book 1, chapter 5.

23   Say, Traité d'économie politique, book 1, chapters 4 and 5.

24   Ibid., book 1, chapter 1.

25   Tracy, Traité de la Volonté (1818 ed.), p. 147. The reference is
to the 1803 edition of Say's Traité. Tracy made a similar remark
a few years earlier in his Commentaire, p. 285.

26   Commentaire, pp. 284ff.

27   Tracy, Traité de la Volonté (1818), p. 148.

28   Ibid., p. 149.

29   Ibid., p. 150.

30   Ibid., p. 151.

31   Commentaire, pp. 281-283. Condorcet gave an extremely generous
assessment of the physiocrats in Sketch, pp. 138-139, omitting to
mention their doctrine of the primacy of agriculture.

32   Traité, pp. 152-153.

33   Ibid., p. 153; cf. pp. 201-203.

34   Ibid., p. 154.

35   Cf. Sieyès, Qu'est-ce que le Tiers-état?, ed. Zapperi (1970),
pp. 121ff.

36   Cf. B.-C. Dunoyer, "Esquisse historique des doctrines auxquelles on
a donné le nom d'industrialisme ...", Revue encyclopédique, vol. 33
(February 1827), pp. 368-395; Saint-Simon, Selected Writings, ed.
K. Taylor (London, 1975), Part III.

37   Tracy, Traité, pp. 154-155; cf. pp. 290-292. The phrase "frelons
de la ruche" (drones of the hive) originally appeared in the
Commentaire, p. 294.

38 Traité, p. 155; cf. Commentaire, p. 287. (For Tracy's views on the productivity of commerce, cf. Traité, pp. 205-215. He is in accord on this point with Say, op.cit., book 1, chapter 2.)

39 Traité, p. 157.

40 Ibid., p. 158.

41 Ibid., p. 159.

42 Ibid., p. 160.

43 Ibidem.

44 Ibid., p. 161.

45 Cf. Commentaire, pp. 290-291.

46 Tracy, Traité, p. 163. Cf. Say, op.cit., book 1, chapter 7, who makes this point forcefully.

47 Traité, p. 164.

48 Ibidem; cf. Traité (1815), p. 99.

49 "Mémoire sur la faculté de penser", p. 401.

50 On the term "industry", cf. F. Brunot, Histoire de la langue française, tome VI, p. 379f; R. Williams, Keywords (London, 1976), pp. 137-138.

51 Cf. G.V. Taylor, "Non-capitalist wealth and the origins of the French Revolution", American Historical Review, vol. 72 (January 1967), pp. 469-496; R. Price, The Economic Modernization of France (London, 1975); F. Braudel and C.E. Labrousse, Histoire économique et sociale de la France, tome III: 1789-années 1830, vol. I (Paris, 1976).

52 Op.cit., article "industrie", p. 253f.

53 Cf. E. Allix, "L'oeuvre économique de Germain Garnier", Revue d'histoire économique et sociale, vol. 5 (1912), pp. 317-342; Allix, "La rivalité entre la propriété foncière et la fortune mobilière sous la Révolution", ibid., vol. 6 (1913), pp. 297-348.

54 Cf. Cambacérès, "Discours sur la science sociale", pp. 3, 5.

55 Cf. Baudeau, Première introduction, in Daire (ed.), Physiocrates, p. 723: "Laissez les faire, as a famous intendant du commerce said [Gournay], that is the whole of legislation for the manufactures and sterile arts ... Qu'on les laisse faire, that is the true legislation, i.e., the function of the guarantor authority".

56 Commentaire, p. 280 (and p. 280n).

57 Cf. the extracts in R.L. Meek (ed.), Precursors of Adam Smith, especially pp. 108ff.

58 For a detailed account of the French and Scottish contributions to the "four-stages" theory of historical development, cf. R.L. Meek, Social Science and the Ignoble Savage (Cambridge, 1976).

59 P. Lévesque, "Considérations sur l'homme, observé dans la vie sauvage, dans la vie pastorale et dans la vie policée", Mémoires de l'Institut, tome I (1798), pp. 209-246. Lévesque (born 1736) did not, however, make a clear distinction between a society whose major "industry" was agriculture and one whose "industry" was increasingly oriented towards manufacturing, commerce and "useful arts".

60 Tracy, Traité (1818), p. 322.

61 Baudeau, Première introduction, pp. 669, 691.

62 Tracy, Traité (1818), p. 154. For the origin of "class" terminology, cf. Brunot, Histoire de la langue française, tome VI, pp. 191f.

63 Condillac, Le Commerce et le Gouvernement considérés relativement l'un à l'autre [1776], in Oeuvres philosophiques, vol. II, pp. 241-367. Cf. I.F. Knight, The Geometric Spirit, chapter 9.

64 Ibid., pp. 311-312.

65 Ibid., pp. 258-262. Condillac's heretical view was strongly attacked by the physiocrat Le Trosne, De l'intérêt social [1777], in Daire (ed.), Physiocrates, especially pp. 929ff.

66 Smith, Wealth of Nations, p. 356; cf. p. 155.

67 Say, Traité, book 1, chapter 5.

68 Ibid., book 1, chapter 6 [Treatise, New York 1880, p. 80].

69 Ibidem.[Treatise, p. 81.]

70 Tracy, Traité (1818), pp. 166-167; cf. pp. 176-177, 214.

71 Ibid., pp. 167-169.

72 Ibid., pp. 170-171. Cf. Say, Traité, book 2, chapter 7 [Treatise, pp. 327-329], who claims that the savant is typically underpaid for the important services he provides.

73 Tracy, Traité (1818), p. 171.

74 Cf. Say, Traité, book 2, chapter 8, section 2 [Treatise, p. 354].

75 M. Dobb, "Entrepreneur", Encyclopaedia of the Social Sciences (New York, 1931), vol. 5, pp. 558-560.

76 Cf. Bert Hoselitz, "The early history of entrepreneurial theory", in Essays in Economic Thought, ed. Spengler and Allen (Chicago, 1960), especially pp. 247-248.

77 Say, Traité, book 2, chapter 7, section 3 [Treatise, p. 332].

78 Hoselitz, op.cit., pp. 250-253; G. Koolman, "Say's conception of
    the role of the entrepreneur", Economica, vol. 38 (1971), pp. 269-
    286; M. James, "P.-L. Roederer, J.-B. Say and the concept of
    'industrie'", History of Political Economy, vol. 9 (1977), pp. 455-
    475.

79 Say, Traité, book 2, chapter 7, section 3 [Treatise, pp. 330-331].

80 Tracy, Traité, pp. 172-173.

81 Ibid., p. 172; cf. pp. 214-215.

82 Ibid., p. 333.

83 Ibid., p. 334.

84 Saint-Lambert, "Luxury", in Diderot et al., Encyclopedia: Selections
    (New York, 1965), especially p. 230.

85 Baudeau, Principes de la Science morale et politique sur le luxe et
    les loix somptuaires [1767], ed. Dubois (Paris, 1912); and for the
    quote, see his Première introduction [1771], p. 736.

86 Commentaire, p. 79.

87 Ibid., pp. 80-81.

88 As he was well aware: ibid., pp. 81-83.

89 Ibid., pp. 83-84.

90 Ibid., p. 85; cf. Traité (1818), p. 343.

91 Commentaire, p. 86.

92 The term rentiers, meaning "idle" capitalists living from rent or
    interest, is used in Traité (1818), pp. 290, 342, 347. Tracy also
    used the term rentiers oisifs in 1798: "Quels sont les moyens", p.470

93 Commentaire, pp. 92-93; Traité, pp. 356-363.

94 Commentaire, p. 88.

95 Ibid., pp. 97-98.

96 Traité, pp. 345, 349.

97 Commentaire, p. 99; Traité, p. 368.

98 Commentaire, pp. 95-96; Traité, p. 364.

99 Traité, p. 335.

100 Ibid., pp. 290-291.

101 Ibid., pp. 335-336. Cf. Commentaire, p. 55, where Tracy points to
    the need for superior classes in earlier societies to repress the
    lower classes which would otherwise accumulate all the wealth by
    their talent and industry.

02 Traité, pp. 336-337.

03 Ibid., pp. 338-339.

04 Ibid., p. 353. Cf. Smith, Wealth of Nations, book 2, chapter 3.

05 Ibid., p. 346.

06 Ibid., p. 341.

07 Ibid., p. 348. Moreover, non-agricultural industry was even more
    productive: ibid., pp. 202-203.

08 Ibid., p. 349.

09 Ibid., pp. 354-355 and 355n.

10 Cf. Condorcet, Sketch, pp. 174, 179-184, on the need to reduce
    economic inequality. That Tracy regarded some kinds of inequality
    as reversible may be judged from the following: "When we deal with
    legislation, it will be seen further that the extremes of inequality
    and of luxury are much more the effects of bad laws than of the
    natural course of events". (Traité, p. 354n.1)

11 Traité, pp. 168-171.

12 Ibid., p. 175.

13 Ibid., p. 176.

14 Ibid., p. 262.

15 Ibid., p. 263.

16 Ibid., p. 264; cf. pp. 288, 513.

17 Ibid., pp. 264-265.

18 Quels sont les moyens, in Commentaire, pp. 464, 466. Tracy gave no
    philosophical justification for this measure: it was more a matter
    of pragmatic intervention.

19 Traité, pp. 270-274.

20 Ibid., pp. 265-266; on population pressures, cf. ibid., chapter 9,
    and Commentaire, book 23. Tracy argues that there is no duty to
    populate the world with miserable and unwanted children, and that
    the welfare of individuals is more important than their multiplication.
    Having recognized the Malthusian problem of resources in relation
    to population, he prescribes no remedies, apparently believing that
    rates of growth and decline in numbers are determined by economic
    factors. Tracy's position here is close to that of Condorcet,
    Sketch, pp. 188-189.

21 Traité, p. 266.

22 Ibid., pp. 267-268.

123 Ibid., p. 268.

124 Ibid., p. 173.

125 Ibid., p. 174.

126 Cf. Smith, Wealth of Nations, pp. 357-359.

127 Traité, p. 175. On the Le Chapelier law of 1791, cf. Godechot,
     Les Institutions (1951), pp. 181ff.

128 Ibid., p. 268.

129 Ibid., p. 290.

130 Ibid., p. 268. This thesis contains the germs of an underconsumption
     theory of crisis; these doctrines are discussed in M. Bleaney,
     Underconsumption theories (London, 1976), especially chapters 1, 3, 5

131 Traité, p. 269.

132 Cf. Dupont de Nemours, Abrégé des principes de l'économie politique,
     p. 383; Baudeau, Première introduction, pp. 740ff, 803ff.

133 Condorcet, Sketch, pp. 128, 184 and especially 192; Condorcet, "Que
     toutes les classes de la société n'ont qu'un même intérêt", Oeuvres
     complètes (1804), vol. 18, pp. 43-50.

134 Traité, p. 269. For the view that class interests are in conflict,
     cf. Mably, Doutes proposés aux philosophes économistes [c.1768]:
     "In a society where landed property and inequality exist, no social
     order can be considered by everyone as the best. Society is divided
     into classes and these classes have antagonistic interests".
     (Cited in Morelly, Code de la Nature, ed. Volguine, Introduction,
     p. 17.)

135 Traité, p. 269.

136 Ibid., p. 288.

137 Cf. ibid., p. 302.

138 Ibid., p. 264.

139 Ibid., p. 294.

140 Ibid., p. 295.

141 Ibid., pp. 295-296.

142 Ibid., p. 296.

143 Cf. Dupont de Nemours, Abrégé, pp. 382-383, for the view that one
     may be misled or mistaken about one's desires, but one's interests
     are objectively given. Cf. Traité (1815), p. 86.

144 Traité (1818), p. 296.

145 Ibid., p. 297.

146 Ibid., p. 298.

147 Ibid., pp. 298-299. On changing conceptions of the desirability of a higher wage structure, cf. the writings of A.W. Coats in Bibliography Part C.

148 Ibid., pp. 299-300.

149 Ibid., pp. 300-301.

150 Ibid., p. 302.

151 Ibid., p. 305.

152 Ibid., p. 306. I have omitted Tracy's discussion of the inflationary effects of paper money, found in ibid., chapters 6 and 12; similarly, I have omitted his discussion of the types of taxes, in Commentaire, chapter 13.

153 On the price-fixing regulations of this period, cf. Godechot, Les Institutions (1951), pp. 349ff.

154 Traité, p. 307.

155 Cf. ibid., p. 327, where he rejected the identification of commercial nations with greed and agricultural nations with moderation.

156 Ibid., p. 309. Tracy added (p. 310) that our security of existence would be greatly improved if foodstuffs could be reduced to a small bulk for easy transportation.

157 Ibid., p. 311.

158 Ibid., p. 312.

159 Ibid., p. 313.

160 Ibidem.

161 Ibid., pp. 313-314.

162 Cf. Say's criticism of Sismondi, in Say, Traité de l'économie politique, book 1, chapter 7 [Treatise, especially p. 90n-91].

163 Tracy, Traité, p. 315.

164 Ibid., p. 316.

165 Ibid., p. 317.

166 Ibid., p. 318.

167 Ibid., p. 319.

168 Ibid., p. 320.

169 Commentaire, pp. 57-58.

170 Traité, p. 321.

171 Ibidem.

172 Ibid., p. 322. Cf. Commentaire, p. 97.

173 Ibid., p. 325. Tracy illustrates the last remark by comparing the
     fate of the Spanish Americas, and the later developments in North
     America under the influence of "Locke and Franklin".

174 Ibid., p. 326.

175 Ibid., p. 329.

176 On the liberal and idéologue belief in philanthropy and sympathy for
     the deserving poor; cf. Chamfort, Oeuvres complètes (1808), vol. II,
     pp. 116-120; R. Fargher, The 'Décade Philosophique', pp. 291ff;
     J. Kitchin, Un journal 'philosophique', pp. 201-203.

177 Cabanis, Quelques principes et quelques vues sur les secours publics,
     in Oeuvres philosophiques, vol. II, pp. 1-63. For the eighteenth-
     century background to the discussion of poverty, cf. M. Leroy,
     Histoire des idées sociales, vol. II, chapter 12; O. Hufton, "Towards
     an understanding of the poor in eighteenth-century France", in
     French Government and Society 1500-1850, ed. Bosher, pp. 145-165.

178 Cf. Kitchin, op.cit., p. 198.

CHAPTER SIX

POLITICS: THE SCIENCE OF "HAPPINESS"

I   Liberal elitism and the Directory

II   Critique of Montesquieu

III Representative government: reason and liberty

I. LIBERAL ELITISM AND THE DIRECTORY

Tracy's political theory may be seen as an attempt to find
a balance between principles of democracy and enlightened leadership.
He advocated a system of representative government, founded on liberal-
constitutional principles and individual rights, which would seek to
extend public instruction and civic-mindedness among the people, and
which was led by an enlightened élite. As will be shown in the last
section of this chapter, Tracy claimed that this type of political
system was the most likely to produce a prosperous, contented and
energetic nation, where individual merit would be rewarded, and the
least talented would nonetheless receive a basic education in citizenship and a trade.

Tracy was firmly convinced that progressive change had to
be initiated by élites, in particular by savants of various kinds,
politicians and educators. In an age before the rise of modern
political parties, parliamentary government was largely a system of
rule by notables.[1] Under the Directory, the notables included certain
idéologues and men sympathetic to that outlook. For Tracy, the
essential quality of the élite should be its understanding of the
"social art" and the science of "legislation" or social science.[2] The
essential test of good government was its principles: was it devoted
to the general interest, individual rights, and the security and
happiness of the people? He was scarcely concerned about the "politics
of experience" in the sense intended by philosophical conservatism.[3]
Experience in the narrow technical sense was useful in the idéologue
view because it implied efficiency. But experience in the broad sense
of historically evolving social practices and traditions, was of small
relevance to the idéologues: this type of experience had been found
guilty by its association with the mass ignorance and oppression of the

past.[4] It was the task of the liberal notables to create the institutional, legislative and educational bases of the society, and shape a social consensus around the new institutions. In time, ordinary citizens might understand the practical wisdom, if not the theoretical principles, embodied in the rational social arrangements. But Tracy never speculated on a future in which a more participatory form of democracy would be made possible by generalized enlightenment.

Tracy's conception of government is essentially that of implementing certain principles; it is not a matter of compromises and bargaining among various socio-economic interests. Given his insistence on a politics of principles, he was almost inevitably bound to desire that men of principles - indeed, his own principles - should occupy the positions of authority and influence. The élite should be a knowledge élite rather than a propertied élite, knowledge here being defined in the sense of the social art or social science. Another way of describing Tracy's views is to say that he believed in a meritocracy whose task was to reconcile order, progress, and individual liberty. The democratic element of his thought emphasized parliamentary government, free elections, civil liberties and legal equality; the elitist element emphasized the role of leadership, guidance, knowledge and principles in achieving a rational society. Pierre Flourens, speaking at Tracy's funeral in March 1836 made the illuminating remark that Tracy had been born into a hereditary nobility, but eventually sought a nobility of merit.[5] If the qualities of the élite were uppermost in Tracy's mind, one might wonder why he professed democratic principles of any kind: why not seek an educational autocracy? The short answer is that he strongly believed in the doctrine that legitimate government is based on the sovereignty of the people. He believed in the superiorit of representative government as the form best able to secure the Rights of Man and the general happiness and progress of society. He did not

claim its superiority stemmed from the intrinsic value of political

participation, or from the most effective articulation of group interests.

(This point will be taken up again at the end of this chapter.)

According to Tracy, the uneducated masses could not be

expected to make any useful contribution to government decision-making:

government should be responsible to the people, and govern in their

interests, but it should be conducted by an educated élite.[6] Mass

political mobilization had no place in Tracy's outlook, other than for

the limited objective of patriotic defence of national boundaries.

Social stability was a value which he never under-estimated. This view-

point had been reinforced by experience of the Terror in 1793-4, when

Tracy and several colleagues spent many months in their prison cells

reflecting on the dangers of populist demagoguery replacing a stable

structure of authority with constitutionally defined procedures and

due process of law. The idéologues in 1795 were content with those

provisions of the new Constitution which introduced a property

qualification for the franchise, declared that private property was the

basis of wealth and of the social order, and defined equality as a

legal category with no economic implications.[7]

The Thermidoreans who drafted the 1795 Constitution were

determined to suppress the egalitarian currents of 1793-4, and were

further convinced by the insurrection in Paris in May 1795. Boissy

d'Anglas, one of the key figures in the constitutional Commission des

Onze, explained rather bluntly on 23 June 1795 that

> We must be governed by the best citizens; the best citizens
> are those who are most educated and most interested in the
> keeping of the law. Now, with very few exceptions, you will
> find such men only among those who possess some property,
> who are attached to the country that contains it, the laws
> that protect it, and the peace that maintains it; men who
> owe to that property and to the affluence it affords the

education which has made them fit to discuss, wisely
and equitably, the advantages and the drawbacks of the
laws that determine the fate of the country.... A
country governed by landowners is in the social order,
whereas one governed by persons other than property
owners is in the state of nature.[8]

Most liberals in the period before the late nineteenth
century held serious reservations about the wisdom of universal
suffrage: they generally recommended that voters should have certain
qualifications of property, gender or education. Tracy shared their
scepticism and caution. He was unwilling, in the first place, to
acknowledge that women should play an active role in public life. He
argued in his Commentaire that although women had the same rights and
probably the same capacities as men, they were most usefully occupied
in domestic functions, in which they excelled. Men were the "natural"
representatives of families in public affairs.[9] The sexes were not
"unequal", simply endowed by "nature" with different functional roles.
He provided no evidence, however, for his assumption that the
division of tasks between men and women was "natural" (thus irreversible
rather than a social convention (and even an oppressive convention).
Tracy's view that public life was - and should remain - a sphere of
exclusively male influence set him apart from Cordorcet, who had
vigorously supported equality of education for girls and boys, and
encouraged the movement of women into various spheres of public life.[10]

Tracy's conception of a "natural" differentiation of functions
based upon supposed differences in needs, inclinations, and abilities,
was potentially open to abuse. Tracy had avoided one possible
inconsistency in his discussion of political and legal equality by
arguing for the equal rights of blacks in the French colonies; this
was an extension of his condemnation of slavery and his support for
the implementation of the Rights of Man. On the issue of universal

uffrage, however, Tracy found it necessary to invoke restrictions.
hese were justified by an appeal to a functionalist version of
tilitarianism. It was not in the general interest of society, he
laimed in 1806, that everyone should participate in every kind of
ctivity. Rather, they should specialize in those activities for
hich they are best fitted.[11] The problem with this doctrine, in my
wn view, is to determine what is the optimal and/or natural division
f labour, and to determine whether the actual role occupied by
particular individual - or category of individuals - is the result
f natural talents or of social and cultural conditions. Tracy's
octrine of the paramount influence of education might have suggested
o him a more critical analysis of any allegedly "natural" division of
abour.

Tracy invoked his principle of utilitarian specialization in
second area of political influence: he was unwilling to allow the
neducated and the propertyless citizens a decisive voice in determining
he composition or the policies of the national legislature. Tracy
ecognized the need to maintain the principle of popular sovereignty;
ut he also saw a tension between that principle and the need for
xpert leadership. He resolved the dilemma in the following way. In
iscussing the procedures by which a new constitutional convention
hould be elected, Tracy made two important claims: (i) no man should
e excluded from participating in the electoral process merely by
virtue of his birth, wealth, or social rank;[12] (ii) however, the poor
nd uneducated masses should participate only in primary assemblies,
vhich would elect representatives to intermediate bodies, whose task
in turn would be to elect the national representatives.[13] Those
hosen to represent the local assemblies would generally be better
educated and less subject to local prejudices, according to Tracy.

Such men would be best suited to choosing the membership of a national convention: c'est là la bonne aristocratie. [14]

By this indirect method of election, the actual capacities of men might best be correlated with the functions to be performed. All men were fit to participate in primary assemblies, [15] but only a select few had enough knowledge and experience to be suitable electors at a higher level. One advantage of an indirect method of election was that there would be little need to specify precise property qualifications for membership of the intermediate body; equality of rights was preserved without odious restrictions on political participation. Tracy believed that education was more important than property as an index of political wisdom. Although it was empirically true that property and education usually co-existed, the correlation was not perfect. Hence, "reason" would not be best strengthened by giving special privileges to certain "fractions of society" whose interests might sometimes be contrary to it. [16]

Tracy, then, did not unequivocally support the viewpoint of Boissy d'Anglas in 1795, cited above, nor indeed the related sentiments of Mme de Staël, who had also urged in the same year that the nation required an enlightened leadership possessing a certain combination of qualities:

> ... should not property and knowledge form a natural
> aristocracy, very favourable to the prosperity of a country
> and to the increase of this very knowledge? [17]

The supposed connection between property, education and political judgement was strongly reiterated twenty years later by Benjamin Constant, a close friend of Mme de Staël. According to him, while the classe laborieuse did not lack patriotism, it lacked the ability to know the true interests of the country. Moreover, the granting of full political rights to the non-proprietors would encourage government policies which undermined property and the work ethic. Electors and representatives

should all be proprietors, if corruption and tyranny were to be

avoided. Leisure, wrote Constant, is

> indispensable for the acquisition of knowledge and for
> making correct judgements. Property alone assures this
> leisure: property alone makes men capable of exercising
> political rights.[18]

Tracy, by contrast, was willing to allow universal male

suffrage providing that the method of election remained indirect. He

believed that class legislation would best be avoided by refusing to

differentiate between the political rights of various socio-economic

groups. The best strategy, he implied, was to emphasize common rights

and interests, not differential class qualities, which would only

encourage social conflict. Reason was more likely to prevail when not

formally attached to the destiny and interest of any social class.[19]

He also assumed that the civil equality embodied in the Rights of Man

posed difficulties for such discrimination.

Tracy's primary political orientation was the liberal-

constitutionalism of the first Assemblée Nationale of 1789-91. The

doctrines of civil equality, universal legal principles and rights,

abolition of traditional privileges, separation of Church and State,

limited powers of government, defence of private property, and minimal

regulation of industry and commerce - these were some of the main

articles of political faith among the liberals of 1791. Tracy remained

committed to these doctrines throughout the following decades of

political upheaval. However, the overthrow of the monarchy, the

changing fortunes of the republican régimes, and the rise of the

Napoleonic Empire, led him to modify his views on some points and

placed strains on the consistency of his outlook. He sometimes felt

obliged to make concessions in order to enhance, as he saw it, the

long-term success of his principles. It is necessary to return briefly to Tracy's reactions to political events in the 1790s.

Tracy's early political career saw him championing a reformed system of constitutional monarchy, which would incorporate guarantees of various legal and political rights of citizens; which would rationalize the administrative and taxation system; and which would acknowledge the fundamental right of the governed, through elected representatives, to make laws and levy the taxes. Tracy's belief in the advantages of representative government in protecting the natural rights of the citizens owed much to the American examples of constitution-making in the 1770s and 1780s, as well as to the general stream of philosophical opinion critical of autocracy and privilege. Tracy assumed, with Locke and Rousseau, that the sovereignty of the people was the basis of legitimate government. During the period of the first Constituent Assembly of 1789-91, Tracy was a firm adherent of a comp-romise between monarchy and democracy, which finally took shape in the 1791 Constitution.[20] There was no hint of republicanism in the views he expressed. On the contrary he agreed with Lafayette on the importance of maintaining public order,[21] and protection for the royal family at times when popular sentiments seemed to threaten their security; and he criticized all manifestations of "mob" rule in the streets and demagoguery in public journals.

The (unsuccessful) flight of the royal family towards the border in June 1791, widely understood as attempting to rally foreign support to defend the king's prerogatives against the encroachments of the Assembly, caused many of the liberals to reassess their loyalties towards the Crown.[22] There is no evidence of Tracy's views at this time, other than his apology to the Assembly for the involvement of his own regiment in aiding the king's flight. Further doubts about the king's sympathies were raised in Tracy's mind six months later when he returned to a military command under Lafayette; he called upon the king

to pay his respects before departing for the front, but was disappointed

to find Louis absorbed in the activities of an aristocrat preparing to

flee abroad.[23] When the dispute between the liberal constitutionalists

(including Lafayette) and the Jacobins reached total breakdown in mid-1792,

Tracy resigned his command to seek a more tranquil life of study and

domesticity away from the turmoil of public life. The monarchy,

alleged to be in collusion with the foreign powers, was declared over-

thrown after the riots of 10 August, and a National Convention was

elected in September 1792 to frame a republican Constitution. The king

was executed in January 1793.

Tracy was undoubtedly appalled by these events of 1792-3.

During the early months of the Republic before his arrest in November

1793, Tracy maintained an aloof propriety, eschewing political involve-

ment, but doing whatever was necessary to demonstrate his continued

"patriotism" and avoid being labelled an erstwhile aristocrat of dubious

civisme. His experience in prison apparently did not colour his later

attitudes to republicanism or to monarchy as such, but it undoubtedly

reinforced his earlier concerns for public order and political stability.

As will be seen later, however, Tracy had become extremely critical of

the principle of hereditary power by 1806 when he wrote his Commentaire,

doubtless in reaction to the development of Napoleon's autocracy.

With the establishment of the 1795 Constitution, the écoles

centrales, and the Institut, Tracy saw that the interest of those who

shared his general persuasion in political philosophy lay with the new

régime. There was no returning to the status quo ante: the 1791 comp-

romise could never be regained, for the doctrinal currents and personal

bitterness of the intervening years made consensus impossible - one

had to create a new consensus, based on republican institutions which upheld legality and constitutionalism. Support for "royalism" became, in the eyes of the idéologues, identified with the more vehement critics of the Directory, those émigrés and priests who wanted the restoration of throne and altar in the old manner and the reversal of all revolutionary reforms.[25] Tracy became a supporter of the post-Thermidorean settlement; for the polarization between extreme left and reactionary right could only be bridged, in his view, by a régime which occupied a new middle ground of constitutional republicanism.

The Directory was a régime without a broad social basis of support. It failed to generate the consensus and political stability desired by the idéologues, but it retained their support during four years of political discord, severe economic difficulties, and fluctuations in military fortunes. The Directory has often been condemned by historians as a period of economic mismanagement, banditry in the provinces, military adventure, political intrigue and moral decadence.[26] We are only concerned, however, to discuss why the idéologues continued to support the Directory, despite its unconstitutiona[l] actions (invalidating the election of alleged royalist deputies in September 1797 and of alleged Jacobin sympathizers in May 1798); and secondly, why the idéologues supported Bonaparte's coup of 18 brumaire abolishing the Constitution of 1795. The main political events of the Directory may be rapidly outlined.

Following the Babeuf crisis (the "Conspiracy of the Equals") in 1796, the elections of April 1797 gave a legislative majority in the lower chamber to royalist sympathizers, who threatened to withdraw the Directory's control over expenditure. A majority of the Directors believed that a coup was the only way to save the republic from an attempted restoration of the ancien régime and a purge of the revolutionary leaders. The coup of 18 fructidor year V (4 September 1797), with the military support of republican Generals, led to the exclusion of 195 deputies (over 50 were deported), the replacement of two Directors, and the annulment of election results in 49 departments. The Directory had judged that the wishes of the electorate were less important than the survival of the régime, at least when the continued existence of that régime was threatened by domestic and external opponents; thus, the possibility of compromise was rejected as impractical in a time of crisis. The Constitution allowed no legal way in which the legislature could be dissolved by the executive; the latter therefore resorted to force in the interests of its own political survival.[27]

In the elections of the following year, the Jacobins gained a majority in the legislature; the Directors again moved to annul the election of 127 deputies, this time by quasi-legal methods without military backing. This second coup of 22 floréal year VI (11 May 1798) showed that the Directory was balanced finely between the left and right, without a substantial social basis of electoral support for its own position. In mid-1799, after a further election, the legislature was able to force substantial changes in the personnel of the Directory, including the entry of Sieyès and others willing to countenance the replacement of the 1795 Constitution.[28] The Thermidoreans had built a series of checks and balances into the 1795 Constitution to prevent a repetition of the executive authoritarianism of 1793-4; but the fatal weakness of the executive had become obvious by 1799. Moreover, article 338 specified that proposals for constitutional change would take at least nine years.[29] No-one was prepared to wait. A strong government was seen to be necessary to control extremism and to deal with the economic and military problems facing the nation. Many of the liberal notables sought the leadership of a republican General: at the decisive moment, Bonaparte was the only one available judged to possess the requisite qualities of republican sympathies, respect for the sciences and arts,[30] and public acclaim for his military and administrative abilities.

The idéologues gave strong support to the Directorial coup against the royalist deputies in 1797, officially justified by the alleged discovery of a conspiracy to overthrow the republic. There is no direct evidence for Tracy's own opinions on the coups of 1797 to 1799, since no correspondence from these years has survived and he published no remarks on contemporary political events under the Directory.[31] However, Cabanis, his close colleague at Auteuil and the Institut, and whose political and philosophical views in the decade after thermidor coincided almost entirely with those of Tracy, was moved to defend the fructidorisation of the royalist deputies in September 1797 and was active in promoting and defending Bonaparte's coup in November 1799. Tracy's general outlook may be inferred from that of his colleague, though it is quite likely that Cabanis was more passionate in his enthusiasms than was Tracy, especially in regard to Bonaparte's coup.[32] These episodes raise critical problems for the character of the idéologues' liberalism and constitutionalism, as was suggested briefly in chapter one.[33]

Writing to a relative in the provinces during the assemblées primaires preceding the elections of April 1797, Cabanis urged the importance of electing deputies who were "attached to neither of the two extreme parties and who have enough firmness to defend the Constitution against open attacks, and enough insight to discern veiled attacks. If they had considerable knowledge, that would be all the better, for that is greatly lacking in the legislature".[34] In July 1797, following the royalist successes, he expressed his fear that the reaction was building up, and that key legislative proposals were being undermined:

> The ardour with which a part of the Council of 500 is
> concerned with useless or dangerous activities, means
> that there is no time remaining for the more important
> and necessary items. Bells and religion turn their
> heads, and they leave aside the finances, the civil code,
> the transactions before and during the depreciation of
> paper money. Mortgages are one of these urgent questions,
> but whose discussion requires considerable maturity, and
> they adjourn it continually. [35]

The Directorial coup, with military support, against the legislature

on 18 fructidor (4 September) was justified by Cabanis in the following

terms:

> Be assured that the 18 fructidor was necessary to avoid
> a civil war, the most frightful that could be imagined.
> The Council of 500 was moving rapidly towards a general
> upheaval. The government has saved the Republic; it has
> steered France away from the devastation which threatened
> it. This will be felt more and more, as the plots of the
> drama are revealed. The Constitution has been violated
> for a moment only in order for it to be preserved.[36]

Further evidence for the idéologues' support of the coup is

contained in the journal le Conservateur (edited by Garat, Daunou,

M.-J. Chénier, and Cabanis), which commenced publication only three days

before the coup. The "Prospectus", issued some time earlier, drew

attention to increasing signs of "struggles and civil war". The title

of the journal indicated its goals, namely, the preservation and security

of the Republic. The Prospectus stated that in any contest between the

legislature and the Directory, which had been established as independent

and equal parts of the constituted authority of the Republic, the part

which was "most devoted to the Republic" would be the more worthy of

support. "We will write in favour of neither the legislature nor the

Directory, but for the Constitution".[37] The early issues of the journal

strongly justified the 18 fructidor coup, interpreted as a defence of

the Constitution against extremist elements of the legislature. Similar

support appeared in la Décade during the same period.[38]

Directorial moves against a Jacobin revival in 1798 also
received idéologue approval, as had the crushing of the Babeuvistes
in 1796.[39]   In the May 1798 elections, Cabanis, Andrieux and
M.-J. Chénier were elected to the Council of 500, joining Daunou
(Garat was already a member of the Council of Ancients). Cabanis and
Andrieux became members of a legislative commission on the press;
although outvoted in the commission, they nevertheless were later able
to persuade the Council of 500 to extend the duration of the Directory's
special powers over press censorship.[40]   This was another example of
invoking restrictions upon political freedom in the name of the long-
term interests of liberal-constitutionalism. The inconsistencies,
exceptions,and special pleading continued to accumulate in the
liberalism of the idéologues during the Directory period. Some of
them began to wonder how to prevent the incessant political turbulence
and the crisis in finances without resort to a "strong man".[41]   Their
manoeuvring in the last months of 1799 helped to prepare the way for
Bonaparte's final blow against the 1795 Constitution.

The events of 18 and 19 brumaire are well known.[42]   Tracy
remained at Auteuil with other idéologues who were not members of the
legislative bodies.[43]   Cabanis, together with Daunou and M.-J. Chénier,
was closely involved in moves in the Council of 500 for the success of
the coup. The desire for stability and an "end to the revolution" was
strongly felt in most quarters of political society.[44]   Cabanis
delivered a strong critique of the Directorial political system in his
speech on 19 brumaire justifying the overthrow of the system. Given
that happiness was the goal of social organization, he claimed,a Constitution which could not uphold the happiness of the people was deficient.[45]
The people could not be free and happy when the common interest was
destroyed by factional strife, when laws threatening property and

liberty were a product of the disordered public life,

> when talents, virtues, wealth, sooner or later become
> grounds for proscription; when industry finds almost no
> more sustenance owing to the flight of capital and almost
> no stimulus owing to the fears of consumers; finally, when
> the laws and government itself are in a continual state
> of instability, which gives no solid guarantee to the
> citizens, breeding uncertainty and fears in every mind.[46]

Much of the blame for this sorry condition, he asserted, had to be placed upon the 1795 Constitution, which, despite its "excellent" principle of the division of powers, contained certain flaws: namely, by failing to guarantee solidity, "it encourages factions to attack it continually, even providing them with periodic opportunities to overthrow it, and constantly obliges conservative patriots to violate it themselves in order to protect it from these blows".[47] It was not possible to provide liberty and security for the people "in a country where annual elections put them in a fever for at least six months in every twelve"; when the large turnover of new deputies constantly changed the majority in the legislature; when the executive had means of usurpation but no means to govern and maintain social peace; and when a complex and expensive administration merely obstructed the laws and individual freedom. Everything encouraged arbitrary rule and civic agitation, menacing the people with both tyranny and rebellion. If one added the problems of a war against the despotic enemies of the Republic, one could see the reasons for the series of hasty measures and disorders, leading to "bad laws on finances, a host of vexatious details, and a system of administration that is wearisome, inquisitorial and tyrannical".[48]

The Jacobins, declared Cabanis, had seen that the existing institutions could not protect liberty and the Republic; but their solution was to seek extraordinary measures by declaring the country in danger. This would not have protected liberty, but only produced

disorganization and disintegration. The crises and failures of the

Directory period, he continued, had been perceived not only by the

politicians and public officials, but by the people themselves, who

wanted their legislators to make whatever changes were necessary to

protect their happiness, liberty, security, industry and possessions.[49]

The ordinary people were firmly opposed to any arbitrary and confis-

catory system; they wanted a secure and just system which guaranteed

the rights of all classes, and if such a system was not rapidly

established, they might unleash a new crisis which would ultimately spell

the end of all the gains of the Revolution:

> I often hear invoked in this Council the name of the
> people, but it is almost always by men who have a poor
> understanding of their opinions, sentiments and real
> wishes. I can speak of them, I dare to say, with
> greater knowledge; everyday I see the indigent class
> of manual labourers, I see this respectable class in
> their cottages or fourth-floor rooms; and I can truly
> claim that nowhere is shown a greater horror for so-
> called popular laws, that nowhere arise stronger
> desires for the return of a system of justice and security,
> which the people now recognize as the only one able to
> allow all the citizens to benefit from the wealth of the
> few and to extend a comfortable life to all parts of the
> society. The people's state of mind has reached a point
> where, unless you [legislators] are seen to make rapidly
> all the legislative changes required by their interest,
> their despair, together with their awareness of their
> rights which nothing can henceforth stifle, could at any
> moment make them rise up as in '89 in a popular and spon-
> taneous movement. But this disordered movement, with no
> precise objective, would inevitably precipitate into the
> same abyss not only the Constitution but the Republic and
> liberty.[50]

Given, then, that the 1795 Constitution was leading rapidly

towards the dissolution of liberty and of the nation itself, Cabanis

urged immediate constitutional changes, to be directed by a "provisional

government" proposed by the "Commission" of the legislature.[51] A

similar message was formulated by Cabanis for proclamation as an

"Address to the French people", which officially justified the coup in terms of the need to restore constitutional guarantees for "the liberty of the citizens, the sovereignty of the people, the independence of the constitutional powers, and the Republic itself", by means of a "firm and wise government" which could ensure peace and happiness. The 1795 Constitution had been ceaselessly undermined by "seditious men", provoking a series of revolutions by various political parties: "even those who most sincerely wanted to maintain this Constitution were forced to violate it constantly to prevent its destruction".[52]

Cabanis was thus one of the foremost spokesmen for the coup, which he desperately hoped would be the coup to end all coups, the guarantee of social stability and liberty. Two days later, he wrote to his cousin in the country, outlining the events of 18-19 Brumaire; he concluded with the "hope that their result will be to save the republic from the sway of bandits and assassins, and to found it at last on a solid base. Such have been, at least, the intentions of the men who were involved in this movement. I myself will always be proud of the part I played in it".[53] Cabanis became a member of the "Commission" of 25 deputies from the Council of 500 - the Bonapartist "rump" of the lower chamber. This group, in conjunction with the provisional government of Sieyès, Roger-Ducos and Bonaparte, met with a similar "Commission" from the Council of Ancients to draft a new Constitution. During the early part of these discussions, Cabanis felt obliged to rebut rumours from both the left and right which claimed that the new régime would threaten the property of those who had bought the confiscated land of the Church or of émigrés. Cabanis stressed instead the continuity between the intentions of the liberal notables in '95, '97 and '99:

> are not the men of the 18 and 19 brumaire the same who
> sought and prepared the 18 fructidor to halt the
> assassinations by royalist brigands, to repress the
> boldness of the émigrés who were then talking of taking
> back their former possessions? You have made these
> revolutionary fanatics see ... what the courage of

reason and conscience is like; you have proved to them
that moderates can be bold, when it is necessary. ... You
will now show them what should be the energy of moderation
after victory ...[54]

The text of the new Constitution of year VIII was completed on

13 December. A Proclamation of the Consuls to the people declared:

The Constitution is founded on the true principles of
representative government, on the sacred rights of
property, equality and liberty. The powers it institutes
will be strong and stable, as they must be to guarantee the
rights of the citizens and the interests of the State.
Citizens, the Revolution is established upon the principles
in which it originated: it is over.[55]

On the following day, Cabanis delivered a major speech to the "Commission"

of the legislature, analyzing and defending the principles of the new

Constitution. His remarks are of significance for two reasons in the

context of this study. The first is his elitist analysis of represent-

ative government, an analysis which Tracy generally followed in his

Commentaire, as will be seen towards the end of this chapter. Secondly,

Cabanis celebrated the Constitution of year VIII as a triumph of the

social art, a claim which he doubtless came to regret.

The new Constitution, wrote Cabanis, was based on the

representative system of government, which alone could ensure both

public liberty and a strong government that could maintain social

peace. The particular complex of representative institutions contained

in the Constitution combined the best aspects of monarchy (unity of

action), aristocracy (excellence of talents) and democracy (broad

support).[56] The essential principle of representative government,

according to Cabanis, was that the people should select men in whom

they had confidence to hold public office; but the people should not

themselves be involved in legislation, administration or making judge-

ments, and indeed should not directly decide which men would fill the

positions. Hence, elections should be indirect; electoral bodies were

better able to select appropriate candidates for office, because the

intermediate electors had a greater "interest in maintaining order
and public liberty, in the stability of institutions and the progress
of ideas, in the fixity of good principles, and in the gradual
improvement of laws and administration".[57] This was la bonne démocratie
with civic equality and responsiveness to public opinion. It was
"democracy without all its [usual] disadvantages", since the populace
did not congregate in the forum or in political clubs, and la classe
ignorante exerted no direct influence over the legislature and government; hence there would be no more demagoguery. "All is done for the
people and in the name of the people; nothing is done by it, or under
its unreflective dictates".[58] Sovereignty remained with the people,
but their control over public authorities was muted and indirect,
mediated by a transmission belt of intermediate élites which interpreted the public interest according to their own lights.

The new Constitution, Cabanis claimed, may also be seen to
include the best aspects of aristocracy, especially in regard to the
Sénat conservateur, composed of men devoted to the public interest and
directed to protect the liberty of all. "The only good aristocracy
is that which summons talents and virtues to public office: the best
of all ... would be that which rests on a popular base".[59] (Tracy
and Cabanis were appointed to this Senate of talent and civic virtue
several days later.) Cabanis noted, in a prediction which was to be
borne out by events, that the "most dangerous coalition against public
liberty" would be that of the strong executive together with the
Senate. Cabanis dismissed this as highly improbable, since the
Senate's duty and interest was to maintain the institutional balance
of forces.[60] Overall, Cabanis' assessment of the Constitution -
whose outlines he attributed to a plan which Sieyès had long been
meditating-was that it was a monumental achievement: it combined "the

fruits of experience" with an "inventive reason". The new
Constitution, he claimed, "would create a new epoch in the history
of the social art".[61]

Cabanis also took up another theme dear to the idéologues,
namely, the link between the progress of society and progress in the
sciences and arts. The "philosophical" ideas arising from the sciences
and arts had gradually undermined the influence of superstition and
weakened the strength of arbitrary power; the useful arts had given
economic independence to the workman as well as wealth to the more
fortunate. Cabanis claimed that knowledge, in conjunction with property
(which in recent centuries had in his view been more equally distributed
by industry and commerce), had created a "force unknown in the ancient
States, that force of la classe moyenne among whom are generally found
great talents and sound virtues".[62] At the present time, said Cabanis
(in words that anticipate the phrases of Saint-Simon and the young
Comte),

> the plan for scientific and industrial work is organized;
> the task of each kind of collaborator and the goal they must
> pursue are determined; the means of achieving the task and
> reaching the goal have been recognized: philosophy has
> placed very sure guiding threads almost everywhere.[63]

It was the task of "all good government", according to Cabanis, to
encourage the development of the "sciences, literature, philosophy and
the arts, for it is in this way that it also perfects itself, and
becomes continually stronger, linking its existence increasingly to
the public liberty and happiness of the citizens".[64]

The Constitution of year VIII, establishing the Consulate, was
ratified in a plebiscite in February 1800.[65] On the last day before
the "Commission" dissolved in favour of the new authorities, Cabanis
addressed his fellow brumairiens:

> To establish the representative system on its true
> foundations; to attach the ideas of morale and happiness

to that of liberty; to consolidate their influence by
means of a government which is strong and wise,
protective and energetic - such are the undertakings
we made on that memorable day [19 brumaire].[66]

The new Constitution had established, in addition to the executive

of three Consuls (granted authority for ten years) three bodies

dealing with legislation and constitutional procedures: the Sénat

Conservateur,the Tribunat and the Corps législatif. The membership

of the Senate was by appointment, and included many idéologues and

their friends. The 60 Senators chose the original 300 members of the

Corps législatif, and the 100 members of the Tribunate.[67]   Just

before these nominations were made, Cabanis made some exaggerated

claims for the new Constitution, claims which he no doubt came to

regret. The "new social pact", to be approved by the people,

combining all the lessons of experience with the views of
the soundest theory, must mark a new stage in the moral
and political sciences. You have rid democracy of the
agitation and disorder which have characterized it until
this time; you have borrowed from aristocracy whatever
utility it can offer for the improvement of selections for
public office, for the perfecting of moeurs and for the
emulation of virtues. You have even enriched your work
by that which has alone made monarchy bearable for so
long in civilized countries: I mean the unity of impulse,
energy, and harmony of movements.[68]

The irony is that this expected contribution to the progress of the

moral and political sciences, this embodiment of the idéologues'

political and philosophical aspirations, rapidly turned into an

instrument which neutralized their political influence, and increasingly

isolated them from the social consensus being forged by Bonaparte's

domestic and foreign policies.

The deterioration of political and personal relationships

between Bonaparte and the idéologues of the Tribunate and Senate,

and the evolution of the Consulate into the Empire with a hereditary

ruling family, have been mentioned in chapter one. The details have

been documented by many historians and require no further discussion

here. Tracy's energies under the Directory had been largely
channelled into his work on educational administration and the
further development of his theory of idéologie; he was not directly
involved in the political struggles of the period. It is difficult
to know how far he shared the illusions of his colleagues. His
nomination to a life-tenure position in the Senate suggests that he
was known to be a supporter of the new order. Tracy's views on the
constitutional problems raised by the Directory, Consulate, and Empire
were made known indirectly through his commentary on Montesquieu,
commenced two years after the coronation of Napoleon. In the following section, the main lines of Tracy's critique of Montesquieu are
discussed, focusing on the forms of government, their sources of
legitimation, and their social effects. In the final section, Tracy's
celebration of representative government is discussed, showing its
supposed connections with happiness, reason, and liberty, and the
constitutional provisions which it should embody.

II. CRITIQUE OF MONTESQUIEU

Tracy's major work of political theory was his _Commentaire_ on
Montesquieu's _l'Esprit des Lois_ (written during 1806-7 under the Empire)
It contained a number of veiled criticisms of Napoleon's régime as part
of a critique of the principle of hereditary authority. The circumstances of the publication of the _Commentaire_, and the light it throws
on Tracy's view of social science, have already been described in
chapter four. It is now necessary to discuss Tracy's political theory
in a more systematic way on the basis of the principles elaborated in
the _Commentaire_.

Tracy, following the structure of Montesquieu's work, began
by discussing the concept of _law_. Rejecting Montesquieu's proposition

that laws are necessary relations deriving from the nature of things,

Tracy substituted the idea that a law in society is

> a rule prescribed for our actions by an authority we
> regard as having the right to make this law: this last
> condition is necessary, for otherwise the prescribed rule
> is no more than an arbitrary order, an act of violence and
> oppression. This idea of law implies that of a penalty
> attached to its infraction, of a tribunal which applies
> this penalty, and a physical force which puts it into
> operation. Without all that, the law is incomplete or
> illusory.[69]

The "positive" laws made by men in society - "artificial and
conventional laws" - are to be distinguished from the "laws of nature",
which are the necessary expression of the operation of phenomena in
specified circumstances. Natural laws are unchangeable, whether
those governing falling objects, or those governing the sensible
qualities of animate beings including their capacity for happiness
and misery. Here again we find Tracy claiming that our "natural"
capacities form a kind of substructure of human action, on
which a social science of needs and their satisfactions could be
built. Natural laws, he claimed, could be discovered through the
observation of phenomena; how such observation could yield laws of
"human nature" was left to the science of idéologie. Tracy posed
the question of the relation between the positive laws of a society
and the natural laws governing our behaviour and capacities. He
claimed, in a way reminiscent of the "natural law" theory of the
physiocrats, that the "good" and "just" laws in a society are those
which conform most closely to the natural laws.[70] The difficulties
of detecting, or facilitating, such a correspondence between the social
and natural realms were glossed over. It was for idéologie to
demonstrate the basic faculties and needs of man, and for the various
human sciences to deduce the social and political institutions which
would maximize individual satisfaction within a social framework of

authority. The naturalistic terminology disguised the speculative character of the enterprise: the search for natural laws, to which social practices should conform, was a form of political philosophy disguised as empiricism.

Tracy regarded the science of politics as concerned to find those institutions and practices which would increase and secure human "happiness". Good and just laws were those which were directed towards this objective. Tracy noted that concepts of the "good" and "just" were applicable only to the second order of laws, those created by men. These laws should be judged in accordance with their effects upon human happiness (understood in terms of reason and liberty). Natural laws, on the other hand, were not subject to moral judgements: a law of nature was simply "necessary", since it could not be changed by our actions.[71] A genuine discourse on the spirit of laws, said Tracy, should investigate the degree of correspondence between positive laws and the natural laws of human action, in relation to the circumstances and organization of various societies.[72] Montesquieu was found inadequate for failing to undertake such a project.

Tracy examined Montesquieu's division of government (republic, monarchy, despotism) and found it of little use for his purpose of assessing how various institutional forms contributed to the happiness of man or conformed to the natural laws of human behaviour. Tracy noted that Montesquieu's first type, republic, was commonly stretched to cover a multitude of diverse historical cases, including various kinds of democracy, oligarchy and aristocracy. Moreover, the term republic was not an appropriate contrast to monarchy, for there were nations like the United States or Holland, usually called republics, which had a single chief magistrate.[73]

Montesquieu's second type, monarchy, should strictly denote

a government where executive power was held by a single person; but this fact alone, said Tracy, did not sufficiently describe the essence of that social organization, and could be found to co-exist with many other diverse characteristics. In Great Britain, for example, authority resided in some respects with a noble aristocracy; and the _ancien régime_ of France was really an ecclesiastical and feudal aristocracy, of both robe and sword.[74] In fairness to Montesquieu, it should be pointed out that Tracy's two examples were not inconsistent with Montesquieu's own view of monarchy, wherein a single person governs by fixed and established laws, and where power flows through intermediate bodies, particularly the nobility and judiciary.[75]

According to Tracy, Montesquieu's third type, despotism, should not be regarded as a separate type of government, but rather as an abuse of power which may enter to some extent into all political forms, whenever the rule of law gives way to the arbitrary will of one man or of a group. No government is ever established with arbitrary rule as its guiding principle - it is rather a degeneration which may occur when people have not taken adequate precautions against its emergence. The nearest approximation, said Tracy, would not be the Oriental empires, but Denmark, where the King had been granted unlimited discretionary power in order to prevent a restoration of influence by the nobles and clergy. Yet his rule had been so moderate that it seemed a misnomer to call his government a despotism. Even the old French monarchy, with its claims to hold authority from God alone, was not a despotism, despite its enormous abuses: it was always a limited monarchy. The term despotism, then, could not stand as a separate type of government. In practice it usually meant simply a brutally conducted monarchy.[76]

The threefold classification of republic, monarchy and despotism, Tracy concluded, was completely unsatisfactory, producing many confusions, and was not applicable to many of the states commonly contained in each category. What alternative classifications were available? Tracy equally rejected a division of governments which had been attributed to Helvétius in a letter allegedly written to Montesquieu.[77] According to this conception, all governments could be simply divided into "the good", which do not yet exist, and "the bad", which variously enrich the governors at the expense of the governed. Tracy's main objection was that since each government may produce some good and some bad practical effects, it could be placed in one or other category at various times.[78] Moreover, Tracy professed to adopt a more detached and objective attitude than Helvétius claiming he did not seek to judge the intrinsic merit of a government's theoretical principles. His Commentaire was more akin to Montesquieu's work in being descriptive and analytical: Tracy wanted only to "describe what exists, show the different consequences arising from the various modes of social organization, and leave to the reader the task of drawing his own conclusions in favour of one or another form".[79]

After this claim to be presenting only the facts, Tracy proposed his own twofold classification of the "fundamental principles" of governments (leaving aside the "diverse forms" which they might take). The first was called gouvernement national ou de droit commun, and the second was called gouvernement spécial ou de droit particulier et d'exceptions. Tracy added in a note that "we could also say public or private, not only because one is founded on the general interest and the other on some private interest, but also because the one effects publicity in all its deliberations and the other, mystery".[80] The reader could be left in no doubt concerning the preference of the author.

Tracy's first type of government, however organized in detail, was based on the principle that "all rights and powers belong to the whole body of the nation, reside in it, emanate from it, and only exist by it and for it". Such a government would proclaim the principle - asserted in the _Parlement_ of Paris in October 1788 - that holders of public office, _qua_ officials, have only duties, while the citizens alone have rights. A "national" government of this type might take one of many possible forms - from absolute democracy (where the whole nation strictly exercises all powers); representative government (where power is delegated to officials elected periodically); various forms of aristocracy (where power is granted wholly or partly to groups of men, whether for life, whether hereditary, or with powers of co-option); or it might even be a monarchy (where power is entrusted to a single man, with hereditary rights or otherwise). Beneath this diversity of possible forms, there would remain the fundamental principle that the system might be changed or abolished if the nation so desired, and that no-one had the right to oppose the general will as manifested in the recognized manner.[81]

The second type of government included all those forms whose authority was based on sources of legitimacy other than the general will - such as divine right, conquest, birth in a certain place or caste, mutual capitulation, or an agreement of some kind. As with the general will, these diverse sources of particular rights could also give rise to many forms of democracies, aristocracies and monarchies: but different kinds of rights would be recognized. The organization of a "special" government was difficult to alter by legal methods because this would require agreement by groups with very different interests and beliefs.[82]

Tracy reiterated that he was not concerned to judge the relative merits of each type of particular right, nor the merits of national and special governments. His point of departure was, with Montesquieu, to examine the nature of "the laws which tend to conserve each form".[83] It soon became evident, however, as the comparative analysis proceeded, that Tracy was a strong advocate of national government based on the general will, and especially a champion of representative government as that form most likely to develop the talents and protect the interests of its citizens. In his distinction between two main forms of government, it is noteworthy that he was less concerned with institutional organization than with types of legitimacy and the effects of policies upon the citizens.

Tracy criticized Montesquieu's discussion of the cultural sources of legitimacy and stability - the sentiments which must be held by the citizens - in each of the forms of government. Montesquieu had claimed that the sentiments of virtue, honour and fear corresponded to his classification of governments: republic, monarchy and despotism. Tracy found this list of sentiments misleading and inappropriate. He conceded that a sentiment such as virtue, honour or fear might be seen as the principe conservateur of a political society, enabling it to continue over time; but that was quite different from the principe moteur of a society, which arose from the actions of its governing power.[84] For example, fear among the population might well facilitate and encourage despotism, but that cannot make fear the "principle" of this government; despotism is a tendency towards the abuse of power found in all types of government, and stems therefore from a variety of sources. Moreover, a reasonable man might prefer to suffer arbitrary abuses to forestall even worse suffering, and this could be seen as motivated by reason and not by fear. Since no-one seeks to increase the abuses he suffers, it may be that citizens would voluntarily grant a government greater powers in response to a temporary crisis.

Montesquieu's principle of honour (and ambition) in a monarchy, and the principle of virtue (and moderation) in a republic, are also found to be deficient by Tracy. All these sentiments may take contradictory forms, some of which are elevating and some of which are despicable. Honour may be either dedicated to the good it produces, or may be merely a glittering exterior indulging in fashionable vices. Ambition may take a generous form, content to obtain the gratitude of one's fellows, or a selfish and power-hungry form which uses any means available. Moderation may likewise vary, being wise or weak, magnanimous or dissimulating, according to circumstances. As for virtue, why is it appropriate only to republics? Would it be out of place in other governments, and is that desirable or inevitable? Does Montesquieu really believe that the vices he portrays in court life are as useful and necessary to monarchy as other more virtuous qualities?[85]

Having rejected Montesquieu's classification of the types of government and the sentiments which sustained them, Tracy pursued his own conception of the types of government and their consequences, beginning with the diverse forms comprised in the type called "national" (where sovereignty lay with the whole nation). The first of these forms was "pure democracy" or "absolute democracy". According to Tracy, this system could be relevant only to a very small territory, and could last for only a short period of time. It was thus an "almost impossible" system of government, confined to a few primitive tribes and peoples in a remote corner of the earth; as soon as social relations become more highly developed, it soon fell into anarchy and, in its quest for peace, was led to aristocracy or tyranny. Even the ancient Greek democracies were of short duration, and were not self-sustaining: they were always protected by their federative links; and in another sense, they were really aristocracies of free citizens, considering the huge numbers of slaves excluded from public life.[86]

If the "original democracy" developed into an aristocracy, and thereby into superior and inferior classes, the principes conservateurs of the system came to consist in the pride and competence of one class and the humility and ignorance of the other. In the same way, if direct democracy was transformed into a monarchy (having a single ruler, whether hereditary or for life), the government was stabilized by such sentiments as the monarch's sense of dignity and superiority; by the arrogance, ambition and devotion of the courtiers, their scorn for the inferior classes; and finally, by the superstitious respect among the lower classes for all this grandeur and their desire to please those who were decked out in it.[87]

All these sentiments, said Tracy, were functionally useful for the maintenance of monarchy, whatever may be our judgement of such ideas from other viewpoints and whatever their other effects on society at large. He suggested that an aristocratic or a monarchical form of government was in theory possible for a "national" type of government, so long as general respect for the rights of man and the sovereignty of the citizens as a whole still predominated. In practice, however, respect for the rights of citizens tended to be soon forgotten. These governments would quickly turn into "special" governments based on the legitimacy of particular rights, as soon as a general respect for the rights of man was abandoned.[88] The only form of "national" government which promised to be long lasting and consistent, in Tracy's view, was representative government. This form will be

discussed in detail in the last section of this chapter; Tracy's views
on the other forms of government are the focus of the present section.

Tracy assumed that a government whose principe conservateur
most closely conformed to the sentiments of "human nature" would not
only have the best chance of survival, but would be the most likely
to encourage the development of individual talents and thereby the
prosperity and happiness of all. Tracy's discussion therefore turned
rapidly from Montesquieu's functionalist preoccupation with the sentiments
needed to sustain a government,[89] towards a concern for the social
consequences of each type of government. Tracy looked primarily at
the kinds of sentiments, opinions, and knowledge typically engendered
and fostered by each type of government: these social and cultural
effects, said Tracy, were "much more important for the happiness of
men".[90]

Perhaps the most important area for an idéologue like Tracy
was the extent to which the various governments tried to curtail or to
encourage the development of knowledge and its diffusion among the
citizens. Tracy examined the monarchical and aristocratic forms of
"special" government. He gave a scathing portrait of the type of
education fostered by a hereditary monarchy.[91] Whether its legitimacy
was based on conquest, ancient possession, social pact, or divine
right, the hereditary monarchy

> is bound to inculcate and propagate the maxims of passive
> obedience, a profound veneration for established forms,
> confidence in the permanence of these political arrange-
> ments, a great antipathy to the spirit of innovation and
> inquiry, and great aversion to the discussion of principles.[92]

To this end, the monarch would draw support from religious ideas
which, influencing the mind from infancy, formed lasting habits and
firm opinions before the age of reflection; the priests should be made
dependent upon the monarch's power, in order to be a source of

stability instead of undermining his authority. And among the religions, he should promote the interests of the one that is most concerned to dominate minds; prohibit inquiry; preach the sanctity of precedent, tradition and hierarchy; uphold faith and credulity; and spread the greatest number of dogmas and mysteries.[93]

In the realm of culture and society, the monarch must seek to induce gay and superficial qualities of mind and manners, whether in the fine arts and literature or in the graceful reaches of high society. Erudition and the exact sciences may be safely encouraged – indeed, remarked Tracy, the success of the French in these accomplishments and their corresponding fame and vanity, long diverted them from serious business and philosophical research, matters which a monarch should seek to repress or discourage. If he succeeds in all these methods of social control, there is little more to be done, to protect his power and stability, than

> encourage in all the classes of society a spirit of individual vanity and a desire for distinction. For this purpose it will suffice to create a multiplicity of ranks, titles, privileges and distinctions, in such a way that the most esteemed honours are those which are most closely associated with his person.[94]

These measures, according to Tracy, captured the general spirit in which the education of the subjects should be directed in a hereditary monarchy. It was necessary that precautions be taken

> to provide only a limited instruction among the lowest classes of the people, and to restrict it virtually to religious teachings. For this class of men needs to be kept in a degraded state of ignorance and crude passions, so that they do not progress from an admiration of all that is above them in society, to a desire to escape their miserable condition; or even to conceive of the possibility of change, which would make them the blind and dangerous instrument of reformers of all kinds, whether fanatical and hypocritical or benevolent and enlightened.[95]

Similarly, the aristocratic form of "special" government, where the nobility claim legitimate authority over the rest of the nation, would be concerned to restrict the content and diffusion of

education. However, wrote Tracy, there were two main differences,

one concerning the role of religion, and the other concerning the

need for serious education among the nobility themselves. In the

first place, the noble aristocrats are less imposing and less united

than a monarch; they therefore cannot plausibly claim the authority

of divine right, nor can they with confidence manipulate religious

ideas and the priesthood. Religion, as an instrument of social

control, must therefore be used with more caution and discretion.

Giving too much importance to religious ideas might place too much

power in the hands of the priests, whose influence over the people

might rival that of the government; or, in forming a party within

the nobility, the priests might divide them and manage to take over

the mantle of power for themselves.[96] In the case of Berne, where

the clergy were not rich or ambitious, the simple teachings of the

local faith could be used peaceably to direct the people and keep

them in a condition of benign ignorance. In Venice, on the contrary,

the nobles had to deal with a powerful and turbulent priesthood,

dangerous on account of their dogmas and their dependence on a foreign

sovereign. Religious ideas could not, therefore, be encouraged by

the nobility lest the priests turned it to their advantage; but neither

could they combat religion by fostering "reason and enlightenment",

for that would "soon destroy the spirit of dependence and servility".

Their solution was to plunge the people into a condition of disorder,

yet controlled by a rigid system of police.[97]

Secondly, the interests of the aristocracy differed from

those of a monarch also in regard to the education of la classe

supérieure of society. Whereas the nobles and courtiers in a monarchy

could be encouraged to adopt a spirit of vanity, levity and lack of reflection, the governing body of an aristocracy required in its members qualities of solid knowledge, hard work, business acumen, capacity for reflection, a circumspection and prudence even in their pleasures, and a certain gravity and simplicity of manners. The ruling nobles had to understand man and society and the interests of various states, if only the better to combat them when necessary. Their principal study and occupation should be la science politique in all its dimensions. Insofar as such knowledge was cultivated, the aristocracy had a strong interest in confining it to themselves. They had even more to fear from an enlightened tiers-état than did a monarch, though the latter also was most threatened from this quarter.[98]

Tracy ignored the educational doctrines appropriate to pure democracies of all kinds because they were largely theoretical or "imaginary" systems, and because those which had existed were operated by primitive peoples among whom there was no "education in a strict sense". Tracy equally passed over what Montesquieu had called despotism because such a government was generally only a brutal form of monarchy.[99] Tracy has a little more to say about the monarchic and aristocratic forms of "national" government, whose interests would be largely the same as those discussed earlier as "special" governments. The difference was that they would have to demonstrate more respect for the governed, since they claimed to derive their legitimacy from the general will. They could not brutalize the people, nor weaken and impair the minds of la classe supérieure, without undermining their own character as a national and patriotic government based on the rights of man, and without thus reverting to a form of "special" government. In the latter case, their legitimacy would be weak if the citizens had previously experienced the benefits of a government of universal rights where "reason and truth" were not neglected.[100]

Tracy regarded legislation as one of the key influences shaping the ideas and behaviour of citizens: all laws had the effect of inspiring certain sentiments and discouraging others, tending to produce certain actions and restraining others of an opposite kind. In the long term, the laws thereby guided the _moeurs_ and habits of men.[101] The question posed by Tracy is what type of laws were most conducive to the various forms of government. Having once more criticized many of Montesquieu's views as inconsistent, imprecise, based upon a faulty classification, and inattentive to the requirements of human nature,[102] Tracy again adopted his own nomenclature to tackle the question of how forms of law were related to forms of government.

Monarchy, in the sense of the authority of a single ruler, had its origins in a condition of ignorance and barbarism. It tended to be despotic, with its administration and revenue-raising conducted by force rather than by a system of legislation. The ruler was obliged to control the nomination of his successor and also to make use of religious authority where possible to control his ignorant subjects. To transcend this precarious form of social organization, the ruler must elaborate a more systematic and complete form of authority, perhaps establishing a precise line of hereditary succession confined to a sovereign family. But such authority would be too isolated to survive unsupported for long - it was necessary to create around it a great number of ennobled families, whose permanent interests were tied to those of the monarchy: the term "honour", said Tracy, was merely a mask for their real interest in securing the obedience of the whole people.[103]

The private rights of the monarch should be buttressed by the private (but subordinate) rights of a nobility who were strong yet submissive. The monarch should make use of respected and established forms, while making them dependent on him; everything should have a certain plausibility that avoids recourse to discussions of original rights and authority. Montesquieu's functionalist advice to monarchs on how to preserve their system was thereby vindicated, according to Tracy. Even the most contentious point, the need for venality of offices, was confirmed by this analysis, because the monarch was still able to maintain his choice of officials, his revenue was increased, and the successful purchasers were sure to uphold that external show and grandeur which was so important in a monarchy.[104]

Finally, this venality helped to impoverish the tiers-état, profit the treasury, and swell the fortunes of la classe privilégiée by the entry of new wealth from below. This was an important consideration, since in this system, all the wealth of society was produced entirely by the industry, commerce and useful arts of la classe inférieure. This class would rapidly become the most wealthy and powerful, were they not constantly repressed and exploited, for they had already accumulated the most knowledge and wisdom by virtue of their occupations. If the members of la classe moyenne (i.e., the more wealthy and educated sections of the tiers-état) were not tempted by foolish vanity to seek entry into the nobility, they might soon take hold of all the benefits in society. The intermarriage between rich plebeians and poor nobles was one way of preventing this from occurring.[105]

Montesquieu's advice to an aristocracy[106] on how best to preserve their authority was also endorsed by Tracy as accurate, except to warn that Montesquieu's prohibition against aristocratic fortunes should be balanced by ensuring that members of la bourgeoisie did not accumulate great wealth; otherwise, the richest commoners would have to be absorbed into the ranks of the aristocracy itself. Monarchies and aristocracies claiming to be based upon popular sovereignty had the same interests and the same methods available as the "special" forms already discussed, except that they had to be more circumspect in their tactics, for they should be seen to rule in the interests of the whole people. It was clear enough, noted Tracy, that all those methods designed to protect the "particular" interests of the governors were "contrary to the general good and to the prosperity of the masses".[107]

This account of Tracy's critique of Montesquieu may be concluded by discussing the "great problem" of arranging the structures of authority so that "none of them may trespass on the limits prescribed by the general interest", and so that the authorities be kept in line by "peaceful and legal means".[108] Montesquieu had devoted considerable attention to the "balance" of power among the executive, legislature, and judiciary, taking England as the best example of such a system of checks and balances. Tracy found that the English system operated in a somewhat different manner from that envisaged by Montesquieu, and that the freedoms enjoyed by Englishmen had little to do with these institutional checks and balances. His critique of Montesquieu and of the English Constitution was inspired partly by his dislike of the influence enjoyed by the Crown and the hereditary nobility in that country, and partly by his admiration for the United States constitutional arrangements. These antipathies and enthusiasms naturally endeared his work to Jefferson, whose reading of Montesquieu as an Anglophile coincided with Tracy's.[109]

The principle of the "division of powers" as a bulwark against arbitrary government was accepted by the idéologues as a major triumph of the social art. There were obvious dangers to the liberty of the citizens if two or more of the branches of authority fell into the same hands. The difficulty, wrote Tracy, was not to perceive this manifest fact, but to discover the methods of avoiding it. Montesquieu, said Tracy, "spared himself the trouble of seeking out these methods; he preferred to think he had found them", namely, in his idealized conception of the English government.[110] Montesquieu too quickly forgot that legislative, executive and judicial functions are really only delegated trusts, and that authority flows by right from the will of the nation. He was preoccupied with his view of these powers as independent rivals, which need only be mutually restrained for public liberty to be protected. He failed to note the crucial importance of executive power, and thus conceded it too readily to a single man, even on a hereditary basis, purely because an individual was alleged to possess more unity of action than a plurality. He should have asked whether such a man would permit other free action to exist around him, and whether a ruler chosen by chance would have the necessary wisdom for governing. Montesquieu had given no satisfactory reason for the continued existence of a privileged hereditary body in the legislature with a veto power over decisions by the freely elected body. The judicial functions of the House of Lords did not give that Chamber an independent regulative function: it was really "an appendage and advance-guard of the executive power,... and to give it a veto power and judicial authority only strengthens the party of the court..."[111]

The English system, according to Tracy, continued to operate not because of any "balance", but because of public sentiments and the ability of the executive to control the machinery of authority. Public attachment to personal liberty and a free press, and the existence of certain civil and criminal procedures, were what protected the citizens from their government. Public opinion could be made known; and when the king had abused his power, he had been overthrown. This

deposition of the monarch, wrote Tracy, is a last resort forced upon
a civilized people, who will endure many evils before turning to such
a remedy. They may even become so conditioned to servility that they
lose the desire or capacity for change. Tracy added, in a note to
the 1819 edition, that when he wrote these remarks under the
Napoleonic régime, "we greatly feared that the oppression would last
so long that people would become accustomed to it."[112] The problem of
the division of powers was better resolved in the United States,
according to Tracy; its Constitution prescribed what should be done
where the executive and legislature were in opposition, where one
exceeded its authority, and where constitutional amendment was necessary.[113]

Tracy's remarks criticizing hereditary monarchy were coloured
by his attitude to the Napoleonic régime; the defender of the 1791
compromise had become a mordant critic of the hereditary principle.
In England, said Tracy, the monarch was really "a parasite, a superfluous wheel in the machine, augmenting its friction and expense".[114]
The monarch depended on his ministers, who actually governed the
country, and his own influence depended on controlling part of the
legislature. Tracy rejected the belief that unity in the executive
was best obtained by granting it to a single individual: this had
been the doctrine of the physiocrats.[115] On the contrary, a plural
executive - as in a council of ministers - could still reach united
decisions by majority; it was better able to implement them than an
individual, and would be more consistent in policy.[116] Tracy outlined
what he saw as the distinction between the American presidency and the
Napoleonic régime. There was a great difference, he claimed, between
a single chief executive who was answerable to the electors at
intervals, whose powers were circumscribed, and who remained "the
first magistrate of a free people" rather than a monarch; and, on the

other hand, a single chief executive whose fate was tied to that of the régime as a whole, whose powers were much broader, and whose succession was established in a governing family. The interest of this second type of ruler becomes separated from that of the people: they want peace and happiness, while he thrives on discord and military adventures Such a man clings to power, or loses it only amid public calamity.[117]

For Tracy, the hereditary principle is false in both theory and practice. It is absurd, he jested, that a man will unthinkingly obey a hereditary monarch, when "he would be considered deranged if he declared hereditary the functions of his coachman or his cook".[118] Rare is the man who could not be corrupted in time by unconstrained power; and it is even less likely that his eldest child would be capable of wise and moderate rule. The greatest problem, however, is that the principle of hereditary power tends naturally to be exclusive and unlimited, and thus inconsistent with the principle of the general will, which tends to be temporary and revocable. Liberty and monarchy are antithetical principles.[119] Montesquieu had been correct to detect corrupt tendencies in monarchist government: luxury, disorder, conquest, and contempt for the knowledge found in moral philosophy. Hereditary power "divides the nation in different classes, to dominate some by means of the others, subjects them all by illusions, and consequently produces misery and error in theory and practice."[120] For Tracy, then, the problem of ensuring the liberty and happiness of citizens could not be resolved "so long as one gives too much power to one man", such that he could not be removed without violence and without changing the whole system.[121] All of Tracy's remarks on the defects of governments which are not based on the general will, serve as background to his discussion of the system most in accordance with human nature, reason, liberty and happiness: representative government.

III. REPRESENTATIVE GOVERNMENT: REASON AND LIBERTY

The conception of representative government outlined by Tracy in his Commentaire is an ideal-type construction, not a description of any existing system nor an average of historical examples.[122] Representative government, in his view, may be demonstrated to be the most advanced form of political organization, and the most in accordance with fully developed human capacities. It is the system created by free and rational men in order to maximize that same reason and liberty. It is the fulfilment of the science of politics, understanding that science as concerned with social happiness.[123] Unlike earlier forms of democracy, founded in ignorance, representative government is "the democracy of enlightened reason".[124]

In representative government, said Tracy, all the citizens participate in electing their delegates, and limit the extent of public authority in accordance with the provisions of an agreed constitution. Whereas direct democracy belongs to primitive peoples in a confined territory and is of short duration, representative government is a democratic form capable of continuous existence and is suitable for states of all sizes. It is the state of la nature perfectionnée.[125] Representative government, in Tracy's view, is "a new invention" still unknown in the time of Montesquieu. It could scarcely have been created before the great effects of the invention of printing had been understood, and in fact was not conceived until three centuries after the discovery of "that art which has changed the face of the world". The written word, Tracy pointed out, facilitates both communication among the citizens, and the delegates' accounting for their actions; and it helps avert those sudden storms aroused by impassioned eloquence.[126]

The _principe conservateur_ among the citizens living under
representative government, according to Tracy, is "love of liberty and
equality, or if one likes, of peace and justice".[127] The spirit of the
citizens is opposed to the spirit of conquest and usurpation (an obvious
critique of Napoleon, and an anticipation of B. Constant's famous brochure
of 1814[128]). They are more concerned to protect their possessions, and
to extend them only through the development of their own talents and
industry, never through violating others' rights or through appropriating
public wealth. They feel threatened themselves by any injustice suffered
by their neighbour at the hands of the public authorities. They are
not deflected from their concern for the rights of all by any prospect
of personal gains or favours - for in the latter case, they would soon be
led to condone arbitrary actions by the government in the hope of obtaining personal reward.[129]

These sentiments which sustain representative government are
closely linked to Tracy's conception of human nature. Man's "natural"
sentiments are held to consist in "simplicity, the habit of work, scorn
of vanity, and love of independence".[130] Tracy did not provide reasons
why such qualities were more inherent in man than vanity, idleness and
submissiveness. His viewpoint was based on an assumption, held by Rousseau
and many philosophes, that "natural man" was unpretentious and uncorrupted.
That so many men were victims of "unnatural" sentiments was an indictment
of the social institutions and culture which facilitated such practices
and values. The metaphor of "nature" as a pristine form of goodness is
a frequent theme in the writings of Tracy and the idéologues. They
simultaneously argued that society is the product of art and labour, and
that a fully developed society in some way recaptures a "natural" archetype.
In any case, men's "natural" sentiments need to be nurtured and encouraged
in order to survive and develop. These simple and industrious qualities,

he claimed, are so much "in our nature" that they can be "infallibly
and necessarily produced" in us through "a little habit, good sense,
some wise laws, and the experience that violence and intrigue seldom
bring success". The virtuous qualities arising from human nature were
quite different, in his opinion, from the sentiments demanded by
Montesquieu's "republican virtue", because the latter was based on self-
renunciation, a motive which Tracy saw as contrary to human nature and
which could thus be sustained only for a temporary period and by
fanaticism.[131]

One of Tracy's main criteria for good government is the extent
to which reason and knowledge are protected and encouraged. Unlike the
governments founded on various kinds of privilege, representative government was closely linked with the pursuit and protection of reason and
truth.

> [Representative government] can in no way fear the truth;
> its constant interest is to protect it. Founded solely on
> nature and reason, its only enemies are error and prejudice.
> It must always try to foster sound and solid knowledge of
> all kinds; it cannot subsist unless they prevail. All that
> is good and true is in its favour, all that is bad or false
> is opposed to it. Thus, it should encourage in every way
> the progress and especially the diffusion of knowledge, for
> it has a greater need of spreading knowledge than of making
> new discoveries. Being essentially united with equality,
> justice, and la saine morale, it must constantly attack that
> most dangerous kind of inequality, connected with all the
> others: the inequality of talents and knowledge in the differ-
> ent classes of society. It must continually try to protect
> la classe inférieure from the vices of ignorance and misery,
> and la classe opulente from those of insolence and false
> knowledge. It must try to bring them both nearer to la classe
> mitoyenne, which is naturally imbued with the spirit of order,
> work, justice and reason, since, by its position and its
> direct interest, it is equally distant from all excesses.[132]

This is a philosophical claim about social and political perfectibility
rather than an analysis of institutional structures and historical
practices. This impression is confirmed when we turn from Tracy's concern
with the effects of government upon education, to the social effects in

general of the various forms of government. After the oppressive and deceitful strategies attributed to other régimes, Tracy's idealized account of representative government appears to be a list of virtues, in systematic opposition to the defects of monarchies and aristocracies. Moreover, they can be read as a series of prescriptions rather than descriptions.

In the first place, representative government does not rest on the use of force, manipulation, intrigue or illusions, but gives free rein to "all inclinations that are not depraved and all industry that is not contrary to good order. Being in accord with nature, it has only to let it act".[133] Secondly, representative government "tends towards equality", but rejects all forcible measures in this direction (for they have only a temporary effect, fail to achieve their goal , and are unjust and oppressive). It seeks to reduce as far as possible the "worst" form of inequality - that of knowledge - and to develop all talents, encourage their free operation, opening up to everyone the roads to fortune and fame.[134]

Thirdly, representative government has an "interest" to ensure that the accumulation of great riches is not perpetuated in the same hands, but should be dispersed and returned to general circulation. This can be done indirectly, without force, by legislating against primogeniture titles and privileges; and establishing measures such as equal distribution of property among children, limiting the freedom of testament, and allowing divorce under certain conditions, thereby preventing marriages and wills from becoming objects of speculation by those unwilling to seek wealth by honest industry.[135] Tracy had advocated similar measures several years earlier in his essay on _la morale_, discussed at the end of chapter three above.

Fourthly, representative government should encourage a "spirit of work, order and economy". There is no need to keep track of all the actions and circumstances of every individual, restrict their choice of occupation, or arouse their anger with sumptuary laws which are an affront to liberty and property. It is enough to avoid impeding men in their reasonable pursuits, to provide no encouragement to pomp and vanity, and to prevent men acquiring rapid wealth as a result of the mismanagement of state finances. With a small number of such measures, said Tracy, most families will be found to practise domestic virtues even if surrounded by external temptations.[136]

Fifthly, representative government, whose interest lies in the diffusion of truths and the dissipation of errors, has no need to protect "what it believes to be the truth" by manipulating public opinion: whether by paying writers, by engaging professors, preachers and actors, by distributing selected elementary texts, almanachs, catechisms, pamphlets, periodical journals, or by multiplying inspections, regulations, and censorship.[137] On the contrary, the government should simply leave each individual in the full enjoyment of his right to say and publish what he pleases, confident that "when opinions are free, it is certain that truth will eventually come to the fore, and become evident and immovable". Representative government has nothing to fear from this, since it is founded upon, and submits readily to, "right reason" and the general will. Government then, should only intervene in the realm of opinion in order to ensure the conditions of calm deliberation necessary for discussions and decision-making.[138]

Finally, since public offices under representative government are generally assigned by the free vote of citizens and the rest by the careful choice of the elected government, and since no such position confers permanent tenure or huge rewards, the venality of offices is quite foreign to representative government. There being no class that it wants to impoverish, nor any class that it wants to make superior, such a practice is repugnant; representative government, Tracy repeats, has need of "enlightened citizens" and not of vain and ignorant men.[139]

Tracy attempted to relate his discussion of the types of government to a notion of historical development, in which a sequence of three main types could be observed. In primitive societies, government is either a pure democracy or a pure monarchy (in the narrow sense of unrestricted rule by one man, or what is commonly called despotism).[140] All societies necessarily commenced with one of these forms, or changed from one to the other according to circumstances, such as the need to wage war. Neither type is capable of enduring for a very long period; they are "intolerable" systems of government, made by crude and ignorant men who understand no principles of social organization. They are founded on ignorance and maintained largely by force; their system of punishments is based on vengeance for wrong-doing, and their more barbarous penalties are destructive of la morale.[141]

At a second state of civilization, the primitive forms of government having broken down through the discontent they produced, there have gradually emerged inequalities of wealth, talents, and power of all kinds. The more powerful use their resources and combine together to take control from the people or from the despot. Thus there gradually developed aristocracies of various types - with plural or single leader-ship - whose original basis of legitimacy seemed to consist simply in possession. They made use of convenient religious or other opinions to support their position, and their system of punishments was justified in terms of divine vengeance. Most nations in history, remarked Tracy, have been aristocracies of one kind or another, including in this category what is called limited monarchy.[142]

In very recent years, wrote Tracy, a third stage of political organization has commenced in a few advanced nations, where the whole people, renouncing all previously established bases of inequality, unite through their freely elected delegates to establish a legally constituted representative government, based on the general will.[143] In this third type of political society, sustained by "reason" and "philosophy", the system of punishments is based on the rational desire to discourage future crimes, not to redress or avenge the wrongs committed by the criminal. In accordance with the liberal jurisprudence of Beccaria, Voltaire and others, Tracy asserted that it is the mark of a liberal and enlightened régime that criminal penalties are less severe and are graduated in accordance with the importance of the crime and the temptation to commit it. Emphasis should be placed on ensuring that criminals cannot escape punishment, which is the greatest deterrent of all.[144]

Representative government is also that system which is most concerned to establish simplicity and uniformity in its civil laws, for, unlike aristocracies with their disparity of social ranks, this government cannot exist without the equality and union of its citizens.[145] The liberty of the citizens requires that certain modes of civil and criminal procedure be adopted. Private or civil cases should be determined by an independent judiciary, rather than by the government itself or by special commissions. In regard to criminal law, it is proper that public authority and not private citizens should initiate prosecutions, for it is one of the tasks of the state to reduce the incidence of crimes. Criminal procedure should strive for simplicity and respect for the rights of man, thereby allowing the accused to mount an adequate defence. Juries, said Tracy, repeating his viewpoint of 1798, are most commendable from a political viewpoint, insofar as they are a strong obstacle to tyranny and encourage men to take greater notice of injustices suffered by their fellows. (From a purely judicial viewpoint, however, there was no high probability that juries were more likely to arrive at the most accurate or just decisions.) Juries were more compatible with governments whose principles upheld liberty, justice and concern for public affairs.[146] Political liberty, claimed Tracy, is most favoured by representative government, for political liberty "cannot exist without individual liberty and freedom of the press, and for the maintenance of these, all arbitrary detention should be proscribed and the use of juries adopted at least in criminal cases".[147]

In seeking a form of government more in accordance with "nature, truth and reason", a few nations had embarked on a new era of social organization. The principe moteur and the principe conservateur of representative government were identical: it was "reason" which both sustained and motivated them.[148] Their main principles could be reduced to three points. Firstly, government is for the people, and exists only by majority will; if the people's will changes the government changes; all citizens should have the right to emigrate; and there should be no hereditary power, or any privileged or oppressed groups. Secondly, public authorities should be able to be changed without violence and without the whole of society changing also; hence, all power should never be entrusted to one individual; there should be a strict separation of executive, legislative, and judicial or conservatory powers; and any constitution-making body should again be separate from these other powers.[149] Thirdly, the government should seek the independence of the nation, the liberty of its citizens, and domestic and external peace; the government should never threaten the security of the citizens, their rights of free speech, or their freedom of religious beliefs. It should seek to obtain international agreement on its proper territorial boundaries,[150] and on this basis seek to make federative links with its neighbouring states, preferably entering

into a "formal federation". This would be the "highest point of international law", where violence gave way to justice, and where the rights
of nations could really be called laws.[151]

A free constitution, said Tracy, should be based on the above
"fundamental laws". They are "immutable" constitutional principles,
"eternal truths" based on our own nature; they should never be changed,
whereas the "positive laws" must always be subject to change in accordance with public opinion. These basic principles would be even more
useful than declarations of the rights of man, which had been attached
to several French constitutions in the 1790s. Such declarations had
been a great contribution to the "social art"; but the essential thing
was to show the constitutional principles by which they could be secured.[152]
Tracy gave further attention to the institutional forms most conducive to
a free and rational system of government in book XI of his Commentaire.
Having rejected Montesquieu's proposed solution (checks and balances on
the English model), Tracy endeavoured to discover "theoretically rather
than historically" the principles of a free and peaceful constitution
for a nation with a unitary system of authority.[153]

A new constitution is best drawn up by an elective assembly
created especially for that task, and which would be dissolved when its
deliberations were concluded. The task should not be entrusted to the
existing authorities, whose tasks are properly confined to legislative or
other specific functions. Nor should it be consigned to a wise theorist
who could perhaps produce a highly coherent document but one which might be
inflexible, lack public support, or which might lead to his being granted
executive power by public acclaim. A constitutional assembly, on the other
hand, would have the advantage of producing a more practical document which
was acceptable to the public; and would pose no threat to the future
security of the nation if it was obliged to be dissolved after finishing

its work.[154]   The election of members to such an assembly, Tracy argued, should be conducted in a two-tiered or indirect manner;[155] the views of Tracy and Cabanis on the importance of indirect elections in represent- ative government have already been discussed in section I of this chapter.

Tracy made a few substantive recommendations on how the three main branches of government should be constituted. The legislative power, he believed, should not be entrusted to a single man but to an elective assembly subject to periodical renewal. This assembly might for conven- ience - or specialization of functions - be divided further into parts, but the principle of its unity should not be impaired, thus avoiding the possibility of its becoming incoherent or fragmented.[156] The executive power should not be confided to one individual: as we saw earlier, Tracy rejected the view that unity of action is best obtained by a single man. He argued that a plural executive - a council of state ministers - was more effective; it could be just as united in carrying out policy, it would be more consistent, and it could be more easily changed. Most important , however, was the fact that the power of a single ruler was dangerous to liberty and popular sovereignty, especially if that man held hereditary power.[157] Both the legislature and executive should be recog- nized as owing their functions to the general will.

Tracy was particularly concerned to specify the functions of a third branch of authority, to "facilitate and regulate the action" of the other two branches. Tracy was not concerned here with the judicial authorities presiding in civil and criminal cases, but with a corps conservateur whose tasks were political and constitutional.[158] The import- ance of such a body was clear from the recent history of France: it was the "keystone" of any free constitution.[159] Its absence from the 1795 constitution had led to internecine warfare between the executive and legislature and the overthrow of the system.[160] The body created for

this function in the 1799 constitution (the Sénat conservateur, of which

Tracy was a member) had failed to perform its task, and voted the

"illegal" provisions creating the Napoleonic Empire; but its manner of

appointing and replacing members had been improper from the very beginn-

ing and had been further corrupted as time went by.[161] The members of a

corps conservateur should be chosen by the electoral bodies. Its members

should consist of men of maturity, "beyond the age of passions and great

projects", who would undertake such functions in recompense for their

past services to the nation; they would hold office for life, but be

excluded from all other public positions.[162] The functions of this body

would be to supervise the elections of members of the legislature and

executive, and the nomination of supreme court judges; to decide upon

questions of the constitutionality of actions by the executive or of

laws passed by the legislature; and to determine procedures for constitut-

ional revision.[163]

Did Tracy believe that all his recommendations were practicable?

Or were they simply "the soundest notions of reason and justice" for an

ideal constitution? Tracy showed that he was sensitive to the variability

of historical conditions and to the impossibility of there being one form

of organization appropriate to all times and places.[164] He conceded that

a plan which carried "the theory of social organization" to a higher degree

of perfection was of little utility by comparison with a plan which had

the support, or suited the various desires, of the citizens.[165] It is

always true, said Tracy, that a nation is free to the extent that its

people support their régime - even if an alternative government is more

in keeping with "the principles of liberty".[166] Institutions can only be

improved in step with the development of general enlightenment. The best

institutions in an absolute or theoretical sense are not always the best in relation to the actual desires of a people. The 1795 Constitution, for example, had been out of step with popular opinion.[167] If an ideal system is opposed by many citizens, it could only be maintained by force, thereby destroying liberty, happiness and stability. It is thus essential to understand the historical variations between societies. The best form of government in each society is that in which the most people are content.[168]

> ... it is not a matter of speculation and theory in the affairs of this world, but of practice and results. It is this which affects individuals, who are sentient and actual beings, not ideal and abstract entities.[169]

Liberty and happiness are inseparable; but happiness, measured in terms of subjective wants, is the real measure of freedom. Thus, the "only thing which makes one social organization preferable to another is that it is better able to make happy the members of the society".[170] However, if there are established ways in which their desires can be made known, this makes it more likely that they will be governed in accordance with their will.[171] These arguments show that Tracy ultimately rejected the _dirigiste_ solution which had lurked in the background of idéologue thought in regard to the reconstruction of society and culture. He declared that politics is about subjective wants, not objective interests. This was to place a considerable distance between his liberal political theory and the centralist solutions of both the physiocrats and the egalitarian Jacobins.

Tracy argued that an abstract ideal must undergo considerable change if it is to be implemented in a society. In the case of France, he concluded (in a note added to the 1819 edition of the _Commentaire_) that

> constitutional monarchy, or representative government with a single hereditary leader, is now, and for a very long time to come, despite its imperfections, the best of all possible governments for all the peoples of Europe and especially for France.[172]

Was Tracy simply inconsistent and opportunistic in making this concession
to historical relativism? He denied it, claiming that he was "only
establishing the very important difference ... between the abstractions
of theory and the realities of practice".[173] Tracy's Commentaire was
nevertheless seen by liberals as an important contribution to the
political debate in Restoration France. The publisher of the anonymous
1817 edition claimed that the publication of a French edition, several
years after the American edition, was "a true service to the liberals of
all countries".[174] While Tracy's critique of the hereditary principle
may have appeared misplaced in the context of the Restoration, his
defence of individual liberty and free speech, his emphasis on the
principle of popular sovereignty, and his view of the need to constrain
the powers of the executive, and restrict the role of the state in economic
regulation,[175] marked his work as belonging to the main currents of liberal
thought. The Commentaire also showed that Tracy's thought had become
more firmly gradualist in outlook under the Empire: the inculcationist
remarks of 1796-1801, seeking to hasten the spread of reason, gave way to
a long-term evolutionary perspective. Tracy did not withdraw his view
that reason would ultimately triumph, or that representative government
of the type he described was the highest form of social organization.
There was an implication, however, that the gap between ideal and reality,
though diminishing, remained large. The subjective wants of men seldom
coincided with theoretical analysis of their objective interests as
rational beings. Tracy also appeared to agree that the stability and
security of established forms of authority were a "good" in themselves,
especially if these forms enjoyed the support of their citizens.

The source of progress in human societies was knowledge and
experience. Education was the means of bridging the gap between ideal
and reality; it was the means by which a society sustained itself

(socialization) and advanced the happiness of its citizens (economic, political and technological progress). The importance of education in the ideologues' thinking can scarcely be underestimated. This is the subject of the final chapter.

FOOTNOTES TO CHAPTER SIX

1   Cf. Max Weber, "Politics as a Vocation", in From Max Weber: Essays in Sociology, ed. Gerth and Mills (New York, 1946), pp. 100ff.

2   In the sense discussed in chapter four.

3   Cf. the writings of Professor Michael Oakeshott, and the collection of essays edited by P.T. King and B.C. Parekh, Politics and Experience (Cambridge, 1968).

4   Cf. the views of the marquis de Mirabeau cited in chapter four, p. 210. Sieyès held a similar view: cf. P. Bastid, Sieyès et sa pensée, p. 388.

5   J.-P.-M. Flourens, Discours (1836), p. 9.

6   Cf. the remark by Amaury Duval, editor of la Décade, on 29 January 1797: "the inequality of talents would serve the equality of happiness". Cited in M. Régaldo, "Lumières, Elite, Démocratie", p. 203.

7   Cf. text of Constitution in J. Godechot, Les Constitutions de la France depuis 1789, p. 101f. The property qualification operated at the second level of a three-tier structure of representation. See also G. Lefebvre, The Thermidoreans (London, 1965), chapter 9; J. Godechot, Les institutions (1951), p. 395f.

8   Boissy d'Anglas, Discours préliminaire au projet de Constitution de l'an III, 5 messidor (23 June 1795): for the translation, see Lefebvre, op.cit., p. 189.

9   Commentaire, pp. 177-178. For another instance of Tracy ascribing certain qualities of mind and temperament to women, cf. De l'amour, pp. 50-51. Tracy, however, condemns social systems in which women are domesticated slaves, "the playthings and victims of men": Commentaire, p. 299. Tracy argues that it is only in countries guided by liberty and reason that women escape various forms of oppression and indignity: ibid., p. 103.

10 For Condorcet's views, cf. Selected Writings, pp. 97-103, 134-140; the latter extract is also reprinted in C. Hippeau (ed.), L'instruction publique (1881), pp. 279-288. For a strong statement of the traditional distinction between male (public) and female (domestic) roles, cf. the "Discours de Mirabeau sur l'instruction publique" [1791], in Hippeau, op.cit., especially pp. 12-14. This discours is usually attributed to Cabanis who was the doctor and friend of the comte de Mirabeau (not to be confused with his father, the physiocratic marquis de Mirabeau). The report on public instruction by Talleyrand in September 1791 made similarly traditionalist distinctions: see Hippeau, op.cit., especially pp. 175-181.

11 Commentaire, pp. 177, 179.

12 Ibid., pp. 170-176.

13   Ibid., pp. 179-180.

14   Ibid., p. 180. For the meaning of the term "aristocracy" in this
      context, see the discussion of Cabanis below, and Cabanis, Oeuvres
      philosophiques, vol. II, pp. 467, 472, 475.

15   Tracy made a few obvious exceptions on grounds of age, infirmity of
      mind, criminality, or employment by foreign powers (ibid., p. 177).

16   Ibid., pp. 175-176.

17   Réflections sur la paix intérieure [1795], cited in G.E. Gwynne,
      Madame de Staël et la Révolution française (Paris, 1969), p. 58.
      Cf. also Moravia, Il tramonto, pp. 233ff.

18   B. Constant, Principes de la politique [1815], chapter 6, in Oeuvres,
      ed. Roulin (Paris, 1957), p. 1113. Constant's remarks are similar
      to those of Boissy d'Anglas reprinted in Moravia, Il tramonto,
      p. 242n.64.

19   Commentaire, pp. 174-176.

20   Cf. M. de Tracy à M. Burke (1790), p. 9. Cf. Cabanis, "Notes pour
      la Cour" (1791).

21   Tracy à Burke, p. 13.

22   Cf. Moravia, "La Société d'Auteuil et la Révolution", pp. 181-191.

23   Mignet, "Notice historique sur ... Destutt de Tracy", p. 252.

24   Cf. the "patriotic gifts" he was forced to pay in 1793: G. Rougeron,
      Destutt de Tracy, p. 7.

25   Cf. M. Lyons, France under the Directory, chapter 3; Cobban, History,
      vol. I, p. 249.

26   For some attempts to re-evaluate the Directory, see the work of
      M. Lyons, op.cit.; A. Goodwin, "The French Executive Directory:
      A Revaluation", History, vol. 22 (1937), pp. 201-218; C.H. Church,
      "In Search of the Directory", in French Government and Society 1500-
      1850, ed. Bosher, pp. 261-294; G. Lefebvre, The Directory (London,
      1965).

27   M. Lyons, op.cit., chapters 2 and 3; Lefebvre, op.cit., chapters 5
      and 7.

28   Lyons, op.cit., chapter 15; Lefebvre, op.cit., chapters 10 and 14.

29   Text in Godechot, Les Constitutions, p. 138.

30   Cf. Moravia, Il tramonto, pp. 299-305; G. Lacour-Gayet, Bonaparte,
      membre de l'Institut (Paris, 1921).

31   The main exception is his 1798 discussion of whether there had
      been a démoralisation under the Directory: see above, pp. 193-194.
      Tracy also made a critical remark about the lack of constitutional

safeguards in the Directorial system, in <u>Commentaire</u>, p. 208.

32 Cf. Victor Jacquemont, letter of 17 November 1824 to Stendhal, in Jacquemont, <u>Lettres à Stendhal</u>, ed. P. Maes (Paris, 1933), p. 107.

33 Above, pp. 27-32.

34 Vermeil de Conchard, <u>Trois études sur Cabanis d'après des documents inédits</u> (Brive, 1914), p. 32: letter of 9 germinal an V (29 March 1797).

35 <u>Ibid.</u>, pp. 34-35: letter of 29 messidor an V (17 July 1797).

36 <u>Ibid.</u>, p. 35: letter of 4 vendémiaire an VI (25 September 1797).

37 <u>Le Conservateur</u>, "Prospectus", pp. 1-2.

38 For secondary analysis of <u>la Décade</u>'s position, cf. Kitchin, <u>op.cit.</u>, pp. 51-53, and Fargher, <u>The 'Décade philosophique'</u>, Part I, chapter 2. B. Constant also rallied to the Directory, and was involved in organizing the <u>cercles constitutionnels</u> supporting the Directorial group: cf. Challamel, <u>Les clubs contre-révolutionnaires</u>, pp. 513-518; E. Asse, "B. Constant et le Directoire", <u>Revue de la Révolution</u>, vols. 15 and 16 (1889); Moravia, <u>Il tramonto</u>, pp. 270ff.

39 Cf. Kitchin, <u>op.cit.</u>, pp. 54, 193-194.

40 Cabanis, <u>Discours ... relatif aux journaux calomniateurs des premières autorités</u>, 1er fructidor an VII (18 August 1799); cf. Kitchin, <u>op.cit.</u>, p. 57n.1.

41 Cf. <u>la Décade</u>, 10 thermidor an VII (28 July 1799), p. 253, for a prescient statement of concern lest the series of convulsions and reactions might lead not to a strengthening of the constitution but to "le despotisme d'un seul".

42 Cf. A. Vandal, <u>L'avènement de Bonaparte</u>, vol. I.

43 Guillois, <u>Le Salon de Mme Helvétius</u>, p. 3.

44 Cf. Moravia , <u>Il tramonto</u>, p. 288.

45 "Discours ... du 19 brumaire an VIII", in <u>Oeuvres philosophiques</u>, vol. II, p. 451.

46 <u>Ibid.</u>, p. 452.

47 <u>Ibid.</u>, p. 453.

48 <u>Ibidem</u>.

49 <u>Ibid.</u>, p. 454.

50 <u>Ibid.</u>, pp. 454-455.

51 <u>Ibid.</u>, p. 456.

52   "Adresse du Corps législatif au peuple français", in ibid., vol.
     II, pp. 457-459.

53   Vermeil de Conchard, Trois études, p. 41: letter of 21 brumaire an
     VIII (12 November 1799).

54   "Cabanis à ses collègues", Amis des lois, 30 brumaire an VIII
     (21 November 1799), no. 1545, pp. 2-3: cited in Aulard, Paris sous
     le Consulat, vol. I, p. 17. In fact, there was no threat to the
     owners of biens nationaux: the new Constitution protected the rights
     of the purchasers (articles 93 and 94: see Godechot, Les Constitution
     p. 162).

55   Proclamation by the Consuls (Bonaparte, Cambacérès and Lebrun),
     15 December 1799, in Godechot, Les Constitutions, p. 162.

56   "Quelques considérations sur l'organisation sociale ...", 16 December
     1799, in Oeuvres philosophiques, vol. II, pp. 470-473.

57   Ibid., p. 474.

58   Ibid., p. 475. (See also p. 481.)

59   Ibidem.

60   Ibid., pp. 488-489.

61   Ibid., p. 482.

62   Ibid., p. 481. (Cabanis' notion of a classe moyenne combining
     education and property is similar to Tracy's idea of a classe
     savante, described in chapter seven. Tracy also discussed the
     importance of a classe mitoyenne in his Commentaire: see the third
     section of this chapter on Tracy's notion of representative govern-
     ment.)

63   Ibidem.

64   Ibid., pp. 481-482.

65   The results were reported in the Moniteur of 22 pluviôse an VIII
     (11 February 1800), p. 565: over 3 millions in favour and 1562
     against.

66   Discours prononcé par Cabanis ... séance du 3 nivôse an VIII (24
     December 1799), p. 2.

67   This procedure was in accordance with sections 20 and 24 of the
     Constitution. See also the Procès-verbal des élections (nivôse an
     VIII), pp. 1-27. The membership of the Senate included Tracy,
     Cabanis, Garat, Volney, Lambrechts, Laplace, Lagrange, Monge,
     Lenoir-Laroche and François de Neufchâteau. The Tribunate included
     Andrieux, M.-J. Chénier, B. Constant, Boisjolin, Daunou, Gallois,
     Ginguené, J.-B. Say, and Laromiguière: they were removed in the
     épuration of 1802.

68   Discours ... du 3 nivôse an VIII [footnote 66 above], p. 2.
     The need for a strong executive was justified by Cabanis in terms
     of the grave problems facing the nation: cf. "Quelques considér-
     ations sur l'organisation sociale", in Oeuvres philosophiques,
     vol. II, pp. 477, 482n. 486.

69   Commentaire (Paris, 1819), pp. 1-2.

70   Ibid., pp. 2-4, and 220.

71   Ibid., pp. 4-5.

72   Ibid., p. 6.

73   Ibid., p. 7.

74   Ibid., p. 8.

75   Montesquieu, De l'esprit des lois [1748] (Paris, 1922), vol. I,
     book 2, chapter 4.

76   Commentaire, pp. 8-10. For further discussion of the three forms,
     cf. ibid., pp. 63-66. See also Cabanis, Oeuvres philosophiques,
     vol. II, pp. 466-473.

77   It has been shown that the letter was probably a forgery, written
     by the editor of the 1795 edition of the Oeuvres of Helvétius, the
     abbé Laroche: cf. R. Koebner, "The authenticity of the letters on
     the 'Esprit des lois' attributed to Helvétius", Bulletin of the
     Institute of Historical Research, vol. 24 (1951), pp. 19-43. Tracy
     had reprinted the letter in the American edition of his work:
     A Commentary and Review of Montesquieu's Spirit of Laws, pp. 285-289.

78   Commentaire, pp. 10-11; cf. Commentary, p. 288 for the distinction
     attributed to Helvétius.

79   Commentaire, p. 12.

80   Ibidem.

81   Ibid., pp. 13-14.

82   Ibid., pp. 14-15.

83   Ibid., p. 15.

84   Ibid., p. 16.

85   Ibid., pp. 17-19.

86   Ibid., pp. 21-22.

87   Ibid., pp. 25-26.

88   Ibid., pp. 26-27.

89   Ibid., p. 31.

90   *Ibid.*, p. 27.

91   Tracy also allowed for an "elective monarchy", *ibid.*, p. 38: one possible example was Bonaparte's authority as Consul for life, and later as Emperor, both ratified by plebiscite. Tracy, however, possibly would have included these systems under his category of national governments, owing to their profession of respect for the rights of man, but would have argued that the rights tended to be undermined by the form of authority itself.

92   *Commentaire*, p. 35.

93   *Ibid.*, pp. 35-36. It would be of some interest to compare and contrast the advice to a prince given by Machiavelli, Montesquieu and Tracy.

94   *Ibid.*, p. 37.

95   *Ibid.*, pp. 37-38.

96   *Ibid.*, p. 39.

97   *Ibid.*, pp. 39-40.

98   *Ibid.*, pp. 41-42.

99   *Ibid.*, pp. 42-43, 64.

100   *Ibid.*, pp. 43-44.

101   "Quels sont les moyens", p. 463; *Commentaire*, p. 46.

102   *Commentaire*, pp. 47-50.

103   *Ibid.*, pp. 51-52.

104   *Ibid.*, pp. 53-54.

105   *Ibid.*, pp. 54-55.

106   *Ibid.*, pp. 48-49; Montesquieu, *De l'esprit des lois*, book 5, chapter 8

107   *Commentaire*, p. 56.

108   *Ibid.*, p. 159.

109   Cf. Chinard, *Jefferson et les idéologues*, chapter 2; Lafayette, *Mémoires*, IV, p. 350-351.

110   *Commentaire*, pp. 150-152, 226.

111   *Ibid.*, pp. 152-154.

112   *Ibid.*, pp. 156-157 and 157n.

113   *Ibid.*, pp. 159-160.

114 Ibid., p. 186. Tracy even argued (pp. 111-112) that representative government would be "cheaper" to operate because the court and idle aristocracy would not be a drain on public funds. Max Weber, a century later, argued that democratic egalitarianism breeds an increasingly expensive bureaucratic structure: cf. From Max Weber, p. 224.

115 Cf. Le Mercier de la Rivière, L'ordre naturel ... [1767], chapters 16, 17, 18; Dupont de Nemours, De l'origine et des progrès ... [1768], ed. Dubois, p. 31; Lefure de Beauvray, Dictionnaire social ... (1770), "Monarchie", pp. 361-367: "In politics as in mechanics the machine which is the most simple and the least complicated is always the best" (p. 361).

116 Commentaire, pp. 185-189.

117 Ibid., pp. 190-192.

118 Ibid., p. 194.

119 Ibid., pp. 194-197.

120 Ibid., p. 198.

121 Ibid., pp. 226-227.

122 I mean to suggest a parallel with Weber's concept of an ideal-type: cf. Max Weber, Methodology of the Social Sciences (New York, 1949), p. 90. Tracy's model of representative government is doubly an ideal-type, given his passionate attachment to that particular type of government.

123 Commentaire, p. 308.

124 Ibid., p. 57.

125 Ibid., p. 22.

126 Ibid., pp. 23, 115.

127 Ibid., p. 23. (The American translation by Jefferson used the words "country and equality": Commentary, p. 19.)

128 B. Constant, "De l'esprit de conquête et de l'usurpation", in Oeuvres, ed. Roulin, pp. 949ff. Constant's ideas also were originally developed in 1806: cf. p. 1570.

129 Commentaire, pp. 23-24.

130 Ibid., p. 24.

131 Ibid., pp. 24, 29-30.

132 Ibid., pp. 44-45. The notion of a "middle class" characterized by reason, work and education is rather similar to Aristotle's discussion in Politics, sections 1221-1222. Tracy's theory on this point is to be distinguished from the somewhat self-congratulatory

conception of a <u>classe moyenne</u> in the work of F. Guizot, who succeeded Tracy in the Académie française: see, for example, Guizot's <u>Discours de réception</u> (1836), p. 17 and the reply by Ségur, p. 30.

133 <u>Commentaire</u>, p. 57.

134 <u>Ibid.</u>, pp. 57-58.

135 <u>Ibid.</u>, p. 58.

136 <u>Ibid.</u>, p. 59.

137 <u>Ibid.</u>, pp. 59-60. The version of this passage in the American edition is quite different in its implications: assuming that Jefferson's translation is accurate and not embellished by additional phrases, Tracy claimed in his original manuscript that such devices as mentioned in the text should be used, in order to establish "new incentives to genius and virtue": <u>Commentary</u>, p. 43. Perhaps Tracy reconsidered his position after seeing how these devices were used by the Napoleonic régime.

138 <u>Commentaire</u>, p. 60.

139 <u>Ibid.</u>, pp. 60-61.

140 <u>Ibid.</u>, pp. 63-64.

141 <u>Ibid.</u>, pp. 66-67, 62, 75.

142 <u>Ibid.</u>, pp. 68, 62, 229.

143 <u>Ibid.</u>, p. 68.

144 <u>Ibid.</u>, pp. 62, 230, 75-76. There is an interesting parallel between the evolutionary conceptions of law and punishment enunciated by Tracy, and those of E. Durkheim 70 years later. Durkheim was also a close reader of Montesquieu.

145 <u>Commentaire</u>, pp. 70-71.

146 <u>Ibid.</u>, pp. 71-73.

147 <u>Ibid.</u>, p. 217; on freedom of individuals and the press, cf. p. 210.

148 <u>Ibid.</u>, pp. 230-231.

149 <u>Ibid.</u>, p. 231.

150 The question of the best territorial boundaries for a state was discussed in <u>Commentaire</u>, book 8. Tracy noted in book 10 that a nation should go to war in self-defence, but never for any other reason; where this led to conquests, it was legitimate to create new independent states, which would be fortunate indeed if they were given representative government: this would be more like being rescued from bondage than being conquered! (<u>ibid.</u>, p. 135).

151 Commentaire, p. 232. The question of international federation was discussed also in ibid., pp. 129-130. On the separate question of the relative advantages of a federal vs. unitary system of government for a single state, cf. ibid., book 9. Tracy allowed that federation was useful for the American system, with a large territory and no hostile neighbours, but claimed that France had needed to be a unitary state to survive its wars with the European coalitions: ibid., p. 121, and also letter of 21 October 1811 in Chinard, Jefferson et les idéologues, p. 90. Chinard points out a resemblance between Tracy's view of the conditions for the success of American federalism, and the view of Tocqueville: op.cit., pp. 93-94.

152 Commentaire, pp. 233-234.

153 Ibid., p. 160.

154 Ibid., pp. 162-168.

155 Ibid., pp. 169-180.

156 Ibid., pp. 181-185.

157 Ibid., pp. 185-199. Jefferson disputed Tracy's preference for a plural executive: cf. Chinard, Jefferson et les idéologues, letter by Jefferson to Tracy, 26 January 1811, pp. 75-77.

158 Commentaire, p. 203.

159 Ibid., p. 206.

160 Ibid., p. 208.

161 Ibid., p. 208n.

162 Ibid., pp. 206-207. Tracy's "upper house" was not hereditary, but based on merit. For a different assessment of the hereditary principle, cf. the views of Mme de Staël, Constant and Lanjuinais, discussed in G.A. Kelly, "Liberalism and Aristocracy in the French Restoration", Journal of the History of Ideas, vol. 26 (1965), pp. 509-530.

163 Commentaire, p. 203-205.

164 Ibid., p. 209.

165 Ibid., p. 166.

166 Ibid., p. 146.

167 Ibid., p. 147.

168 Ibid., p. 148.

169 Ibid., p. 149.

170 Ibidem.

171 *Ibid.*, p. 150.

172 *Ibid.*, p. 211.

173 *Ibidem.* Cf. a similar distinction in his letter to Jefferson of 14 July 1814, in Chinard, *Jefferson et les idéologues*, p. 125.

174 *Commentaire* (Liége, 1817), p. v ("Avertissement de l'éditeur").

175 On the proper role of the state in economic affairs, cf. Tracy, *Traité*, pp. 350–352, 358–363, chapter 12; and *Commentaire*, chapters 13 and 22. A more activist conception appears in Condorcet's *Sketch*, pp. 131–132, 180–181. Tracy's position is close to that of Adam Smith in most respects: cf. Reisman, *A. Smith's Sociological Economics*, chapter 7.

CHAPTER SEVEN
PUBLIC INSTRUCTION AND IDÉOLOGIE

I   Public instruction and the Directory

II   Idéologie in education

III Defence of the "écoles centrales"

I. PUBLIC INSTRUCTION AND THE DIRECTORY

Tracy had argued in 1798 that legislators and rulers were the true teachers of humanity, and that a sound moral instruction was dependent on a proper framework of legislation and administration.[1] It was necessary, however, that these authorities should be suitably enlightened in their actions: "truth is the sole road to well-being", and truth consisted in a knowledge of the laws of our own nature and those governing our environment.[2] The elitist character of the educational writings of Tracy and other idéologues arose partly from their environmental determinism and partly from their scientism. Progress could be achieved by modifying the institutional environment which conditioned the people's actions and beliefs; but only an élite equipped with scientific knowledge of men and their environment could intervene in a decisive manner to control the direction of social change.

It had become a commonplace in eighteenth-century social philosophy that education was the key to reforming moral and political practices and improving the material prosperity of the people. Ignorance and habitual prejudice were taken to be the main obstacles to human improvement, for they were seen as the pillars supporting all forms of oppression, injustice, inequality and superstition . If the individual's ideas were shaped, as Helvétius[3] emphasized, by his social milieu, this implied that the cycle of repression and determinism would be reproduced by each generation unless an "external" force intervened to alter the institutional pattern. This was the role of the savants. The determinist theory implied the possibility of social engineering by the élite. A different pattern of values and beliefs could be encouraged by carefully modifying the social and cultural environment, so that virtue, honesty and co-operation would be rewarded, for example, instead of selfish and dishonest behaviour. It was this theory of education and environment which Marx summarized in his

critical claim that the "materialist doctrine concerning the changing of
circumstances and education forgets that circumstances are changed by
men and that the educator must himself be educated. This doctrine has
therefore to divide society into two parts, one of which is superior to
society".[4]

The educational theories of Tracy and the idéologues were
directly related to their project of making the people "free and happy".[5]
Education was what "made" man, and education could change him for the
better if properly planned. Instruction in "making good judgements
habitual"[6] was essential for moral and social behaviour as well as for
advances in the sciences of physical nature. The argument of this
chapter is that the idéologues' conception of knowledge in terms of
propositions derived by "ideological" deduction from the observation of
man's natural capacities, and their emphasis upon the diffusion of a
scientific model of thought, led to a "transmission" conception of
education. The task of the enlightened élite of legislators and educators
was to frame rational institutions, distil the essential principles of
scientific knowledge, and ensure that these ideas were widely extended
throughout the society. Public instruction was the necessary adjunct to
rational political and legal authorities.

It was no accident that the idéologues were deeply involved in
the educational projects of the 1790s: the diffusion of science, and
especially of "scientific" approaches to social and moral questions, was
central to their reforming enterprise. Moreover, the educational developments after thermidor may be regarded as essentially idéologue in characte'
This direct connection between idéologie and public instruction makes
necessary an account of the educational system of the Directory, as part
of my discussion of Tracy's educational activities and writings. This
chapter is concerned to discuss the "ideological" principles which infused

the educational system of 1794-1801, Tracy's contribution to the theory
and practice of this system, and his defence of the system when it was
about to be disbanded under the Consulate.

The physiocrats had been among the forerunners of the idéologues
in calling for a national system of public instruction, and in regarding
it as the state's responsibility to ensure that all citizens received a
basic training in literacy, civic duties and vocational skills. They
regarded such education as necessary for social organization in accordance
with knowledge of the "laws of nature". Instruction was seen as a key
element of the "social art".[7] The idéologues, as we saw in chapter one
(pp. 25-27), further developed the educational plans of the early years
of the Revolution and made them the foundation for their programme of
political socialization and the diffusion of scientific thought. Public
instruction was seen by Daunou as the means to end the years of turmoil,
secure the positive gains of the Revolution, and promote social harmony.[8]

The role of the state in public instruction was to be strictly
limited, however: schooling was not compulsory, private schools and
domestic education co-existed with government schools, and fees were
payable in state schools to supplement the meagre salaries. There was
also a large degree of independence for teachers in deciding what to
teach and by what methods; the idéologues maintained that a government
should not use the schools to preach a particular doctrine.[9] Tracy and
Cabanis strongly attacked the neo-Spartan proposal for compulsory state
education, formulated by L.-M. Lepelletier and championed by Robespierre
in July 1793, according to which all children aged five years would be
sent to state boarding-schools for six or seven years.[10] The illiberalism
and coercion of such a proposal alarmed them, and in this fear of the
potential abuses of a national system of education they might have
sympathized with William Godwin's eloquent criticisms.[11]

On the other hand, Tracy and Cabanis were concerned to ensure that the inequality of lumières among the various parts of society should be reduced. If left to the parents and to private schools, the situation would hardly improve. Hence, public schools - organized and partly financed by the state - were urgently necessary.[12] Philosophers and economists had been divided on the "applicability of the free-market principle to education".[13] Smith extolled the advantages of fee-paying schools and competition for students, opposed state training for teachers, and wished to confine state financial aid to provision of buildings. The idéologues modified this doctrine, believing that the state, as concerned with the general interest, had a special duty in the area of primary education. This was reflected in the creation of a teacher-training institute, the école normale, at the end of 1794 (discussed below); in the section of the 1795 Constitution providing that, from the year 1804, all people wishing to be inscribed on their civic register would have to demonstrate their literacy and knowledge of a trade;[14] and in the concern throughout the 1790s to commission the publication of elementary textbooks for use in government schools.[15]

The debate on public instruction in France in the 1790s was highly politicized. The question of fees, levels of government funding, and competition between the private and public schools, was only one side of the debate. The other concerned the content of education. Governments and their spokesmen asserted the necessity of an explicit civic and political component in public instruction. For example, the idéologue M.-J. Chénier had bluntly stated in November 1793 under the Jacobin régime that the duty of the Convention in organizing public instruction was "to form republicans" and "to form Frenchmen".[16] After thermidor, Chénier's concerns remained constant: the Committee of public instruction of the Convention, he said in May 1795, should "take all the necessary means of encouragement to steer the schools, theatres, and the arts and sciences in general" towards the overriding objective of "consolidating the republic".[17] According to the typical viewpoint of the 1790s, government schools would have to supervise the development of both the intellectual and moral faculties of the individual; and everyone, regardless of abilities and interests, should be instructed in the rights and duties of the French citizen. Formal schooling in such areas was supplemented by a series of public festivals and holidays celebrating key dates in the revolutionary calendar and supporting the moral virtues associated with republican citizenship.[18] Daunou had regarded these *fêtes nationales* as crucial adjuncts to formal instruction.[19] Teachers themselves became subjected to scrutiny, during the Directory period, to ensure that they would approach their task with the requisite zeal and spirit.[20] The propaganda potentialities of public instruction had come to the foreground; the education system became a locus for ideological battle between revolutionaries, reformers and traditionalists of all kinds; it had been politicized by successive governments in the 1790s, and continued to be so under the Napoleonic régime.

In addition to their concern with the moral and political content of instruction, the reformers of the 1790s were anxious to increase the importance of science, and the use of the French language[21] (vis-à-vis ancient languages) in the curriculum. In this, they were continuing a tendency already begun in the schools of the *ancien régime* and rapidly increased in the early years of the Révolution. The idéologues were very critical of the *collèges* in which they had themselves been educated: Tracy attacked their "metaphysical" or scholastic conceptions of philosophy, and emphasis on ancient literature to the detriment of all else;[22] Lakanal attacked the use of Latin as "the almost exclusive vehicle for all ideas", thus retarding "the progress of the mind";[23] Daunou described the colleges as "bizarre institutions" devoted only to learning by rote, and claimed

that the local primary schools had been sources of "ignorance, fanaticism

and prejudice".[24] The idéologues' position was well summed up in

Lakanal's speech introducing the legislation establishing the _école_

normale:

> Whilst political liberty and the complete freedom of
> industry and commerce will destroy the monstrous in-
> equality of wealth, [the use of philosophical] analysis
> applied to all types of ideas in all the schools will
> destroy the inequality of _lumières_, which is even more
> fatal and humiliating. Analysis is thus essentially an
> indispensable instrument in a great democracy; the light
> which it sheds has such a capacity to penetrate every-
> where, that, like all fluids, it tends constantly to
> find its own level.[25]

The Thermidoreans in 1794 placed a high priority upon re-estab-

lishing a national system of education, as part of their attempt to

conserve and stabilize a republican system based on property rights and

secular reason. The system formulated by Lakanal and his colleagues in

1794 and revised by Daunou and others in 1795 was explicitly directed

towards the development and diffusion of scientific knowledge, the practical

arts, and utilitarian social and political doctrines. Many of the details

had been foreshadowed by such legislative proposals as those by Talleyrand

(1791) and Condorect (1792), whose projects were singled out for praise

by Daunou in October 1795.[26] The new system of public instruction and

the creation of the Institut National were the institutional embodiment

of idéologue educational doctrines. In the remainder of this section, we

will examine briefly each of the main components of the scientific and

educational system under the Directory.[27]

The primary schools were seen after thermidor as the area of

greatest neglect and urgency. The Jacobin law of December 1793 declaring

education compulsory had been inoperative. Lakanal's project in November

1794 sought to establish one primary school for every district of one

thousand inhabitants. Schools would cater for children of at least six

years of age, with separate sections for boys and girls. Instruction
was to include reading and writing in the French language, arithmetic,
geography, studies of natural phenomena, the history of "free peoples",
and details of the Rights of Man and the French constitution. A local
jury d'instruction appointed by the district administration would select
teachers, who would receive a fixed salary from the state. Similarly,
in the law of 25 October 1795 which consolidated all previous education
laws, primary schools were to be established in each canton, departmental
administrations were to issue regulations for the operation of the schools,
and each local jury d'instruction would control appointment and dismissal
of teachers. However, students had to pay their teacher an annual fee,
determined by the departmental administration, with the proviso that one
quarter of students might be exempted on grounds of poverty. The state
thus avoided a heavy expenditure on teachers' salaries, but undertook to
provide a dwelling and school buildings.[28] A proposal to pay salaries
from public revenues was defeated in the Council of 500 in 1799.[29]

The new Constitution of August 1795 (article 296) had decreed
that primary schools would teach reading, writing, and the elements of
arithmetic and of morale. It had also guaranteed the freedom to establish
private schools (article 300).[30] These were indeed established in fairly
large numbers during the Directory years, and competed very successfully
with the public schools. Many private schools were devoted to religious
instruction and neglected the republican propaganda which they were
required to disseminate. Several decrees were issued by the Directory to
counter the popularity and the religious basis of the private schools. In
November 1797, it was decreed that all applicants for public positions would
have to prove they had attended state schools and that their children were
also doing so; and in February 1798 a decree required local administrations
to determine that the Rights of Man were being taught and republican

festivals observed. Some private schools were closed as a result, but
others were opened and some authorities failed to execute such laws,
either through their own religious beliefs or in deference to popular
opinion.[31]

The public primary schools suffered from additional problems
of their own. There was a lack of buildings and facilities; rental allow-
ances for teachers without a dwelling were seldom paid; incomes from
fees were generally inadequate; and there was a shortage of qualified
teachers. The quality of primary education was, therefore, heavily
criticized by some parents. The church schools of the previous era had
probably not provided a better education, but there had been more schools
available for children to attend. The old system, said Daunou in October
1795, was misguided, "but it was organized".[32] Most importantly, however,
the public schools encountered two sources of resistance among the local
populations. Firstly, there was widespread religious and even political
hostility to the secular republican schools; secondly, the very need for
education was not widely recognized, especially by the poorer classes who
could not afford to send their children to school or to spare them from
the fields. Consequently, actual attendance at primary schools constituted
only a very small proportion of those who were eligible to attend, a
situation which did not improve significantly for several decades.[33]
Public education was neither compulsory nor universal in the period under
discussion, and several of the idéologues and their colleagues in the
Institut and legislature expressed great concern lest the advances achieved
by the Revolution should be allowed to languish through a failure to
provide elementary literacy and moral and civic instruction.[34]

The primary schools were not, however, the area of public
instruction in which Tracy and the idéologues were most interested or
energetic. The secondary and tertiary levels attracted far more of their

attention, for these involved the instruction of the élites in all

spheres of science, government and industry. Lakanal submitted a project

in December 1794 which became the law of February 1795, establishing a

series of superior secondary schools known as écoles centrales, replacing

the colleges of the ancien régime.[35] The idéologues' two-class meritocratic

conception of public instruction was clearly evident in the scheme.

According to Lakanal, most students would find that their education in

the improved and revitalized primary schools would be sufficient to equip

them for the workforce and citizenship; one would learn in the primary

schools the preliminaries of all the studies which would be taught in

the écoles centrales.[36] It was necessary, said Lakanal,

> that the greatest number of young citizens, without
> aspiring to a more extended education, should upon
> leaving school go out into the fields, the workshops,
> the stores, on your ships and into your armies. All
> those who form the majority of the generation will
> have found in the primary schools all that was necessary
> for them to fill with honour, in these diverse callings,
> their status as citizens.[37]

It would be wasteful, said Lakanal, for children of only mediocre ability

to be trained for several more years in the new schools. On the other

hand, the more gifted children deserved a maximum extension of their

education:

> ... for the glory of the motherland, for the advancement
> of the human mind, it is necessary that young citizens
> excepted by nature from the ordinary class should find
> a sphere in which their talents can be given scope.[38]

The select few would attend the écoles centrales, which Lakanal

fervently commended to the Convention as the key to rekindling the flame

of science which had been almost stifled during the years of tyranny.

No expense should be spared, and no further delay allowed; for such

schools were essential to the good of the nation itself. The name

"central" schools arose because one would be placed at the centre of the

primary schools in each department, normally in the main town. Children aged from eleven or twelve years might attend. The curriculum was to be broad and ambitious, covering the physical sciences and mathematics; history and the economic and political sciences; and literature, fine arts and languages. Classes were to be conducted in French. The Committee of public instruction was to maintain a general responsibility for regulating the écoles centrales and for the composition of suitable text books.[39]

Daunou's law of 25 October 1795 retained the écoles centrales with little alteration, other than a reduction in the subjects offered, following a report by five commissioners appointed by the Convention in April to investigate the problems of re-establishing the schooling system. The main difficulties could be overcome, according to Daunou, only by the "suitable selection of teachers, the concern of the government, and the composition of elementary texts".[40] The legislation stipulated that there would be one école centrale in each department, with its own library, garden, and collections of equipment for natural history, chemistry and physics. Teachers would be appointed and dismissed by the jury d'instruction, subject to confirmation by the departmental administration, which also made regulations governing the operation of the schools, and determined the fees payable by students (of whom one quarter might be given free places). The legislation nominated ten chairs for each school and divided the curriculum into three sections. The first, open to students of at least twelve years, would comprise drawing, natural history, and ancient languages; modern languages could be added if deemed appropriate by the department administration. The second section, open to students over fourteen years, would comprise mathematics, physics and chemistry. The third section, for students over sixteen years, would comprise grammaire générale, literature, history, and legislation.[41]

Much has been written for and against the viability of the
écoles centrales under the Directory and the first years of the Consulate.
Some historians have condemned them as a disastrous experiment which
placed secondary education far behind the ancien régime both in standards
and in availability.[42] There were also many contemporary observers who
pointed to severe problems concerning staffing, finance, student attendance, lack of entry standards, lack of cohesion in the curriculum, absence
of textbooks, the republican and anticlerical content of certain courses,
and competition from private schools.[43] In short, the écoles centrales
faced problems similar to those of the primary schools (above p. 376).
Public education was the responsibility of the Minister of the Interior.
Bénézech, the first of four such Ministers under the Directory, issued
regulations establishing the first 68 écoles centrales: there were about
100 operating by 1800, which, together with the private schools, were
attempting to fill the gap left by 562 colleges operating before 1789.[44]
It is not part of my task to assess the strengths and weaknesses of the
écoles centrales; it is necessary only to have shown that these schools,
whose curriculum included new "ideological" subjects such as general
grammar, legislation, and a particular view of history, were embroiled
in a deep controversy (which was resolved, against the wishes of Tracy
and his friends, by the reforms of the Consulate in 1802). This debate
will be raised again at the end of this chapter in discussing Tracy's
defence of the écoles centrales. For the moment, we continue with our
examination of the scientific and educational institutions established
after thermidor.

The level of public instruction beyond secondary schooling was
the province of the écoles spéciales. The law of 25 October 1795 rationalized and extended these technical and professional schools, which had been
developed over a long period. In addition to the schools for artillery,

military and civil engineering[45],the navy,and other types of military

training including field medicine which had all been re-organized in

1793-94, the Convention now decreed in 1795 that there would be ten kinds

of écoles spéciales, devoted to astronomy; geometry and mechanics;

natural history; medicine; veterinary studies; rural economy; antiquities;

political sciences; painting, sculpture and architecture; and finally,

music. Moreover, there would be special schools for the teaching of deaf-

mutes and the blind.[46] The twenty-one universities which had operated

during the ancien régime had all been abolished, and none of these

institutions was resurrected until the centralized Imperial University

was established in 1808.[47] However, the Collège de France, an independent

institution of higher edcuation founded in 1530, managed to survive the

political vicissitudes owing to its innovative approach and the excellence

of its teaching, and its staff received state salaries from 1793. The

idéologues had little but praise for its work.[48]

The shortage of qualified teachers, the abolition of religious

seminaries for teachers, and the need to instil a new set of principles

among students, led to the project of creating a centre in Paris for

training teachers. In October 1794, just before the Convention disbanded

in favour of the new Constitution, Lakanal introduced legislation establish-

ing an école normale.[49] Citizens from all over France, already educated

in the "useful sciences" and noted for their civisme, were to learn the

arts of teaching from the most eminent men in all fields. After their

course in Paris, students would return to their provinces to pass on their

skills to prospective teachers at the local level. Lakanal conceived of

the école normale in Baconian terms as forming the "renovators of the human

mind". They would initiate a revival of the sciences and of republican

sentiment, a "regeneration of the human understanding", based firmly on

the analytical principles of Bacon, Locke and Condillac:

> For the first time on earth, nature, truth, reason and
> philosophy are also going to have a seminary. For the
> first time the most eminent men in every type of science
> and talent ..., men of genius are going to be the first
> school-masters of a people ...[50]

The "pure" and lofty ideas deriving from "the first men of the Republic"

would be transmitted by the "disciples" in local écoles normales; the

diffusion of enlightenment would thereby be guaranteed, and the same

principles would be taught throughout the nation. Children of every

social class would have access to the finest minds in the land.

> Human reason, cultivated everywhere with an equally
> enlightened industry, will produce everywhere the same
> results, and these results will be the re-creation of
> the human understanding in a people who are going to
> become the example and model of the world.[51]

The idéologues' "transmission" conception of scientific instruction was

seldom stated so forcefully.

The école normale opened in Paris on 20 January 1795 with about

1400 students, and fourteen professors selected mainly from the new

Institut National. The courses and professors were designated as follows:

Mathematics (Lagrange and Laplace), Physics (Haüy), Geometry (Monge),

Natural History (Daubenton), Chemistry (Berthollet), Agriculture (Thouin),

Geography (Buache and Mentelle), History (Volney), Morale (Bernardin de

Saint-Pierre), Grammar (Sicard), Analysis of Understanding (Garat), and

Literature (La Harpe). There was a large overlap between these professors

and the list of experts commissioned by the Committee of public instruction

in October 1794 to write a series of elementary textbooks for use in

primary schools.[52] The general approach of the professors, urged on by

Garat in particular, was to use the analytical method of Condillac to

develop pedagogical methods appropriate to their various disciplines.

But their unity was only apparent - only a few attempted to apply the

analytical method to pedagogy; others (like La Harpe and Bernardin de

Saint-Pierre) ignored or attacked l'analyse.

Several professors concentrated on expounding the substantive content of their subject instead of developing the arts of teaching. There were additional problems arising from large numbers of students being obliged to sit through several sessions of lectures without a break, and from the lack of supervision of students. The most common criticism was that the lectures were too concerned with theory and not enough with the practical problems of prospective teachers, despite the discussion sessions built into the programme. The Committee of public instruction decided that the _école normale_ had outlived its usefulness, having become incoherent and expensive.[53] Daunou, in his speech explaining the decision to close the institution after only one four-month session, defended the professors' emphasis on imparting knowledge instead of teaching methods on the grounds that students had been brought up to date with current knowledge. However, he noted that the school had been very costly to operate, and many students wanted to join the new _écoles centrales_ being established in their provinces[54] (although the _école normale_ had originally been intended for primary teachers). The provincial _écoles normales_, then, were never established, and the teacher-training experiment at the expense of the state was very short-lived.

Of all the institutions devoted to the promotion of the sciences and the philosophy of enlightenment, the pinnacle was the Institut National des Sciences et des Arts. The conception of such a body had been put forward earlier by Talleyrand and Condorcet, to replace the Académies of the _ancien régime_.[55] The Constitution of August 1795 (article 298) provided that there would be "for the whole Republic a national institute designed to record discoveries and to perfect the arts and sciences".[56] The organization of the Institut was specified two months later in Daunou's law, which defined its aims as (i) perfecting the sciences and arts by research, publications, and correspondence with learned societies abroad; and (ii) pursuing scientific and literary works whose object would be "general utility" and the "glory of the Republic".[57] The structure of the Institut has already been outlined.[58] The most notable aspects of the Institut for our present discussion were the encyclopedic breadth of areas it encompassed; its concern with practical and applied sciences as well as the less utilitarian or more traditional academic pursuits; and the creation of a separate Class of moral and political sciences, which had never been recognized in the old Académies.[59] All of these features were in accordance with the outlook of the idéologues.

The legislation established that a member could belong only to one Class but might attend the working sessions of any Class; each Class would publish its own research papers; there would be quarterly public sessions of the Institut as a whole; each Class would conduct an annual prize competition; the legislature would vote an annual sum for the maintenance of the Institut; and the Institut would submit an annual report on the progress and activities of each Class.[60] The first public session of the Institut was held on 4 April 1796 in the Louvre, with great pomp and ceremony, and in the presence of the five Directors.[61]

The Second Class was the locus par excellence of the idéologues (even though some members, such as Garat, became more concerned with politics than with the activities of the Institut). The intellectual style and tone of the Institut were set by their optimism and scientism. The five volumes of Mémoires of the Second Class, containing a selection of papers delivered during the period 1796-1802, attest to the idéologues' wide range of enquiry and their search for new discoveries about man and society; and equally to their desire to create a systematic understanding of fundamental social principles which could guide legislators and educators. Idéologie was widely accepted as providing the correct method for approaching the human sciences (not to mention the sciences of nature); moreover,

a direct connection was always made between scientific method and the
social applications of idéologie in politics, economics, morality, and
public instruction. The political and educational thrust of idéologie
was undoubtedly the main reason for Bonaparte's increasing hostility
to the idéologues and their favoured institutions - such as the écoles
centrales,suppressed in April 1802, and the Second Class of the Institut,
abolished in January 1803.

Their enthusiastic sense of reforming zeal, and their mission
to "change the face of the world",[62] was captured by Cabanis at the
conclusion of his first mémoire at the Institut on the physical and
moral aspects of man.

> After overthrowing the monstrous temple of error and tyranny,
> it is time that the new building ... is shown to be entirely
> based on immovable foundations .... The republican government,
> which alone is strengthened by public enlightenment, has alone
> been able to join thinkers concerned especially with the science
> of man and science of society with savants, artists and men of
> letters. This government does not fear that the people invest-
> igate, or become enlightened; it does not fear to see its
> principles ... and powers ... submitted to the most serious
> examination. Far from repelling or stifling sound ideas, it
> encourages and propagates them with confidence. In fact, the
> habits of reason can alone make it stable and peaceful ...
> [It] is by enlightening opinion that it achieves by sentiments
> [moeurs] what the laws and police cannot undertake without
> endangering this very liberty of which it is the protector.
> It is for you , citizens, to fulfil a great part of its task
> in this respect: it is here [in the Institut] that is placed,
> so to speak, the telegraph of science and reason, whose signals
> must be constantly relayed throughout the Republic.[63]

Here we find a repetition of the conception behind the école normale:
science and truth, formulated by the enlightened élite, is to be transmitted through all the available channels of communication. The difference
here between the Institut and the école normale, however, was that the
Institut had no supervisory functions of any kind in relation to the other
levels of educational and scientific institutions under the Directory.
Its influence was to be won by its excellence and inspiration, not decreed
by a formal structure of authority.

Having reviewed the idéologues' system of public instruction under the Directory, it is necessary to examine more closely the writings and activities of Tracy during this period, and the extent to which idéologie actually became embodied in the curricula.

II. IDÉOLOGIE IN EDUCATION

Tracy emphasized the importance of institutional practices as the main agency in shaping moral judgements and actions. Moreover, he argued that formal schooling or instruction was only one part of an individual's educational life-experience, and that it was not necessarily the most effective agency of moral socialization for most people. Where direct instruction could not succeed, it might still be possible to arrange circumstances in such a way that individuals were indirectly prompted to value certain forms of action and to avoid other forms.[64] Tracy assumed that what is true of men's linguistic usage is also true of their social behaviour, namely, that people are primarily creatures of habit (rather than of ratiocination). This assumption led to his distinctive statement of the foundation of progressive education: the essential thing, said Tracy, is "to make correct judgements habitual".[65]

The practical task of the science of idéologie in education was to provide a pedagogical methodology, by means of which students could be taught how to draw correct judgements from the basic data of experience. The truths which emerged from this procedure were held to be capable of demonstration (proof) and of systematic presentation as a series of connected propositions stemming from a scientific understanding of human nature. Idéologie, applied to the content of the schooling system, could provide a systematic demonstration of the rationality and social wisdom embodied in the Rights and Duties of Man and Citizen, thereby helping to stabilize the new social and political order and preserve republican institutions. What was the proper relationship between government and education? To what extent should the system of public instruction be used by the government as a functional support for the political régime?

Montesquieu had argued in Book IV of l'Esprit des Lois (1748) that the educational laws of a society are always in fact related to the principles of the government; education within the family will mirror the content of the education received in the grand famille of the society as a whole; both levels prepare us to be citizens in our own type of community.[66] Tracy in his Commentaire agreed that our education should "dispose us to have sentiments and opinions which are not in opposition with established institutions; otherwise, we would want to overthrow them".[67] The three levels of education - our parents, our teachers and the world around us - should complement each other if they are to act effectively; a wise government will take quiet measures to ensure that the three levels tend to operate in the same direction and tend to maintain the principles of the government.[68]

The limits of interference had to be carefully defined. No government, said Tracy, should ever interfere with the natural authority and custody of parents over their children. Hence, the Jacobin proposals for compulsory state boarding-schools could not be tolerated; nor should any religious doctrine be enforced, for this should be a matter of family concern. However, it was legitimate, in Tracy's view, for a government to try to influence - but not control - public opinion. If public opinion could be enlightened, this would have some effect upon even the private or family sphere of education, and would certainly affect the general education which people received from their institutional environment. The other type of education, in the schooling system, was

more open to direct influence because the majority of children attended
government schools and the minority at private schools would still be
influenced by the tendencies followed in the state schools. Tracy
concluded that all three levels of education were subject to the direct
or indirect influence of government principles.[69] The unstated premise
of Tracy's analysis is that all governments will in practice try to
influence the opinions of children and of adult citizens, but that this
attempt is really legitimate only where the content of this influence is
in accordance with "reason" and social happiness. Tracy undoubtedly
believed that reason, happiness and liberty had a special status of some
kind as goals of politics and education. However, he stopped short of
autocratic schemes to enforce his own "ideological" view of these goods.
Even under the Empire, he professed his faith that reason and truth would
triumph by peaceful means over prejudice.[70]

The line between reasoned supervision and illiberal control was
sometimes very fine indeed under the Directory. It is of considerable
interest to trace the supervisory role played by the idéologues in the
education system after 1798, when the "ideological" influence over the
content of curricula and operation of the schools became more noticeable.
As we saw earlier,[71] Tracy became directly involved in state supervision
of the écoles centrales, owing to his membership of a Council of public
instruction established by the Minister of the Interior, François de
Neufchâteau. The work of this Council, during the twelve months following
Tracy's appointment in February 1799, provides invaluable insights into
the general conceptions of public education held by Tracy and the idéologues,
and more particularly the ways in which they tried to devise pragmatic
methods for remedying the widely perceived defects of the écoles centrales.

In his first brief term of office in 1797, Neufchâteau had taken
up the pressing question of elementary textbooks. He invited the

professors in the écoles centrales to submit their cahiers for "examination by the Institut National, this great jury d'instruction of the French Republic", and promised rewards for those efforts judged worthy of being published as elementary texts at government expense.[72] Returning to the Ministry of the Interior in July 1798 after ten months as a member of the Directory, Neufchâteau took up the same problem. His creation of an advisory Council of public instruction, drawn from members of the Institut,[73] was evidently designed to facilitate the work of examining cahiers, and offering constructive criticisms of each course and the overall programme of studies. The official announcement of the creation of the Council on 6 October 1798 stated that its objectives were

> to examine elementary texts whether printed or manuscript,
> the cahiers, the views of the professors, and to be occupied
> continuously with the means of perfecting republican
> instruction.[74]

Tracy was appointed to strengthen the Council's supervision of the courses on grammaire générale and legislation.[75] The work of the Council consisted largely of conducting an extensive correspondence with professors and administrators in the écoles centrales and primary schools, gathering information on the content and organization of instruction, and drafting circulars and instructions for consideration by the Minister. There are several documents of particular interest for understanding the role of idéologie in public education - a series of four circulars to professors in the écoles centrales in August-September 1799, and a lengthy Report in February 1800 on the current state of public education and some suggested reforms. Tracy's publisher claimed in the last edition of his Elémens d'idéologie that all these documents were drafted by Tracy on behalf of the Council:[76] indeed, they were printed as his own work in volume IV of that edition. However, since they represent the collective views of the Council, and since Tracy's exact role in their production cannot be verified, all we may assume is that they reflect accurately both his own views and those of the other idéologues in the Council. The fact that the terms _idéologie_ and _idéologique_ appear in these documents adds further evidence of Tracy's intimate involvement.

The freedom in teaching given to professors in the _écoles centrales_ had resulted in an enormous diversity of course contents and teaching hours; in many cases this led to a lowering of teaching standards. There was a lack of co-ordination among teachers of related subjects, there was no coherent sequence of studies with appropriate pre-requisites set for more advanced courses, and teachers were often unsure what should be taught.[77] The invitations by Neufchâteau to the professors to forward their _cahiers_ produced few results, most of which were very disheartening to the members of the Council. Nothing worthy of reproduction as a student text had been forthcoming. The greatest problems occurred in the courses on ancient languages, _grammaire générale_, legislation and history; a circular signed by the Minister was therefore prepared for teachers in each of those subjects in August-September 1799. We have already examined the latter two circulars when discussing Tracy's conception of social science.[78] Here we will examine only those concerned with ancient languages and _grammaire générale_.

One problem with the teaching of ancient languages was that one appointee had been found insufficient to teach both Latin and Greek at various levels: an extra teacher had been recommended on a number of occasions, but without result except in the Paris schools. The Council seemed more concerned in its circular, however, with the content of such courses and their relationship to idéologie and _grammaire générale_. Each teacher of ancient languages was addressed in the following terms:

> You are not unaware, citizen, that the young cannot learn
> properly the principles of any language unless they are
> first given some notions of _grammaire générale_; and that

> they cannot understand the general rules of language unless
> one begins by explaining to them what goes on in their minds
> when they think and when they try to express their thoughts.
> This path is the only one to follow if the students are not
> to contract the fatal habit of being satisfied with words
> whose meaning they cannot grasp, and if the study of a single
> language is not to take up many years of repulsive and often
> fruitless labour .... Accordingly you see, citizen, that it is
> necessary for your course on the Latin or Greek language to
> be preceded by some treatment of idéologie and grammaire
> générale. No doubt, these two sciences do not have to be
> dealt with in great detail at this point, since the students
> will make a deeper study of them at a later stage when they
> take the course by the professor of grammaire générale: but
> it is still necessary that they know the fundamentals, for
> therein is the true introduction to the study of languages.[79]

The circular recommended that suitable books might include works by

"Condillac, Dumarsais, or some other grammairien métaphysicien". It

repeated the earlier requests for the teachers to send their cahiers for

examination, especially in regard to these preliminary studies which

were the "most important" and the "most neglected" part of the course.[80]

The circular to the professors of grammaire générale emphasized

the importance of going beyond grammar as such, and recognizing instead

that the course should comprise four parts: "idéologie, grammaire générale

French grammar, and logic". Understood in this broad manner, "your course

should be the complement and the completion of the courses on ancient

languages, and the introduction to the courses on literature, history and

legislation". The professors of grammaire générale were reminded that

their courses were preceded by those on ancient languages, whose professors

should have commenced by teaching "some elementary notions of idéologie"

appropriate to their students' level of understanding, based on the

principle of proceeding "from the known to the unknown".[81]

The later courses should build upon this elementary knowledge

by providing "more advanced lessons on idéologie and grammaire générale;

for this is the stage where they should learn properly these two sciences"

These principles might then be applied to French grammar, necessary for

the study of literature; and finally applied to the art of reasoning, or logic, which is the guiding thread which helps the young "to
understand men and things, facts and institutions, in the courses on
history and legislation, and which guides them for the rest of their
lives". The art of reasoning, or logic, was said to comprise the study
of "what constitutes the certainty of our knowledge, the truth of our
propositions, and the correctness of our deductions." Logic was based on
"the careful examination of our intellectual faculties, and the effects
produced by the frequent repetition of the same operations and by the
constant use of the signs by which we combine and communicate our ideas".[82]
Tracy's principles of idéologie clearly had the support of the Council
of public instruction. Some unfortunate teachers of general grammar
were upbraided by the Minister on the advice of the Council: their
mistake was to have relied too heavily on Condillac's Traité des sensations
(which Tracy and others regarded as in many respects too mechanistic),
or to have proclaimed the immortality of the soul and the qualities of
the Supreme Being. Such things were beyond empirical demonstration: "the
character of the new metaphysics is, and should be, to deal only with
subjects which are clearly within the grasp of our intellect".[83]

The acknowledged difficulties facing the écoles centrales, the
public criticism of their performance, and the problems of making improvements in the absence of sufficient information about the abilities of the
teachers and the achievements of the students, led the idéologues into
a defensive campaign to protect the écoles centrales, to rebut the more
hostile critics, and to seek urgent reforms within the schools themselves.
The pages of la Décade in 1799-1801 contained many articles praising the
more noteworthy écoles centrales, suggesting modifications, and attacking
traditionalist critics.[84] In the early weeks of the Consulate, on the
basis of further information obtained from the teachers and school admin-

istrations, the Council of public instruction was able to draw up a
comprehensive Report to the Minister,[85] outlining

> the true state of public instruction in France, the hopes
> and fears which may be held for it, and the improvements
> which can be introduced, without, however, giving too great
> a shock to the vast system which is established; for ...
> whenever a plea to change or reform the system of public
> education is announced in the legislature or in the acts
> of the government, this has been a signal in the departments
> for a coolness among the professors, discouragement of
> students, and desertion of the schools.[86]

The Report, dated 5 February 1800, did not receive a reply from the new
Minister of the Interior, Lucien Bonaparte, and the Council was quietly
dissolved later in the year.[87] The Report, however, is of great interest,
not only because Tracy claimed it as his own work in the 1825 edition of
his works, but also because it provides the first detailed account by
the idéologues of how they interpreted the strengths and weaknesses of
the education system begun in 1795, and shows their willingness to modify
their ideas in the light of practical experience.

Having first reminded the new Minister of the original terms
of reference of the Council some fifteen months earlier, the Report raised
the matter of elementary texts and listed the authors most commonly recommended by the professors in each course. These works, supplemented by
a few others nominated by the Council, were held to be adequate for the
moment, inspiring "sound, liberal and philosophical ideas" among students.
Secondly, the Report raised the question of how each course was interpreted and organized by the professors, a matter which could only be
judged on the basis of their cahiers and correspondence with the Council.
Some were held to require further guidance, especially in those "sciences
with a novel title in French schools such as grammaire générale, morale,
and législation". For this reason, circulars had been written for
professors in those courses which seemed to need more precise directions
concerning the content and duration of instruction, and relations with

other courses. Subsequent correspondence had confirmed the value of these circulars, according to the Report. Moreover, the cahiers and plans of study judged most useful were communicated to the other professors, especially in new courses such as general grammar and legislation. The examination of the cahiers was not, then, intended to be "a rigorous surveillance and censorship", but a way of sharing among all the schools the benefits of the best methods of teaching.[89]

The Council had asked the professors and administrations for precise details of their existing programmes. Eighty per cent supplied the required information. Their replies were analyzed in regard to the nine courses taught in the following sequence in the écoles centrales. The course on drawing (dessin) had been the most popular in attracting students, but the Council refrained from judging the merit of this non-"academic" course separated from la chaîne d'études. The course on ancient languages suffered from the inadequate preparation of students by the primary schools; many students were illiterate, for the law of 1795 had stipulated only a minimum age for entry to the courses. There was a great variety in the length and intensity of courses, and the single professor was overburdened by having to take classes at different levels. However, said the Report, the circular to teachers had already improved the situation by suggesting some introductory lessons on grammaire générale and idéologie as background for the study of languages, and thereby establishing closer links between the various courses.[90] The course on natural history, which attracted solid enrolments, varied in content according to the particular interests of the locality, with botany emphasized in some areas, mineral science in others; and the connections with local commerce or the arts were generally pointed out. The mathematics course was second to the drawing course in attracting students, followed by the course on physics and chemistry.[91]

The idéologues of the Council were more defensive about their
favoured courses, such as <u>grammaire générale</u>. This course, according
to the Report, was one in which the professors included a large proportion
of "men distinguished by their knowledge and their zeal". In a few
schools, classes were large, but this was "far from being common". In
some schools, the course could not be implemented because the students
had not sufficient preparatory education - which only emphasized the
need for a clear sequence of courses. The course lasted for two years
in half the schools, and one year in others. Some teachers had originally
included only French grammar; but the recent circular had shown them that
it should contain idéologie, general grammar, French grammar, and logic,
and that the course should be preceded by that on ancient languages and
followed by those on legislation and history. Without the art of correct
reasoning, how could one appreciate the men and institutions examined in
these later courses? The course on literature had the smallest attendance
it had been given no links with the courses on ancient languages or
general grammar which preceded it, nor with history, which followed. It
clearly required the sort of guidance given in the circulars drawn up for
other courses.[92]

In history, said the Report, enrolments had been small, and
the teachers had shown a great diversity in their conceptions of the
content and organization of the course: some had concentrated on historical
geography, others on chronology. The circular to professors had clarified
such uncertainties and imparted a more precise direction for the course,
and had "shown them the philosophical objective which should be attained".
There had also been low enrolments in the course on <u>législation</u>, where
the idéologues again had a vested interest. The professors had taken
advantage of the great latitude offered them to present courses of variabl
duration on very different areas, such as French jurisprudence or a comment

on the Constitution. The circular had resolved these problems by pointing out that the course on morality and legislation should not be too specialized, but should attempt to form men of virtue, who knew their own interest and that of their country.[94] Knowledge of one's rights and duties would emerge from a proper study of "the principles of private and public morality, of social organization, and of social economy".[95]

According to the Report, the greatest defect of the écoles centrales, upon which there was a general agreement among the teachers themselves, was "the lack of liaison and relations between the different studies". Each course was isolated from those coming before and after it, and there were no pre-requisites for entry except a minimum age specified in the law of October 1795. This not only prevented able youngsters from entering the schools, thereby driving them into the arms of private tutors who were hostile to the écoles centrales; it also failed to tackle the important problem of ensuring that students had reached an adequate level before beginning any given course. Since the primary schools were not yet doing their job properly, it was incumbent on the écoles centrales to set aside some time for elementary studies. The main defects of the law of October 1795, in summary, were the lack of structure in the course of studies, the minimum age regulations, and insufficient attention to ancient languages.[96] Teachers had also drawn attention to problems of interference by department administrations and non-payment of monies owing to them; but they were agreed on a number of other important reforms involving centralized directives:

> that the government, by a general measure, should prevent
> students from taking too many courses at once; that it
> oblige them at the beginning of the school year to undergo
> an examination whose format is regulated by the government;
> that it determine the period of vacations, which are nowhere
> the same; that it establish the obligation to have passed a
> certain course in order to proceed to another; that it

encourage, by all means in its power, the creation of
pensionnats near the écoles centrales and the permanence
of those already existing ...[97]

The notable feature of all these reforms is that they could readily be accommodated within the existing system. The idéologues were determined to improve the efficiency and co-ordination of the system in order to forestall larger criticisms of its whole philosophical approach. The Council's Report thus stressed that the system was improving rapidly and needed only minor changes to become completely satisfactory. Despite the organizational problems of a new system and the long interruption of public education caused by the years of turmoil, the evidence showed that there was good reason to have faith in the existing system of schooling. The ranks of the teachers included many men of distinction and energy; the number of students had recently increased; and the standards of instruction were improving.[98] The report strongly urged the retention of the system:

> To attain all the perfection of which it is capable, all it
> needs is time. That is something that nothing can replace,
> and is all the more necessary with every modification. The
> Council thus believes that any upheaval, or even any displace-
> ment of the écoles centrales now operating, would be a public
> calamity and would amount to nothing less than abolishing
> once more the instruction of a whole generation.[99]

The Report concluded with a number of further measures, the most important of which was the Plan d'études[100] which it had formulated after extensive examination, to replace the vague programme established in the Daunou law. Without a suitably integrated plan of studies, instruction would inevitably fail to bear fruit. Students required a mutual reinforcement of courses and a gradual development of knowledge, to obtain most profit from their studies.[101] The Council pointed out that the practice of corresponding with the teachers and administrations, to monitor the implementation of the new procedures and the use of text-books, would have to be continued for at least several years. Moreover,

the teachers should be encouraged to produce complete <u>cahiers</u> so that
the best could be used to redress the absence of good elementary texts.
It also emphasized the need for privately-administered <u>pensionnats</u>
attached to the <u>écoles centrales</u>, so that students could be given
properly supervised conditions of study outside the schoolroom; parents
would be wary of sending their children to <u>écoles centrales</u> so long as
most continued to lack such facilities.[102]

Finally, the Council proposed the creation of a special school
in Paris for the moral and political sciences, just as the <u>école poly-
technique</u> existed for advanced studies in the physical and mathematical
sciences. A school for the moral and political sciences had been envisaged
in the Daunou law of 1795, and it became a constant complaint by Tracy
and the idéologues that such a school had never been organized.[103] It
was essential, according to the Report, to produce men who were capable
of teaching the moral and political sciences; moreover, it was to be hoped
that all holders of high public office should have undertaken advanced
studies in these fields.

> In the meantime, given that the study of the moral and
> political sciences is absolutely necessary to form good
> citizens, and given that it is nevertheless very neglected
> because it is rejected by all the prejudiced, and is not
> required for entry into any useful positions in society,
> the Council thinks it would be necessary to announce that,
> in a few years to come, no-one will be admitted into places
> in the various <u>écoles spéciales</u> or the public service unless
> he has proof that he has taken a course on legislation in an
> <u>école centrale</u>.[104]

The Report reminded the Minister that the stability of the
government could be derived "above all from the progress and diffusion of
knowledge".[105] The Consulate, however, was not convinced by the ideologues'
self-justificatory plea for continuing the existing system, albeit with
several modifications; nor was it satisfied with the quality and quantity
of the evidence alluded to in the Report concerning the viability of the

écoles centrales. Chaptal repeated to the Council of State in November 1800 many of the organizational criticisms made in the idéologues' Report, but argued that most schools were deserted, and recommended the creation of a different system of secondary education and the abolition of such courses as general grammar and legislation.[106]

III. DEFENCE OF THE ÉCOLES CENTRALES

In March 1801 an enquiry was ordered into national education, conducted by department prefects and members of Bonaparte's Council of State. Their replies were generally unfavourable[107] towards the écoles centrales, although several schools were undoubtedly of excellent quality. In April 1802, the écoles centrales were replaced by secondary schools and a new élite of thirty state-financed lycées. In introducing the new legislation, Roederer accused the écoles centrales of having tried "to populate France with living Encyclopedias";[108] and Fourcroy argued that, while the new institutions of 1795 had been inspired by "grander and more liberal ideas" than those of the old régime, they had met with little success or utility.[109]

In the meantime, Tracy had decided - probably as a result of his experience during 1799 on the Council of public instruction - to write a series of texts for students to overcome the absence of suitable course materials for general grammar. The first volume appeared in 1801, under the lengthy title: Project d'Eléments d'idéologie à l'usage des écoles centrales de la République française. In the preface to this volume, Tracy noted that until the professors themselves, through experience, could produce suitable student texts, there remained an important lacuna to be filled. The course on general grammar, he believed, would demonstrate that "all languages have common rules which are derived from the

nature of our intellectual faculties", and that this knowledge is
necessary "not simply for the study of languages but is also the only
solid basis of the moral and political sciences". Hence, in teaching
the philosophy of language, one would be providing an introduction to
the course on private and public morale.[110]

But the intentions of the educational legislation of 1795 were
now threatened, he noted: the Jacobin fureur de tout détruire had been
replaced by the present government's manie de ne rien laisser s'établir.[111]
The finest results of the revolution were being abandoned in the name of
redressing the errors of the past. The wisdom of "practical knowledge"
was now being championed as an antidote to "theories", but the critics
had not troubled themselves to understand these theories and wrongly
attributed all the evils of the revolution to the philosophers whose
ideas were embodied in the highly useful educational institutions. The
production of excellent texts would require a number of years, taking
account of experience in the classroom; this was an additional reason
for hoping that the government would not halt

> the teaching of the ideological, moral and political
> sciences which, after all, are sciences like the others,
> with the difference that those who have not studied them
> believe so sincerely that they know them, that they
> believe they are in a position to decide the issue.[112]

Tracy's worst fears were proving to be correct, and he rapidly
wrote a last defence of the écoles centrales, based closely on the ideas
contained in the Report of February 1800. His brochure, entitled
Observations sur le système actuel d'instruction publique, appeared in
about June 1801.[113] The Observations, said Tracy in his foreword, had
been published out of sequence; he had wanted to wait until suitable texts
had appeared for the courses on general grammar, and perhaps also for
the course on morals and legislation and for history. Without such texts,
a programme of studies was difficult to discuss or to justify, especially

when the content was new and not well understood.[114] The Observations

had to be published in haste owing to the imminent decision on the future

of public instruction. Tracy's starting point and general objective was:

> to prove that we have an excellent [system of public
> instruction]; that its bases leave absolutely nothing
> to be desired; that it has already produced many good
> results and no bad effects; that to obtain from it all
> the advantages we have a right to expect, it is necessary
> only to know properly its character [esprit], in order to
> put successively into activity all the parts and to inter-
> relate them, and especially in order to avoid partial
> measures which, departing from the general system,
> disturb the totality and make it unrecognizable.[115]

This viewpoint was re-affirmed in his conclusion that, if the reforms

proposed were carried out, it would become relatively easy "to spread

among the mass of citizens a pure and quite extensive knowledge". The

purpose of his pamphlet was

> to prove that the fundamental principles of our present
> institutions are excellent, and that to produce their
> best effects they have only to be completed. I would
> be happy if, by developing their character, I had
> forestalled their disorganization![116]

The Observations contain two inter-related kinds of arguments:

the first and somewhat truncated argument concerned the relationship

he saw between the schooling system and the class structure of society.

The second concerned his detailed recommendations for reorganizing the

curriculum of the écoles centrales, based on the plan d'études which had

emerged in 1799-1800 from the deliberations of the Council of public

instruction.

Echoing Lakanal's speech of December 1794,[117] Tracy began by

proposing a permanent social division between two classes of men in terms

of their educational needs and abilities:

> one, who draw their subsistence from their manual labour;
> the other, who live from the revenue of their properties,
> or from the product of certain functions in which the
> work of the mind is more important than the work of the
> body. The first is the classe ouvrière, the second is
> what I will call the classe savante.[118]

These two classes were regarded by Tracy as absolutely "invariable data" of social life, and as independent of human volition or intentionality: "they derive necessarily from the very nature of men and of societies; it is not in the power of anyone to change them".[119] These two classes differed from one another in all important respects: "_moeurs_, needs, means, everything is different between these two types of men".[120] Their educational needs and desires were therefore different. The children of the _classe ouvrière_ were required for labour by their parents, and the children must acquire the skills and become accustomed to the habits of "laborious toil for which they are destined". For these reasons, such children cannot spend many years in school; they must be given an abridged or summary education, complete in itself, before they enter the workshops or return to domestic or agricultural labour. Schools must be plentiful and easily accessible in every locality so that boarding schools are not required for these children, who are the vast majority.[121]

The educational needs and expectations of the children of the _classe savante_ require a distinct set of educational responses. They are fortunately able to give more time to their studies; they are obliged to undertake a long period of education if they are to fulfil their social "destiny"; and they must study certain fields of knowledge which can be grasped only by minds with a certain maturity. Moreover, they are in a position to attend a more distant school or a boarding school, or to have private tutors; such arrangements are probably necessary, since their studies demand close supervision.[122]

The content of instruction for the two social classes should also be quite different, according to Tracy. The education of the masses should not consist simply in the first few years of the extended curriculum followed by the élite. Mass education should be an "abridgement" but not a "part" of the élite education. The objects and the methods of teaching should remain distinct. A carefully considered system of national education should really be two separate systems. Tracy claimed that this had been envisaged in the law of 1795:

> the primary schools and the apprenticeships in various trades, these are the education of the classe ouvrière; the écoles centrales and écoles spéciales are the education of the classe savante. And I would no more advise sending a child destined to be a workman to the latter schools, than sending to the former a child who would become a man of state or man of letters ...[123]

It was erroneous to believe that the primary schools were intended to form the first step in a graded system and thus to be linked to the écoles centrales. It might even be necessary to change the name "primary" in order to overcome this "false view". Children of the élite would have a private education in the family home until they could enter the écoles centrales at about the age of nine or ten; the majority of children would attend primary school from the age of about six, followed by vocational training of some kind as a skilled labourer or tradesman.[124]

Tracy's Observations are overwhelmingly concerned to discuss ways of improving the education of the classe savante, a class which he also describes as classe éclairée and classe supérieure.[125] Tracy gave two reasons for this preoccupation. In the first place, the lower levels of education could not yet be fully organized for lack of "resources, teachers and students", and could only be established gradually over a long period.[126] Secondly, since the content of primary education should be a simplified resumé of the knowledge acquired by the educated élite, it was the task of the latter to propagate these "sound ideas and good methods" and to become the teachers of the whole society. The education of the élite, then, was a pre-requisite for the generalized instruction of the "lowest classes of society". Tracy's transmission concept of education is well illustrated by this conception of the relation between élite and the ordinary people. He drew an analogy between the diffusion of ideas and military instruction (with which he was very familiar), where the teaching of new exercises follows a chain of command from the senior officers, through junior officers, to the ordinary ranks.

> It is the same with all instruction. Once the education of the classe savante in society has been successful, one will see formed among them some excellent teachers for the classe ouvrière, see them provide many methods of instruction and instil in the latter the desire to profit from that instruction.[127]

This was the same idea as that envisaged in the operation of the école normale.[128]

Tracy's discussion of the education of the classe savante began by asserting that youths at the age of twenty years must take their place in the adult world, so that their formal schooling should be concluded by this time. Three stages could be specified as a "natural" division of instruction.[129] Young children, who are incapable of "sustained concentration", should not attend formal classes. Instead, the first eight or nine years of life should be spent under parental supervision, learning elementary skills of reading and writing, and acquiring those good habits of mind which result from the "company of men of good education and liberal moeurs".[130] A primary school was generally not a suitable place for acquiring the abilities and dispositions required by the classe savante, said Tracy. Primary schools were for the children of the working classes. Tracy did not explain why the latter should not also stay at home until the age of nine years - presumably it was a matter of wealth (the classe savante could employ private tutors) and not a matter of which children were more capable of "sustained concentration".

At the second stage of instruction, children of the classe savante would attend an école centrale for about eight years; the student would learn "all those forms of general knowledge needed by every well-

educated man". This would be followed by three or four years at an
école spéciale, where he would learn professional skills for his career.[13]
In the écoles centrales, it would be necessary to present a well-rounded
education, covering all three areas of knowledge embodied in the three
Classes of the Institut National: languages and literature, physical and
mathematical sciences, and moral and political sciences. This tripartite
division of studies appears to be largely a matter of convenience, since
it does not rigorously correspond to Tracy's conception of the hierarchy
of knowledge which we noted earlier.[132] Nor is there any place for
"literature" in a rigorous "ideological" schema: its inclusion in the
curriculum of the écoles centrales is simply traditional. Tracy argued
on practical grounds that these three areas are the "bases of all the
learned professions", and that members of every learned profession need an
acquaintance with all such areas.[133] The education law of 1795 had
established three divisions of the curriculum along broadly similar lines.
The important thing, in Tracy's view, was to have a coherent and systemati
plan of studies, whose content was carefully graded and mutually inter-
related.[134]

The details of his plan need not concern us here, other than to
note some of his remarks on the moral sciences. In years five and six,
the students would study morals and legislation and public morality. The
latter includes the origins of authority and the source of wealth, that
is, the principles of "social organization and political economy". In
years seven and eight, the history course would be a "continual applicatio
of the ideological, moral, political and economic observations which have
already been made"; the student, while continuing to "learn the facts",
would eventually be able to "make sound judgements on men and things in
accordance with the true principles of the moral sciences". At the end
of such studies, a student is equipped either to proceed to a special

school for professional training in one of the three fields described above, or simply to "live as a sensible man, as a good father of a family, as a sufficiently enlightened citizen - in a word, as a reasonable being ..."[135]

To ensure that courses conformed to the general intentions of the plan d'études, Tracy advocated the reactivation of a body such as the Council of public instruction, a body of learned men who would draw up detailed instructions for each course, and "while not positively dictating the teacher's lesson",[136] would give details of course content, the spirit in which it should be undertaken, its links with other courses, and a few words on teaching methods. The co-ordinating body would also invite professors to send their written lessons, so the best might be printed as texts and the authors rewarded by the government; and publicize the general objectives and character of the écoles centrales. A wider understanding among the people of these goals would greatly contribute to the schools' success, for "the biggest obstacle to the implementation of the new public instruction arises from the fact that it is too far in advance of generally received ideas ...; such that few people have grasped the whole, and parents, students and even some teachers do not really know what is being proposed".[137]

The success of the education of the classe savante, in Tracy's view, depended partly on the public acceptability of the écoles centrales. One important step in this direction would be the establishment of privately-organized pensionnats so that students would receive additional supervised study,[138] a measure which had been advocated also in the Report of the Council a year earlier. Pensionnats should also be available for students at the écoles spéciales.[139] Students who successfully completed their studies at the écoles centrales should be able to pursue more advanced training in any of the three main fields they had already studied.

For this purpose, it was necessary to open advanced institutions in the fields of the moral and political sciences, and in languages and literature.[140] In the short-term, it would suffice to attach additional positions to the <u>Collège de France</u> and the <u>Bibliothèque Nationale</u>. Tracy declared that an institution like the Collège de France should be preserved owing to its demonstrated excellence: "All my life I have proposed to increase what is good and never to destroy it; the long existence of an institution is part of its merit since this adds to its effect".[141] In a refashioned Collège directed towards perfecting the "ideological, moral and political" sciences, said Tracy,

> ... I would want not only professors who demonstrated the
> principles of political economy or of social organization
> in general. I would want there to be some who taught in
> particular the statistics of the various states, the theory
> of taxation, of the money system, of exchange, of the diverse
> branches of commerce, etc., for the individual utility of
> certain diplomats, administrators, merchants. There should
> also be some courses on the various parts of positive law,
> for the benefit of those destined for judicial positions ...[142]

There were many citizens, besides those in legal and judicial careers, who needed a detailed knowledge of the legal system. The course on morals and legislation at the <u>écoles centrales</u> was not intended to give this knowledge; a number of <u>écoles spéciales</u> for legal studies should thus be established. It should be borne in mind, however, that

> Positive law is a consequence, an application of the
> principles of <u>morale</u> and of <u>la science sociale</u>. No field
> of study, with the possible exception of history, is more
> likely to damage the mind and seriously corrupt the judgement
> on the most essential points, if one gets used to confusing
> what <u>is</u> with what <u>should be</u>. And that is bound to happen if
> one is concerned with the positive before having enough know-
> ledge of the principles. That is why the best lawyers have
> not always been the best legislators or the best judges of
> the wisdom of a legislative measure. It is then absolutely
> necessary to oblige young people to pass through an <u>école
> spéciale des sciences morales et politiques</u> before entering
> a professional school of law, just as one attends the <u>école
> polytechnique</u> before reaching a school for engineering, or,
> as in the medical schools, the courses on theory are done
> before taking those on clinical medicine.[143]

The idéologue position was clear: principles must precede detailed factual

knowledge, in order to ensure that a proper framework of education is

used by the students. It was the task of idéologie, in its application

to the analysis of institutions, to elaborate the principles of a social

science which could be used to judge the effects of various measures and

practices upon the happiness and freedom of men. Tracy showed a boundless

confidence that the principles were correct - and indeed, that they were

permanent laws governing the human condition, since they were derived

from an analysis of human nature.

Tracy believed that a satisfactory framework already existed

for the education of the classe savante: all that was needed was "stability,

permanence and consistency".[144] On the other hand, public instruction

for the classe ouvrière - which Tracy also called la classe pauvre and

la classe ignorante - lagged behind considerably. Tracy's view of how

the ideas of the lower classes are formed is highly suggestive for under-

standing his theory of education in general.

Of all the classes, the poor and ignorant are the most strongly

influenced by social institutions in general rather than by formal schooling.

"The less a man receives explicit lessons, the more his ideas are due

simply to his association with his fellows and to the chance circumstances

of his life". Among the poor, almost all they learn is acquired "without

their suspecting it". Tracy's image of the uneducated classes is one of

passively accepting habitual ideas; they "invent nothing". Tracy assumes

that their education is dependent entirely on the standards of those who

write the almanacs used by the poor, and upon the knowledge of those who

do business with them - namely, the educated élite. The education of

the poor, he concludes, "is three-quarters accomplished if we have properly

arranged that of la classe savante", who also provide the teachers and

programmes of instruction. The material and intellectual possessions of

the poor are "those which have become common" in a given society.[145]
Through their ignorance, the poor are always several steps behind in
accepting the truths discovered by the élite. "They are always behind
the times: that is their only fault. And the task of those who attend
to their instruction must continually and solely be to impart the ideas
which have superseded those presently held by the people, on every point
of theory and practice".[146]

Tracy makes the assumption that on every question, "there are
a thousand ways of going astray, but only one way to decide correctly".[147]
How can one avoid the errors and follow the truth? This is a difficult
process, according to Tracy: a great deal of knowledge in related areas
is required to be certain one has properly decided a question. The
highly educated have enough difficulty in attaining certain knowledge,
since no-one has the strength to suspend judgement on various matters
until he has reason to be completely sure of his conclusions. The poor
majority, by implication, are never in a position to know anything with
certainty unless they are instructed by men who have gained such knowledge.
Tracy's solution is not to attempt to educate the majority to a high level
of knowledge - which would have been consistent with his environmentalist
view of education - but to urge that the élite present to the masses a
digest of truths about man, morality, social organization, and productive
technology. The poor have little time for instruction and little capacity
for making correct judgements from subtle discussions. They should simply
be given the sound results of modern science, in all three areas of
knowledge: for the ignorant man has (erroneous) ideas on the same range of
subjects as the most highly educated man.

Every man has his ideas of grammar and logic; history and
morality; physics and arithmetic. It is thus necessary to shape opinions
on all these points, or leave such ideas to the fortuitous conjunction of

circumstances which has produced so much error and deception in the past.[148] In a perfect society, education of the masses could safely be left to the "slow but sure effect of the social organization and private industry"; this would be preferable to instruction given by the state, which might contain a serious flaw which was buttressed by the weight of public authority.[149] In the present circumstances, what should the government do about the instruction of the classe ouvrière? In regard to vocational training or apprenticeships, the best thing would be to help the masters become aware of modern scientific information and techniques: this would involve focusing on the classe savante rather than the workers themselves.[150] Secondly, the primary schools should be gradually improved as resources and teachers become available. But primary instruction should not be completely free, according to Tracy. Parents should pay fees amounting to perhaps half the operating costs of the schools. This was not only to lift some burden from the public treasury, but also because "no lesson is useful except where it is desired to receive it", and the best evidence of this desire was an agreement to contribute towards the costs.[151] Fees would also stimulate local interest in the school, ensure its economical operation, and lead to higher standards of achievement. Other improvements depended upon the prior education of the classe savante and the perfection of its own curriculum from which the instruction of the "less fortunate" would be extracted and distilled.[152]

Tracy corresponded with teachers in the écoles centrales, exchanging ideas, and rallying support, believing that the threat to the schools was motivated by political and religious prejudices.[153] The opinion of Tracy and the idéologues, that the main bases of the 1795 system should be preserved with a few changes in detail, was ignored in the reforms to the schools in 1802 and to the Institut in 1803. In the foreword to his Grammaire in 1803, Tracy expressed his sorrow that his

texts could no longer be subtitled "for the use of the écoles centrales",
and that his second volume would be deprived of the stimulating exchange
of ideas with teachers which arose from the first volume. Tracy also
expressed his anger that idéologie, or "sound logic", which alone could
throw light on all the other sciences, was no longer part of public
instruction in France.[154] Tracy claimed that the scientific climate of
opinion was now coming to demand the formulation of la méthode des
méthodes or la science des sciences based on the theory of signs.[155]
Finally, he expressed the hope that the Institut (which no longer contained
sections on analyse des idées or grammaire générale) would not regard
"la philosophie rationnelle" as outside its proper concerns, nor occupy
itself with the French language to the exclusion of "the general theory
of language".[156] Tracy's defiant belief that his views were correct and
irrefutable only increased during the period of the Consulate. In the
1804 reprint of his first volume, he declared that he was now convinced
he had "reached the truth", that his later work had confirmed that his
early opinions were well founded, and that his initial "hesitations and
uncertainties" could now be abandoned.[157] In the three years of rapid
change since 1801, he said, idéologie had   given an "immense impetus"
to knowledge, even though it had now been abolished in the Institut and
the schools.[158]

Tracy, who had wanted to become, through his textbooks, "the
secretary of all the enlightened men" of his time,[159] had lost the battle
for an education system based upon rationalist principles of morality and
politics. In his Commentaire of 1806, he ruefully joked that the only
unproductive workers of any merit were those who studied the science of
man: and they were the only ones persecuted. This, he said, was because
they pointed out the errors of all les oisifs. Returning to this passage
in 1819, Tracy noted that theorists were producers of the greatest of all

utilities, that of truth.[160] The idéologue had not forgotten his

dictum of 1798: _la vérité est le seul chemin du bien-être_.[161]

44444444

FOOTNOTES TO CHAPTER SEVEN

1   "Quels sont les moyens", in Commentaire, p.463.

2   Ibid., p. 456; cf. Elémens, vol. I, p. 388.

3   Cf. Helvétius, De l'esprit (1758) and De l'homme (1773); I. Cumming, Helvétius: his life and place in the history of educational thought (London, 1955); A. Keim, Helvétius, sa vie et son oeuvre (Paris, 1907).

4   Marx, "Theses on Feuerbach", no. 3; cf. The Holy Family, chapter 6, section (d) on French materialism.

5   "The most certain means of rendering a people free and happy is to establish a perfect method of education": Beccaria, cited on title page of Tracy, Commentary (1811).

6   Elémens, vol. I, p. 273. See also chapter three above, pp. 177-178.

7   See Mirabeau, Leçons économiques (1770), Avertissement, pp. i-xliv; Baudeau, Première introduction, pp. 663-665, 671-672, 792; Dupont de Nemours, De l'origine et des progrès d'une science nouvelle, pp. 19-20, 34.

8   Daunou, speech of 19 October 1795 introducing the new education law, in Hippeau (ed.), L'instruction publique (1881), pp. 485-486.

9   Ibid., p. 479; see also my discussion above, pp. 177, 195, 228.

10   The Lepelletier proposal is described in H.C. Barnard, Education and the French Revolution, p. 119f. For Tracy's reaction, defending parental rights, see Commentaire, p. 32; for Cabanis' criticism, see Oeuvres philosophiques, vol. II, pp. 429, 447.

11   W. Godwin, Enquiry concerning political justice [1793], book 6, chapter 8.

12   Cf. Cabanis, Oeuvres philosophiques, vol. II, pp. 433-436.

13   Cf. E.G. West, "Private versus Public Education, a Classical Economic Dispute", in The Classical Economists and Economic Policy, ed. A.W. Coats (London, 1971), pp. 123-143.

14   Article 16: cf. Godechot, Les Constitutions, p. 105. This provision was never implemented, since it was omitted from the new Constitution in 1799.

15   Cf. Talleyrand, September 1791, in Hippeau (ed.), L'instruction publique (1881), p. 172.

16   Cited in Van Duzer, Contribution of the idéologues, p. 93n.

17   Ibid., p. 114. Cf. the statement by Barère (1793), cited in Duruy, L'instruction publique et la Révolution, p. 261.

18   On these festivals, cf. Duruy, op.cit., chapter 6 and pp. 456f;
      Woronoff, Nouvelle histoire, pp. 151-153; A. Sicard, L'éducation
      morale et civique, especially pp. 271-290, 368-405; and section 301
      of the 1795 Constitution, which gave them formal recognition. For
      these festivals during the Jacobin period, cf. Barnard, op.cit.,
      pp. 115-117, 132; and Sicard, op.cit., pp. 243f, 352f. We saw in
      chapter three above, p. 192, that Tracy was sceptical about the
      usefulness of such festivals unless public authority was already
      well organized.

19   Daunou, 19 October 1795, in Hippeau, op.cit., p. 483.

20   Duruy, op.cit., pp. 345-347, 460-461; Van Duzer, op.cit., pp. 132f.

21   Cf. the discussion in F. Brunot, Histoire de la langue française,
      tome IX, part I.

22   Logique (1805), p. 287n; Observations sur l'état actuel de l'instruc-
      tion publique [1801], in Elémens (Bruxelles, 1826-1827), vol. IV,
      pp. 334-335.

23   Lakanal, speech of 16 December 1794, in Hippeau, op.cit., p. 427.

24   Daunou, speech of 19 October 1795, in Hippeau, op.cit., pp. 472-473.
      The colleges had been criticized for similar kinds of reasons in
      the Encyclopédie: see Diderot's article "Collège, in The Encyclopédie
      of Diderot and d'Alembert, ed. Lough, pp. 21-32.

25   Lakanal, in Hippeau, op.cit., p. 417. I have previously pointed out
      that this speech was probably written by Garat.

26   Daunou, in ibid., pp. 476-478.

27   The écoles primaires, the écoles centrales, the écoles spéciales,
      the école normale, and the Institut National des Sciences et des
      Arts.

28   J.E. Helmreich, "The establishment of primary schools in France under
      the Directory", French Historical Studies, vol. 2 (1961), pp. 189-
      208; Barnard, op.cit., pp. 166ff; Van Duzer, op.cit., p. 104; Duruy,
      op.cit., chapter 3, and pp. 375-376; C. Bloch, "L'instruction
      publique dans l'Aude pendant la Révolution", Revue internationale
      de l'enseigement, vol. 27 (1894), pp. 36-62.

29   Woronoff, Nouvelle histoire, pp. 156-157.

30   Text in Godechot, Les Constitutions, p. 133.

31   Helmreich, op.cit., pp. 204-205; Barnard, op.cit., pp. 181ff;
      L. Grimaud, Histoire de la liberté de l'enseignement en France
      (Paris, 1898), pp. 62-72. On the February 1798 decree, see Duruy,
      op.cit., pp. 460-466.

32   Daunou, in Hippeau, op.cit., p. 471.

33   Helmreich, op.cit., pp. 194-203; Bloch, op.cit., pp. 50-60.

34   Cf. the paper read by Dupont de Nemours at the Institut in March
      1799: "Mémoire sur le nombre des écoles primaires que l'on doit
      établir", in Mémoires de l'Institut, Classe des Sciences morales et
      politiques, vol. 5 (1804), pp. 317-330. The publication of this
      mémoire five years after its presentation suggests that a critical
      point was being made about the level of primary education under
      the Napoleonic régime.

35   Lakanal, 16 December 1794, in Hippeau, op.cit., pp. 423-435.

36   Ibid., p. 426.

37   Ibid., p. 427.

38   Ibid., pp. 427-428.

39   Ibid., pp. 428-435; Duruy, op.cit., chapter 4, and p. 387 for an
      organizational decree of March 1795; Barnard, op.cit., pp. 169-171.

40   Daunou, in Hippeau, op.cit., p. 480; cf. Barnard, op.cit., p. 172-
      175.

41   Text of law of 25 October 1795, in Duruy, op.cit., pp. 376-377.

42   Cf. E. Allain, L'oeuvre scolaire de la Révolution (Paris,
      1891); Duruy, op.cit., p. 256, is also rather scathing in his
      criticisms.

43   Cf. Barnard, op.cit., pp. 186-198; Bloch, "L'instruction publique
      dans l'Aude", pp. 193-223; G. Coirault, Les écoles centrales dans
      le Centre-Ouest (Tours, 1940), chapters 4-11 and Conclusion; Duruy,
      op.cit., chapters 4 and 7.

44   Duruy, op.cit., pp. 258-259, 416-417; Barnard, op.cit., pp. 9, 186.

45   Renamed the école polytechnique in September 1795: Barnard, op.cit.,
      p. 140.

46   Ibid., pp. 136-151; text of law of October 1795 in Duruy, op.cit.,
      p. 378; L. Liard, L'enseignement supérieur en France 1789-1889
      (Paris, 1888), vol. I, pp. 288-296.

47   Aulard, Napoléon 1er et le monopole universitaire (Paris, 1911).

48   Barnard, op.cit., pp. 156-157; Tracy wanted to extend the Collège
      de France to include chairs in the moral and political sciences, as
      we will see in section III below. Daunou took a chair in history
      at the Collège de France in 1819.

49   Lakanal, speech of 23 October 1794, in Hippeau, op.cit., pp. 408-422
      [see footnote 25 above]. Cf. Van Duzer, op.cit., pp. 109-110. The
      term "normale" is explained in Barnard, op.cit., p. 153 and Duruy,
      op.cit., pp. 105-106: the Paris institution was to be the model for
      similar local institutions.

50   Lakanal, in Hippeau, op.cit., p. 419.

51 Ibid., p. 421.

52 Duruy, op.cit., pp. 58-59; P.M. Dupuy, "L'école normale de l'an III", p. 103. These elementary texts were never published.

53 Dupuy, op.cit., pp. 110-112, 177-179; Van Duzer, op.cit., pp. 117-127.

54 Moniteur, 29 April 1795, cited by Van Duzer, op.cit., pp. 127-128.

55 Cf. Talleyrand's report of 1791 in Hippeau, op.cit., especially pp. 228-237.

56 Text in Godechot, Les Constitutions, p. 133.

57 Text in Duruy, op.cit., pp. 378-380.

58 Cf. chapter one above, p. 26, and Appendix II.

59 J. Simon, Une Académie sous le Directoire, chapters 1 and 3.

60 Ibid., chapters 4 and 6; text in Duruy, op.cit., p. 380.

61 Cf. la Décade philosophique, 30 germinal an IV (19 April 1796), pp. 148-155. However, the working sessions of the Institut had begun in February 1796.

62 Letter by Maine de Biran to the abbé de Féletz, 11 thermidor an X (30 July 1802), reporting the views of Tracy and Cabanis: in Maine de Biran, Oeuvres philosophiques, vol. VI, p. 140.

63 Mémoires de l'Institut, vol. I (1798), pp. 95-96; and also in Cabanis, Oeuvres philosophiques, vol. I, pp. 161n-162. These remarks were omitted from the book versions of the Rapports du physique et du moral de l'homme published in 1802 and subsequent editions.

64 See section III of chapter three, above.

65 See footnote 6, above.

66 Montesquieu, De l'esprit des lois (Paris, 1922), vol. I, p. 29f.

67 Tracy, Commentaire, p. 28.

68 Ibid., pp. 28, 33.

69 Ibid., pp. 33-34. For a strong statement of the need for unity of principles between government and education, cf. Lakanal's speech on the école normale in Hippeau, op.cit., p. 412.

70 Logique, p. 146.

71 See above, pp. 46, 226.

72 Duruy, op.cit., pp. 265-266.

73 They were thus savants rather than teachers, as Duruy pointed out, ibid., p. 286. The original appointees were Daunou, Garat,

Jacquemont, Lebreton, Palissot, Domergue, Lagrange and Darcet; Daunou was replaced almost at once by Ginguené, and Tracy was added four months later: cf. ibid., pp. 241n, 266-267, 284f.

74   Duruy, op.cit., p. 241n.

75   Cf. Tracy's letter of appointment, 23 February 1799, reprinted in Elémens, 5 vols. (Bruxelles, 1826-1827), vol. IV, p. 259.

76   Ibid., pp. 257-258.

77   Cf. Duruy, op.cit., p. 235f.

78   See chapter four above, pp. 226-229.

79   Reprinted in the appendix of Duruy, op.cit., p. 447.

80   Ibidem.

81   Ibid., p. 444.

82   Ibid., p. 445.

83   Cited in ibid., p. 233: letter of about September 1799.

84   For secondary analysis, cf. Kitchin, op.cit., pp. 179-192; Van Duzer, op.cit., pp. 137-142.

85   Reprinted in Elémens, 5 vols. (Paris, 1824-1825), vol. IV, pp. 294-324; ibid., (Bruxelles, 1826-27), IV, pp. 288-318; Duruy, op.cit., pp. 391-411.

86   Duruy, op.cit., p. 391.

87   Cf. letter by Lucien Bonaparte, 12 October 1800, cited in Elémens, IV, pp. 291-293 (Paris ed.) or pp. 285-287 (Bruxelles ed.).

88   Duruy, op.cit., p. 393. For the list of authors, see ibid., pp. 392-393: some of the names included Condillac, Dumarsais, Duclos, Court de Gebelin, Locke, Harris, Voltaire, Montesquieu, Hobbes, Filangieri and Beccaria.

89   Duruy, op.cit., p. 394.

90   Ibid., pp. 396-397.

91   Ibid., pp. 397-398.

92   Ibid., p. 399.

93   Ibid., p. 400.

94   Ibid., p. 401.

95   Ibid., p. 408.

96   Ibid., pp. 401-402.

97   Ibid., p. 402.

98   Ibid., pp. 403-405.

99   Ibid., pp. 403-404.

100 Reprinted in Tracy, Elémens, IV, following p. 318 (Bruxelles ed.).

101 Duruy, op.cit., p. 406.

102 Ibid., pp. 407-410.

103 Ibid., p. 409. Cf. the call by Boisjolin in la Décade philosophique,
     30 pluviôse an VII (18 February 1799), p. 338; Tracy, Quels sont
     les moyens ... (Paris an VI [1798]), p. 30n [cf. Commentaire (1819),
     p. 473n.]; circular to professors of legislation, September 1799,
     in Duruy, op.cit., p. 443; Tracy, Observations (1801), reprinted in
     Elémens, IV, pp. 358-360 (Bruxelles ed.); and Tracy, "Aux rédacteurs
     de la Revue [sur l'école polytechnique]", Revue philosophique,
     12 October 1805, pp. 125-126.

104 Duruy, op.cit., pp. 409-410.

105 Ibid., p. 411.

106 Barnard, op.cit., pp. 199-202.

107 See the replies in Duruy, op.cit., pp. 467-500.

108 Roederer, speech of 11 May 1802, in Oeuvres, vol. VII, p. 210.

109 Fourcroy, speech of 20 April 1802, in Hippeau, op.cit., pp. 488-489.

110 Elémens, vol. I (Paris, 3e ed. 1817), préface of 1801, pp. xxiii-
     xxiv.

111 Ibid., p. xxv.

112   Ibid., pp. xxviii-xxix.

113 Cf. the favourable review in la Décade philosophique, 10 messidor an
     IX (29 June 1801), pp. 14-31. The review is unsigned, but is
     attributed to Garat by J. Kitchin, op.cit., p. 190n. A critical
     review appeared in the Mercure de France on 1er thermidor an IX
     (20 July 1801), pp. 192-197 (signed "P"): the critic believed that
     the moral and political sciences deserved to be omitted from the
     curriculum and that the Council of public instruction had been
     useless.

114 Observations sur le système actuel d'instruction publique, in Elémens,
     IV, pp. 319-375 (Bruxelles ed.), at pp. 321-322.

115 Ibid., p. 325.

116 Ibid., p. 375.

117 Cited above, p. 377 of this chapter.

118 Observations, pp. 325-326.

119 Ibid., p. 327.

120 Ibid., p. 328.

121 Ibid., p. 326.

122 Ibid., p. 327.

123 Ibid., p. 328.

124 Ibid., p. 330.

125 Ibid., pp. 368, 370.

126 Ibid., pp. 329, 371.

127 Ibid., p. 329.

128 See above, p. 381 of this chapter. Dupont de Nemours had envisaged a system in rural primary schools where the teachers would instruct senior students, who would in turn instruct junior students: "Mémoire sur le nombre des écoles primaires", p. 317.

129 Observations, pp. 329-330; the same idea had occurred in the circular to teachers of legislation, September 1799, in Duruy, op.cit., pp. 440-441.

130 Observations, p. 330.

131 Ibid., p. 331.

132 Above, pp. 90-91.

133 Observations, pp. 331-333.

134 Ibid., p. 336.

135 Ibid., pp. 342-343.

136 Ibid., p. 349.

137 Ibid., pp. 350-351.

138 Ibid., pp. 351-353.

139 Ibid., pp. 364-366.

140 Ibid., pp. 357-358. The legislation of 1795 had envisaged special schools for the moral and political sciences, but had not contemplated such an institution for language and literature.

141 Ibid., p. 359.

142 Ibid., p. 360.

143 Ibid., pp. 361-362.

144 Ibid., p. 367.

145 Ibid., p. 368-369. Cf. Elémens, vol. I, p. 295, on the stunted
     intellectual development of the lower classes.

146 Observations, p. 370.

147 Ibid., p. 369.

148 Ibid., pp. 323, 344, 346-347, 370.

149 Ibid., p. 371.

150 Ibid., p. 372.

151 Ibid., p. 373. Cf. "Quels sont les moyens", p. 476, on the import-
     ance of encouraging parents of students in the poorer classes,
     which composed 90% of the people. Cabanis seemed to be less
     content about the operation of market principles in primary
     education: see note 12 above.

152 Observations, p. 374. Tracy's two-class approach was supported by
     Garat in his review of Tracy's pamphlet (see note 113 above);
     the more conservative reviewer in the Mercure was more critical of
     Tracy's distinction, regarding it as an overly strenuous reaction
     to the "equality of 1793" (loc.cit., p. 193). Guizot in 1816
     happily adopted a distinction similar to that of Tracy: cf.
     D. Johnson, Guizot (London, 1963), pp. 111-112.

153 Cf. Tracy, letter to Droz, 27 vendémiaire an X (19 October 1801),
     reprinted by A. Aulard in la Révolution française, vol. 58 (1910),
     pp. 361-362; and the fragment of a letter by Tracy cited in
     la Décade, 20 fructidor an IX (7 September 1801), pp. 496-497.

154 Grammaire [1803] (Paris, 2e ed. 1817), pp. vi-vii.

155 Ibid., pp. viii-ix.

156 Ibid., p. xi.

157 Elémens, vol. I, 1804 foreword (Paris, 3e ed. 1817), pp. v-vi.

158 Ibid., pp. vii-viii.

159 Grammaire, p. viii.

160 Commentaire, p. 97n.

161 "Quels sont les moyens", p. 456.

APPENDICES

I. Speech by Destutt de Tracy, 1 December 1791

II. Structure of the Institut National, 1795

APPENDIX I

Speech by Destutt de Tracy, président du Conseil du Département de l'Allier, 1 December 1791

"Messieurs, Vous voilà parvenus aux termes de vos travaux. Vous avez vérifié les nombreuses opérations que nos collègues ont execute [sic] depuis la dernière session du Conseil général; vous avez rendu un juste tribut d'éloges à leur zèle et à leurs lumières; vous avez adjoint à leurs fonctions des hommes dont le choix vous garantit les succès à l'avenir; vous avez, autant que les circonstances l'ont permis, réglé les affaires instantes qui réclamoient votre attention. Alliant la prudence avec le zèle, vous n'avez voulu vous occuper que de ce qui étoit indispensable. Vous avez senti qu'une administration naissante devoit avant tout prendre une concistance; que c'étoit beaucoup faire pour la patrie et la liberté que de maintenir et d'affermir le nouvel ordre de choses, et de travailler à l'établissement complet du nouveau sistême d'impositions et d'administration.

Cette session sera mémorable, moins par ce qu'elle a exécuté, que par ce qu'elle a proposé. Un jour on se rappellera qu'elle est la première depuis l'achèvement complet de la Constitution. Les citoyens de ce département, datant de cette époque chérie le commencement de leur prospérité, penseront avec reconnoissance que ceux qui ont écartés [sic] les premiers obstacles, sont les premiers auteurs de la félicité publique; et, s'ils peuvent se rappeller, ce qui n'est malheureusement que trop vrai, que, dans ces tems d'orages, il existe un grand nombre de personnes auxquelles il est difficile de faire aimer le nouveau gouvernement, ils nous sauront gré d'avoir, par sentiment, devancé les lumières de l'expérience.

Après avoir rempli dignement vos importantes fonctions, vous allez retourner dans vos foyers et là vous servirez encore la patrie, en échauffant tous les coeurs du feu de votre patriotisme, en éclairant tous les esprits de vos lumières, en expliquant, en faisant aimer les loix dont vous venez d'ordonner l'exécution, et en donnant l'exemple d'y être soumis. C'est ainsi que la vie d'un bon citoyen est une magistrature perpétuelle; c'est ainsi, Messieurs, que dans tous les moments vous acquérerez de nouveaux droits à l'estime et à la reconnoissance de vos concitoyens.

Pour moi, Messieurs, pénétré de la bienveillance que vous m'avez montré [sic] et de la confiance dont vous m'avez honoré, je vais savourer dans ma retraite ce souvenir flatteur; et, soit que je puisse y goûter les douceurs de la paix et de l'étude, soit que le vif intérêt que je prends aux affaires publiques m'attire au foyer des évènements, soit que mon devoir m'oblige à voler à la deffense des frontières, quelque part enfin que je sois, je n'existerai que pour sentir le prix des bontés de cette Assemblée et pour hâter par mes voeux le jour qui doit la réunir."

(Source: F. Claudon and P. Flament (ed.), Inventaire sommaire des Archives départementales postérieures à 1790. Allier, série L (Moulins 1912), vol. I, pp. 47-48.)

APPENDIX II

Structure of the Institut National des Sciences et des Arts, 1795

CLASSES	SECTIONS		MEMBRES À PARIS	ASSOCIÉS DANS LES DÉPARTEMENTS
I. Sciences Physiques et Mathématiques	1	Mathématiques	6	6
	2	Arts mécaniques	6	6
	3	Astronomie	6	6
	4	Physique expérimentale	6	6
	5	Chimie	6	6
	6	Histoire naturelle et minéralogie	6	6
	7	Botanique et physique végétale	6	6
	8	Anatomie et zoologie	6	6
	9	Médecine et chirurgie	6	6
	10	Economie rurale et arts vétérinaires	6	6
			60	60
II. Sciences morales et politiques	1	Analyse des sensations et des idées	6	6
	2	Morale	6	6
	3	Sciences sociales et législation	6	6
	4	Economie politique	6	6
	5	Historie	6	6
	6	Géographie	6	6
			36	36
III. Littérature et Beaux-Arts	1	Grammaire	6	6
	2	Langues anciennes	6	6
	3	Poésie	6	6
	4	Antiquités et monuments	6	6
	5	Peinture	6	6
	6	Sculpture	6	6
	7	Architecture	6	6
	8	Musique et déclamation	6	6
			48	48

(Source: law of 3 brumaire an IV: 25 October 1795)

BIBLIOGRAPHY

Part A   Published Writings of
          Antoine-Louis-Claude Destutt de Tracy

Part B   Other Primary Sources

Part C   Secondary Sources and Miscellaneous

Part A: Published Writings of Antoine-Louis-Claude Destutt de Tracy

Destutt de Tracy, Antoine-Louis-Claude, comte de,

[D.T.] "Aux Rédacteurs de la Revue [sur l'école polytechnique]",
    Revue philosophique, littéraire et politique, 12 Octobre 1805/
    20 vendémiaire an XIV, pp. 123-126.

[Anon.] "Avis important [review of Villers' Philosophie de Kant]",
    la Décade philosophique, politique et littéraire, 10 vendémiaire
    an X, pp. 54-57.

[Anon.] Analyse de l'origine de tous les cultes par le citoyen
    Dupuis, et de l'abrégé qu'il a donné de cet ouvrage (Paris:
    Agasse, an VII [1799].

[Anon.] Analyse raisonnée de 'l'Origine de Tous les Cultes, ou
    Religion Universelle' (Paris: Courcier, An XIII=1804).

Commentaire sur l'Esprit des Lois de Montesquieu (Paris: Théodore
    Desoer, 1819).

[Anon.] A Commentary and Review of Montesquieu's Spirit of Laws
    [trans. Thomas Jefferson] (Philadelphia: William Duane, 1811).

De l'Amour [c. 1813] ed. and intro. Gilbert Chinard (Paris: Les
    Belles Lettres, 1926).

"De la métaphysique de Kant, ou observations sur un ouvrage intitulé:
    'Essai d'une exposition succinte de la critique de la raison
    pure', par J. Kinker, traduit du hollandais par J. le F. en
    1 vol. in -8°, à Amsterdam, 1801", in Mémoires de l'Institut
    National, Classe des Sciences morales et politiques, tome IV
    (1802), pp. 544-606.

[Discours au Conseil général du département de l'Allier, 1er décembre
    1791] in F. Claudon and P. Flament (eds.), Inventaire sommaire
    des archives départementales postérieures à 1790. Allier, série L
    (Moulins: Imprimerie du progrès de l'Allier, 1912), tome I,
    pp. 47-48.

"Discours prononcés dans la séance publique tenue par la classe de
    la langue et de la littérature françaises de l'Institut de
    France, pour la réception de M. de Tracy ... le 21 décembre
    1808" (Paris: Baudouin, décembre 1808).

"Dissertation sur l'Existence, et sur les hypothèses de Mallebranche
    et de Berkeley à ce sujet", in Mémoires de l'Institut National,
    Classe des Sciences morales et politiques, tome III (1801),
    pp. 515-534.

"Dissertation sur quelques questions d'idéologie", in Mémoires de
    l'Institut National, Classe des Sciences morales et politiques,
    tome III (1801), pp. 491-514.

Projet d'éléments d'idéologie à l'usage des écoles centrales de
    la République française (Paris: Didot, an IX [1801]).

Destutt de Tracy, Antoine-Louis-Claude, comte de,

Elémens d'idéologie. Première partie. Idéologie proprement dite
(Paris: Courcier, an XIII=1804) [the second edition of
Projet, 1801]

Elémens d'idéologie. Première partie. Idéologie proprement dite
(Paris: Courcier, 1817) [reprinted (Paris: Vrin, 1970),
ed. H. Gouhier] [3rd ed. of Projet, 1801].

Elémens d'idéologie. Seconde partie. Grammaire (Paris: Courcier,
an XI=1803).

Elémens d'idéologie. Second partie. Grammaire (Paris: Courcier,
1817) [reprinted (Paris: Vrin, 1970), ed. H. Gouhier] [the
second edition of Grammaire, 1803].

Elémens d'idéologie. Troisième partie. Logique (Paris: Courcier,
an XIII=1805).

Elémens d'idéologie. Troisième partie. Logique (Paris: Courcier,
1818) [the second edition of Logique, 1805]

Elémens d'idéologie. IVe et Ve parties. Traité de la Volonté et
de ses effets (Paris: Courcier, 1815)

Elémens d'idéologie. IVe et Ve Parties. Traité de la Volonté et
de ses effets (Paris: Courcier, 1818) [the second edition of
Traité de la Volonté, 1815].

Elémens d'idéologie, 5 vols. (Paris: Lévi, 1824-26).

Elémens d'idéologie, 5 vols. (Bruxelles: A. Wahlen, 1826-27).

"Extrait raisonné servant de Table analytique", attached to Cabanis,
P.-J.-G., Rapports du physique et du moral de l'homme, 2 vols.
(Paris: Bibliothèque Choisie, 1830), I, pp. 23-65.

"Le Mémoire de Berlin" [written 1806, in response to the question:
Y a-t-il des aperceptions internes immédiates?" in the essay
competition conducted by the Academy of Berlin], ed. Pierre
Tisserand, Revue philosophique de la France et de l'étranger,
tome 116 no. 8 (September 1933), pp. 161-187.

[Lettres du Ministre de l'Intérieur aux professeurs des écoles
centrales, 1799], in Elémens d'idéologie, 5 vols. (Paris:
Lévi, 1824-26), IV, pp. 266-291, and in ibid., 5 vols.
(Bruxelles: A. Wahlen, 1826-27), IV, pp. 260-285.

"Mémoire sur la faculté de penser", in Mémoires de l'Institut National
des Sciences et Arts pour l'An IV de la République, Sciences
morales et politiques, tome I (1798), pp. 283-450.

"M. de Tracy à M. Burke" (Paris: De l'Imprimerie Nationale, 1790).

Observations sur le système actuel d'instruction publique (Paris:
Panckouche, an IX [1801]).   [Also reprinted in Elémens
d'idéologie, 5 vols. (Paris: Lévi, 1824-26), IV, 325-382,
and in ibid., 5 vols. (Bruxelles: A. Wahlen, 1826-27), IV,
pp. 319-375].

Destutt de Tracy, Antoine-Louis-Claude, comte de,

"Opinion de M. de Tracy, sur les affaires de Saint-Domingue, en septembre 1791" (Paris: Imprimerie de Laillet, 1791).

Principes logiques, ou recueil de faits relatifs à l'intelligence humaine (Paris: Courcier, 1817) [Also in Elémens d'idéologie, 5 vols. (Paris: Lévi, 1824-26), IV, pp. 197-219, and ibid., 5 vols. (Bruxelles: A. Wahlen, 1826-27), IV, pp. 191-253].

"Quels sont les moyens de fonder la morale chez un peuple?" par le Cit. D.T. *** (Paris: Agasse, an VI [1798]) [reprinted in Commentaire sur l'Esprit des Lois de Montesquieu (Paris: Théodore Desoer, 1819), pp. 435-477].

"Rapport de M. Destutt-Tracy [on behalf of a commission of the Institut examining mémoires on the question: Déterminer quelle est l'influence de l'habitude sur la faculté de penser]", (1802), attached to Maine de Biran, L'influence de l'habitude sur la faculté de penser, ed. Pierre Tisserand (Paris: Presses Universitaires de France, 1954), pp. 207-224.

[Rapport du Conseil d'instruction publique au Ministre de l'Intérieur sur l'état au vrai de l'instruction publique dans la France, 16 pluviôse an VIII (5 February 1800)], in Albert Duruy, L'Instruction publique et la Révolution (Paris: Hachette, 1882), Appendix No. 6, pp. 391-411 [also in Tracy, Elémens d'idéologie, 5 vols. (Paris: Lévi, 1824-26), IV, pp. 294-324, and in ibid., 5 vols. (Bruxelles: A. Wahlen, 1826-27), IV, pp. 288-318].

"Réflexions sur les projets de pasigraphie", in Mémoires de l'Institut National, Classe des Sciences morales et politiques, tome III (1801), pp. 535-551.

Supplément à la première section des Elémens d'idéologie [1805], in Traité de la Volonté (1815), pp. 7-50, or in ibid., (1818), pp. 7-48.

[Anon.] "Sur les Lettres de Descartes", Revue philosophique, littéraire et politique [formerly la Décade ...], 1 juin 1806, pp. 392-401.

"Sur un systême méthodique de bibliographie", Gazette National ou Moniteur Universel, 8, 9 brumaire an VI, pp. 151-152, 155-156.

Traité d'Economie Politique (Paris: Bouget et Lévi, 1823).

A Treatise on Political Economy [trans. rev. Thomas Jefferson] (Georgetown, D.C.: Joseph Milligan, 1817) [reprinted New York: A.A. Kelley, 1970].

Part B: Other Primary Sources

Académie des Sciences morales et politiques, Séances et Travaux de
    l'Académie des Sciences morales et politiques, 1ère Série (Paris,
    1842-).

Académie française, Dictionnaire de l'Académie française,
    2 vols. (Nismes: Pierre Beaume, nouv. ed. 1787)
    2 vols. (Paris: J.J. Smits, 5e ed. an VII [1798])
    2 vols. (Paris: Moutardier, an X [1802])
    3 vols. (Paris: F. Didot, 6e ed. 1835-6).

Adams, John, The Adams-Jefferson Letters, ed. L.J. Cappon, 2 vols.
    (Chapel Hill: Uni. of North Carolina Press, 1959).

Aimé-Martin, L., "Essai sur la Vie et les Ouvrages de Bernardin de
    Saint-Pierre", in J.-H. Bernardin de Saint-Pierre, Oeuvres complètes,
    ed. L. Aimé-Martin, 12 vols. (Paris: Mequignon-Marvis, 1818),
    vol. 1, pp. 1-271.

Ampère, André-Marie and Jean-Jacques, Correspondance et Souvenirs (de
    1805 à 1864), 2 vols. (Paris: J. Hetzel, 2e ed. 1875).

Andrieux, François-Guillaume-Jean-Stanislas, Oeuvres, 3 vols. (Paris:
    Nepveu, 1818).

Andrieux, François-Guillaume-Jean-Stanislas, Opinion ... sur l'instruction
    publique dans les écoles primaires, Séance du 1er floréal an 7
    [20 April 1799] (Paris: Imprimerie nationale, floréal an 7).

Annales de la Religion, 18 vols. (Paris, 1795-1803).

Annales encyclopédiques, rédigées par A.-L. Millin, 12 vols. (Paris,
    1817-1818) [Continuation of Magazin encyclopédique, 1795-1816].

[Anonymous], A Narrative of Memorable Events in Paris Preceding the
    Capitulation and During the Occupancy of that City by the Allied
    Armies in the year 1814 ... (London, 1828).

[Anonymous], Biographie des Quarante de l'Académie française (Paris: les
    Marchands des Nouveautés, 1826).

[Anonymous], Dictionnaire de la Constitution et du Gouvernement
    français ... (Paris: chez Guillaume, an III de la liberté française
    [1791]).

Archives Parlementaires, Première Série (1787-1799) - sous la direction
    de J. Maridal et E. Laurent (Paris: Paul Dupont, 1875-).

Aulard, François-Victor-Alphonse (ed.), Paris pendant la Réaction
    thermidoriénne et sous le Directoire: Recueil de documents pour
    l'histoire de l'esprit public à Paris, 5 vols. (Paris: Noblet;
    Quantin; Cerf, 1898-1902).

Aulard, François-Victor-Alphonse (ed.), Paris sous le Consulat: Recueil
    de documents pour l'histoire de l'esprit public à Paris, 4 vols.
    (Paris: Noblet; Quantin; Cerf, 1903-09).

Aulard, François-Victor-Alphonse (ed.), Paris sous le Premier Empire: Recueil de documents pour l'histoire de l'esprit public à Paris, 3 vols. (Paris: Noblet; Quantin; Cerf, 1912-23).

Bacon, Francis, The New Organon and Related Writings, intro. F.H. Anderson (New York: Bobbs-Merrill, 1960).

Bailly, Jean-Sylvain, Histoire de l'astronomie ancienne, depuis son origine jusqu'à l'établissement de l'école d'Alexandrie (Paris: chez les frères Debure, 1775).

Bailly, Jean-Sylvain, Histoire de l'astronomie moderne depuis la fondation de l'école d'Alexandrie, jusqu'à l'époque de MDCCXXX, 3 vols. (Paris: chez les frères Debure, 1779-82).

Bailly, Jean-Sylvain, Lettres sur l'origine des sciences, et sur celle des peuples de l'Asie, addressées à M.de Voltaire ... (Paris: chez les frères Debure, 1777).

Ballanche, Pierre-Simon, Essai sur les institutions sociales dans leur rapport avec les idées nouvelles (Paris: Renouard, 1818).

Barbier, Antoine-Alexandre, Dictionnaire des ouvrages anonymes et pseudonymes ..., 4 vols. (Paris: Imprimerie Bibliographique, 1806-08).

Barnave, Joseph, Power, Property and History: Joseph Barnave's 'Introduction to the French Revolution' [1792] and other writings, trans. and intro. Emanuel Chill (New York: Harper & Row, 1971).

Barrière, Jean-François (ed.), Bibliothèque des mémoires relatifs à l'histoire de France pendant le XVIIIe siècle, 37 vols. (Paris, 1846-81).

Baudeau, Nicolas, abbé de, Première introduction à la philosophie économique; ou analyse des états policés [1771], in Eugène Daire (ed.), Physiocrates (Paris: Guillaumin, 1846), pp. 655-821.

Baudeau, Nicolas, abbé de, Principes de la Science morale et politique sur le Luxe et les Loix somptuaires [1767], ed. A. Dubois (Paris: P. Geuthner, 1912).

[Beauvray, C.R. Lefure de], Dictionnaire social et patriotique, ou précis raisonné de connoissances relatives à l'économie morale, civile et politique (Amsterdam, 1770).

Beccaria, Cesare, On Crimes and Punishments, trans. Henry Paolucci (New York: Bobbs-Merrill, 1963).

Bentham, Jeremy, A Fragment on Government, and An Introduction to the Principles of Morals and Legislation, ed. and intro. Wilfrid Harrison (Oxford: Blackwell, 1948).

Bentham, Jeremy, Traités de législation civile et penale ..., trans. and ed. Etienne Dumont (Paris: Bossange, Masson, Besson, an X-1802).

Bentham, Jeremy, Bentham's Theory of Fictions, intro. C.K. Ogden (London: Paul, Trench, Trubner, 1932).

Bérenger, Laurent-Pierre, Esprit de Mably et de Condillac relativement à la morale et à la politique, 2 vols. (Grenoble, 1789).

Bernardin de Saint-Pierre, Jacques-Henri, Oeuvres Complètes, ed. L. Aimé-Martin, 12 vols. (Paris: Mequignon-Marvis, 1818).

Beyle, Marie-Henri [Stendhal], Love, trans. J. Stewart and B. Knight (Harmondsworth: Penguin, 1975).

Beyle, Marie-Henri [Stendhal], Oeuvres Complètes, 34 vols. (Paris, 1913-1940).

Beyle, Marie-Henri [Stendhal], The Life of Henry Brulard, trans. J. Stewart and B. Knight (Harmondsworth: Penguin, 1973).

Boissy d'Anglas, François-Antoine, comte de, Discours préliminaire au projet de Constitution de l'an III, prononcé à la séance du 5 messidor (Paris: Imprimerie de la République, messidor an III).

Bonald, Louis-Gabriel-Ambroise, vicomte de, Essai analytique sur les lois naturelles de l'ordre social ou du pouvoir, du ministre et du sujet dans la société (Paris, 1800).

Bonald, Louis-Gabriel-Ambroise, Législation primitive ..., 3 vols. (Paris, 1802).

Bonald, Louis-Gabriel-Ambroise, Mélanges littéraires, politiques et philosophiques, 2 vols. (Paris: Adrien Le Clerc, 1819).

Bonaparte, Lucien, Lucien Bonaparte et ses Mémoires, 1775-1840, ed. H.F.T. Jung, 3 vols. (Paris: G. Charpentier, 1882-3).

Broglie, Achille-Léonce-Victor-Charles, duc de, Ecrits et discours, 3 vols. (Paris: Didier, 1863).

Broglie, Achille-Léonce-Victor-Charles, Souvenirs, 1785-1870, 4 vols. (Paris: Calmann Lévy, 1886).

Brun, Jean-Baptiste, Leçons Idéologiques, pour apprendre à la jeunesse à contracter des habitudes sociales et des habitudes morales (Paris: chez Renard, 1821).

Brun, Joseph-André, Science de l'organisation sociale, demontrée dans ses premiers élémens (Paris: Cerioux; Moutardier, an VII).

Brunot, Ferdinand, Histoire de la langue française des origines à 1900, 13 tomes (Paris: Armand Colin, 1905-1953).

Buchez, P.-J.-B., and Roux-Lavergne, P.-C., Histoire parlementaire de la Révolution française, ou journal des assemblées nationales, 1789-1815, 40 vols. (Paris, 1834-8).

Buffon, Georges-Louis Le Clerc, comte de, Oeuvres philosophiques, ed. Jean Piveteau (Paris: Presses Universitaires de France, 1954).

Burke, Edmund, Reflections on the Revolution in France [and other writings], intro. A.J. Grieve (London: Dent, 1964).

Cabanis, Pierre-Jean-Georges, "Cabanis à ses collègues", Ami des Lois 30 brumaire an 8 [21 November 1799], in Paris sous le Consulat, ed. F.V.A. Aulard (Paris: Cerf; Noblet; and Quantin, 1903), vol. I, p. 17.

Cabanis, Pierre-Jean-Georges, Cabanis: choix de textes et Introduction par Georges Poyer (Paris: Louis-Michaud, n.d.).

Cabanis, Pierre-Jean-Georges, Discours de Cabanis en offrant au Conseil des Cinq-Cents la gravure du portrait de Mirabeau [suivi de] Discours de Cabanis en offrant au Conseil des Cinq-Cents l'édition des 'Oeuvres' de Condillac, Séance du 13 thermidor an 6 [31 July 1798] (Paris: Imprimerie Nationale, thermidor an 6).

Cabanis, Pierre-Jean-Georges, Discours prononcé par Cabanis, en offrant au Conseil [des Cinq-Cents] la nouvelle édition du Dictionnaire de la ci-devant Académie française, Séance du 18 brumaire an 7 [8 November 1798] (Paris: Imprimerie nationale, brumaire an 7).

Cabanis, Pierre-Jean-Georges, Discours prononcé par Cabanis en offrant au Conseil [des Cinq-Cents] un ouvrage posthume de Condorcet sur l'arithmétique, Séance du 26 vendémiaire an 7 [17 October 1798] (Paris: Imprimerie Nationale, vendémiaire an 7).

Cabanis, Pierre-Jean-Georges, Discours prononcé par Cabanis, Membre de la Commission du Conseil des Cinq-Cents, Séance du 3 nivôse an 8 [24 December 1799] (Paris: Imprimerie Nationale, nivôse an 8).

Cabanis, Pierre-Jean-Georges, Discours prononcé par Cabanis, sur le message du Conseil des Anciens, relatif aux journaux calomniateurs des premières autorités, Séance du premier fructidor an 7 [18 August 1799] (Paris: Imprimerie Nationale, fructidor an 7)

Cabanis, Pierre-Jean-Georges, "Notes pour la cour", 19 and 20 avril 1791, in Correspondance entre le comte de Mirabeau et le comte de la Marck pendant les années 1789, 1790 et 1791, ed. A. de Bacourt, 3 vols. (Paris: Le Normant, 1851), vol. III, pp. 134-142.

Cabanis, Pierre-Jean-Georges, Oeuvres Complètes, ed. F. Thurot, 5 vols. (Paris: Didot; Bossange frères, 1823-25).

Cabanis, Pierre-Jean-Georges, Oeuvres philosophiques, ed. Claude Lehec and Jean Cazeneuve, 2 vols. (Paris: Presses Universitaires de France, 1956).

Cabanis, Pierre-Jean-Georges, Opinion de Cabanis contre le projet de partage des biens communaux, Séance du 7 pluviôse an 7 [26 January 1799] (Paris: Imprimerie Nationale, pluviôse an 7).

Cabanis, Pierre-Jean-Georges, Opinion de Cabanis sur l'emprunt forcé, Séance du 25 brumaire an 8 [16 November 1799] (Paris: Imprimerie Nationale, brumaire an 8).

Cabanis, Pierre-Jean-Georges, Opinion de Cabanis sur l'impôt du sel à l'extraction [Séance du 11 fructidor an 6 (28 August 1798)] (Paris: Baudouin, n.d. [fructidor an 6]).

Cabanis, Pierre-Jean-Georges, Opinion de Cabanis sur les réunions s'occupant d'objets politiques (Paris: Baudouin, n.d. [therimdor an 5: July-August 1797]).

Cabanis, Pierre-Jean-Georges, Rapports du physique et du moral de l'homme, précédés d'une table analytique par M. le comte Destutt de Tracy et suivis d'une table alphabétique [par P. Sue], 3 vols. (Paris: Baillière, 1824).

Cabanis, Pierre-Jean-Georges, "Science, Philosophie", Le Conservateur, no. 30 (Paris: 9 vendémiaire an 6: 30 September 1797), pp. 236-238.

Cahier de l'Ordre de la Noblesse du Bourbonnais et Pouvoirs remis à MM. D.-M.-P. Dubuisson ..., A.-L.-C. de Stutt ..., H. Coiffier ..., députés aux Etats-Généraux (n.p., n.d. [1789]).

Cambacérès, Jean-Jacques Régis, comte de, "Discours sur la science sociale", in Mémoires de l'Institut National, Classe des Sciences morales et politiques, vol. III (1801), pp. 1-14.

Cambacérès, Jean-Jacques Régis, comte de, Lettres inédites à Napoléon, ed. Jean Duhamel, 2 vols. (Paris: Klincksieck, 1974).

Chamfort, Sébastian-Roch-Nicolas, Oeuvres complètes, 2 vols. (Paris: Colnet, 2e ed. 1808).

Chaptal, Jean-Antoine-Claude, comte de Chanteloup, De l'industrie française, 2 vols. (Paris, 1819).

Chateaubriand, François-René, vicomte de, Génie du Christianisme [1802], intro. Pierre Reboul, 2 vols. (Paris: Garnier-Flammarion, 1966).

Chateaubriand, François-René, vicomte de, Mémoires d'outre-tombe, ed. V. Giraud, 2 vols. (Genève: La Palatine, n.d. [1946]).

Chénier, Marie-Joseph Blaise de, Oeuvres, ed. D. Ch. Robert, précedées d'une Notice sur Chénier par M. Arnault, 5 vols. (Paris: Guillaume, 1824-26).

Chénier, Marie-Joseph Blaise de, Tableau historique de l'état et des progrès de la littérature française depuis 1789 (Paris: Maradan, 3e ed. 1818).

Chinard, Gilbert, Jefferson et les idéologues d'après sa correspondence ... (Baltimore: John Hopkins Press, 1925).

Claudon, F., and Flament, P. (eds.), Inventaire sommaire des Archives Départementales postérieures à 1790. Allier, Série L., vol. I (Moulins: Imprimerie du progrès de l'Allier, 1912).

Comte, Auguste, Cours de philosophie positive, 6 vols. (Paris, 1830-42).

Comte, Auguste, The Crisis of Industrial Civilization: the Early Essays of Auguste Comte, trans. H.D. Hutton, intro. R. Fletcher (London: Heinemann, 1974).

Condillac, Etienne Bonnot, abbé de, Oeuvres Philosophiques, ed. Georges Le Roy, 3 vols. (Paris: Presses Universitaires de France, 1947-51).

Condorcet, Marie-Jean-Antoine-Nicolas Caritat, marquis de, Esquisse d'un tableau historique du progrès de l'esprit humain [1793], ed. O.H. Prior (Paris, 1933).

Condorcet, Marie-Jean-Antoine-Nicolas Caritat, marquis de, Oeuvres complètes, 21 vols. (Brunswick: Vieweg, et à Paris: Henrichs, an XIII = 1804).

Condorcet, Marie-Jean-Antoine-Nicolas Caritat, marquis de, Selected Writings, trans. and ed. Keith M. Baker (Indianapolis: Bobbs-Merrill, 1976).

Condorcet, Marie-Jean-Antoine-Nicolas Caritat, marquis de, Sketch for a Historical Picture of the Progress of the Human Mind, trans. June Barraclough, intro. Stuart Hampshire (London: Weidenfeld and Nicolson, 1955).

Condorcet, Marie-Jean-Antoine-Nicolas Caritat, marquis de, "Un 'éloge' officieux de Condorcet: sa notice historique et critique sur Condillac", intro. Keith M. Baker, Revue de synthèse, vol. 88, nos. 47-48 (1967), pp. 227-251.

Condorcet, Sophie Grouchy, marquise de, Lettres sur la Sympathie ... [attached to] Adam Smith, Théorie des sentiments moraux, suivi d'une Dissertation sur l'origine des langages, 2 vols. (Paris: F. Buisson, an 6 [1798]).

Le Conservateur, journal politique, philosophique et littéraire par les citoyens Garat, Daunou, Chénier (Paris, 1 September 1797- 20 July 1798)

Constant, Benjamin-Henri (de Rebecque), Choix de textes politiques, ed. Olivier Pozzo di Borgo (Paris: J.-J. Pauvet, 1965).

Constant, Benjamin-Henri (de Rebecque), Ecrits et discours politiques, ed. Olivier Pozzo di Borgo, 2 vols. (Paris: J.-J. Pauvet, 1964).

Constant, Benjamin-Henri (de Rebecque), Mélanges de littérature et de politique (Paris: Pichon; Didier, 1829).

Constant, Benjamin-Henri (de Rebecque), Oeuvres, ed. Alfred Roulin (Paris: Pléiade, 1964).

Constant, Benjamin-Henri (de Rebecque), Oeuvres politiques, ed. Charles Louandre (Paris: Charpentier, 1874).

Cornet, Mathieu-Augustin, comte de, Souvenirs Sénatoriaux ... (Paris: Baudouin, 1824).

Cousin, Victor, "Adam Smith", Séances et Travaux de l'Académie des Sciences morales et politiques, 1ère série, vol. X (Paris, 1846), pp. 441-462.

Cousin, Victor, Cours de l'histoire de la philosophie moderne: Deuxième série, 3 vols. (Paris: Didier, nouv. ed. 1847).

Cousin, Victor, Cours d'histoire de la philosophie morale au 18e siècle, professé ... en 1819 et 1820, 3 vols. (Paris, 1839-42).

Cousin, Victor, Fragmens philosophiques (Paris: Sautelet, 1826).

Daire, Eugène (ed.), Physiocrates: Quesnay, Dupont de Nemours, Mercier de la Rivière, l'abbé Baudeau, Le Trosne, 2 vols. (Paris: Guillaumin, 1846).

d'Alembert, Jean Le Rond, Preliminary Discourse to the Encyclopedia of Diderot, trans. and intro. R.N. Schwab (New York: Bobbs-Merrill, 1963).

Damiron, Jean-Philibert, Essai sur l'histoire de la philosophie en France au dix-neuvième siècle (Bruxelles: Librairie Polymathique, 3e ed. 1829).

Damiron, Jean-Philibert, Mémoires pour servir à l'histoire de la philosophie au dix-huitième siècle, 2 vols. (Paris, 1858).

Daube, L.-J.-J., Essai d'idéologie servant d'introduction à la grammaire générale (Paris: Gide; Levrault frères, an XI-1803).

Daunou, Pierre-Claude-François, Discours d'Ouverture du Cours d'Histoire et de Morale au Collège Royal de France, prononcé le mardi 13 avril 1819 (Paris: Foulon, 1819).

Daunou, Pierre-Claude-François, Discours prononcé par P.-C.-F. Daunou, président du Conseil des Cinq-Cents, pour l'anniversaire de la fondation de la République, Séance du premier vendémiaire an 7 [22 September 1798] (Paris: Imprimerie nationale, vendémiaire an 7).

Daunou, Pierre-Claude-François, Essai sur les garanties individuelles que réclame l'état actuel de la société (Paris: Bobée, 3e ed. 1822).

Daunou, Pierre-Claude-François, Discours prononcé aux funérailles de M. le comte Destutt de Tracy ... le 12 mars 1836, par M. Daunou (Paris: typographie de Firmin Didot frères, n.d. [1836]).

Daunou, Pierre-Claude-François, Mémoires, in J.-F. Barrière (ed.), Bibliothèque des mémoires relatifs à l'histoire de France pendant le XVIIIe siècle, tome 12 (Paris, 1848), pp. 409-464.

Daunou, Pierre-Claude-François, Mémoires pour servir à l'histoire de la Convention Nationale, in A.-H. Taillandier, Documents biographiques sur P.-C.-F. Daunou (Paris: Firmin Didot, 1841), pp. 174-197.

Daunou, Pierre-Claude-François, Notice des travaux de la Classe des Sciences morales et politiques pendant le premier trimestre de l'an XI (Paris: Baudouin, an XI).

Daunou, Pierre-Claude-François, Rapport fait à la Convention Nationale, dans sa séance du 13 germinal, au nom du comité d'instruction publique (Paris: Imprimerie Nationale, germinal an III [April 1795]).

La Décade philosophique, littéraire et politique (Paris, 1794-1807) [entitled la Revue ... after October 1804].

Descartes, René, Discourse on Method and other writings, trans. F.E. Sutcliffe (Harmondsworth: Penguin, 1968).

Desné, Roland (ed.), Les matérialistes français de 1750 à 1800 (Paris: Buchet/Chastel, 1965).

Destutt de Tracy, Sarah Newton, "Notice sur M. Destutt de Tracy", in Essais divers, Lettres et Pensées, de Madame de Tracy, 3 vols. (Paris: Typographie Plon, 1852-5), vol. I, pp. 305-404.

Diderot, Denis, et al., Encyclopedia: Selections, trans. and intro. N.S. Hoyt and T. Cassirer (New York: Bobbs-Merrill, 1965).

Diderot, Denis, et al., The Encyclopedia: Selections, ed. and trans. S.J. Gendzier (New York: Harper and Row, 1967).

Diderot, Denis, Oeuvres Philosophiques, ed. Paul Vernière (Paris: Garnier, 1964).

Diderot, Denis, Oeuvres politiques, ed. Paul Vernière (Paris: Garnier, 196?

Diderot, Denis, Selected Writings, trans. D. Coltman, ed. L.G. Crocker (New York: Macmillan, 1966).

Diderot, Denis, et al., The Encyclopédie of Diderot and d'Alembert: Selected Articles, ed. and intro. John Lough (Cambridge: Cambridge University Press, 1969).

Doyon, André, and Fleury, Marie-Antoinette, "Amitiés Parisiennes de Stendhal. Emile Desages et Sarah de Tracy (avec deux lettres inédites à Stendhal)", Stendhal Club, no. 41 (1968), pp. 7-14.

Dumont, Etienne, Recollections of Mirabeau, and of the Two First Legislativ Assemblies of France (London: Edward Bull, 1832).

Dunoyer, Barthélemy-Charles-Pierre-Joseph, "Esquisse historique des doctrines auxquelles on a donné le nom d'industrialisme, c'est-à-dire, des doctrines qui fondent la société sur l'industrie", Revue encyclopédique, vol. 33 (February 1827), pp. 368-395.

Dupont de Nemours, Pierre-Samuel, De l'origine et des progrès d'une science nouvelle [1768], ed. A. Dubois (Paris: P. Geuthner, 1910).

Dupont de Nemours, Pierre-Samuel, De Staël - Du Pont Letters, trans. and ed. James F. Marshall (Madison: University of Wisconsin Press, 1968).

Dupuis, Charles-François, Abrégé de 'l'Origine de tous les Cultes' (Paris, an VI [1798]).

Dupuis, Charles-François, Origine de tous les Cultes, ou Religion universelle, 7 tomes (Paris, an III [1795]).

Ecole Normale, Séances des écoles normales recueillies par les Sténographes 13 vols. (Paris, 1801).

Escher, J.-B., Exercice public d'idéologie et de logique (Strasbourg: Levrault, an 10-1802).

Fabre, Marie-Jacques-Joseph-Victorin, Oeuvres, 2 vols. (Paris: Paulin, 1844

Fabre, Marie-Jacques-Joseph-Victorin, Tableau littéraire du dix-huitième siècle ou essai sur les grands écrivains de ce siècle et les progrès de l'esprit humain en France (Paris: Baudouin, avril 1810).

Fabre (de l'Aude), Jean-Pierre, comte de, Histoire secrète du Directoire, 4 vols. (Paris: Ménard, 1832).

Fabre (de l'Aude), Jean-Pierre, comte de, Mémoires et souvenirs, 4 vols. (Paris, 1829).

Fauriel, Claude-Charles, Les derniers jours du consulat [1804], ed. Ludovic Lalanne (Paris: Calmann Lévy, 1886).

Fauvelet de Bourrienne, Louis-Antoine, Mémoires sur Napoléon, le Directoire, Le Consulat, l'Empire et la Restauration, 10 vols. (Paris: Ladvocat, 1829).

Ferguson, Adam, An Essay on the History of Civil Society [1767], ed. Duncan Forbes (Edinburgh: Edinburgh University Press, 1967).

Fiévée, Joseph, Correspondance et relations de Joseph Fiévée avec Bonaparte pendant les ans 1802 à 1813, 3 vols. (Paris, 1836).

Flourens, J.-P.-M., Discours prononcé aux funerailles de M. le comte Destutt de Tracy ... le 12 mars 1836, par M. Flourens (Paris: typographie de Firmin Didot frères, n.d. [1836].

Fourcroy, Antoine-François, comte de, Philosophie chimique ... (Paris, 2e ed. 1795).

Franck, Adolphe (ed.), Dictionnaire des sciences philosophiques par une société de professeurs et de savants, 6 vols. (Paris: Hachette, 1844-1852).

Garat, Dominique-Joseph, Discours prononcés à l'Institut dans la séance publique du 6 nivôse an XII [28 December 1803]: Discours du citoyen Parny ... [suivi de] Réponse du citoyen Garat, président de la Classe de littérature et de langue françaises ... (Paris: Baudouin, nivôse an XII).

Garat, Dominique-Joseph, Mémoires historiques sur la vie de M. Suard, sur ses écrits, et sur le XVIIIe siècle, 2 vols. (Paris: Belin, 1820).

Garat, Dominique-Joseph, Mémoires sur la Révolution ... (Paris, an III [1795]).

Gérando, Joseph-Marie, baron de, "Considérations sur les diverses méthodes à suivre dans l'observation des peuples sauvages" [1800], Revue d'anthropologie, vol. 12 (1883), pp. 153-182).

Gérando, Joseph-Marie, baron de, Des Signes et de l'art de penser considérés dans leurs rapports mutuels, 4 vols. (Paris: Goujon; Fuchs; Henrichs, an VIII [1800]).

Gérando, Joseph-Marie, baron de, Histoire comparée des systèmes de philosophie, relativement aux principes des connoissances humaines, 3 vols. (Paris: Henrichs, an XII = 1804).

436

Gérando, Joseph-Marie, baron de, The Observation of Savage Peoples, trans. and introduction by F.C.T. Moore (London: Routledge and Kegan Paul, 1969).

Ginguené, Pierre-Louis, Journal de Ginguené, 1807-1808, ed. Paul Hazard (Paris: Hachette, 1910).

Ginguené, Pierre-Louis, Notice des travaux de la Classe des Sciences morales et politiques pendant le troisième trimestre de l'an 10, séance publique du 17 messidor an 10 [6 July 1802] (Paris: Baudouin, an 10).

Ginguené, Pierre-Louis, "Notice sur la vie de Chamfort", in Oeuvres de Chamfort, recueillies et publiées par un de ses amis, 4 vols. (Paris: Imprimerie des Sciences et Arts, an III [1795]), vol. I, pp. vi-lxxx.

Girardin, Stanislas-Cécile-Xavier-Louis, Discours et opinions, journal et souvenirs, 4 vols. (Paris: Moutardier, 1828).

Glachant, Paul and Victor, Lettres à Fauriel conservées à la Bibliothèque de l'Institut (Paris: La Nouvelle Revue, 1902).

Glachant, Victor, Benjamin Constant sous l'oeil du guet (Paris: Plon-Nourrit, 1906).

Godwin, William, Enquiry concerning political justice, ed. K.C. Carter (Oxford: Clarendon Press, 1971).

Grégoire, Henri-Baptiste, abbé de, "Réflexions extraites d'un ouvrage du citoyen Grégoire sur les moyens de perfectionner les sciences politiques", in Mémoires de l'Institut National, Classe des Sciences morales et politiques, vol. I (1798), pp. 552-566.

Guerard, Benjamin-Edmé-Charles, Notice sur M. Daunou (Paris, 1855).

Guillaume, James (ed.), Procès-verbal du Comité d'instruction publique de la Convention Nationale, 6 vols. (Paris, 1891-1907).

Guizot, François-Pierre-Guillaume, Discours prononcés dans la séance publique tenue par l'Académie française, pour la réception de M. Guizot, le 22 décembre 1836 (Paris: Firmin Didot, 1836).

Guizot, François-Pierre-Guillaume, Mémoires pour servir à l'histoire de mon temps, 8 vols. (Paris, 1858-67).

Guizot, François-Pierre-Guillaume, The History of Civilization in Europe [1828] (London: Cassell, 1911).

Guizot, François-Pierre-Guillaume, Trois générations, 1789, 1814, 1848 (Paris, 1863).

Helvétius, Claude-Adrien, A Treatise on Man, His Intellectual Faculties and his Education, trans. W. Hooper, 2 vols. (London, 1777).

Helvétius, Claude-Adrien, Helvétius: Collection des plus belles pages ed. Albert Keim (Paris: Mercure de Paris, 1909).

437

Helvétius, Claude-Adrien, De l'esprit [1758], intro. François Châtelet
    (Paris: Marouet, 1973).

Helvétius, Claude-Adrien, De l'esprit, or Essays on the mind and its
    several faculties [1758] (London, 1810).

Hobbes, Thomas, Body, Man and Citizen: Selections from Thomas Hobbes,
    ed. and intro. R.S. Peters (New York: Collier, 1967).

Hobbes, Thomas, Leviathan, ed. M. Oakeshott, intro. R.S. Peters
    (New York: Collier, 1973).

Hobbes, Thomas, Man and Citizen: Thomas Hobbes' "De Homine" and "De Cive"
    ed. and intro. B. Gert (New York: Doubleday, 1972).

Hoefer, Ferdinand (ed.), Nouvelle Biographie Générale ..., 46 vols.
    (Paris: Firmin Didot, 1853-1866).

d'Holbach, Paul-Heinrich-Dietrich Thiry, baron, Ethocratie, ou le
    gouvernement fondé sur la morale (Amsterdam, 1776).

d'Holbach, Paul-Heinrich-Dietrich Thiry, baron, Morale Universelle,
    3 vols. (Amsterdam, 1776).

d'Holbach, Paul-Heinrich-Dietrich Thiry, baron, Politique Naturelle,
    2 vols. (Londres, 1773).

d'Holbach, Paul-Heinrich-Dietrich Thiry, baron, Système de la Nature,
    2 vols. (Londres, 1775).

d'Holbach, Paul-Heinrich-Dietrich Thiry, baron, Système Sociale, 3 vols.
    (Londres, 1773).

Institut National, Mémoires de l'Institut National des Sciences et Arts,
    Classe des Sciences morales et politiques, 5 tomes (Paris: Imprimerie
    Nationale, 1798-1804).

Institut National, Morceaux de poésie lus dans la séance publique tenue
    par la Classe de la langue et de la littérature françaises de
    l'Institut le 21 décembre 1808, pour la réception de M. de Tracy,
    élu à la place de feu M. Cabanis (Paris: Baudouin, janvier 1809).

Jacquemont, Victor-Vinceslas, Correspondance inédite, 2 vols. (Paris, 1867).

Jauffret, L.-F., Dictionnaire étymologique de la langue française à
    l'usage de la jeunesse, 2 vols. (Paris, 1799).

Jefferson, Thomas, Correspondance de Thomas Jefferson et Dupont de
    Nemours, intro. G. Chinard (Baltimore: John Hopkins Press, 1931).

Jefferson, Thomas, Correspondance of Thomas Jefferson and Dupont de
    Neumours, trans. L. Lehman, ed. D. Malone (Boston: Houghton Mifflin,
    1930).

Jouffroy, Théodore-Simon, Mélanges philosophiques (Paris: Ladrange, 2e
    ed., 1838).

Jouffroy, Théodore-Simon, Nouveaux mélanges philosophiques (Paris: Hachette, 2e ed., 1861).

Journal d'économie publique, de morale et de politique, ed. P.-L. Roederer, 4 vols. (Paris, 1796-98).

Journal de la Société de 1789, 15 numéros (Paris, 1 juin-15 septembre 1790).

Journal d'Instruction sociale, par les citoyens Condorcet, Sieyès et Duhamel, 6 numéros (Paris, 1793).

Jung, Henri-Félix-Théodore (ed.), Lucien Bonaparte et ses Mémoires, 1775-1840, 3 vols. (Paris: G. Charpentier, 1882-83).

Kant, Immanuel, On History, ed. L.W. Beck, trans. L.W. Beck, R.E. Anchor and E.L. Fackenheim (New York: Bobbs-Merrill, 1963).

Laboulinière, Pierre Toussaint de, De l'influence d'une grande révolution, sur le commerce, l'agriculture et les arts (La Haie, 1808).

Laboulinière, Pierre Toussaint de, Précis de l'idéologie, dans lequel on relève des erreurs accréditées, et où l'on établit quelques vérités neuves et importantes sur cette matière (Paris: F. Cocheris fils, 1805).

Lachabeaussière, Auguste-Etiene-Xavier Poisson de, Catéchisme français ou principes de la morale républicaine (Paris: Dupont, an IV [1796])

La Chesnaye des Bois, François-Alexandre-Aubert, Dictionnaire de la Noblesse, 15 vols. (Paris: Antoine Boudet, 2e ed., 1770-1786).

Lacretelle, Jean-Charles-Dominique de, Dix années d'épreuves pendant la Révolution (Paris: A. Allouard, 1842).

Lacroix, Silvestre-François, Essais sur l'enseignement en général et sur celui des mathématiques en particulier (Paris: Bachelier, 3e ed., 1828).

Lafayette, Marie-Joseph-Paul du Motier, marquis de, Mémoires, correspondance et manuscrits, 6 vols. (Paris: H. Fournier, 1837-1838).

de Lafontainerie, Frank (ed.), French Liberalism and Education in the Eighteenth Century (New York: McGraw-Hill, 1932).

Lagrange, Joseph-Louis, comte de, Oeuvres, 14 vols. (Paris, 1867-92).

La Harpe, Jean-François de, Du fanaticisme dans la langue révolutionnaire ... (Paris, 1797).

La Harpe, Jean-François de, Oeuvres, 16 vols. (Paris, 1820-21).

La Harpe, Jean-François de, Philosophie du dix-huitème siècle, 2 tomes (Paris, 1818).

La Harpe, Jean-François de, Refutation du livre "De l'esprit" (Paris, 1797).

Lakanal, Joseph, Rapport fait au Conseil des Cinq-Cents ... sur les livres
élémentaires présentés au concours ouvert par la loi du 9 pluviôse
an II, séance du 14 brumaire an IV [5 November 1795] (Paris:
Imprimerie Nationale, an IV).

Lambrechts, Charles-Joseph-Mathieu, comte de, Principes politiques, avec
des additions ... (Paris: Marchant; Delaunay, 1815)

La Mettrie, Julien-Jan Offray de, L'homme-machine, ed. Aram Vartanian
(Princeton: Princeton University Press, 1960).

Lami, Pierre-Rémy-Crussolle, Notice sur les traductions de deux ouvrages
de M. le Comte Destutt de Tracy, Pair de France, Membre de
l'Institut, etc. ... les Elémens d'idéologie et les Principes
d'économie politique (Paris, n.d. [1818]).

Lancelin, P.-F., Introduction à l'analyse des sciences ...,3 vols.
(Paris, an IX-an XI [1801-1803]).

Lanjuinais, Jean-Denis, Oeuvres, 4 vols. (Paris: Dondey-Dupré, 1832).

Laplace, Pierre-Simon, marquis de, Discours ... au nom de l'Institut
National des Sciences et des Arts, séance du premier jour
complémentaire, an 4 [17 September 1796] (Paris: Imprimerie
Nationale, an IV).

Laplace, Pierre-Simon, marquis de, Exposition du système du monde, 2 vols.
(Paris, 1796).

La Revellière-Lépeaux, Louis-Marie de, Essai sur les moyens de faire
participer l'universalité des spectateurs à tout ce qui se pratique
dans les fêtes nationales (Paris, an VI).

La Revellière-Lépeaux, Louis-Marie de, Mémoires, 3 vols. (Paris, 1895).

La Revellière-Lépeaux, Louis-Marie de, Réflexions sur le culte, sur les
cérémonies civiles et sur les fêtes nationales (Paris, an V).

Laromiguière, Pierre, Leçons de Philosophie, 3 vols. (Paris: Brunot-
Labbe, 4ᵉ ed. 1826).

Laromiguière, Pierre, Projet d'Eléments de métaphysique (Toulouse, n.d.
[1793]).

La Vicomterie, Essai sur la morale calculée (Paris: Convention Nationale,
17 vendémiaire an III [18 October 1794]).

Lavoisier, Antoine-Laurent, marquis de, et al., Méthode de nomenclature
chimique (Paris, 1787).

Lavoisier, Antoine-Laurent, marquis de, Traité élémentaire de chimie
(Paris, 1789).

Le Mercier de la Rivière, Pierre, L'ordre naturel et essentiel des
sociétés politiques [1767], ed. E. Depitre (Paris: P. Geuthner, 1910).

Lerminier, Jean-Louis-Eugène, De l'influence de la philosophie du XVIIIe siècle sur la législation et la sociabilité du XIXe (Bruxelles: Louis Hauman, 1834).

Lévesque, Pierre-Charles, "Considérations sur l'homme, observé dans la vie sauvage, dans la vie pastorale et dans la vie policée", in Mémoires de l'Institut National, Classe des Sciences morales et politiques, vol. 1 (1798), pp. 209-246.

Lévesque, Pierre-Charles, "Extrait d'un mémoire sur quelques acceptions du mot 'nature'", in Mémoires de l'Institut National, Classe des Sciences morales et politiques, vol. III (1801), pp. 231-239.

Locke, John, Locke on Politics, Religion and Education, ed. and intro. M. Cranston (New York: Collier, 1965).

Locke, John, Two Treatises of Government, ed. and intro. P. Laslett (New York: Mentor, 1965).

Magasin Encyclopédique (Paris 1795-1816) [continued as Annales Encyclopédiques]

Maine de Biran, Marie-François-Pierre-Gonthier, L'influence de l'habitude sur la faculté de penser, intro. Pierre Tisserand (Paris: Presses Universitaires de France, 1954).

Maine de Biran, Marie-François-Pierre-Gonthier, Mémoire sur la décomposition de la pensée précédé de la Note sur les Rapports de l'idéologie et des mathématiques, intro. Pierre Tisserand, 2 vols. (Paris: Presses Universitaires de France, 1952).

Maine de Biran, Marie-François-Pierre-Gonthier, Oeuvres Philosophiques, ed. V. Cousin, 3 tomes (Paris, 1834-41).

Maine de Biran, Maire-François-Pierre-Gonthier, Oeuvres Philosophiques, ed. Pierre Tissérand and Henri Gouhier, 14 tomes (Paris: Alcan, 1920-1949).

Maistre, Joseph, comte de, The Works of Joseph de Maistre, trans. and ed. Jack Lively (London: Allen and Unwin, 1965).

Maistre, Joseph, comte de, Oeuvres complètes de J. de Maistre, 14 vols. (Lyons, 1884-1893).

Marx, Karl Heinrich and Engels, Friedrich, Collected Works (London: Lawrence and Wishart, 1975-).

Mathiez, Albert, "Lettres de Volney à La Révellière-Lépeaux (1795-1798)", Annales Révolutionnaires, vol. 3 (1910), pp. 161-194.

Meek, Ronald Lindley, Precursors of Adam Smith 1750-1775 (London: Dent, 1973).

Mercier, Louis-Sébastien, Néologie, ou Vocabulaire de mots nouveaux ..., 2 vols. (Paris: Moussard; Maradan, an IX-1801).

Mercure de France, littéraire et politique (Paris, 1800-1807).

Mignet, François-Auguste-Marie, Notices et Mémoires Historiques, 2 vols. (Paris: Paulin, 1843).

Mignet, François-Auguste-Marie, Portraits et Notices historiques et littéraires, 2 vols. (Paris: Didier, 2e ed. 1852).

Millot, J.-A., L'art d'améliorer et de perfectionner les hommes, au moral comme au physique (Paris, an X [1801]).

Milot de Melito, André-François, comte, Mémoires du comte Milot de Melito, 1799-1815, 3 vols. (Paris: Calmann Lévy, 3e ed., 1880).

[Mirabeau, Victor Riquette, marquis de], Leçons économiques (Amsterdam, 1770).

Monglond, André, La France Révolutionnaire et Impériale: Annales de Bibliographie Méthodique ..., 9 vols. (Grenoble and Paris, 1930-63).

[Moniteur Universel], Réimpression de l'ancien Moniteur [Mai 1789 - Novembre 1799], 32 vols. (Paris: Plon frères, 1850-54).

[Moniteur Universel], Gazette Nationale ou le Moniteur Universel (Paris, 1800-1814).

Montesquieu, Charles-Louis Secondat, baron de, De l'Esprit des Lois [1748], 2 vols. (Paris: Garnier, 1922).

Monthly Magazine and British Register (London, 1796-   ).

Monthly Review or Literary Journal (London, 1790-1825).

Morellet, André, abbé de, Mélanges de littérature et de philosophie du 18e siècle, 4 vols. (Paris: Lepetit, 1818).

Morellet, André, abbé de, Mémoires, 2 vols. (Paris: Baudouin, 2e ed. 1823).

Morelly, Code de la Nature [1755], intro. V.P. Volguine (Paris: Editions sociales, 1970).

Morgan, Lady Sydney [née Owenson], France, 2 vols. (London: Henry Colburn, 1817).

Morgan, Lady Sydney [née Owenson], France in 1829-30, 2 vols. (London: Saunders and Otley, 1830).

Morgan, Lady Sydney [née Owenson], Lady Morgan's Memoirs: Autobiography, Diaries and Correspondence, ed. W.H. Dixon, 2 vols. (London: Allen and Co., 1862).

Napoléon 1er, Correspondance de Napoléon I, 32 vols. (Paris, 1858-69).

Napoléon 1er, Entretiens avec Napoléon, ed. Léon Pautré (Paris: Belfond, 1969).

Napoléon 1er, Voix de Napoléon: Paroles Authentiques, ed. P.-L. Couchoud, (Genève: Milieu du Monde, 1949).

Neufchâteau, François de, Discours pour l'ouverture de la Société en faveur des Savans et des Hommes de lettres (Paris: Everat, an XI).

Nodier, Jean-Emmanuel-Charles, Souvenirs, 2 vols. (Paris, nouv. éd. 1872).

Ordinaire, J.-J., Méthode pour l'enseignement des langues (Paris: Colas, 1820).

Pasquier, Etienne-Denis, duc de, Histoire de mon temps: Mémoires ..., 6 vols. (Paris, 1893-1895).

Peltier, Jean-Gabriel (ed.), Paris, pendant l'année 1795 [etc.], 35 vols. (Londres, 1795-1802).

Pinel, Philippe, Rapport fait à la Société des Observateurs de l'homme sur l'enfant connu sous le nom de sauvage de l'Aveyron [1800], in Revue Anthropologique, vol. 21 (1911), pp. 441-454.

Pinel, Philippe, Traité médico-philosophique sur l'aliénation mentale, ou la Manie (Paris: Richard, Caille et Ravier, an IX [1801]).

Prévost, Pierre, Des signes envisagés relativement à leur influence sur la formation des idées (Paris, an VIII [1800]).

[Proisy d'Eppe, César de], Dictionnaire des Girouettes, ou nos contemporains peints d'après eux-mêmes, ... par une société de Girouettes (Paris: Alexis Eymery, 3e ed. 1815).

Proudhon, Pierre-Joseph, Qu'est-ce que la propriété? [1840], ed. E. James (Paris: Garnier-Flammarion, 1966).

Rabbe, Boisjolin and Saint-Preuve, Biographie universelle et portative des Contemporains, ou Dictionnaire historique des hommes vivants, et des hommes morts depuis 1788 jusqu'à nos jours, 5 vols. (Paris: Levrault, 1834).

Reichardt, J.-F., Un Hiver à Paris sous le Consulat, 1802-1803, d'après les lettres de J.-F. Reichardt, trans. and ed. Arthur Laquiante (Paris: Plon-Nourrit, 1896).

Rémusat, Charles-François-Marie, comte de, Essais de Philosophie, 2 vols. (Paris: Ladrange, 1842).

Rémusat, Charles-François-Marie, comte de, Mémoires de ma vie: Enfance et Jeunesse, La Restauration Libérale (1797-1820), ed. Charles H. Pouthas (Paris: Plon, 1958).

Rémusat, Charles-François-Marie, comte de, Politique libérale ou Fragments pour servir à la défense de la Révolution française (Paris: Michel Lévy frères, 1860).

Rey, Joseph-Auguste, Théorie et pratique de la science sociale, ou exposé des principes de morale, d'économie publique et de politique, et application à l'état actuel de la société de moyens généraux, immédiats et successifs d'améliorer la condition des travailleurs et même des propriétaires, 3 vols. (Paris: Prudhomme, 1842).

Rey, Joseph-Auguste, Traité des principes généraux du droit et de la
législation (Paris: Alex-Gobelet, 1828).

Ricardo, David, The Principles of Political Economy and Taxation [3rd ed.
1821], intro. M.P. Fogarty (London: J.M. Dent, 1962).

Ricardo, David, The Works and Correspondence of David Ricardo, 11 vols.,
ed. P. Sraffa (Cambridge: Cambridge University Press, 1962).

Rivarol, Antoine de, De la philosophie moderne (Paris, 1799).

Rivarol, Antoine de, Discours préliminaire du nouveau Dictionnaire
(Paris, 1797).

Rivarol, Antoine de, Oeuvres complètes, 5 vols. (Paris, 1808).

Robespierre, Maximilien, "Sur les rapports des idées religieuses et
morales avec les principes républicains et sur les fêtes nationales",
18 floréal an 2 (7 mai 1794), in Textes Choisis, ed. Jean Poperon
(Paris: Editions Sociales, 1974), vol. III, pp. 155-180.

Roederer, Pierre-Louis, Bonaparte me disait ... Conversations notées
par le comte P.-L. Roederer (Paris: Horizons de France, 1942).

Roederer, Pierre-Louis, Oeuvres, 8 vols. (Paris: F. Didot, 1853-1859).

Rousseau, J.-J., and von Herder, J.-G., On the Origin of Language: Two
Essays, trans. J.H. Moran and A. Gode (New York: Frederick Ungar,
1966).

Rousseau, J.-J., The Social Contract and Discourses, trans. G.D.H. Cole,
revised J.H. Brumfitt and J.C. Hall (London: J.M. Dent, 1973).

Saint-Lambert, Jean-François de, Oeuvres, 3 vols. (Paris, 1798).

Saint-Lambert, Jean-François de, Principes des moeurs chez toutes les
nations ou catéchisme universel, 3 vols. (Paris, 1798).

Saint-Martin, Louis-Claude de, De l'ésprit des choses ..., 2 vols
(Paris, an VIII [1800]).

Saint-Martin, Louis-Claude de, Essai sur les signes et sur les idées
(Paris, an VII [1799]).

Saint-Martin, Louis-Claude de, Lettre à un ami (Paris, 1795).

Saint-Martin, Louis-Claude de, Mon Portrait historique et philosophique,
1789-1803 (Paris, 1961).

Saint-Martin, Louis-Claude de, Réflexions d'un observateur sur la question:
Quelles sont les institutions les plus propres à fonder la morale d'un
peuple? (Paris, n.d. [1798]).

Saint-Simon, Claude-Henri, comte de, Oeuvres, 6 vols. (Paris: Anthropos,
1966).

Saint-Simon, Claude-Henri, comte de, Henri Saint-Simon 1760-1825: Selected Writings on Science, Industry and Social Organization, trans. and intro. by Keith Taylor (London: Croom Helm, 1975).

Saint-Simon, Claude-Henri, comte de, The Political Thought of Saint-Simon, trans. and intro. by Ghita Ionescu (London: Oxford University Press, 1976).

Saint-Simon, Claude-Henri, comte de, Social Organization, the Science of Man, and other Writings, trans. and ed. Felix M.H. Markham (New York: Harper and Row, 1964).

Say, Jean-Baptiste, Mélanges et correspondance d'économie politique, éd. Charles Comte (Paris: Chamerot, 1833).

Say, Jean-Baptiste, Oeuvres diverses (avec des notes par Charles Comte, E. Daire, Horace Say) (Paris: Guillaumin, 1848).

Say, Jean-Baptiste, Olbie, ou essai sur les moyens de réformer les moeurs d'une nation (Paris: Deterville; Treuttel et Wurtz, an VIII [1800]).

Say, Jean-Baptiste, Traité d'économie politique, ou simple exposition de la manière dont se forment, se distribuent, et se consomment les richesses, 2 vols. (Paris: Deterville, an XI - 1803).

Say, Jean-Baptiste, Traité d'économie politique [etc.], 2 vols. (Paris: Renouard, seconde édition 1814).

Say, Jean-Baptiste, A Treatise on Political Economy, trans. C.R. Prinsep (Philadelphia, 1880).

Sieyès, Emmanuel-Joseph, Qu'est-ce que le Tiers-état?, édition critique avec une introduction et des notes par Roberto Zapperi (Genève: Droz, 1970).

Sieyès, Emmanuel-Joseph, What is the Third Estate?, trans. M. Blondel, intro. P. Campbell (London: Pall Mall, 1963).

Simon, William M. (ed.), French Liberalism 1789-1848 (London/New York: John Wiley, 1972).

Smith, Adam, Essais Philosophiques, trans. Prévost (Paris, 1797).

Smith, Adam, Recherches sur la Nature et les Causes de la Richesse des Nations (Londres, 1788).

Smith, Adam, The Wealth of Nations [1776], ed. Andrew Skinner (Harmondsworth: Penguin, 1974).

Staël-Holstein, Anne-Louise-Germaine Necker de, Dix années d'exil, intro. Simone Balayé (Paris: Bibliothèque 10/18, 1966).

Stryienski, Casimir (ed.), "Lettres Inédites de Jeremy Bentham", Journal des Economistes, série 5, vol. 1 (1890), pp. 367-374.

Taillandier, A.H. (ed.), Documents Biographiques sur P.-C.-F. Daunou (Paris: Firmin Didot frères, 1841).

Talleyrand-Périgord, Charles-Maurice de, Mémoires, 8 vols. (Paris, 1953-55).

Teggart, Frederick John (ed.), The Idea of Progress: a collection of readings (Berkeley: University of California Press, 1949).

Thibaudeau, Antoine-Claire, Bonaparte and the Consulate, trans. and ed. G.K. Fortescue (London: Methuen, 1908).

Thibaudeau, Antoine-Claire, Le Consulat et l'Empire ... de 1799 à 1815, 10 vols. (Paris: Jules Renouard, 1834-1835).

Thierry, Augustin, Augustin Thierry (1795-1856) d'après sa correspondance et ses papiers de famille, préface de Gabriel Hanotaux (Paris: Plon-Nourrit, 1922).

Thierry, Augustin [review article on Tracy's Commentaire], Le Censeur Européen, vol. VII (1818), pp. 191-260.

Thurot, Jean-François, De l'Entendement de la Raison, 2 vols., intro. P.-C.-F. Daunou (Paris, 1833).

Thurot, Jean-François, Mélanges (Paris: Firmin Didot, 1880).

Tourneux, Maurice, Bibliographie de l'histoire de Paris pendant la Révolution française, 5 vols. (Paris: Ville de Paris, 1890-1913).

Turgot, Anne-Robert-Jacques, baron de l'Aulne, Turgot on Progress, Sociology and Economics: Three Major Texts, trans. and ed. Ronald L. Meek (Cambridge: Cambridge University Press, 1973).

Vermeil de Conchard, Colonel Paul-Prosper, Trois Etudes sur Cabanis d'après des documents inédits (Brive: Imprimerie Roche, 1914).

Volney, Constantin-François Chasseboeuf, comte de, La loi naturelle, ou catéchisme du citoyen français, ed. Gaston-Martin (Paris: Armand Colin, 1934).

Volney, Constantin-François Chasseboeuf, comte de, Leçons d'histoire, prononcées à l'école normale en l'an III de la république française (Paris: Brousson, an VIII).

Volney, Constantin-François Chasseboeuf, comte de, Oeuvres complètes, ed. Adolphe Bossange, 8 vols. (Paris: Bossange frères, 1821).

Voltaire, François-Marie Arouet de, Dictionnaire Philosophique [1764], ed. R. Pomeau (Paris: Garnier-Flammarion, 1964).

Voltaire, François-Marie Arouet de, Lettres Philosophiques [1734], ed. R. Pomeau (Paris: Garnier-Flammarion, 1964).

ADDENDUM

Dupont de Nemours, Pierre-Samuel, "Mémoire sur le nombre des écoles primaires que l'on doit établir", Mémoires de l'Institut National, Classe des Sciences morales et politiques, vol. V (1804), pp. 317-330.

Jacquemont, Victor-Vinceslas, Lettres à Stendhal, ed. Pierre Maes (Paris: A. Poursin, 1933).

Procès-verbal des élections des membres du Sénat conservateur, de ceux du corps législatif, et de ceux du Tribunat, en exécution de la constitution [3, 4 and 5 nivose, an VIII] (Paris: Imprimerie Nationale, nivose an VIII [December 1799]).

Part C: Secondary Sources and Miscellaneous

Acton, Henry B., "The Philosophy of Language in Revolutionary France",
    in Studies in Philosophy: British Academy Lectures, ed. J.N. Findlay
    (London: Oxford University Press, 1966), pp. 143-167.

Airiau, Jean, L'Opposition aux Physiocrates à la fin de l'Ancien Régime.
    Aspects économiques et politiques d'un Libéralisme éclectique
    (Paris: Pichon; Durand-Auzias, 1965).

Aldridge, A.O., Franklin and his French Contemporaries (New York: New
    York University Press, 1957).

Aldridge, A.O., "The State of Nature", Studies on Voltaire and the
    Eighteenth Century, vol. 98 (1972), pp. 7-26.

Alfaric, Prosper, Laromiguière et son école: étude biographique (Paris:
    Les Belles Lettres, 1929).

Allain, Ernest, L'oeuvre scolaire de la Révolution, 1789-1802: Etudes
    critiques et documents inédits (Paris: Firmin-Didot, 1891).

Allix, Edgard, "Destutt de Tracy, économiste", Revue d'économie
    politique, vol. 26 (1912), pp. 424-451.

Allix, Edgard, "J.-B. Say et les Origines de l'Industrialisme", Revue
    d'économie politique, vol. 24 (1910), pp. 303-313, 341-363.

Allix, Edgard, "La Déformation de l'économie politique libérale après
    J.-B. Say: Charles Dunoyer", Revue d'histoire économique et
    sociale, vol. 4 (1911), pp. 115-147.

Allix, Edgard, "La Méthode et la Conception de l'économie politique dans
    l'oeuvre de J.-B. Say", Revue d'histoire économique et sociale,
    vol. 4 (1911), pp. 321-360.

Allix, Edgard, "La rivalité entre la Propriété foncière et la Fortune
    mobilière sous la Révolution", Revue d'histoire économique et
    sociale, vol. 6 (1913), pp. 297-348.

Allix, Edgard, "Le Physicisme des Physiocrates", Revue d'économie
    politique, vol. 25 (1911), pp. 563-586.

Allix, Edgard, "L'oeuvre économique de Germain Garnier ...", Revue
    d'histoire économique et sociale, vol. 5 (1912), pp. 317-342.

Althusser, Louis, Politics and History: Montesquieu, Rousseau, Hegel and
    Marx, trans. Ben Brewster (London: New Left Books, 1972).

Apt, Leon, Louis-Philippe de Ségur: an intellectual in a revolutionary
    age (The Hague: Nijhoff, 1969).

Arbelet, Paul, La Jeunesse de Stendhal, 2 vols. (Paris, 1919).

Asse, Eugène, "Benjamin Constant et le Directoire", Revue de la
    Révolution, vol. 15 (1889), pp. 337-356, 433-453, and vol. 16
    (1889), pp. 5-26, 105-125.

Aubenque, Pierre, "Philosophie et idéologie", Archives de philosophie, vol. 22 (1959), pp. 483-520.

Aulard, François-Victor-Alphonse, Christianity and the French Revolution, trans. Lady Frazer (London: Benn, 1927).

Aulard, François-Victor-Alphonse, Histoire politique de la Révolution française (Paris, 1913).

Aulard, François-Victor-Alphonse, "La politique scolaire du Directoire", Revue Bleue (12 mai 1900), pp. 585-588.

Aulard, François-Victor-Alphonse, Le culte de la raison et le culte de l'être suprême, 1793-1794 (Paris: Alcan, 1892).

Aulard, François-Victor-Alphonse, Napoléon 1er et le monopole universitaire (Paris: Colin, 1911).

Bakalar, H.N., "The Cartesian Legacy to the Eighteenth-Century Grammarians", Modern Language Notes, vol. 91 no. 4 (May 1976), pp. 698-721.

Baker, Keith Michael, Condorcet: From Natural Philosophy to Social Mathematics (Chicago: University of Chicago Press, 1975).

Baker, Keith Michael, "Politics and Social Science in Eighteenth-Century France: The 'Société de 1789'", in French Government and Society 1500-1850: Essays in Memory of Alfred Cobban, ed. J.F. Bosher (London: Athlone Press, 1973), pp. 208-230.

Baker, Keith Michael, "Scientism, Elitism and Liberalism: the case of Condorcet", Studies on Voltaire and the Eighteenth Century, vol. 55 (1967), pp. 129-165.

Baker, Keith Michael, "State, Society and Subsistence in Eighteenth-Century France", Journal of Modern History, vol. 50 no. 4 (December 1978), pp. 701-711.

Baker, Keith Michael, "The Early History of the term 'Social Science'", Annals of Science, vol. 20 no. 3 (September 1964), pp. 211-226.

Bagge, Dominique, Les idées politiques en France sous la Restauration (Paris: Presses Universitaires de France, 1952).

Balayé, Simon, "'Corinne' et la presse parisienne de 1807", in Approches des Lumières: Mélanges offerts à Jean Fabre (Paris: Klincksieck, 1974), pp. 1-16.

Baldensperger, Philippe-Jules-Fernand, Le Mouvement des idées dans l'émigration française, 1789-1815, 2 vols. (Paris, 1925).

Balteau, Dictionnaire de Biographie française (Paris: Letouzey et Ané, 1933-).

Barbu, Zev, "The New Intelligentsia", in John Cruickshank (ed.), French Literature and its Background, vol. 3: The Eighteenth Century (Oxford: Oxford University Press, 1968), pp. 80-99.

Barclay, Leigh, "Louis de Bonald, prophet of the past?", Studies on Voltaire and the Eighteenth Century, vol. 55 (1967), pp. 167-204.

Barnard, Howard Clive, Education and the French Revolution (Cambridge: Cambridge University Press, 1969).

Barnard, Howard Clive, The French Tradition in Education (Cambridge: Cambridge University Press, 1970).

Barni, Jules, R., Les moralistes français au dix-huitième siècle (Paris: Baillière, 1873).

Barth, Hans, Truth and Ideology, trans. F. Lilge, foreword R. Bendix (Berkeley: University of California Press, 1976).

Bastid, Paul, Benjamin Constant et sa doctrine, 2 vols. (Paris: Armand Colin, 1966).

Bastid, Paul, Sieyès et sa pensée (Paris: Hachette, nouv. ed. 1970).

Bay, Christian, "Needs, wants and political legitimacy", Canadian Journal of Political Science, vol. 1 no. 3 (September 1968), pp. 241-260.

Bayet, Albert, and Albert, Francois (eds.), Les écrivains politiques du dix-neuvième siècle (Paris, 1907).

Beal, M.W., "Condillac as Precursor of Kant", Studies on Voltaire and the Eighteenth Century, vol. 102 (1973), pp. 193-229.

Becker, Carl, The Heavenly City of the Eighteenth-Century Philosophers (New Haven: Yale University Press, 1932).

Beik, Paul H., The French Revolution, seen from the Right: social theories in motion, 1789-1799 (Philadelphia: American Philosophical Society, 1956).

Belin, Jean-Paul, La logique d'une idée-force: l'idèe d'utilité sociale et la Révolution française (Paris: Hermann, 1939).

Benewick, Robert, et al. (eds.), Knowledge and Belief in Politics: the Problem of Ideology (London: Allen and Unwin, 1973).

Berrian, A.H., Stendhal and the Idéologues (Ph.D. thesis, New York University, 1954).

Berry, C.J., "Adam Smith's 'Considerations' on Language", Journal of the History of Ideas, vol. 35 no. 1 (January 1974), pp. 130-138.

Bertauld, Alfred, Deux Individualistes, Benjamin Constant et Daunou (Caen: A. Hardel, 1862).

Berthelot, Philippe, "Auteuil: Histoire littéraire", La Grande Encyclopédie (Paris: H. Lamirault, 1887-1902), vol. 4, pp. 749-751.

Besterman, Theodore, Voltaire (London: Longmans, 1969).

Bezanson, Anna, "The Early Use of the Term Industrial Revolution", Quarterly Journal of Economics, vol. 36 (1922), pp. 343-349.

Biffault, V., "Volney et l'enseignement de l'histoire à l'école normale", Revue pédagogique, vol. 55 (1900), pp. 527-552.

Biernawski, Louis, Un département sous la Révolution française: (1'Allier de 1789 à 1'an III) (Moulins: Librairie historique du Bourbonnais, 1909).

Bingham, Alfred J., "Marie-Joseph Chénier, idéologue and critic", Studies on Voltaire and the Eighteenth Century, vol. 94 (1972), pp. 219-276.

Bleaney, Michael F., Underconsumption Theories: A History and Critical Analysis (London: Lawrence and Wishart, 1976).

Blet, Henri, Histoire de la colonisation française, 3 vols. (Paris: Arthaud, 1946-1950).

Bloomfield, Arthur I., and Allen, W.R., "The Foreign-Trade Doctrines of the Physiocrats", in Essays in Economic Thought, ed. J.J. Spengler and W.R. Allen (Chicago: Rand McNally, 1960), pp. 215-233.

Boas, George, French Philosophies of the Romantic Period (Baltimore: John Hopkins Press, 1925).

Boas, George, "In Search of the Age of Reason", in Aspects of the Eighteenth Century, ed. E.R. Wasserman (Baltimore: John Hopkins Press, 1965), pp. 1-19.

Bonar, James, Philosophy and Political Economy (London: Allen and Unwin, 1893).

Bosher, John Francis, French Finances, 1770-1795: From Business to Bureaucracy (Cambridge: Cambridge University Press, 1970).

Bosher, John Francis (ed.), French Government and Society 1500-1850: Essays in Memory of Alfred Cobban (London: Athlone Press, 1973).

Boss, R.I., "The development of social religion: a contradiction of French free thought", Journal of the History of Ideas, vol. 34 no. 4 (October 1973), pp. 577-589.

Bottomore, Thomas B., and Nisbet, Robert A. (eds.), A History of Sociological Analysis (London: Heinemann, 1979).

Bouillier, Francisque, Histoire de la philosophie cartésienne, 2 vols. (Paris, 3e ed. 1868; reprinted: Bruxelles, 1969).

Bourget, Paul-Charles-Joseph, Nouvelles pages de critique et de doctrine, 2 vols. (Paris: Plon, 1922).

Bouteiller, (Mlle) M., "La Société des Observateurs de l'Homme, ancêtre de la Société d'Anthropologie de Paris", Bulletins et mémoires de la Société d'Anthropologie de Paris, vol. 7, série 10, nos. 1-2 (1956), pp. 448-465.

Brailsford, H.N., Shelley, Godwin, and their circle (London: Butterworth, 1930).

Bramsted, E.K., and Melhuish, K.J., Western Liberalism: A History in Documents from Locke to Croce (London: Longmans, 1978).

Braudel, Fernand, Capitalism and material life 1400-1800, trans. M. Kochan (London: Fontana, 1974).

Braudel, Fernand, and Labrousse, C. Ernest, Histoire économique et sociale de la France, tome 3: 1789 - années 1800, Première volume (Paris: Presses Universitaires de France, 1976).

Bredvold, Louis I., The Brave New World of the Enlightenment (Ann Arbor: University of Michigan Press, 1962).

Bréhier, Emile, The History of Philosophy, trans. W. Baskin, 7 vols. (Chicago: University of Chicago Press, 1965-1969).

Brinton, Crane, A Decade of Revolution 1789-1799 (New York: Harper and Row, 1963).

Brooks, Richard A., "Condorcet and Pascal", Studies on Voltaire and the Eighteenth Century, vol. 55 (1967), pp. 297-307.

Brotonne, Léonce de, Les Sénateurs du Consulat et de l'Empire ... (Paris: Etienne Charavay, 1895).

Brown, Philip Anthony, The French Revolution in English History (London: Frank Cass, 1965).

Brunel, Lucien, Les philosophes et l'Académie française au dix-huitième siècle (Paris, 1884).

Brunet, Pierre, L'introduction des théories de Newton en France au dix-huitième siècle (Paris: A. Blanchard, 1931).

Bruun, Geoffrey, Europe and the French Imperium, 1799-1814 (New York: Harper and Row, 1965).

Bryson, Gladys, Man and Society: The Scottish Inquiry of the Eighteenth Century (Princeton: Princeton University Press, 1945).

Buchdahl, G., The image of Newton and Locke in the Age of Reason (London: Sheed and Ward, 1961).

Buriot-Darsiles, Henri, "Destutt de Tracy", Bulletin de la société d'émulation du Bourbonnais, vol. 32 (1929), pp. 119-122.

Burns, J.H., "J.S. Mill and the Term 'Social Science'", Journal of the History of Ideas, vol. 20 no. 3 (June 1959), pp. 431-2.

Burtt, E.J., Social Perspectives in the History of Economic Theory (New York: St. Martin's Press, 1972).

Bury, J.P.T., "The End of the Napoleonic Senate", Cambridge Historical Journal, vol. 9 no. 2 (1948), pp. 165-189.

Butterfield, Herbert, The Origins of Modern Science, 1300-1800 (London: Bell, 1968).

Cabanis, André, "Le courant contre-révolutionnaire sous le Consulat et l'Empire (dans le 'Journal des Débats' et le 'Mercure de France')", Revue des Sciences Politiques, vol. 24 no. 2 (1971), pp. 9-85.

Cabanis, André, La Presse sous le Consulat et l'Empire (1799-1814) (Paris: Société des études Robespierristes, 1975).

Cahen, Léon, "La Société des Amis des Noirs et Condorcet", La Révolution française, vol. 50 (1906), pp. 481-511.

Cailliet, Emile, La Tradition littéraire des Idéologues, Introduction by Gilbert Chinard (Philadelphia: American Philosophical Society, 1943).

Cambridge Modern History, ed. A.W. Ward, G.W. Prothero, S. Leathes, Vol. VIII: The French Revolution (Cambridge: Cambridge University Press, 1904; reprint 1934).

Campardon, E., Le tribunal révolutionnaire de Paris, 2 vols. (Paris, 1866).

Campbell, Blair, "Helvétius and the Roots of the Closed Society", American Political Science Review, vol. 68 no. 1 (March 1974), pp. 153-168.

Campbell, Blair, "La Mettrie: the Robot and the Automaton", Journal of the History of Ideas, vol. 31 no. 4 (October 1970), pp. 555-572.

Canivez, André, "Les idéologues", in Histoire de la Philosophie, vol. III [Encyclopédie de la Pléiade, vol. 38] (Paris: Gallimard, 1974), pp. 99-120.

Canivez, André, "Les Traditionalistes, de J. de Maistre à B. Constant", in Histoire de la Philosophie, vol. III [Encyclopédie de la Pléiade, vol. 38] (Paris: Gallimard, 1974), pp. 70-83.

Capaldi, Nicholas, "Hume as Social Scientist", Review of Metaphysics, vol. 32 no. 1 (September 1978), pp. 99-123.

Cappadocia, Ezio, The History of the Liberal Party in France, 1814-1824 (Ph.D. thesis, University of Chicago, 1957).

Cappadocia, Ezio, "The Liberals and Madame de Staël in 1818", in Ideas in History: Essays presented to Louis R. Gottschalk, ed. R. Herr and H.T. Parker (Durham, N.C.: Duke University Press, 1965), pp. 182-198.

Carey, Raymond Giddens, The Liberals of France and their relation to the development of Bonaparte's dictatorship, 1799-1804 (Ph.D. thesis, University of Chicago, 1947).

Cassirer, Ernst, The Philosophy of the Enlightenment, trans. F.C.A. Koelln and J.P. Pettegrove (Princeton: Princeton University Press, 1951).

Cavanaugh, Gerald J., "Turgot: the rejection of Enlightened Despotism", French Historical Studies, vol. 6 no. 1 (Spring 1969), pp. 31-58.

Challamel, Jean-Baptiste-Marie-Augustin, Les Clubs Contre-révolutionnaires. (Paris, 1895).

Charavay, Etienne, "Le centenaire de l'Institut de France", Revue Bleue (4e série, tome IV) (19 and 26 Octobre 1895), pp. 482-487, 522-527.

Charavay, Etienne, "Le Sénateurs du Consulat et de l'Empire ayant fait partie des Assemblées républicaines", La Révolution française, vol. 13 (1887), pp. 524-529.

Charlton, D.G., Secular Religions in France, 1815-1870 (London: Oxford University Press, 1963).

Charpentier, John, Napoléon et les hommes de lettres de son temps (Paris: Mercure de France, 2e ed. 1935).

Chevalier, Louis, Classes laborieuses et classes dangereuses à Paris pendant la première moitié du dix-neuvième siècle (Paris, 1958).

Chevallier, J.-J., "Le XVIIIe siècle et la naissance des idéologies", Res Publica, vol. 2 no. 3 (1960), pp. 194-204.

Chinard, Gilbert, "Introduction: A Neglected Province of Literary History", in Emile Cailliet, La Tradition littéraire des Idéologues (Philadelphia: American Philosophical Society, 1943), pp. 1-23.

Chinard, Gilbert, "Jefferson among the Philosophes", Ethics, vol. 53 no. 4 (July 1943), pp. 255-268.

Chinard, Gilbert, "Jefferson and the Physiocrats", University of California Chronicle, vol. 33 no. 1 (January 1931), pp. 18-31.

Chinard, Gilbert, Volney et l'Amérique (Baltimore: John Hopkins Press, 1923).

Chomsky, Noam, Cartesian Linguistics (New York: Harper and Row, 1966).

Chomsky, Noam, Language and Mind (New York: Harcourt, Brace and World, 1968).

Church, Clive H., "Bureaucracy, Politics and Revolution: the Evidence of the Commission des Dix-Sept", French Historical Studies, vol. 6 (1970), pp. 492-516.

Church, Clive H., "In Search of the Directory", French Government and Society 1500-1850: Essays in memory of Alfred Cobban, ed. J.F. Bosher (London: Athlone Press, 1973), pp. 261-294.

Church, Clive H., "The social basis of the French central bureaucracy under the Directory, 1795-1799", Past and Present, no. 36 (April 1967), pp. 59-72.

Clapham, J.H., Economic development of France and Germany, 1815-1914 (Cambridge: Cambridge University Press, 4th ed. 1936).

Coats, A.W., "Changing Attitudes to Labour in the mid-eighteenth century", Economic History Review (second series), vol. XI (1958), pp. 35-51.

Coats, A.W. (ed.), The Classical Economists and Economic Policy (London: Methuen, 1971).

Coats, A.W., "The Classical Economists, Industrialisation, and Poverty", in R. Hartwell et al., The Long Debate on Poverty (London: The Institute of Economic Affairs, 1972), pp. 143-168.

Cobb, Richard, Paris and its Provinces, 1792-1802 (Oxford: Oxford University Press, 1975).

Cobb, Richard, The Police and the People: French Popular Protest, 1789-1820 (Oxford: Oxford University Press, 1970).

Cobban, Alfred B.C., A History of Modern France, 3 vols. (Harmondsworth: Penguin, 1973).

Cobban, Alfred B.C., Aspects of the French Revolution (London: Paladin, 1973).

Cobban, Alfred B.C., In search of humanity: the role of the Enlightenment in modern history (London: Jonathan Cape, 1960).

Cobban, Alfred B.C. (ed.), The Debate on the French Revolution, 1789-1800 (London: Black, 2nd ed., 1960).

Cobban, Alfred B.C., The Social Interpretation of the French Revolution (Cambridge: Cambridge University Press, 1968).

Coirault, Gaston, Les Ecoles Centrales dans le Centre-Ouest (Tours: Arrault, 1940).

Collins, Irene, Liberalism in nineteenth-century Europe (London: Historical Association, 1957).

Collins, Irene, The Government and the newspaper press in France, 1814-1881 (Oxford: Oxford University Press, 1959).

Colonna d'Istria, F., "Ce que la médecine expérimentale doit à la philosophie: Pinel", Revue de Métaphysique et de Morale, vol. 12 (1904), pp. 186-210.

Colonna d'Istria, F., "La logique de la médecine d'après Cabanis", Revue de Métaphysique et de Morale, vol. 24 (1917), pp. 59-73.

Compayré, Gabriel, Histoire critique des doctrines de l'éducation en France depuis le seizième siècle, 2 vols. (Paris: Hachette, 1879).

Copleston, Frederick Charles, A History of Philosophy, Vol. IX: Maine de Biran to Sartre (London: Search Press, 1975).

Cornillon, Jean, Le Bourbonnais sous la Révolution française, 5 vols. (Vichy and Riom: Bougarel and Girerd, 1888-1895).

Corréard, François, La France sous le Consulat (Paris: L.-H. May, n.d. [c.1899]).

Coser, Lewis A., Men of Ideas: A Sociologist's View (New York: Free Press, 1965).

Courtney, C.P., Montesquieu and Burke (Oxford: Blackwell, 1963).

Couturat, L. and Leau, L., Histoire de la Langue Universelle (Paris: Hachette, 1907).

Cox, Richard H. (ed.), Ideology, politics and political theory (Belmont: Wadsworth, 1969).

Cox, Richard H., "On the Origins of Ideology: the Problem of Theory and Practice". Unpublished paper, Southern Political Science Association Conference (Atlanta, Georgia, 6 November 1970).

Cranston, Maurice, "Ethics and Politics", Encounter (June 1972), pp. 16-26.

Cranston, Maurice, "Ideologies, Past and Present", Survey, nos. 70-71 (Winter-Spring 1969), pp. 3-11.

Cranston, Maurice, "Ideology" Encyclopaedia Britannica, 30 vols. (Chicago, 15th ed. 1975), Macropaedia, vol. 9, pp. 194-198.

Cranston, Maurice, "Ideology and Mr Lichtheim", Encounter (October 1968), pp. 70-74.

Cranston, Maurice, "Knowledge versus Information: On the New 'Propaedia'", Encounter (July 1974), pp. 46-49.

Cranston, Maurice, "The Positivism of Baron d'Holbach", The Listener (9 January 1969), pp. 37-38.

Cranston, Maurice, "Voltaire: Man of Feeling", The Listener (23 April 1970), pp. 541-542.

Creighton, Douglas George, "Man and Mind in Diderot and Helvétius" Publications of the Modern Language Association of America, vol. 71 (1956), pp. 705-724.

Crocker, Lester Gilbert, An Age of Crisis: Man and World in Eighteenth Century French Thought (Baltimore: John Hopkins Press, 1959).

Crocker, Lester Gilbert, Diderot: The Embattled Philosopher (New York: Free Press, rev. ed. 1966).

Crocker, Lester Gilbert, Nature and Culture: Ethical Thought in the French Enlightenment (Baltimore: John Hopkins Press, 1963).

Crocker, Lester G. (ed.), The Age of Enlightenment (London: Macmillan, 1969).

Crosland, Maurice Pierre, The Society of Arcueil: a review of French science at the time of Napoléon I (London: Heinemann, 1967).

Cruet, Jean, La philosophie morale et sociale de Destutt de Tracy (1754-1836) (Tours: Bousrez, 1909).

Cumming, Ian, Helvétius: his life and place in the history of educational thought (London: Routledge and Kegan Paul, 1955).

Cunningham, D.J., "Anthropology in the Eighteenth Century", Journal of the Royal Anthropological Institute of Great Britain and Ireland, vol. 38 (1908), pp. 10-35.

Dansette, Adrien, Histoire Religieuse de la France Contemporaine: de la Révolution à la Troisième République, 2 vols. (Paris: Flammarion, 1948).

Dawson, John Charles, Lakanal the Regicide: a biographical and historical study of the career of Joseph Lakanal (Alabama: University of Alabama Press, 1948).

Delbos, Victor, La Philosophie française (Paris: Plon-Nourrit, 1919).

Delbos, Victor, Maine de Biran et son oeuvre philosophique (Paris, 1931).

Deslandres, M.-C.-E., Histoire constitutionnelle de la France depuis 1789 jusqu'à 1870, 2 vols. (Paris: Armand Colin; Sirey, 1932).

De Soto, J., "La Constitution Sénatoriale du 6 avril 1814", Revue internationale d'histoire politique et constitutionnelle (nouvelle série), no. 12 (1953), pp. 268-304.

Didier, Béatrice, [Collection de littérature française] Le XVIIIe siècle, III: 1778-1820 (Paris: Arthaud, 1976).

Dobb, Maurice, "Entrepreneur", Encyclopaedia of the Social Sciences (New York: Macmillan, 1931), vol. 5, pp. 558-560.

Dobb, Maurice, Theories of Value and Distribution since Adam Smith: Ideology and economic theory (Cambridge: Cambridge University Press, 1973).

Dorsey, John Morris, Psychology of Political Science, with special consideration for the political acumen of Destutt de Tracy (Detroit: Center for Health Education, 1973).

Driver, C.H., "Morelly and Mably", in The Social and Political Ideas of some great French Thinkers in the Age of Reason, ed. F.J.C. Hearnshaw (London: Harrap, 1930), pp. 217-252.

Drucker, Henry Matthew, The Nature of Ideology and its place in modern political thought (Ph.D. thesis, University of London, 1967).

Drucker, Henry Matthew, The Political Uses of Ideology (London: Macmillan, 1974).

Dumolard, Henri, "Joseph Rey de Grenoble (1779-1855) et ses 'mémoires politiques'", Annales de l'Université de Grenoble (nouvelle série), vol. 4 no. 1 (1927), pp. 71-111.

Dumolard, Henri, Pages Stendhaliennes (Grenoble: Arthaud, 1928).

Dupuy, Paul M., "L'école normale de l'an III", in P.M. Dupuy et al., Le Centenaire de l'Ecole Normale, 1795-1895 (Paris: Hachette, 1895), pp. 21-209.

Durkheim, Emile, "Les Principes de 1789 et la Sociologie", Revue internationale de l'enseignement, vol. 19 (1890), pp. 450-456.

Durkheim, Emile, Montesquieu and Rousseau: Forerunners of Sociology, foreword by Henri Peyre (Ann Arbor: University of Michigan Press, 1965)

Durkheim, Emile, The Evolution of Educational Thought: Lectures on the formation and development of secondary education in France, trans. P. Collins (London: Routledge and Kegan Paul, 1977).

Duruy, Albert, "L'instruction publique en 1789", Revue des Deux Mondes, vol. 44 (1881), pp. 862-892.

Duruy, Albert, L'instruction publique et la Révolution (Paris: Hachette, 1882).

Dutruch, Roger, Le Tribunat sous le Consulat et l'Empire (Paris: Rousseau, 1921).

Duvergier de Hauranne, Prosper, Histoire du gouvernement parlementaire en France 1814-1848, 10 vols. (Paris: Michel Lévy frères, 1857-1872).

Echeverria, Durand, Mirage in the West: A history of the French image of American society to 1815, foreword by Gilbert Chinard (Princeton: Princeton University Press, 1957).

Ehrard, Jean, L'idée de Nature en France à l'aube des lumières (Paris: Flammarion, 1970).

Elton, Godfrey, The Revolutionary Idea in France, 1789-1871 (London: Arnold, 1923).

Engel-Janosi, Friedrich, Four Studies in French Romantic Historical Writing (Baltimore: John Hopkins Press, 1955).

Epsztein, Léon, L'économie et la morale aux débuts du capitalisme industriel en France et en Grande-Bretagne (Paris: Armand Colin, 1966).

Espinas, Alfred, La Philosophie sociale du XVIIIe siècle et la Révolution (Paris: F. Alcan, 1898).

Faivre, Jean-Paul, "Les Idéologues de l'an VIII et le voyage de Nicolas Baudin en Australie (1800-1804)", Australian Journal of French Studies, vol. 3 no. 1 (January 1966), pp. 3-15.

Fargher, Richard, The "Décade Philosophique" and the Defence of Philosophy at the Beginning of the Nineteenth Century (D.Phil. thesis, Oxford University, 1940).

Fargher, Richard, "The Literary Criticism of the Idéologues", French Studies, vol. 3 (1949), pp. 53-66.

Fargher, Richard, "The Retreat from Voltairianism, 1800-1815", in The French Mind: Studies in Honour of Gustave Rudler, eds. W.G. Moore, R. Sutherland and E. Starkie (Oxford: Clarendon Press, 1952), pp. 220-237.

Fayolle, Roger, "Le XVIIIe siècle jugé par le XIXe ...", in Approches des Lumières: Mélanges offerts à Jean Fabre (Paris: Klincksieck, 1974), pp. 181-196.

Ferraz, Martin, Histoire de la philosophie pendant la Révolution (1789-1804) (Paris: Perrin, 1889).

Finer, S.E., "The Transmission of Benthamite Ideas, 1820-50", in Studies in the Growth of Nineteenth-Century Government, ed. G. Sutherland (London: Routledge and Kegan Paul, 1972), pp. 11-32.

Fink, Beatrice C., "Benjamin Constant on Equality", Journal of the History of Ideas, vol. 33 no. 2 (April 1972), pp. 307-314.

Fitzgerald, Ross (ed.), Human Needs and Politics (Sydney: Pergamon Press, 1977).

Forbes, Duncan, Hume's Philosophical Politics (Cambridge: Cambridge University Press, 1975).

Forster, Robert, "The Survival of the Nobility during the French Revolution", Past and Present, no. 37 (July 1967), pp. 71-86.

Foucault, Michel, The Archaeology of Knowledge, trans. A.M. Sheridan Smith (London: Tavistock, 1974).

Foucault, Michel, The Order of Things: an archaeology of the human sciences (London: Tavistock, 1974).

Foulquié, Paul (avec Saint-Jean, Raymond), Dictionnaire de la langue philosophique (Paris: Presses Universitaires de France, 2e ed., 1969)

Fox, Robert, "Enlightened entanglements", Times Literary Supplement, 16 April 1976, p. 474.

Fox, Robert, "Scientific Enterprise and the Patronage of Research in France 1800-1870", in The Patronage of Science in the Nineteenth Century, ed. G. Turner (Leyden: Noordhoff, 1976), pp. 9-51.

Fox-Genovese, Elizabeth, The Origins of Physiocracy: Economic Revolution and Social Order in Eighteenth-Century France (New York: Cornell University Press, 1976).

Frankel, Charles, The Faith of Reason: The Idea of Progress in the French Enlightenment (New York: King's Crown Press, 1948).

Frankel, Charles, "The Plight of the Humanist Intellectual", Encounter (August 1974), pp. 11-17.

Franquet de Franqueville, Alfred-Charles-Ernest, Le premier siècle de l'Institut de France, 25 Octobre 1795 - 25 octobre 1895, 2 vols. (Paris: J. Rothschild, 1895-6).

Friedrich, Carl J. (ed.), Liberty [Nomos, vol. IV] (New York: Atherton, 1962).

Friedrich, Carl J. (ed.), Revolution [Nomos, vol. VIII] (New York: Atherton, 1967).

Gaffarel, Paul, "L'opposition militaire sous le Consulat", La Révolution française, vol. 12 (1887), pp. 865-887, 982-997, 1096-1111.

Gaffarel, Paul, "L'opposition républicaine sous le Consulat", La Révolution française, vol. 13 (1887), pp. 530-550 and vol. 14 (1888), pp. 609-639.

Gaffarel, Paul, "L'opposition littéraire sous le Consulat", La Révolution française, vol. 16 (1889), pp. 307-326, 397-432.

Galley, Jean-Baptiste, Claude Fauriel, membre de l'Institut, 1772-1843 (Saint-Etienne: Imprimerie de la "Loire Républicaine", 1909).

Garnham, Barry G., The Social, Moral and Political Thought of Destutt de Tracy (Ph.D. thesis, University of Durham, 1974).

Gassier, Emile, Les cinq cent immortels: histoire de l'Académie française 1634-1906 (Paris, 1906).

Gaulmier, Jean, L'idéologue Volney 1757-1820: Contribution à l'Histoire de l'Orientalisme en France (Beyrouth: Imprimerie Catholique, 1951).

Gaulmier, Jean, Un grand témoin de la Révolution et de l'Empire, Volney (Paris: Hachette, 1959).

Gaulmier, Jean, "Volney et ses leçons d'histoire", History and Theory, vol. 2 (1962), pp. 52-65.

Gay, Peter Jack (editor), Eighteenth century studies presented to Arthur M. Wilson (Hanover, N.H.: University Press of New England, 1972).

Gay, Peter Jack, The Enlightenment: An Interpretation, 2 vols. (London: Wildwood House, 1973).

Gay, Peter Jack, The Party of Humanity: Essays in the French Enlightenment (New York: Norton, 1971).

Gay, Peter Jack, Voltaire's Politics: The Poet as Realist (Princeton: Princeton University Press, 1959).

Gellner, Ernest, "French Eighteenth-Century Materialism", in A Critical History of Western Philosophy, ed. D.J. O'Connor (New York: Free Press, 1964), pp. 275-295.

Gentile, Francesco, "La trasformazione dell' idea di progresso da Condorcet a Saint-Simon", Revue Internationale de Philosophie, vol. 14 (1960), pp. 417-444.

Germino, Dante, Beyond Ideology: The Revival of Political Theory (New York: Harper and Row, 1967).

Gillispie, Charles Coulston, "Probability and Politics: Laplace, Condorcet and Turgot", Proceedings of the American Philosophical Society, vol. 116 no. 1 (February 1972), pp. 1-20.

Gillispie, Charles Coulston, "Science in the French Revolution", Behavioural Science, vol. 4 no. 1 (January 1959), pp. 67-73.

Gillispie, Charles Coulston, The Edge of Objectivity: An essay in the history of scientific ideas (Princeton: Princeton University Press, 1960).

Gillispie, Charles Coulston, "The Encyclopédie and the Jacobin philosophy of science", in Critical Problems in the History of Science, ed. M. Clagett (Madison: University of Wisconsin Press, 1959), pp. 255-289.

[Giraudeau, Louis], Biographie des représentans du peuple à l'Assemblée Nationale Constituante (Paris: Bureau de "Notre Histoire", 1848).

Girdlestone, Cuthbert, Louis-François Ramond (1755-1827): sa vie, son oeuvre littéraire et politique (Paris: Minard, 1968).

Girdlestone, Cuthbert, "Ramond and the Ecole Centrale des Hautes-Pyrénées", in The French Renaissance and its Heritage: essays presented to Alan Boase, ed. D.R. Haggis, et al. (London: Methuen, 1968), pp. 63-73.

Gobert, Adrienne, L'opposition des Assemblées pendant le Consulat, 1800-1804 (Paris: Ernest Sagot, 1925)

Godechot, Jacques (ed.), Les Constitutions de la France depuis 1789 (Paris: Garnier-Flammarion, 1970).

Godechot, Jacques, Les Institutions de la France sous la Révolution et l'Empire (Paris: Presses Universitaires de France, 1951).

Goldstein, Doris S., "'Official Philosophies' in modern France: the example of Victor Cousin", Journal of Social History vol. I (1968), pp. 259-279.

Goncourt, Edmond-Louis-Antoine and Jules, Histoire de la société française pendant la Révolution (Paris: Quantin, 1889).

Goodwin, A., "The French Executive Directory: A Revaluation", History, vol. 22 no 3 (December 1937), pp. 201-218.

Gottschalk, Louis, "Three generations: a plausible interpretation of the French philosophes?", in Studies in Eighteenth-Century Culture, vol. 2: Irrationalism in the Eighteenth Century, ed. H.E. Pagliaro (Cleveland: Case Western Reserve University Press, 1972), pp. 3-12.

Gottschalk, Louis and Maddox, Margaret, Lafayette in the French Revolution, 2 vols. (Chicago: University of Chicago Press, 1969-1973).

Gouhier, Henri, La jeunesse d'Auguste Comte, 3 vols. (Paris: J. Vrin, 1933-41).

Gouhier, Henri, Les conversions de Maine de Biran (Paris: J. Vrin, 1947).

Gouhier, Henri, "L'idéologie et les idéologues: esquisse historique", Archivio di filosofia (1973, nos. 2-3), pp. 83-92.

Gouhier, Henri, "Un 'Projet d'Encyclopédie' de Saint-Simon", Revue Internationale de Philosophie, vol. 14 (1960), pp. 384-398.

Goyard-Fabre, Simone, La Philosophie des Lumières en France (Paris: Klincksieck, 1972).

Grange, Henri, "Necker, Madame de Staël et la Constitution de l'an III", in Approches des lumières: Mélanges offerts à Jean Fabre (Paris: Klincksieck, 1974), pp. 225-239.

Granger, Gilles-Gaston, La mathématique sociale du marquis de Condorcet (Paris: Presses Universitaires de France, 1956).

Granger, Gilles-Gaston, "Langue universelle et formalisation des sciences: un fragment inédit de Condorcet", Revue d'histoire des sciences et leurs applications, vol. 7 (1954), pp. 197-219.

Greifer, Elisha, "Joseph de Maistre and the Reaction against the Eighteenth Century", American Political Science Review, vol. 55 (1961), pp. 591-598

Grimaud, Louis, Histoire de la liberté d'enseignement en France (Paris: A. Rousseau, 1898).

Grimsley, Ronald, From Montesquieu to Laclos (Genève: Droz, 1974).

Grimsley, Ronald, Jean d'Alembert, 1717-1783 (Oxford: Oxford University Press, 1963).

Grimsley, Ronald, Maupertuis, Turgot et Maine de Biran (Genève: Droz, 1971).

Grimsley, Ronald, "Maupertuis, Turgot and Maine de Biran on the origin of language", Studies on Voltaire and the eighteenth century, vol. 62 (1968), pp. 285-307.

Grimsley, Ronald, "Some aspects of 'Nature' and 'Language' in the French Enlightenment", Studies on Voltaire and the eighteenth century, vol. 56 (1967), pp. 659-677.

Groenewegen, Peter D., "Labour and the Classical Economists", Labour History, no. 16 (May 1969), pp. 20-29.

Groenewegen, Peter D., The Economics of A.-R.-J. Turgot (The Hague: Nijhoff, 1977).

Groenewegen, Peter D., "Turgot and Adam Smith", Scottish Journal of Political Economy, vol. 16 (1969), pp. 271-287.

Gruner, Shirley M., "Destutt de Tracy - a Forgotten Idéologue", Durham University Journal, vol. 63 (June 1971), pp. 186-195.

Gruner, Shirley M., Economic materialism and social moralism: a study in the history of ideas in France from the latter part of the eighteenth century to the middle of the nineteenth century (The Hague/Paris: Mouton, 1973).

Gruner, Shirley M., "Political Historiography in Restoration France", History and Theory, vol. 8 (1969), pp. 346-365.

Guerci, Luciano, "Gli idéologues tra filosofia e politica: intorno a un contributo di Sergio Moravia", Rivista Storica Italiana, vol. 86 no. 1 (1974), pp. 101-122.

Guerlac, Henry, "Newton's Changing Reputation in the Eighteenth Century", in Carl Becker's Heavenly City Revisited, ed. R.O. Rockwood (New York: Cornell University Press, 1958), pp. 3-26.

Guerlac, Henry, "Some Aspects of Science during the French Revolution", The Scientific Monthly, vol. 80 (February 1955), pp. 93-101.

Guerlac, Henry, "Three Eighteenth-Century Social Philosophers: Scientific Influences on their thought", in Science and the Modern Mind, ed. G. Holton (Boston: Beacon Press, 1958), pp. 1-18.

Guillois, Antoine, La Marquise de Condorcet, sa famille, son salon, ses amis, 1764-1822 (Paris: Ollendorff, 2e ed. 1897).

Guillois, Antoine, Le Salon de Madame Helvétius: Cabanis et les idéologues (Paris: Calmann Lévy, 2e ed. 1894) [reprint, New York: B. Franklin, 1971].

Gusdorf, Georges, Introduction aux sciences humaines: essai critique sur leurs origines et leur développement (Paris: "Les Belles Lettres", 1960).

Gusdorf, Georges, L'avènement des sciences humaines au siècle des lumières (Paris: Payot, 1973).

Guyot, Raymond, "Du Directoire au Consulat: les transitions", Revue historique, vol. CXI (1912), pp. 1-31.

Gwynne, G.E., Madame de Staël et la Révolution française: politique, philosophie, littérature (Paris: Nizet, 1969).

Hahn, Roger, The Anatomy of a Scientific Institution: the Paris Academy of Sciences, 1666-1803 (Berkeley: University of California Press, 1971).

Halévy, Elie, The Growth of Philosophic Radicalism, trans. Mary Morris (London, Faber, 1949).

Hallie, Philip P., Maine de Biran: reformer of empiricism, 1766-1824 (Cambridge, Mass.: Harvard University Press, 1959).

Hampson, Norman, A Social History of the French Revolution (London: Routledge and Kegan Paul, 1966).

Hampson, Norman, The Enlightenment (Harmondsworth: Penguin, 1976).

Hankins, Thomas Leroy, Jean d'Alembert: Science and the Enlightenment (Oxford: Clarendon Press, 1970).

Hanotaux, G.-A.-A. and Martineau, A., Histoire des colonies françaises, 6 vols. (Paris, 1929-1934).

Harnois, Guy, Les théories du langage en France de 1660 à 1821 (Paris: Les Belles Lettres, n.d. [1929]).

Harpaz, Ephraïm, "'Le Censeur européen': Histoire d'un journal industrialiste", Revue d'histoire économique et sociale, vol. 37 (1959), pp. 185-218 and 328-357.

Harpaz, Ephraïm, L'école libérale sous la Restauration: le 'Mercure' et la 'Minerve' (1817-1820) (Genève: Droz, 1968).

Hastings, Hester, Man and Beast in French thought of the Eighteenth Century (Baltimore: John Hopkins Press, 1936).

Hatin, Eugène, Bibliographie historique et critique de la Presse périodique française (Paris: Firmin Didot, 1866).

Hatin, Eugène, Histoire politique et littéraire de la Presse en France, 8 vols. (Paris, 1859-61).

Hayek, Friedrich August von, The Counter-Revolution of Science: studies on the abuse of Reason (Glencoe: Free Press, 1952).

Hazard, Paul, "Etude sur le Journal de Ginguené", in P.-L. Ginguené, Journal de Ginguené 1807-1808, ed. P. Hazard (Paris: Hachette, 1910), pp. 23-76.

Hazard, Paul, European Thought in the Eighteenth Century, trans. J.L. May (Harmondsworth: Penguin, 1965).

Hazard, Paul, The European Mind, 1680-1715, trans. J.L. May (Harmondsworth: Penguin, 1964).

Head, Brian William, "The Origin of 'idéologue' and 'idéologie'", Studies on Voltaire and the Eighteenth Century, vol. 183 (1980), pp. 257-264.

Heimann, Peter M., "The Scientific Revolution", in New Cambridge Modern History, vol. XIII: Companion Volume, ed. Peter Burke (Cambridge: Cambridge University Press, 1979), pp. 248-270.

Helmreich, Jonathan E., "The Establishment of Primary Schools in France under the Directory", French Historical Studies, vol. 2 (1961), pp. 189-208.

Herold, J.C., Bonaparte in Egypt (London: Hamish Hamilton, 1963).

Hervé, Georges, "Le premier programme de l'anthropologie", Revue Scientifique (23 Octobre, 1909), pp. 520-528.

Hervé, Georges, "Le Sauvage de l'Aveyron devant les Observateurs de l'homme (avec le rapport retrouvé de Philippe Pinel)", Revue Anthropologique, vol. 21 (1911), pp. 383-398 and 441-454.

Hervé, Georges, "Les premiers cours d'anthropologie", Revue Anthropologique, vol. 24 (1914), pp. 255-276.

Higgs, Henry, The Physiocrats (London: Macmillan, 1897).

Hine, E.M., "Condillac and the Problem of Language", Studies on Voltaire and the Eighteenth Century, vol. 106 (1973), pp. 21-62.

Hippeau, Célestin (ed.), L'instruction publique en France pendant la Révolution: discours et rapports ... (Paris: Didier, 1881).

Hippeau, Célestin (ed.), L'instruction publique en France pendant la Révolution: débats legislatifs ... (Paris: Didier, 1883).

Hirschman, Albert O., The Passions and the Interests: Political Arguments for Capitalism before its triumph (Princeton: Princeton University Press, 1977).

Horowitz, Irving Louis, Claude Helvétius: Philosopher of Democracy and Enlightenment (New York: Paine-Whitman, 1954).

Hoselitz, Bert F., "The Early History of Entrepreneurial Theory", in Essays in Economic Thought, ed. J.J. Spengler and W.R. Allen (Chicago: Rand McNally, 1960), pp. 234-257.

Hubert, René, Les Sciences sociales dans l'Encyclopédie (Lille: Université de Lille, 1923).

Iggers, George G., "Further Remarks about Early Uses of the Term 'Social Science'", Journal of the History of Ideas, vol. 20 no. 3 (June 1959), pp. 433-36 .

Iggers, George G., The Cult of Authority: the Political Philosophy of the Saint-Simonians (The Hague: Martinus Nijhoff, second edition, 1970).

Imbert, Pierre-Henri, Destutt de Tracy, Critique de Montesquieu (Paris: A.G. Nizet, 1974).

Ions, Edmund, Against Behaviouralism: A Critique of Behavioural Sciences (Oxford: Blackwell, 1977).

James, Michael, "Pierre-Louis Roederer, Jean-Baptiste Say, and the concept of 'industrie'", History of Political Economy, vol. 9 no. 4 (1977), pp. 455-475.

Janet, Paul-Alexandre-René, Histoire de la science politique dans ses rapports avec la morale, 2 vols. (Paris: Félix Alcan, 3e ed. 1887).

Jeanvrot, Victor, "L'instruction primaire en l'an VII et François de Neufchâteau", La Révolution française, vol. 13 (1887), pp. 197-209.

Johnson, Douglas, Guizot: Aspects of French History, 1787-1874 (London: Routledge and Kegan Paul, 1963).

Joyau, Emmanuel, La Philosophie en France pendant la Révolution (1789-1795): son influence sur les institutions politiques et juridiques (Paris: A. Rousseau, 1893).

Juliard, Pierre, Philosophies of Language in eighteenth-century France (The Hague/Paris: Mouton, 1970).

Kafker, Frank A., "Les encyclopédistes et la Terreur", Revue d'histoire moderne et contemporaine, vol. 14 no. 3 (juillet 1967), pp. 284-295.

Kaufman, Arnold S., "Wants, Needs and Liberalism", Inquiry, vol. 14 (1971), pp. 191-206.

Keim, Albert, Helvétius: sa vie et son oeuvre (Paris: Félix Alcan, 1907).

Kelly, George A., "Liberalism and Aristocracy in the French Restoration", Journal of the History of Ideas, vol. 26 no. 4 (October 1965), pp. 509-530.

Kemp, Tom, Economic forces in French history (London: Dobson, 1971).

Kennedy, [Robert] Emmet,Jr., A Philosophe in the Age of Revolution: Destutt de Tracy and the Origins of 'Ideology' (Philadelphia: American Philosophical Society, 1978).

Kennedy, [Robert] Emmet,Jr., "Destutt de Tracy and the Unity of the Sciences", Studies on Voltaire and the Eighteenth Century, vol. 171 (1977), pp. 223-239.

Kennedy, [Robert] Emmet,Jr., "'Ideology' from Destutt de Tracy to Marx", Journal of the History of Ideas, vol. 40 no. 3 (July 1979), pp. 353-368.

Kettler, David, The Social and Political Thought of Adam Ferguson (Columbus, Ohio: Ohio University Press, 1965).

Kiernan, Colm, "Helvétius and a science of ethics", Studies on Voltaire and the Eighteenth Century, vol. 60 (1968), pp. 229-243.

Kiernan, Colm, "Science and the Enlightenment in Eighteenth-Century France", Studies on Voltaire and the Eighteenth Century, vol. 59 (1968), pp. 1-219.

King, Preston T., "An Ideological Fallacy", in P.T. King and B.C. Parekh (eds.), Politics and Experience (Cambridge: Cambridge University Press, 1968), pp. 341-394.

King, Preston T., Fear of Power: an analysis of anti-statism in three French writers (London: Frank Cass, 1967).

Kitchin, Joanna, Un journal "philosophique": La Décade (1794-1807) (Paris: Minard, 1966).

Knight, Isobel F., The Geometric Spirit: The Abbé de Condillac and the French Enlightenment (New Haven: Yale University Press, 1968).

Knowlson, James, Universal language schemes in England and France, 1600-1800 (Toronto: University of Toronto Press, 1975).

Koebner, Richard, "The Authenticity of the letters on the 'Esprit des Lois' attributed to Helvétius", Bulletin of the Institute of Historical Research, vol. 24 (1951), pp. 19-43.

Kohler, Oskar, Die Logik des Destutt de Tracy (Borna-Leipzig: Noske, 1931).

Koolman, G., "Say's Conception of the Role of the Entrepreneur", Economica, vol. 38 (1971), pp. 269-286.

Koyré, Alexandre, "Condorcet", Journal of the History of Ideas, vol. 9 no. 2 (April 1948), pp. 131-152.

Koyré, Alexandre, "Louis de Bonald", Journal of the History of Ideas, vol. 7 no. 1 (January 1946), pp. 56-73.

Koyré, Alexandre, Metaphysics and Measurement: Essays in Scientific Revolution (London: Chapman and Hall, 1968).

Koyré, Alexandre, Newtonian Studies (London: Chapman and Hall, 1965).

Koyré, Alexandre, "The Origins of Modern Science: a new interpretation", Diogenes, vol. 16 (1956), pp. 1-22.

Krailsheimer, A.J., Studies in Self-Interest: from Descartes to La Bruyère (Oxford: Clarendon Press, 1962).

Kuehner, Paul, Theories on the origin and formation of language in the eighteenth century in France (Philadelphia: University of Pennsylvania, 1944).

Kuhn, Thomas S., The Structure of Scientific Revolutions (Chicago: University of Chicago Press, 2nd ed. 1970).

Laboulle, M.-J., "La mathématique sociale: Condorcet et ses prédécesseurs", Revue d'histoire littéraire de la France, vol. 46 (1939), pp. 33-55.

Labrousse, François, Quelques notes sur un médecin-philosophe, P.-J.-G. Cabanis (Paris, 1903).

Lacour-Gayet, G., Bonaparte, membre de l'Institut (Paris: Gauthier-Villars, 1921).

Ladd, Everett C., Jr., "Helvétius and d'Holbach: 'La Moralisation de la Politique'", Journal of the History of Ideas, vol. 23 (1962), pp. 221-238.

Lakatos, Imre and Musgrave, Alan (eds.), Criticism and the Growth of Knowledge (Cambridge: Cambridge University Press, 1970).

Lalande, André (ed.), Vocabulaire technique et critique de la Philosophie (Paris: Presses Universitaires de France, 8e ed. 1960).

Lamartine de Prat, Marie-Louis-Alphonse, Histoire des Constituants, 4 vols. (Paris: Pagnerre; Victor Lecou, 1855).

Lamb, Robert Boyden, "Adam Smith's System: Sympathy not Self-Interest", Journal of the History of Ideas, vol. 35 no. 4 (October 1974), pp. 671-682.

Lane, Harlan, The Wild Boy of Aveyron (London: Allen & Unwin, 1977).

Lanfrey, Pierre, Etudes et Portraits politiques (Paris: Charpentier, 1864).

Lanson, Gustave, Etudes d'histoire littéraire (Paris: Honoré Champion, 1929).

Laski, Harold J., "The Age of Reason", in The Social and Political Ideas of Some Great French Thinkers of the Age of Reason, ed. F.J.C. Hearnshaw (London: Harrap, 1930), pp. 9-38.

Laski, Harold J., The Rise of European Liberalism (London: Allen and Unwin, 1936).

Laski, Harold J., The Socialist Tradition in the French Revolution (London: Fabian Society, 1930).

Lasky, Melvin J., "The English Ideology" Encounter (December 1972), pp. 25-38, and (January 1973), pp. 19-34.

Lassaigne, Jean, Maine de Biran: homme politique, préface par Henri Gouhier (Paris, 1958).

Lebrun, Richard, "Joseph de Maistre, Cassandra of Science", French Historical Studies, vol. 6 (1969), pp. 214-231.

Lefebvre, Georges, Napoleon, trans. H.F. Stockhold, 2 vols. (London: Routledge and Kegan Paul, 1974).

Lefebvre, Georges, The Directory, trans. Robert Baldick (London: Routledge and Kegan Paul, 1965).

Lefebvre, Georges, The Thermidorians, trans. Robert Baldick (London: Routledge and Kegan Paul, 1965).

Lefèvre, Roger, "Condillac, maître du langage", Revue internationale de philosophie, vol. 21 (1967), pp. 393-406.

Lehmann, A.G., "Saint-Beuve and the Historical Movement", in The French Mind: Studies in Honour of Gustave Rudler, ed. W.G. Moore et al., (Oxford: Clarendon Press, 1952), pp. 256-272.

Leith, James A., "Modernisation, Mass Education and Social Mobility in French Thought, 1750-1789", in Studies in the Eighteenth Century ed. R.F. Brissenden (Canberra: A.N.U. Press, 1973), vol. II, pp. 223-238.

Lenoir, Raymond, "Psychologie et logique de Destutt de Tracy", Revue philosophique de la France et de l'étranger, vol. 84 (1917), pp. 527-556.

Léonard, Emile-G., "La question sociale dans l'armée française au XVIIIe siècle", Annales: Economies, Sociétés, Civilisations, vol. 3 no. 1 (January 1948), pp. 135-149.

Leroy, Georges, La Psychologie de Condillac (Paris: Boivin, 1937).

Leroy, Maxime, Histoire des idées sociales en France, 3 vols. (Paris: Gallimard, 1946-54: reprint 1962).

Leroy, Maxime, Le Socialisme des producteurs: Henri de Saint-Simon (Paris: Marcel Rivière, 1924).

Letwin, Shirley Robin, The Pursuit of Certainty (Cambridge: Cambridge University Press, 1965).

Letwin, William, The Origins of Scientific Economics. English Economic Thought, 1660-1776 (Connecticut: Greenwood Press, 1963).

Levasseur, Emile, Histoire des classes ouvrières et de l'industrie en France depuis 1789 à 1870, 2 vols. (Paris, 2e ed. 1903-1904).

Lévy-Bruhl, Lucien, History of Modern Philosophy in France, trans. G. Coblence (Chicago: Open Court, 1899).

Liard, Louis, L'enseignement supérieur en France, 1789-1889, 2 vols. (Paris: Armand Colin, 1888).

Lichtenberger, André, Le Socialisme et la Révolution française (Paris, 1899).

Lichtenberger, André, Le Socialisme français au XVIIIe siècle (Paris, 1895).

Lichtheim, George, The Concept of Ideology and Other Essays (New York: Vintage Books, 1967).

Lively, Jack F. (ed.), The Enlightenment (London: Longmans, 1966).

Lively, Jack F., "The Problem of Evil", in John Cruickshank (ed.), French Literature and its Background, vol. 3, The Eighteenth Century (Oxford: Oxford University Press, 1968), pp. 177-195.

Loté, René, "Histoire de la Philosophie", in Histoire de la Nation française, ed. G.A. Hanotaux, 15 vols. (Paris: Plon-Nourrit, 1920-24) vol. XV, pp. 297-605.

Lough, John, An Introduction to Eighteenth Century France (London: Longmans, 1962).

Lough, John, "Helvétius and d'Holbach", Modern Language Review, vol. 23 no 3 (July 1938), pp. 360-384.

Lough, John, "Who were the Philosophes?" in Studies in Eighteenth-Century French Literature presented to Robert Niklaus, ed. J.H. Fox, M.H. Waddicor and D.A. Watts (Exeter: University of Exeter Press, 1975), pp. 139-150.

Lukes, Steven, Essays in Social Theory (London: Macmillan, 1977).

Lukes, Steven, Individualism (Oxford: Blackwell, 1973).

Luppé, Robert de, Les idées littéraires de Madame de Staël et l'héritage des lumières (1795-1800) (Paris: J. Vrin, 1969).

Lyons, Martyn, France under the Directory (Cambridge: Cambridge University Press, 1975).

McKie, Douglas, Antoine Lavoisier: Scientist, Economist, Social Reformer (London: Constable, 1952).

McManners, John, "France", in A. Goodwin (ed.), The European Nobility in the Eighteenth Century (London: Black, 2nd ed., 1967), pp. 22-42.

McManners, John, The French Revolution and the Church (London: Society for the Promotion of Christian Knowledge, 1969).

McRae, Robert, "'Idea' as a philosophical term in the seventeenth century", Journal of the History of Ideas, vol. 26 no. 2 (April, 1965), pp. 175-190.

McRae, Robert, The Problem of the Unity of the Sciences: Bacon to Kant (Toronto: University of Toronto Press, 1961).

McRae, Robert, "The Unity of the Sciences: Bacon, Descartes and Leibniz", Journal of the History of Ideas, vol. 18 no. 1 (January 1957), pp. 27-48.

Madinier, Gabriel, Conscience et mouvement: étude sur la philosophie française de Condillac à Bergson (Paris: Presses Universitaires de France, 1938; and Louvain: Nauwelaerts, 2e ed. 1967).

Maes, Pierre, Un ami de Stendhal, Victor Jacquemont (Paris: Desclée; Brouwer, n.d. [1953]).

Malson, Lucien and Itard, Jean, Wolf Children, and The Wild Boy of Aveyron, trans. E. Fawcett, P. Ayrton and J. White (London: New Left Books, 1972).

Manning, David J., Liberalism (London: J.M. Dent, 1976).

Manuel, Frank E., Shapes of Philosophical History (London: Allen and Unwin, 1965).

Manuel, Frank E., The New World of Henri Saint-Simon (Notre Dame: University of Notre Dame Press, 1963).

Manuel, Frank E., The Prophets of Paris: Turgot, Condorcet, Saint-Simon, Fourier and Comte (New York: Harper and Row, 1965).

Martin, Kingsley, French Liberal Thought in the Eighteenth Century: A Study of Political Ideas from Bayle to Condorcet, ed. J.P. Mayer (London: Phoenix House, revised ed., 1962).

Masson, Frédéric, "Les Conspirations du Général Malet", Revue des Deux Mondes, tome 53 (1919): 1 September 1919, pp. 24-58; 15 September 1919, pp. 358-389; 15 October 1919, pp. 870-905; 15 November 1919, pp. 364-396.

Mathiez, Albert, "La Constitution de 1793", Annales historiques de la Révolution française (1928), pp. 497-521.

Mathiez, Albert, La Théophilanthropie et le culte décadaire, 1796-1801 (Paris: Félix Alcan, 1904).

Mauzi, Robert, L'idée du bonheur dans la littéraire et la pensée françaises au XVIIIe siècle (Paris: A. Colin, 1960).

Maxwell, Constantia, "Chateaubriand and the French Romantics", in The Social and Political Ideas of Some Representative Thinkers of the Age of Reaction and Reconstruction 1815-1865, ed. F.J.C. Hearnshaw (London: Harrap, 1932), pp. 29-51.

Maynial, Eduard, "Les Grammairiens Philosophes du XVIIIe siècle", Revue Bleue, 7 March 1903, pp. 317-320.

Meek, Ronald Lindley, Social Science and the Ignoble Savage (Cambridge: Cambridge University Press, 1976).

Meek, Ronald Lindley, The Economics of Physiocracy (London: Allen and Unwin, 1962).

Mensard, Paul, Histoire de l'Académie française depuis sa fondation jusqu'en 1830 (Paris, 1857).

Meyer, Paul H., "Politics and Morals in the Thought of Montesquieu", Studies on Voltaire and the Eighteenth Century, vol. 56 (1967), pp. 845-891.

Michaud, Louis-Gabriel (ed.), Biographie universelle ancienne et moderne, 45 tomes (Paris: Desplaces, nouv. ed., n.d. [1843-65]).

Michel, Francisque, Les Ecossais en France, Les Français en Ecosse, 2 vols. (Londres: Trübner, 1862).

Michel, Henry, L'idée de l'état: essai critique sur l'histoire des théories sociales et politiques en France depuis la Révolution (Paris: Hachette, 1896).

Michon, Georges, Essai sur l'histoire du parti feuillant: Adrien Duport (Paris: Payot, 1924).

Miliband, Ralph, "Barnave: a case of bourgeois class consciousness", in Aspects of History and Class Consciousness, ed. I. Meszaros (London: Merlin Press, 1971), pp. 22-48.

Miller, Eugene F., "Hume's Contribution to Behavioral Science", Journal of the History of the Behavioral Sciences, vol. 7 no. 2 (April 1971), pp. 154-168.

Minogue, Kenneth R., The Liberal Mind (London: Methuen, 1963).

Moore, F.C.T., The Psychology of Maine de Biran (Oxford: Clarendon Press, 1970).

Moore, F.C.T., "Translator's Introduction", to J.-M. De Gérando, The Observation of Savage Peoples (London: Routledge, 1969), pp. 1-58.

Moravia, Sergio, "Aspetti della 'science de l'homme' nella filosofia degli 'idéologues'", Rivista critica di storia della filosofia, vol. 21 (1966), pp. 398-425 and vol. 22 (1967), pp. 54-86.

Moravia, Sergio, "Filsofia e 'sciences de la vie' nel secolo XVIII", Giornale critico della filosofia italiana, vol. 21 (1966), pp. 64-109.

Moravia, Sergio, "From 'Homme Machine' to 'Homme Sensible': Changing Eighteenth-Century Models of Man's Image", Journal of the History of Ideas, vol. 39 no. 1 (January 1978), pp. 45-60.

Moravia, Sergio, Il Pensiero degli Idéologues: scienza e filosofia in Francia, 1780-1815 (Firenze: La Nueva Italia, 1974).

Moravia, Sergio, Il tramonto dell'illuminismo: filosofia e politica nella società francese, 1770-1810 (Bari: Laterza, 1968).

Moravia, Sergio, "Intellettuali e vita politica nell'età del direttorio: Gli 'idéologues'", Rivista storica italiana, vol. 78 (1966), pp. 614-676.

Moravia, Sergio, "La scienza della società in Francia alla fine del secolo XVIII", Atti e memorie dell'Accademia Toscana di scienze e lettere La Colombaria, vol. 33 (1968), pp. 305-420.

Moravia, Sergio, La scienza dell'uomo nel settecento (Bari: Laterza, 1970).

Moravia, Sergio, "La Société d'Auteuil et la Révolution", Dix-huitième siècle, no. 6 (1974), pp. 181-191.

Moravia, Sergio, "Logica e psicologia nel pensiero di D. de Tracy", Rivista critica di storia della filosofia, vol. 19 (1964), pp. 169-213.

Moravia, Sergio, "Philosophie et géographie à la fin du XVIIIe siècle", Studies on Voltaire and the Eighteenth Century, vol. 57 (1967), pp. 937-1011.

Moravia, Sergio, "Philosophie et médecine en France   à la fin du XVIIIe siècle", Studies on Voltaire and the Eighteenth Century, vol. 89 (1972), pp. 1089-1151.

Mornet, Daniel, Les Origines intellectuelles de la Révolution française 1715-1787 (Paris, 6e ed. 1967).

Moro, Roberto, "L'Arte Sociale e l'Idea di Società nel Pensiero Politico di Sieyès", Rivista Internazionale di Filosofia del Diritto, vol. 45 (1968), pp. 226-266.

Morrow, Glenn R., "The significance of the doctrine of sympathy in Hume and Adam Smith", The Philosophical Review, vol. 32 (1923), pp. 60-78.

Mortier, Roland, "Les héritiers des 'philosophes' devant l'expérience révolutionnaire", Dix-huitième siècle, no. 6 (1974), pp. 45-57.

Mortier, Roland, "The 'Philosophes' and Public Education", Yale French Studies, no. 40 (1968), pp. 62-76.

Naess, Arne, Democracy, Ideology and Objectivity (Oxford: Blackwell and Oslo University Press, 1956).

Napoleoni, Claudio, Smith, Ricardo, Marx: Observations on the history of economic thought, trans. J.M.A. Gee (Oxford: Blackwell, 1975).

Naville, Pierre, d'Holbach et la Philosophie scientifique au XVIIIe siècle (Paris: Gallimard, nouv. éd., 1967).

Necheles, Ruth F., The Abbé Grégoire, 1787-1831: The Odyssey of an Egalitarian (Westport, Conn.: Greenwood, 1971).

Neill, Thomas P., "Quesnay and Physiocracy", Journal of the History of Ideas, vol. 9 no. 2 (April 1948), pp. 153-173.

Nettement, Alfred-François, Histoire politique, anecdotique, et littéraire du Journal des Débats, 2 vols. (Paris, 1838).

Nisbet, Robert A., "Conservatism and Sociology", American Journal of Sociology, vol. 58 no. 2 (September 1952), pp. 167-175.

Nisbet, Robert A., "The French Revolution and the Rise of Sociology in France", American Journal of Sociology, vol. 49 no. 2 (September 1943), pp. 156-164.

Nisbet, Robert A., The Social Philosophers: Community and Conflict in Western Thought (New York: Thomas Crowell, 1973).

Nisbet, Robert A., The Sociological Tradition (London: Heinemann, 1970).

Nisbet, Robert A., "Turgot and the Contexts of Progress", Proceedings of the American Philosophical Society, vol. 119 no. 3 (June 1975), pp. 214-222.

Oakeshott, Michael, On Human Conduct (Oxford: Clarendon Press, 1975).

Oakeshott, Michael, Rationalism in Politics and other Essays (London: Methuen, 1967).

Oczapowski, Joseph, "Montesquieu économiste", Revue d'économie politique, vol. 5 (1891), pp. 1039-1070.

Orieux, Jean, Talleyrand, ou le sphinx incompris (Paris: Flammarion, 1971).

Ossowski, Stanislas, Class Structure in the Social Consciousness, trans. S. Patterson (London: Routledge and Kegan Paul, 1963).

O'Sullivan, Noël, Conservatism (London: J.M. Dent, 1976).

Outhwaite, William, "Social Thought and Social Sciences", in New Cambridge Modern History, vol. XIII: Companion Volume, ed. Peter Burke (Cambridge: Cambridge University Press, 1979), pp. 271-292.

Palmer, R.R., "Man and Citizen: Applications of Individualism in the French Revolution", in Essays in Political Theory presented to George H. Sabine, ed. M.R. Konvitz and A.E. Murphy (New York: Cornell University Press, 1948), pp. 130-152.

Pappas, John Nicholas, Voltaire and d'Alembert (Bloomington: Indiana University Press, 1962).

Pariset, Georges, Etudes d'Histoire révolutionnaire et contemporaine (Paris: Société d'Edition Les Belles Lettres, 1929).

Passmore, John A., "The Malleability of Man in Eighteenth-century thought", in Aspects of the Eighteenth Century, ed. E.R. Wasserman (Baltimore: John Hopkins Press, 1965), pp. 21-46.

Passmore, John A., The Perfectibility of Man (London: Duckworth, 1972).

Perroud, Claude, "La Société française des Amis des Noirs", La Révolution française, vol. 69 (1916), pp. 122-147.

Perroud, Claude, "Quelques notes sur le Club de 1789", La Révolution française, vol. 39 (1900), pp. 255-262.

Pesciarelli, Enzo, "The Italian Contribution to the Four-Stages Theory", History of Political Economy, vol. 10 no. 4 (Winter, 1978), pp. 597-607.

Peyre, H., "The influence of eighteenth-century ideas on the French Revolution", Journal of the History of Ideas, vol. X (1949), pp. 63-87.

Picavet, François, "Destutt de Tracy", La Grande Encyclopédie (Paris: H. Lamirault, 1887-1902), vol. XIV, pp. 297-298.

Picavet, François, Les Idéologues: essai sur l'histoire des idées et des théories scientifiques, philosophiques, religieuses, etc. en France depuis 1789 (Paris: Félix Alcan, 1891).

Plamenatz, John Petrov (ed.), Readings from Liberal Writers, English and French (London: Allen and Unwin, 1965).

Plamenatz, John Petrov, The Revolutionary Movement in France, 1815-1871 (London: Longmans, 1952).

Plongeron, Bernard, "Nature, métaphysique et histoire chez les idéologues", Dix-huitième siècle, no. 5 (1973), pp. 375-412.

Ponteil, Félix, Histoire de l'enseignement en France: Les grandes étapes, 1789-1964 (Paris: Sirey, 1966).

Ponteil, Félix, La Pensée politique depuis Montesquieu (Paris: Sirey, 1960).

Ponteil, Félix, Napoléon 1er et l'organisation autoritaire de la France (Paris: Armand Colin, 2e éd., 1965).

Pos, H.J., "Remarks on the materialism of the eighteenth century", in Philosophy for the Future: the quest of modern materialism, ed. R.W. Sellars, V.J. McGill and M.B. Farber (New York: MacMillan, 1949), pp. 33-40.

Potiquet, François-Gabriel-Alfred, L'Institut National de France: ses diverses organisations, ses membres, ses associés et ses correspond-ants (20 novembre 1795-19 novembre 1869) (Paris: Didier, 1871).

Prélot, Marcel, Histoire des idées politiques (Paris: Dalloz, 2e ed. 1961).

Price, Roger, The Economic Modernization of France 1730-1880 (London: Croom Helm, 1975).

Rambaud, A., "L'Agriculture, l'industrie, le commerce, le crédit pendant la Révolution et l'Empire", La Révolution française, vol. 13 (1887), pp. 210-238.

Rastier, François, Idéologie et théorie des signes: Analyse structurale des Eléments d'idéologie d'Antoine-Louis-Claude Destutt de Tracy (Paris/The Hague: Mouton, 1972).

Reboul, Robert-Marie, Louis-François Jauffret. Sa vie et ses oeuvres (Paris: Baur et Detaille, 1869).

Régaldo, Marc, "La Décade et les Philosophes du XVIIIe siècle", Dix-huitième siècle, no. 2 (1970), pp. 113-130.

Régaldo, Marc, "Lumières, Elite, Démocratie: la difficile position des idéologues", Dix-huitième siècle, no. 6 (1974), pp. 193-207.

Régaldo, Marc, "Matériaux pour une Bibliographie de l'Idéologie et des Idéologues", Répertoire analytique de littérature française, vol. I (1970), no. 1, pp. 33-49, and nos. 2-3, pp. 27-41.

Régaldo, Marc, "Profil Perdu: l'Idéologue Chaussard", in Approches des lumières: Mélanges offerts à Jean Fabre (Paris: Klincksieck, 1974), pp. 381-401.

Régaldo, Marc, Un Milieu intellectuel: La Décade philosophique, 1794-1807 (Paris/Lille, 1976).

Reinhard, Marcel, "Elite et noblesse dans la seconde moitié du XVIIIe siècle", Revue d'histoire moderne et contemporaine, vol. 3 (1956), pp. 5-37.

Reisman, David A., Adam Smith's Sociological Economics (London: Croom Helm, 1976).

Remmling, G.W., Road to Suspicion: a study of modern mentality and the Sociology of Knowledge (New York: Appleton-Century-Crofts, 1967).

Rémond, René, La droite en France de la première Restauration à la 5e République, 2 vols. (Paris: Editions Montaigne, 3e éd., 1968).

Reynaud, L., L'influence allemande en France au XVIIIe et au XIXe siècles (Paris: Hachette, 1922).

Riese, Walther, The Legacy of Philippe Pinel (New York: Springer Publishing Co., 1969).

Rioux, Jean-Pierre, La Révolution industrielle 1780-1880 (Paris: Seuil, 1971).

Robert, Paul, Dictionnaire alphabétique et analogique de la Langue française (Paris: Presses Universitaires de France, 1957).

Robinet (ed.), Dictionnaire historique et biographique de la Révolution et de l'Empire, 1789-1815, 2 vols. (Paris: Librairie historique de la Révolution et de l'Empire, 1899).

Robison, Georgia, [La] Revellière-Lépeaux Citizen-Director, 1753-1824 (New York: Columbia University Press, 1938).

Rockwood, Raymond O. (ed.), Carl Becker's Heavenly City Revisited (New York: Cornell University Press, 1958).

Rocquain, Félix, L'état de France au 18 brumaire (Paris, 1874).

Rosen, George, "The Philosophy of Ideology and the Emergence of Modern Medicine in France", Bulletin of the History of Medicine, vol. 14 (1946), pp. 328-339.

Rosenberg, Nathan, "Adam Smith on the Division of Labour: Two Views or One?", Economica, vol. 45 (1965), pp. 127-139.

Rosenfield, Leonora C., From Beast-Machine to Man-Machine (New York, 1941).

Rothkrug, Lionel, Opposition to Louis XIV: the political and social origins of the French Enlightenment (Princeton: Princeton University Press, 1965).

Roucek, Joseph S., "A History of the Concept of Ideology", Journal of the History of Ideas, vol. 5 no. 4 (October 1944), pp. 479-488.

Rougeron, Georges, Antoine-Louis-Claude Destutt de Tracy, Président du département de l'Allier (1754-1836) (Montluçon: Grande Imprimerie nouvelle, Biographies Départementales XII, 1966).

Rougeron, Georges, "Lafayette et le Bourbonnais", Bulletin de la Société d'Emulation du Bourbonnais (1958), 3e trimestre, pp. 317-331.

Rougeron, Georges, "Les Noms Bourbonnais des rues de Paris" (2e partie), Bulletin de la Société d'Emulation du Bourbonnais (1959), 3e trimestre, pp. 554-562.

Rude, Fernand, Stendhal et la pensée sociale de son temps (Paris: Plon, 1967

Sagnac, Philippe, La Formation de la Société française moderne, 2 vols. (Paris: Presses Universitaires de France, 1945-46).

Sagnac, Philippe, La Législation civile de la Révolution française, 1789-1804 (Paris, 1898).

Sainte-Beuve, Charles-Augustin, Causeries du lundi, 15 vols. (Paris: Garnier, 3e ed. [1874]).

Sainte-Beuve, Charles-Augustin, Chateaubriand et son groupe littéraire sous l'Empire, 2 vols. (Paris, nouv. éd., 1878).

Sainte-Beuve, Charles-Augustin, Portraits Contemporains, 3 vols. (Paris: Didier, 1847).

Sainte-Beuve, Charles-Augustin, Portraits littéraires, 3 vols. (Paris: Garnier, nouv. éd. 1880).

Salomon, Albert, In Praise of Enlightenment (Cleveland: Meridian Books, 1963).

Salomon, Albert, "The Religion of Progress", Social Research, vol. 13 no. 4 (December 1946), pp. 441-462.

Salomon, Albert, The Tyranny of Progress: reflections on the origin of Sociology (New York: Noonday Press, 1955).

Sampson, R.V., Progress in the Age of Reason: the Seventeenth Century to the Present Day (London: Heinemann, 1956).

Samuels, W.J., "The Physiocratic Theory of Property and State", Quarterly Journal of Economics, vol. 75 (1961), pp. 96-111.

Saricks, Ambrose, Pierre-Samuel Du Pont de Nemours (Lawrence: University of Kansas Press, 1965).

Sasso, Robert, "Voltaire et le 'Système de la Nature' de d'Holbach", Revue Internationale de Philosophie, vol. 32 (1978), pp. 279-296.

Schapiro, Jacob Selwyn, Condorcet and the Rise of Liberalism (New York: Harcourt, Brace and Co., 1934).

Sée, Henri, La France économique et sociale au dix-huitième siècle (Paris, 5e ed. 1952).

Sée, Henri, L'évolution de la pensée politique en France au 18e siècle (Paris, 1925).

Seillière, Baron de, "Les Sciences Morales et Politiques dans l'Institut de France à l'Epoque Révolutionnaire", Revue Internationale de l'Enseignement, 15 January 1940, pp. 21-31.

Senn, Peter R., "Earliest use of the term 'Social Science'", Journal of the History of Ideas, vol. 19 no. 4 (October 1958), pp. 568-570.

Shklar, Judith N., After Utopia: the Decline of Political Faith (Princeton: Princeton University Press, 1957).

Shklar, Judith N., [review of K.M. Baker's Condorcet], Political Theory, vol. 3 no. 4 (November 1975), pp. 469-474.

Sicard, Augustin, L'éducation morale et civique avant et pendant la Révolution (1700-1808) (Paris: Poussielgue, 1884).

Siedentop, Larry Alan, The Limits of Enlightenment: A Study of Conservative Social and Political Thought in Early Nineteenth-Century France (with special reference to Maine de Biran and Joseph de Maistre), 2 vols. (D.Phil. thesis, Oxford University, 1966).

Simon, Jules-François, Une Académie sous le Directoire (Paris: Calmann Lévy, 1885).

Simon, Pierre, L'Elaboration de la Charte Constitutionnelle de 1814 (1er avril - 4 juin 1814) (Paris: E. Cornély, 1906).

Simon, William Michael, European Positivism in the Nineteenth Century (Ithaca: Cornell University Press, 1963).

Sklair, Leslie, The Sociology of Progress (London: Routledge and Kegan Paul, 1970).

Skocpol, Theda, States and Social Revolutions: A Comparative Analysis of France, Russia, and China (Cambridge: Cambridge University Press, 1979).

Smith, Colin, "Aspects of Destutt de Tracy's Linguistic Analysis as adopted by Stendhal", Modern Language Review, vol. 51 no. 4 (October 1956), pp. 512-521.

Smith, Colin, "Destutt de Tracy and the Bankruptcy of Sensationalism", in Balzac and the Nineteenth Century, ed. D.G. Charlton, J. Gaudon and A.R. Pugh (Leicester: Leicester University Press, 1972), pp. 195-207.

Smith, Colin, "Destutt de Tracy's Analysis of the Proposition", Revue Internationale de Philosophie, vol. 21 (1967), pp. 475-485.

Smith, David Warner, Helvétius: a Study in Persecution (Oxford: Clarendon Press, 1965).

Soltau, Roger H., French Political Thought in the Nineteenth Century (New Haven: Yale University Press, 1931).

Sorel, Albert, Europe and the French Revolution: The Political Traditions of the Old Régime, trans. A. Cobban and J.W. Hunt (London: Collins, 1969).

Sorel, Georges, The Illusions of Progress, trans. John and Charlotte Stanley (Berkeley: University of California Press, 1972).

Sowell, Thomas, Classical Economics Reconsidered (Princeton: Princeton University Press, 1974).

Spengler, Joseph J., "The Physiocrats and Say's Law of Markets", in Essays in Economic Thought, ed. Spengler and Allen (Chicago: Rand McNally, 1960), pp. 161-214.

Spink, John Stephen, French Free-Thought from Gassendi to Voltaire (London: Athlone Press, 1960).

Stark, Werner, Montesquieu: pioneer of the Sociology of Knowledge (London: Routledge and Kegan Paul, 1960).

Stark, Werner, "The Conservative Tradition in the Sociology of Knowledge", Kyklos, vol. 13 (1960), pp. 90-101.

Staum, Martin Sheldon, Cabanis and the Science of Man (Ph.D. thesis, Cornell University, 1971).

Staum, Martin Sheldon, "Cabanis and the Science of Man", Journal of the History of the Behavioral Sciences, vol. 10 (1974), pp. 135-143.

Stein, Jay Wobith, "Beginnings of 'Ideology'", South Atlantic Quarterly, vol. 55 no. 2 (1956), pp. 163-170.

Stein, Jay Wobith, The Mind and the Sword (New York: Twayne Publishers, 1961).

Stepanowa, Vera, Destutt de Tracy: eine historisch-psychologishe untersuchung (Zürich: Zürcher and Furrer, 1908).

Stocking, George W., "French Anthropology in 1800", Isis, vol. 55 (1964), pp. 134-150.

Stricklen, C.G., "The Philosophes' Political Mission: The Creation of an Idea, 1750-1789", Studies on Voltaire and the Eighteenth Century, vol. 86 (1971), pp. 137-228.

Suckling, Norman, "The Enlightenment and the Idea of Progress", Studies on Voltaire and the Eighteenth Century, vol. 58 (1967), pp. 1461-1480.

Swingewood, Alan, "Origins of Sociology: The Case of the Scottish Enlightenment", British Journal of Sociology, vol. 21 no. 2 (June 1970), pp. 164-180.

Sydenham, Michael John, The First French Republic, 1792-1804 (London: Batsford, 1974).

Taine, Hippolyte-Adolphe, Les Origines de la France Contemporaine, 6 vols. (Paris, 1876-1894).

Taine, Hippolyte-Adolphe, Les Philosophes français du XIXe siècle (Paris, 1857).

Talmon, Jacob Laib, Political Messianism: the Romantic Phase (London: Secker and Warburg, 1960).

Talmon, Jacob Laib, "The Age of Revolution", Encounter (September 1963), pp. 11-18.

Talmon, Jacob Laib, The Origins of Totalitarian Democracy (London: Sphere Books, 1970).

Taylor, George V., "Noncapitalist Wealth and the Origins of the French Revolution", _American Historical Review_, vol. 72 no. 2 (January 1967), pp. 469-496.

Teggart, Frederick J., _Theory and Processes of History_ (Berkeley: University of California Press, 1960).

Thibaudet, Albert, _Histoire de la Littérature française de 1789 à nos jours_ (Paris: Stock, 1963)

Thiry, Jean, _Le Coup d'Etat du 18 brumaire_ (Paris, 1947).

Thiry, Jean, _Le Sénat de Napoléon (1800-1814)_ (Paris: Berger-Levrault, 1932).

Thomas, Keith, _Religion and the decline of magic_ (Harmondsworth: Penguin, 1971).

Thompson, J.M., _Napoleon Bonaparte: his rise and fall_ (Oxford: Blackwell, 1952).

Tocqueville, Alexis de, _The Ancien Régime and the French Revolution_ trans. S. Gilbert (London: Fontana, 1971).

Tocqueville, Alexis de, _The Recollections_, trans. A.T. de Mattos, ed. J.P. Mayer (New York: Meridian Books, 1959).

Topazio, Virgil W., _D'Holbach's Moral Philosophy: its Background and Development_ (Genève: Institut et Musée Voltaire, 1956).

Trevor-Roper, Hugh, "The Scottish Enlightenment", _Studies on Voltaire and the eighteenth century_, vol. 58 (1967), pp. 1635-1658.

Tribe, Keith, _Land, Labour and Economic Discourse_ (London: Routledge and Kegan Paul, 1978).

Underwood, Edgar Ashworth (ed.), _Science, Medicine and History_, 2 vols. (London: Oxford University Press, 1953).

Vacheron, Louis, _Souvenirs historiques et littéraires: une grande famille du Bourbonnais_, 2 Parties (Paris: Alphonse Lemerre, 1900-1901).

Vachet, André, _L'idéologie libérale: l'individu et sa propriété_ (Paris: Anthropos, 1970).

Vandal, Albert, _L'Avènement de Bonaparte_, 2 vols. (Paris: Plon-Nourrit, 1907).

Van Duzer, Charles Hunter, _Contribution of the Idéologues to French Revolutionary Thought_ (Baltimore: John Hopkins Press, 1935).

Vartanian, Aram, _Diderot and Descartes_ (Princeton: Princeton University Press, 1953).

Vartanian, Aram, _La Mettrie's l'Homme-Machine: A Study in the Origins of an Idea_ (Princeton: Princeton University Press, 1960).

479

Vauthier, Gabriel, "L'enseignement secondaire libre à Paris sous le Directoire", Annales historiques de la Révolution française, vol. 6 (1929), pp. 465-475.

Vauthier, Gabriel, Villemain 1790-1870: essai sur sa vie, son rôle et ses ouvrages (Paris: Perrin, 1913).

Vereker, Charles, Eighteenth-century optimism (Liverpool: Liverpool University Press, 1967).

Vereker, Charles, The Development of Political Theory (London: Hutchinson, 2nd ed., 1964).

Vial, Francisque, Trois siècles d'histoire de l'enseignement secondaire (Paris: Delagrave, 1936).

Viel-Castel, Charles-Louis-Gaspard-Gabriel Salviac, baron de, Histoire de la Restauration, 20 vols. (Paris: Michel Lévy frères, 1860-1877).

de Villefosse, Louis, and Bouissounouse, Janine, L'Opposition à Napoléon (Paris: Flammarion, 1969).

de Villefosse, Louis, and Bouissounouse, Janine, The Scourge of the Eagle: Napoleon and the Liberal Opposition, trans. and ed. Michael Ross (London: Sidgwick and Jackson, 1972).

Villemain, Abel-François, Choix d'études sur la littérature contemporaine (Paris: Didier, 1857).

Viner, Jacob, "Mercantilist Thought", in International Encyclopedia of the Social Sciences (New York: Collier-Macmillan, 1968), vol. 4, pp. 435-442.

Viner, Jacob, The Long View and the Short: Studies in economic theory and policy (Glencoe, Illinois: The Free Press, 1958).

Voegelin, Eric, From Enlightenment to Revolution (Durham, N.C.: Duke University Press, 1975).

Voegelin, Eric, The New Science of Politics (Chicago: University of Chicago Press, 1971).

Vyverberg, Henry Sabin, Historical Pessimism in the French Enlightenment (Cambridge, Mass.: Harvard University Press, 1958).

Wallon, Henri-Alexandre, Histoire du Tribunal Révolutionnaire de Paris avec le Journal de ses Actes, 6 vols. (Paris: Hachette, 1880-1882).

Watkins, Frederick Mundell, The Age of Ideology: Political Thought, 1750 to the present (Englewood Cliffs: Prentice-Hall, 1964).

Watkins, Frederick Mundell, The Political Tradition of the West (Cambridge, Mass.: Harvard University Press, 1948).

Watt, Edward D., "Joseph de Maistre and the Thoughts of Chancellor Bacon", Australian Journal of Politics and History, vol. 17 no. 3 (December 1971), pp. 406-411.

Weightman, John, "Madame de Staël", Encounter (October 1973), pp. 45-54.

Weill, Georges, "Destutt de Tracy" in Encyclopedia of the Social Sciences, ed. E.R.A. Seligman (New York: Macmillan, 1931), vol. 5, p. 108.

Weill, Georges, Histoire du parti républicain en France de 1814 à 1870 (Paris: Félix Alcan, 1900).

Weill, Georges, "Les Mémoires de Joseph Rey", Revue Historique, vol. 157 (1928), pp. 291-307.

Weinberger, J., "Hobbes's Doctrine of Method", Americal Political Science Review, vol. 69 no. 4 (December 1975), pp. 1336-1353.

Welschinger, Henri, La Censure sous le Premier Empire (Paris, 1882).

West, E.G., "Adam Smith's Two Views on the Division of Labour", Economica, vol. 44 (1964), pp. 23-32.

West, E.G., "Private versus Public Education, A Classical Economic Dispute", in The Classical Economists and Economic Policy, ed. A.W. Coats (London: Methuen, 1971), pp. 123-143.

Westfall, Richard S., The Construction of Modern Science: Mechanisms and Mechanics (Cambridge: Cambridge University Press, 1977).

Weulersse, Georges, La Physiocratie à la fin du règne de Louis XV, 1770-1774 (Paris, 1959).

Weulersse, Georges, La Physiocratie sous les Ministères de Turgot et de Necker, 1774-1781 (Paris, 1950).

Weulersse, Georges, Le Mouvement Physiocratique en France de 1756 à 1770, 2 vols. (Paris, 1910).

Weulersse, Georges, "The Physiocrats" in Encyclopaedia of the Social Sciences, ed. E.R.A. Seligman (New York: Macmillan, 1931), vol. 5, pp. 348-351.

Whitehead, Alfred North, Adventures of Ideas (New York: Macmillan, 1933; reprinted, Free Press, 1967).

Whitfield, Ernest A., Gabriel Bonnot de Mably (London: Routledge, 1930).

Wickwar, William H., Baron d'Holbach: A Prelude to the French Revolution (London: Allen and Unwin, 1935).

Wickwar, William H., "Helvétius and Holbach", in The Social and Political Ideas of Some Great French Thinkers of the Age of Reason, ed. F.J.C. Hearnshaw (London: Harrap, 1930), pp. 195-216.

Wiener, Phillip P. (ed.), Dictionary of the History of Ideas, 4 vols. (New York: Charles Scribner's Sons, 1973).

Willey, Basil, The Eighteenth-century background (Harmondsworth: Penguin, 1965).

Williams, L. Pearce, "Science, Education and the French Revolution", Isis, vol. 44 (December 1953), pp. 311-330.

Williams, L. Pearce, "The Politics of Science in the French Revolution", in Critical Problems in the History of Science, ed. M. Clagett (Madison: University of Wisconsin Press, 1959), pp. 291-308.

Williams, Raymond, Culture and Society 1780-1950 (Harmondsworth: Penguin, 1963).

Williams, Raymond, Keywords, a Vocabulary of Culture and Society (London: Fontana, 1976).

Williams, Raymond, Marxism and literature (Oxford: Oxford University Press, 1977)

Wilson, Arthur M., Diderot (New York: Oxford University Press, 1972).

Wilson, Arthur M., "The Concept of Moeurs in Diderot's Social and Political Thought", in The Age of Enlightenment: Studies Presented to Theodore Besterman, ed. W.H. Barber and others (Edinburgh: Oliver and Boyd, 1967), pp. 188-199.

Wilson, Arthur M., "The Philosophes in the light of present-day theories of modernization", Studies on Voltaire and the Eighteenth Century, vol. 58 (1967), pp. 1893-1913.

Wilson, Arthur M., "Why did the Political Theory of the Encyclopedists not prevail? A Suggestion", French Historical Studies, vol. 1 no. 3 (Spring 1960), pp. 283-294.

Wolin, Sheldon S., "Paradigms and political theories", in Politics and Experience: Essays presented to Professor Michael Oakeshott ..., eds. P. King and B.C. Parekh (Cambridge: Cambridge University Press, 1968), pp. 125-152.

Woronoff, Denis, Nouvelle Histoire de la France Contemporaine, 3: La République Bourgeoise de Thermidor à Brumaire,1794-1799 (Paris: Editions du Seuil, 1972).

ADDENDUM

Meek, Ronald Lindley, Studies in the Labour Theory of Value (London: Lawrence and Wishart, 1958).

Weber, Max, From Max Weber: Essays in Sociology, trans. and ed. H. Gerth and C.W. Mills (New York: Oxford University Press, 1946).

Weber, Max, The Methodology of the Social Sciences, trans. and ed. E. Shils and H. Finch (New York: Free Press, 1949).

Bloch, Camille, "L'instruction publique dans l'Aude", Revue internationale de l'enseignement, vol. 27 (1894), pp. 36-62, 193-223.